The 200
Arriva
Bus Handb

CW00430217

British Bus Publishing

Body codes used in the Bus Handbook series:

Type:
A   Articulated vehicle
B   Bus, either single-deck or double-deck
BC   Interurban - high-back seated bus
C   Coach
M   Minibus with design capacity of 16 seats or less
N   Low-floor bus (*Niederflur*), either single-deck or double-deck
O   Open-top bus (CO = convertible - PO = partial open-top)

Seating capacity is then shown. For double-decks the upper deck quantity is followed by the lower deck.

Door position:-
C   Centre entrance/exit
D   Dual doorway.
F   Front entrance/exit
R   Rear entrance/exit (no distinction between doored and open)
T   Three or more access points

Equipment:-

L	Lift for wheelchair	TV	Training vehicle.
M	Mail compartment	RV	Used as tow bus or engineers vehicle.
T	Toilet	w	Vehicle is withdrawn and awaiting disposal.

e.g. - B32/28F is a double-deck bus with thirty-two seats upstairs, twenty-eight down and a front entrance/exit.
N43D is a low-floor bus with two or more doorways.

Re-registrations:-
Where a vehicle has gained new index marks the details are listed at the end of each fleet showing the current mark, followed in sequence by those previously carried starting with the original mark.

Regional books in the series:
The Scottish Bus Handbook
The Ireland & Islands Bus Handbook
The North East Bus Handbook
The Yorkshire Bus Handbook
The North West Bus Handbook
The East Midlands Bus Handbook
The West Midlands Bus Handbook
The Welsh Bus Handbook
The Eastern Bus Handbook
The London Bus Handbook
The South East Bus Handbook
The South West Bus Handbook

Annual books are produced for the major groups:
The Stagecoach Bus Handbook
The Go-Ahead Bus Handbook
The First Bus Handbook
The Arriva Bus Handbook
The National Express Handbook (bi-annual)
Most editions for earlier years are available direct from the publisher .

Associated series:
The Hong Kong Bus Handbook
The Malta Bus Handbook
The Leyland Lynx Handbook
The Model Bus Handbook
The Postbus Handbook
The Overall Advertisment Bus Handbook - Volume 1
The Toy & Model Bus Handbook - Volume 1 - Early Diecasts
The Fire Brigade Handbook (fleet list of each local authority fire brigade)
The Police Range Rover Handbook

2004 Arriva Bus Handbook

The 2004 Arriva Bus Handbook is a special edition of the Bus Handbook series which contains the various fleets of Arriva plc. The Bus Handbook series is published by British Bus Publishing, an independent publisher of quality books for the industry and bus enthusiasts. Further information on these may be obtained from the address below.

Although this book has been produced with the encouragement of, and in co-operation with, Arriva plc management, it is not an official group fleet list and the vehicles included are subject to variation, particularly as the vehicle investment programme continues. Some vehicles listed are no longer in regular use on services but are retained for special purposes. Also, out of use vehicles awaiting disposal are not all listed. The services operated and the allocation of vehicles to subsidiary companies are subject to variation at any time, although accurate at the time of going to print.

To keep the fleet information up to date we recommend the Ian Allan publication *Buses*, published monthly or, for more detailed information, the PSV Circle monthly news sheets.

Edited by Bill Potter and David Donati

Acknowledgments:
We are most grateful to Keith Grimes, Fred Huppertz, Mark Jameson, Harry Laming, Colin Martin, Stuart Martin, Kevin O'Leary, the PSV Circle and the management and officials of Arriva Group plc, and their operating companies, for their kind assistance and co-operation in the compilation of this book.

The front cover photo shows one of the Wrightbus-bodied Volvo B7L 'Bus of the Future' which is owned by the Arriva and used on, loan to the operating companies. It was pictured on the Wirral while with Arriva North West and Wales. The fronticepiece illustrates a Wrightbus Gemini double-deck operating with Arriva London.
Bill Potter, Mark Lyons.

ISBN 1 897990 93 6

Published by *British Bus Publishing Ltd*
16 St Margaret's Drive, Wellington, Telford, TF1 3PH

© British Bus Publishing Ltd, June 2004
Telephone 01952 255669 - Facsimile 01952 222397 - www.britishbuspublishing.co.uk

Contents

Pictured in Whitby, while operating route X56 to Middlesbrough, Arriva North East's 4025, R425RPY is DAF SB220 with Plaxton Prestige bodywork. *Tony Wilson*

ARRIVA plc

The Arriva Group: A Company Profile

Arriva plc is firmly established as one of Britain's top 250 companies quoted on the London Stock Exchange and is one of the largest transport services organisations in Europe, providing more than one billion passenger journeys a year. Its operations include an extensive range of services including buses, trains, commuter coaches and water buses. It operates a national vehicle rental business in the UK and is engaged in bus and coach distribution. In 2003, Arriva bus' Group turnover was £1.751 billion, and it employed around 30,000 staff.

Arriva is one of the UK's largest bus operators, with over 6,000 vehicles serving customers in the North East, North West, London and the South East of England, Yorkshire, the Midlands, Wales and Scotland. Many of Arriva's UK Bus division's operating companies are long established but the grouping emerged out of the privatisation of public sector transport companies, pursuant to the Transport Act 1985, and the subsequent consolidation of the sector. The division is organised into autonomous operating subsidiaries in order that management teams and staff can focus upon the discrete local and regional markets that they serve.

The core activity is the operation of urban, interurban and rural local bus services, demand-responsive transit, commuter and express coach services within England, Scotland and Wales. Arriva is the second largest bus operator in the UK, and is the largest operator in London covering 18.5 per cent of the scheduled network.

Additionally, Arriva operates bus, train, coach, demand responsive and disabled persons travel in Denmark, Germany, Italy, the Netherlands, Portugal, Spain and Sweden. Arriva offers local and regional rail passenger services in the UK, Denmark, Germany and the Netherlands. The Group makes significant capital investment in the replacement and improvement of assets. Over the last five years, £250 million was spent on capital investment in equipment and facilities for Arriva's UK Bus division alone. As a result of recent investment, the bus fleet has been substantially modernised.

Recent years have witnessed a renewed interest in rapid transit systems and the development of intermediate technologies. Arriva has been actively positioning itself within this broadened public transport market. It has been a leading member of a number of consortia bidding to fund, design, build and operate tram and guided bus systems. With FirstGroup, Arriva is one of the operators of the East Leeds guided bus system, Elite. In addition, Arriva is working with Luton Borough Council on the proposed Luton-Dunstable Translink system.

After the original South Leeds scheme fell, West Yorkshire PTE continued to press the case for its tramway scheme and received initial approval in 2001. The Leeds Supertram project, based on the South Leeds route plus a northern and an eastern route was agreed by Government and new bids for the concession were invited. To bid for this concession, Arriva formed a new consortium, named Airelink. The other partners in the consortium are Transdev, AMEC and Siemens. The two consortia listed for the project submitted bids in 2002. West Yorkshire PTE and the Government have been involved since that date in a continuing dialogue about the costs and benefits of the scheme, which should be resolved in 2004.In the UK, Arriva's UK Trains division operates two rail passenger operating companies. Arriva Trains Wales/Trenau Arriva Cymru operates interurban, commuter and rural passenger services throughout Wales and the border counties. Northern operates extensively across the north of England. Arriva continues to pursue a European strategy, which has resulted in acquisitions in Denmark, Germany, Italy, the Netherlands, Portugal, Spain and Sweden recently, with opportunities being actively pursued in other countries and geographical regions in Europe. A fundamental aspect of the European strategy is to invest both in companies and in management teams in order to ensure local market knowledge and expertise.

Arriva Bus and Coach is the group's bus and coach distribution business with exclusive import rights for all VDL chassis supported by a wide range of bus and coach bodywork options, from Van Hool of Belgium, Ikarus from Hungary and Plaxton from the UK, to meet new market demands.

In 2001, Arriva took the first double-deck buses built by Wrights of Ballymena. Many similar buses are now in service with London operators, mostly on Volvo chassis but Arriva London is currently taking delivery of its second batch on DAF chassis, which will bring its fleet of Wrights double-decks to 199 on Volvo and 93 on DAF chassis. Arriva has also made its first purchases of East Lancs bodywork for some years.

In 2004, Arriva invested in excess of £10 million in Project Overdrive – an investment programme in the Medway Towns which saw 61 new vehicles together with a further 40 refurbished modern vehicles introduced in a single day. The investment was complemented by improvements to service levels and infrastructure. Now to some historical background to a group with a complex pedigree.

COWIE

The Cowie name - early years

In 1931, the Cowie family started a motorcycle repair business in Sunderland. In 1934 the first sales outlet opened on what became the location of the Group Head Offices. Business came to a halt in 1942 because of the effects of the war, but reopened in 1948 and benefited from the boom in personal mobility offered by the motorcycle. A second motorcycle shop was opened in Newcastle in 1952. Further expansion occurred in 1955 with another branch in Newcastle, and new branches in Durham and Stockton-on-Tees. A move into the Scottish market was taken with the acquisition of the J R Alexander motorcycle dealerships in Edinburgh and Glasgow in 1960. However, there were signs that the market was moving against the motorcycle, and in favour of the motor car which was becoming a more mass market item in availability and price.

In 1962, Cowie acquired its first car dealership in Sunderland, and such was the pace of change that, by 1963, motor car sales constituted 80% of revenue. On the back of this change, a public company, T Cowie plc, was formed in 1965 and, in that year, a further two car dealerships were acquired, one in Redcar and a second in Sunderland. In 1967, there was investment in new car showrooms for the Ford franchise in Sunderland; there has been a long association with Ford over the years. In 1971, this was strengthened with the acquisition of Ford Blackburn and a further Ford dealership, this time in Middlesbrough. By 1971, the group turnover reached £8m per annum.

Growing on the motor business

In 1972 a new business was set up in the form of Cowie Contract Hire. This and its successors grew to be a large element of the present group.

The first exposure to the bus and coach industry came in 1980. In that year, Cowie took over The George Ewer Group which had various motor interests including Eastern Tractors and these assets were bought with the business. It also included the long established Grey Green coach operation and this was to lead to a sea change in the make-up of the business.

In 1984 Cowie acquired the Hanger Group and this brought Ford dealerships in Nottingham and Birmingham and, significantly, Interleasing, the contract hire business. Expansion continued in 1987 when seven main dealerships were acquired from the Heron Group. On the leasing side, Marley Leasing was acquired. Further growth in this business area came in 1991 when RoyScot Drive and Ringway Leasing were also acquired, adding to the prominence of this activity for the group.

1992 was the year that Cowie very nearly took another step into the bus and coach market, narrowly failing to purchase Henlys which, by that time, had ownership of Plaxtons along with several car franchises. Consolation came with the addition of a Ford dealership in Swindon, a Peugeot dealership in Middlesbrough, and a Toyota dealership in Wakefield. In 1993, the Keep Trust Group was acquired, the dealership network being boosted by 70%.

Another notable event in 1993 was the retirement of Sir Tom Cowie, the Chairmanship of the business being taken up by Sir James McKinnon in 1994 and continuing until he retired at the end of 1999 when Gareth Cooper took over the role.

Explosion into Buses!

The Cowie group's first involvement with the bus and coach sector came with the purchase of the Ewer Group in 1980. Its subsidiary, Grey Green, was a most distinguished name in coaching but, under the Ewer Group, had already started to operate bus services for London Transport.

Grey Green, which had operating bases at Stamford Hill and Dagenham in London, and at Ipswich in East Anglia, participated in historic operations such as East Anglian Express, the Eastlander Pool, and joint services to Scotland in association with Scottish Bus Group. Private Hire coaching also played a large part in the business.

Great opportunities were perceived in the 1980s in commuter coaching after the deregulation of coach services under the 1980 Act. Commuter coach services thrived for a while, but the involvement in British Coachways was not successful. In the mid 1980s, Grey Green's involvement in the East Anglian Express Pool was taken into the National Express operation.

Early success in London Bus tendering brought Grey Green operation into to the very heart of London, notably on route 24 which passes the Palace of Westminster. After that, Grey Green gradually ceased all coach activities and concentrated entirely on tendered bus services in London.

The privatisation of the newly created subsidiaries of London Buses offered the opportunity to build on the favourable experience of Grey Green in the London bus market. Leaside was acquired in 1994 and was renamed Cowie Leaside. Later in 1995, the South London company was purchased, becoming Cowie South London. These two acquisitions made Cowie the largest single operator in the London Buses area. As the London operations were tidied up, the former Kentish Bus/Londonlinks operations at Cambridge Heath, Battersea, Croydon (Beddington Farm) and Walworth, and the East Herts & Essex operations from Edmonton were gradually incorporated into the London operation.

In 1996, Cowie purchased County Bus from the National Express Group, adding to the group's presence in the south east of England. Then, in August 1996, Cowie completed the acquisition of British Bus plc and, at a stroke, became the second largest bus operating group in the United Kingdom. The acquisition of British Bus plc added a whole raft of bus companies across the country and very nearly brought all the disparate elements of the former London Country company, including Green Line Travel, under one ownership. There was a Monopolies and Mergers Commission inquiry into the acquisition of British Bus, with particular focus on the situation in London and the South East, but the report did not require any divestment.

The final acquisition of 1996, also in August, brought another previously divided company back under common ownership. In 1986, United Automobile Services had been split into two separate companies for privatisation: North East Bus and Northumbria. Northumbria was sold to Proudmutual, a company which had been set up to facilitate the management buyout and was acquired by Cowie in 1994. United Auto was sold in December 1987 to Caldaire who sold it on, as North East Bus, to West Midlands Travel. West Midlands Travel itself then merged with the National Express Group which decided to concentrate on its core operations and, in 1996, sold first County Bus then North East Bus to Cowie/Arriva. The former British Bus headquarters at Salisbury, which dated back to Drawlane days, was wound down and closed at the end of 1996, with the group administration being moved to Sunderland.

BRITISH BUS

The growth of British Bus plc

With the acquisition of British Bus plc, Cowie became the second largest bus operating group in the United Kingdom. This move led to the reclassification of the enlarged group from being motor trade to Transport.

Drawlane Ltd

The privatisation of the National Bus Company followed the 1985 Transport Act with the National Bus Company becoming a vendor unit selling its subsidiaries to pre-qualified parties. Endless Holdings Ltd was one of those interested parties, being a group of companies based in the cleaning and building management sector with a head office on Endless Street in Salisbury. The prime mover in Endless was Ray McEnhill. Endless set up a subsidiary called Drawlane Ltd to bid for NBC companies as they were made ready for sale.

The first company bought by Drawlane was Shamrock & Rambler in July 1987. This was the major part of the coaching activities of Hants and Dorset and was based at a modern depot in Bournemouth. The business was heavily dependent on National Express contracts, although a minibus operation was set up to compete with Yellow Buses in the Bournemouth area. Shamrock & Rambler did not survive for long: their bus operations were quickly reduced in scale, and difficulties with the National Express contracts led to notice of termination being given to Shamrock & Rambler which sealed its fate. National Express set up a local joint venture company called Dorset Travel Services Ltd to take over the workings of Shamrock & Rambler using other vehicles and based as a tenant of Yellow Buses at Mallard Road. Yellow Buses eventually purchased Dorset Travel Services. The Shamrock & Rambler vehicles were dispersed around the then Drawlane Group fleets and Shamrock & Rambler was wound up.

Drawlane was preferred bidder for three more companies: Southern National, North Devon, and London Country (South West). Each purchaser was limited to three NBC companies in the first instance. However there was concern that Drawlane might be related to another bidder called Allied Bus which had been selected as preferred bidder for another three companies: Lincolnshire Road Car, East Midland Motor Services and Midland Red North. The concern was sufficient for the preferred bidder status to be withdrawn from both and offers were re-invited.

Drawlane was successful in acquiring Midland Red (North) in January 1988 which, at the time of purchase, had 248 vehicles and 491 employees. The following month, London Country (South West) Ltd was purchased with 415 vehicles and 1250 employees, although the garages were purchased separately by Speyhawk Properties, who then leased them to the bus company with varying securities of tenure, reflecting the premium value of property in London and the South East. Finally, in March 1988, Drawlane acquired the 'new' North Western Road Car Company Ltd based in Bootle, with 340 vehicles and 870 staff.

Drawlane had also bought East Lancashire Coachbuilders from the industrial conglomerate John Brown. East Lancs was based in Blackburn and had a strong customer base in the local authority sector.

Further expansion for Drawlane would now come from acquiring bus operations from other sources. ATL (Western) Ltd had purchased Crosville Motor Services from NBC in March 1988 and in early 1989 was ready to sell. Drawlane purchased the company adding a further 470 vehicles. A quick overview of the future of Crosville is appropriate here. In an exercise to realise value from the company, the South Cheshire operations at Crewe and Etruria were transferred to Midland Red North, the Runcorn and Warrington depots were transferred to North Western, and the Macclesfield and Congleton depots were merged into Bee Line Buzz, of which more later. The remaining operations at Rock Ferry and Chester, together with the vehicles, were sold to PMT Ltd along with the 'Crosville' trading name which PMT, now part of First Group, still uses. The original Crosville Motor Services Company was renamed North British Bus Ltd, and, though it existed for some time thereafter, it did not trade as a bus company.

Midland Fox was bought from its management team in September 1989 along with a minority share holding in the company from Stevensons of Uttoxeter. Bee Line Buzz operations in Manchester had been started up by BET, which had sold its bus operations in 1968, venturing back into bus operation in the UK. A similar operation was started in Preston. Both were sold to Ribble's management buyout team who, in turn, sold Ribble Buses to the Stagecoach Group. As part of an exchange of assets with Stagecoach in the Manchester area, Drawlane bought Bee Line Buzz from Stagecoach along with Hulme Hall Road depot in Manchester and added into the company the former Crosville operations at Macclesfield and Congleton. Bee Line had an independent existence within the group until 1993 when its operations were merged into North Western, with Macclesfield depot going to Midland Red North.

Drawlane in Transition

In 1991, Drawlane became a partner in a consortium with several banks setting up a company called Speedtheme Ltd in a bid to buy National Express Holdings from its management team. As well as the main National Express business, National Express Holdings owned Crosville Wales Ltd and its Liverpool subsidiary Amberline Ltd, Express Travel in Perth, and Carlton PSV the Neoplan coach dealer in Rotherham. Speedtheme Ltd did not want Crosville Wales and Amberline/Express Travel, and these were immediately sold to a company, called Catchdeluxe Ltd, set up by two of the main shareholders of Drawlane, Ray McEnhill and Adam Mills. Although not part of Drawlane at this time, these two companies were under common management, and it was not long before they became part of the Drawlane Group.

Ray McEnhill became the Chairman and Chief Executive of National Express Group and, as this group prepared for its floatation on the Stock Exchange, Ray McEnhill and Adam Mills severed their involvement with Drawlane. The London & Country business called Speedlink Airport Services was sold by Drawlane to National Express at this time, though Drawlane retained the Green Line Travel Company, along with the Green Line trading name.

There was, in effect, a management buyout of Drawlane in the autumn of 1992 to coincide with the successful floatation of National Express and shortly thereafter Drawlane was renamed British Bus plc. (British Bus Ltd had been a dormant subsidiary of National Express Holdings, originally set up by NBC to market the Britexpress card overseas.)

British Bus grows

Throughout this period, there were various smaller acquisitions by the group companies but these are dealt with in the short histories of these companies that follow.

In 1993, British Bus purchased Southend Transport and Colchester Transport, both former municipal operations which had been offered for sale after being weakened by competition from Badgerline subsidiaries, Thamesway in Southend and Eastern National in Colchester. After acquisition, the two companies were put under common management and the supervision of London & Country. A programme of rationalisation put both back onto a firm footing, though down-sized.

In 1993, North Western acquired Liverline of Liverpool which, by then, had grown to a fifty-one vehicle company. It was run as a separate subsidiary until 1997. North Western had by this time absorbed the bus operations of Amberline.

Also in 1993, Tellings Golden Miller was sold back to its original owners. Tellings had been taken over by Midland Fox and came into the group. At the time of its sale, it had bases in Surrey and Cardiff. In the latter location, Tellings had become the joint operator of the Trawscambria service with Crosville Cymru! That role then passed to Rhondda Bus in which British Bus had a share holding for a while.

At the end of 1993, British Bus became the preferred bidder for the purchase of GM Buses North, but the position was overturned by the vendors and new bids invited. The outcome of this exercise was a winning bid from an employee-based team which was eventually completed in the spring of 1994. They subsequently sold out to First.

Further growth was funded by expanding the capital base of the group through investment by two merchant banks who took a share of the increased equity in a new parent company British Bus Group, though operational control remained with British Bus plc.

During 1994, ownership of both East Lancashire Coachbuilders Ltd and Express Travel was transferred out of the group, though they were still associated companies. East Lancs in particular was still a preferred supplier to the group for bus bodywork.

The National Greenway programme was coming to an end at this point. This programme involved the stripping down and re-engineering of Leyland National shells with new a Gardner or Volvo engine, new gearbox and new body panels mounted on the shell framework. The stripping down and mechanical overhaul work was carried out at London and Country's Reigate garage, though later some of this work was carried out by Blackburn Transport, as this was closer to East Lancs. East Lancs then did the body work with customer options as to the front design. Notable numbers were carried out both for Group companies and other operators.

Luton, Derby ,and Clydeside

In July 1994, British Bus acquired Luton and District Transport from its employees. By this time, the business included the former London Country Bus North West and a large part of the Stevenage operations bought from Sovereign Bus. This meant that a sizeable part of the former London Country company was now back in common ownership.

Luton and District had also assisted other employee buyouts such as Derby City Transport in which it had a 25% share holding, and Clydeside 2000 plc, where there was a 19% share holding. In both companies, the shareholders voted to accept offers from British Bus for the balance of the shares and they became fully owned members of the British Bus group. A third company, Lincoln City Transport, had not met with success and the employees had already agreed its sale to Yorkshire Traction-owned Lincolnshire Road Car Company Ltd before the British Bus take-over.

At the same time, there were discussions about the acquisition of Stevensons of Uttoxeter. Stevensons had grown dramatically after deregulation and operated well away from its traditional area. A strong expansion in the West Midlands was initially successful but West Midlands Travel responded to the competition and used its Your Bus acquisition to start up operations in Burton on Trent which was by then the heartland of Stevensons. A long struggle looked in prospect and a sale to British Bus was agreed. Operations in the West Midlands were scaled down and surplus vehicles were distributed around the group. After this process was complete, the geographically separated Macclesfield depot of Midland Red North was transferred to Stevensons control in January 1995.

Proudmutual and Caldaire Holdings

In the summer of 1994, British Bus also acquired the Proudmutual group. Proudmutual had been the buyout vehicle for the management team of Northumbria Motor Services to buy their business from NBC. It had also acquired some smaller businesses in the North East, including Moor-Dale.

Proudmutual had previously purchased Kentish Bus, the former London Country South East from NBC in March 1988. They had considerable success in the London Transport tendering process and further LT work was added when the LT contracts of Boro'line were purchased in February 1992. The Proudmutual acquisition thus gave British Bus a very strong position in LT tendering when the activities of London and Country and the LDT group were taken into account. It also brought another part of the former London and Country into common ownership.

The privatisation of the London Transport Bus companies brought no success for British Bus but, as we have seen earlier, the Cowie Group was successful in acquiring two of the subsidiaries.

In March of 1995, the Caldaire group was acquired. Caldaire was the buyout vehicle with which the management of West Riding Group had purchased their business from NBC in January 1987. In the December of that year they also bought United Auto from NBC. A demerger later on saw the United business being separated off again into North East Bus. The long established independent South Yorkshire Road Transport was acquired and formed one of the trading identities of the Caldaire Group, the others being West Riding, Yorkshire Woollen, and Selby & District. After acquisition, the group of companies was renamed Yorkshire Bus Group by British Bus.

Maidstone & District

What turned out to be the last major acquisition by British Bus was made in April 1995. Maidstone and District had been one of the earliest of NBC sales in late 1986. It had purchased New Enterprise of Tonbridge in 1988, and the assets of Boro'line Maidstone in 1992. Under British Bus ownership, the company was put under common management with Kentish Bus and Londonlinks as the Invictaway Group with its head office at Maidstone.

Floatation or Trade Sale?

Throughout 1995, preparations for floatation had been underway with the appointment of advisors. However, in the summer of 1995, these plans were thrown off course by reports of alleged irregularities involving support from the Bank of Boston for British Bus at an earlier point in the group's history. The timing of these allegations led to the postponement of the floatation. The alternative route for shareholders and the investing banks to realise their investment was a trade sale of the group and discussions were held with various interested parties.

Concurrently, the group was also looking to expand its interests into other modes of transport as the opportunities in the bus industry were becoming scarce due to the growth of the major players. The subsequent sales of the two former GM Buses companies by their employee owners and that of Strathclyde Buses were opportunities for growth, but British Bus was not successful.

In June 1996 the Cowie Group made an offer to acquire British Bus, (which has already been covered). There was a Monopolies and Mergers Commission investigation into the take-over in view of the concentration of operation in London and the South East in the combined business. However, the resulting report made no recommendation about disinvestment, recognising the considerable presence of the other groups in the area. The acquisition by Cowie was completed in August 1996

Trams and trains

As part of its drive to expand its business, British Bus pursued tramway operations and had become a partner in the Eurotrans consortium which bid for both the Leeds Supertram and Manchester Metrolink concessions. British Bus was also part of a consortium bid for the Croydon Tramlink project.

Eurotrans was selected as the preferred bidder for the South Leeds Supertram Project which was being promoted by West Yorkshire PTE. This was a PFI project where bidders were fighting for the concession to design, build, operate, and maintain the tramway for a period of thirty years. The Eurotrans consortium included big construction companies such as Taylor Woodrow, Morrison Construction, and Christiani & Neilsen. The tram supplier was Vevey Technologies of Switzerland, now part of the Bombardier Group. The intention was for Arriva Yorkshire to set up a tram operating subsidiary to operate the tramway for the concession life on behalf of Eurotrans. The project stalled waiting for UK Government funding commitment, but was revived, in expanded form, in 2001 when funding was secured.

British Bus was also active in the process of franchising of the Train Operating Companies by OPRAF although none of their bids were successful. However, the exposure to the process paid off in arranging through ticketing deals with the successful bidders later on.

ARRIVA

In 1997 the group started a rebranding of all its business interests under the new trading identity of 'Arriva'. The bus division became a separate legal identity on 1 January 1998, becoming Arriva Passenger Services (APS). The group livery and identity started to replace the former colours and names progressively from 1999.

A link with the past was broken when the Group Headquarters relocated in the latter part of 1998 from Hylton Road in Sunderland to new purpose built premises on the Doxford International Business Park on the outskirts of Sunderland near the A19.

Arriva Passenger Services shared the head office premises of Arriva Fox, first at Millstone Lane and then, from September 1997, at Thurmaston, although several staff were quartered at offices in bus depots around the country. Then, in August 1999, APS moved to purpose built offices in the Meridian Business Park on the other side of Leicester.

In September 1997, Arriva made its first acquisition outside Britain with the purchase of Unibus Holdings in Denmark. Arriva continues to expand within Europe, and now has operations in Denmark, Germany, Italy, the Netherlands, Portugal, Spain and Sweden.

In 2000, Arriva purchased MTL, the Liverpool-based transport group, which included the major bus operator in Merseyside plus the two rail franchises. A subsidiary operation at Heysham was soon sold on and the MTL bus operation was absorbed into Arriva North West. Gilmoss depot and its operations were sold on to meet the terms required by the Office of Fair Trading for its approval of the purchase of MTL.

Arriva in London

When the Arriva name was introduced, Grey Green was renamed Arriva London North East. Cowie Leaside became Arriva London North, and Cowie South London became Arriva London South. The three companies have moved gradually closer to functioning as one unit, and the London North East operations were absorbed into London North in 2003. The head office for both London companies is at Wood Green. The Beddington Farm depot of Londonlinks transferred from Southern Counties to London South in October 1999. The Leaside Travel coach and bus contract hire fleet still retains a separate livery.

Arriva provided the first low-floor double-deck buses in London and deliveries continue apace. The first buses were DAF with Alexander bodies but Volvo chassis and Plaxton bodies are now in fleet service. In 2001, Arriva London took the first Wrightbus double-deck bodies, on Volvo chassis. More recent orders for Wright double-decks have been on DAF chassis, while Alexander bodies have also switched from Volvo to DAF chassis.

In line with the Mayor's strategy for transport in London, which includes the introduction of Congestion Charging, the Arriva London fleet has seen growth of over 200 extra buses together with rapid fleet renewal. The fleet is now close to being entirely low-floor, a process which should be completed during 2005. To accommodate this growth, Stamford Hill garage has been reopened, the former tram shed at Brixton was brought back into use in February 2003, and facilities elsewhere are being expanded. Premises at Tottenham Hale have been leased for storing vehicles to make room at operational depots, and further new depot sites are being sought.

County Bus and Coach into Arriva East Herts and Essex

County Bus & Coach came into being at the beginning of 1989 to carry on the eastern operations of the former London Country North East, which in itself was one of the four parts into which London Country was divided. Operations were based at Harlow, Hertford and Grays. Ownership had progressed through the AJS group in 1988, the South of England Travel group in 1989 and the Lynton Travel group in 1990. The company was then purchased by the West Midlands Travel holding company, becoming part of the National Express Group when WMT merged into NEG. A retraction into core business led NEG to sell County to Cowie in 1996. A significant acquisition in 1989 was the bus interests and depot of Sampsons of Hoddesdon.

A restructuring of responsibilities saw County Bus take over the controlling supervision of Southend Transport and Colchester Borough Transport from London & Country and, during 1998, this responsibility passed to Arriva The Shires, along with overall control of what was now Arriva East Herts and Essex. The Edmonton operation passed to the Arriva London group in a rationalisation of responsibilities within London. During 1999 the fleets of these various component operations were renumbered into a single series.

In a further restructuring in 2001, responsibility for Colchester, Grays and Southend passed to Arriva Southern Counties.

The Shires becomes Arriva the Shires and Essex Ltd

In 1986, United Counties Omnibus Company Ltd was divided into three parts, the southern most of these being Luton and District Transport Ltd which took over operations in Aylesbury, Dunstable, Hitchin and Luton. The new head office of the company was in Luton.

In August 1987 Luton and District became the first employee owned bus operator in the UK when its employees bought it from NBC. In the period from January 1988 to October 1990, LDT expanded the size and the area of its operations through a number of acquisitions. The assets and business of Red Rover Omnibus Ltd, operating bus services from a depot in Aylesbury, were acquired in January 1988. In June 1988, Milton Keynes Coaches was acquired, joined in May 1990 by two thirds of the bus services operated in the Stevenage area latterly Sovereign Bus Ltd.

In October 1990, LDT acquired London Country North West Ltd. LCNW operated a vehicle fleet of a similar size to LDT from a head office and depot in Garston and other depots in Hemel Hempstead, High Wycombe, Amersham, and Slough. LDT assisted in the employee buyouts of two other companies and acquired a share holding in both, Derby City Transport in 1989, and Clydeside 2000 plc in 1991.

In July 1994 LDT became part of British Bus. In October 1994, the bus operations of Stuart Palmer Travel based in Dunstable was taken over, followed in May 1995 by Buffalo Travel of Flitwick, and Motts Travel of Aylesbury in July 1995.

April 1995 saw the launch of a brand new blue and yellow company livery with local trading names replacing the previous red and cream of LDT and green and grey of LCNW. The legal name was changed to LDT Ltd in May and the corporate operating name became The Shires. In late 1997, Lucketts Garages (Watford) Ltd was acquired. In addition to local bus services in Watford there were substantial dial-a-ride operations and a commercial workshop.

Lutonian Buses was acquired in March. Since then, there has been a ruling that the business should be sold under Competition regulations. The Group's challenge was unsuccessful and Lutonian was sold during 2000.

The Arriva branding saw vehicles carrying the name 'Arriva serving the Shires', except at Garston garage which carries 'Arriva serving Watford'. Management responsibility for Arriva East Herts & Essex now falls to Arriva the Shires and Essex Ltd. Responsibility for Colchester, Grays and Southend passed to Arriva Southern Counties in 2001.

Kentish Bus part of Arriva Southern Counties

Kentish Bus started as London Country South East on the division of London Country Bus Services in 1986. It had its Head Office at Northfleet and in April 1987 was relaunched as Kentish Bus and Coach Ltd with a new livery of cream and maroon.

In March 1988 Kentish Bus was sold to Proudmutual on privatisation. There was considerable expansion into the LT tender market for which new buses were added, many with registration indices originating in the North East. In February 1992 there was further expansion in this area when Kentish acquired the LT tendered work of the troubled Boro'line Maidstone operation, along with some 57 vehicles.

After the acquisition of the Proudmutual group by British Bus in 1994, Kentish Bus and Londonlinks were jointly managed from Northfleet. However, on the acquisition of Maidstone and District by British Bus, the management was relocated to Armstrong Road, Maidstone under the Invictaway grouping. The balance of the operation continued to be controlled from Maidstone after the reallocation of the two London depots to South London and Leaside.

Its size was significantly reduced by the transfer of operations at Battersea to the control of South London and the operations at Cambridge Heath to Leaside.

However the local Kent Thameside network was expanded and upgraded with low floor vehicles upon the opening or the Bluewater shopping centre in 1999.

The Arriva identity was applied as 'Arriva serving Kent Thameside' to the operations at Dartford and Northfleet.

London & Country into Arriva Surrey and West Sussex

London & Country was the trading name of London Country Bus (South West) Ltd, which was one of the four operations that London Country Bus Services Ltd was divided into prior to the privatisation of NBC. The former head office of LCBS at Reigate became that of L&C. The company was bought by Drawlane, as outlined above, in February 1988. However, the properties were leased back having been sold separately. The company was relaunched with a new livery and trading name in April 1989.

London & Country was successful in winning LT tenders and this led to the addition of new vehicles and the high profile opening of an impressive new garage at Beddington Farm in Croydon. Responsibility for this operation passed to Arriva London in 1999.

In 1990 the Woking, Guildford, and Cranleigh operations of the former Alder Valley business were purchased, and though kept as a separate operating company - Guildford and West Surrey - they were put under the same management as L&C. Also in 1990, a separate company called Horsham Buses was established for operations in the Horsham area.

Spare capacity at the Reigate garage allowed the development of the National Greenway concept in conjunction with East Lancs and many vehicles were prepared at Reigate.

Briefly, London & Country had two subsidiaries in Dorset: Stanbridge and Crichel and Oakfield Travel. Both of these were later sold to Damory Coaches. Another subsidiary was Linkline Coaches of Harlesden in London, which specialised in coaching and corporate work. This was later sold to its management.

1993 saw the acquisition of Southend Transport and Colchester Transport and many L&C influences followed. These companies transferred to the supervision of County Bus but returned to Southern Counties in 2001.

The Croydon based operations and other LT tender operations at Walworth were transferred into a new company called Londonlinks. In 1995 Londonlinks was put under common management with Kentish Bus and Maidstone and District as part of the Invictaway Group. Reallocation of responsibilities in the enlarged group later saw the Croydon depot of Londonlinks return to L&C control before finally passing to London South.

A consequence of the property sales was the vacation of Reigate garage and its replacement by a facility at Merstham. The Head Office functions were consolidated in 1997 when the Reigate office closed as the functions moved to other premises including Crawley garage.

The three companies were renamed as Arriva Croydon and North Surrey, Arriva West Sussex, and Arriva Guildford and West Surrey. However the trading identity used is Arriva Surrey & West Sussex. In August 1998 the Countryliner coaching operation was sold to its manager. In 2001, the Crawley operation and depot was sold to Metrobus and the Merstham depot was closed.

In Guildford, significant investment has taken place with the depot completely rebuilt in 2002 and the fleet updated.

Maidstone and District becomes Arriva Kent & Sussex

This is the original Maidstone and District Motor Services Ltd which was founded in 1911. Under NBC, it shared common management with East Kent from 1972 to 1983. In 1983 the Hastings and Rye area services were hived off as Hastings and District.

Maidstone and District was one of the first NBC companies to be privatised, being bought by its management team in November 1986. In 1988 New Enterprise of Tonbridge was purchased and is still kept as a separate entity. In June 1992 the assets of Maidstone Boro'line Maidstone including the premises at Armstrong Road were purchased.

In April 1995 the company was sold to British Bus, and in November the Head Office at Chatham was closed and staff moved along with Kentish Bus head office staff from Northfleet to the former Maidstone Boro'line premises at Maidstone under the Invictaway banner.

Under British Bus Cowie control, the group acquired a number of additional operatorions including Mercury Passenger Services of Hoo, Wealden Beeline of Five Oak Green, and the Grey Green (Medway) bus operation. In May of 1997 the Green Line operations in Gravesend and the Medway Towns were sold to the Pullman Group (London Coaches).

The Arriva branding used three identities, 'Arriva serving the Medway Towns', 'Arriva serving Kent and East Sussex', and 'Arriva serving Maidstone'.

Midland Fox turns into Arriva Fox County Ltd

Midland Red East Ltd was formed in 1981 to take over the Leicestershire operations of Midland Red. In 1984 the company name was changed to Midland Fox Ltd, and there was a major relaunch of the company with a new livery and fox logo. There was also the launch of a new minibus network in Leicester under the, now discontinued, Fox Cub brand.

In 1987 the company was bought from NBC by its management with the help of the directors of Stevensons of Uttoxeter who, separately, bought the Swadlincote depot. Several smaller operators were also taken over. These included Wreake Valley of Thurmaston, Fairtax of Melton Mowbray, Astill and Jordan of Ratby, Shelton Orsborn of Wollaston, Blands of Stamford, and Loughborough Coach and Bus.

In 1989 Midland Fox was acquired by Drawlane. The following year it acquired Tellings-Golden Miller in Byfleet and this business, in turn, acquired the Coach Travel Centre in Cardiff, amongst others. Tellings bus operations eventually became part of London and Country, while Tellings was sold back to its management in 1994 before its expansion into bus operation in Cardiff.

In 1994 Pickering Transport was purchased by British Bus. Pickering build lorry bodies at their extensive site at Thurmaston, and now offer body repair and painting services which has resulted in many group vehicles appearing there. The site also houses one of Fox's three Leicester area depots. 1996 saw a launch of high quality services under the Urban Fox brand in a striking new blue livery.

Derby City Transport Ltd was a long established municipally owned bus company. In August 1989 it was sold to its employees who were assisted by Luton and District Transport. Luton and District took a 25% share holding in the business. There was a competitive interlude in Derby where Midland Red North started operations, but this ended with Derby buying out the competition in February 1990.

In 1994, after the acquisition of Luton and District by British Bus, the shareholders in Derby decided to accept an offer from British Bus for the rest of the share capital of the company. After a period of autonomy, the business was relaunched under the City Rider brand name and a yellow, red and blue livery. In January 1996, Derby City Transport was incorporated into the Midland Fox group; full integration and renumbering of the fleet taking place at the start of 2000.

In 1990, "75" Taxis started as a division of Derby City Transport, building up a fleet of London style taxis. In September 1994, Midland Fox launched a new taxi service in Leicester marketed as Fox Cabs, but this operation was sold in 2001.

In September 1996, the Head Office of Midland Fox moved to the Pickering of Thurmaston premises along with a depot facility. It was later joined by the British Bus head office, now Arriva Passenger Services Ltd, which has since moved to new premises on the other side of Leicester.

The Arriva branding had vehicles carrying the 'Arriva serving the Fox County', or 'Arriva serving Derby' identities as appropriate. The taxi business remains under its previous brand. Special liveries include four vehicles in Quick Silver Shuttle for Leicester Park and Ride, Airport Car Park Shuttle and Airport Rail Link, three vehicles in a blue livery for East Midland Airport, two buses in a Corby to Kettering Rail Link for Midland Main Line, and two vehicles in a green livery for a Marks and Spencer shuttle service.

In 2003 Arriva Fox County and Arriva Midlands North merged to become Arriva Midlands.

Midland Red North & Stevensons become Arriva Midlands North

Midland Red North Ltd was founded in 1981 when the Midland Red company was divided into four operating parts by NBC. The company traded with local network names such as Chaserider for a considerable time. These were based upon the networks generated from the Viable Network Project later carried out across NBC as Market Analysis Project (MAP). The area included the then new town of Telford where a network of new services was introduced displacing many of the long-traditional operators.

The company was sold to Drawlane in January 1988 after a false start as described earlier. In 1989, it took over the Crewe and Etruria depots of fellow Drawlane subsidiary Crosville Motor Services Ltd. In 1992, Midland Red North purchased the Oswestry and Abermule operations of

Crosville Wales Ltd, then an associated company. In 1993, with the dispersion of the Bee Line Buzz Company, the Macclesfield depot of that company which had traded as C-Line was taken over, having been part of Crosville for some time.

Stevensons of Uttoxeter commenced services in that part of Staffordshire in 1926 and continued as a small but successful family owned business. During the 1980s, and particularly after deregulation, significant growth occurred. In 1985 a controlling interest was acquired in the East Staffordshire Borough Council's bus operations in Burton-on-Trent. In 1987, the Swadlincote depot of Midland Fox and the Lichfield out station were purchased from NBC.

Growth in the West Midlands and the acquisition of a number of small companies including Crystal Coaches in Burslem and Viking Tours and Travel saw the company become a major independent operator in the early 1990s.

In April 1994, however, West Midlands Travel used its Your Bus subsidiary to retaliate in the Burton area against the significant level of operation Stevensons then had in the West Midlands area. This led to the sale of the company to British Bus in August 1994 and a significant scaling down of Stevensons operations in the West Midlands.

Macclesfield depot was transferred from Midland Red North into Stevensons in January 1995. From April 1995, Midland Red North and Stevensons were jointly managed. The closure of the Stevensons Head Office at Spath with the provision of central administration services from the Cannock head office became effective in 1996. A common livery was established between the two fleets though the Stevensons fleet name was retained on vehicles allocated to former Stevensons depots. Viking coaches retained a separate livery of two shades of grey until the operation was sold.

The application of Arriva livery and branding saw the trading identity 'Arriva serving the North Midlands' applied to all buses.

In May 1998, the Shifnal depot of Timeline was acquired along with nineteen vehicles. The bus operations of Matthews Handybus in the Newcastle under Lyme area were acquired in February 1998, but no buses were involved. In August of the same year, the local bus operations of Williamsons of Knockin Heath were taken over and four vehicles came with the work.

1999 saw many SLF Dennis Darts arrive and these were followed by thirty Volvo B6BLE buses fitted with Wright Crusader 2 bodywork. All private hire coaching operations along with the vehicles were disposed of during the year.

Arriva Midlands

In February 2003, Macclesfield, Crewe and Winsford depots were transferred from Arriva Midlands North to Arriva North West. The remaining depots of Midlands North were combined with Arriva Fox County to become Arriva Midlands.

North Western Road Car Co Ltd becomes Arriva North West

Ribble Motor Services was another NBC company divided in preparation for privatisation. The dormant Mexborough & Swinton Traction Company was renamed as above to take over the Merseyside, West Lancashire and Wigan operations of Ribble in September 1986. The head office of the new company was sited at Hawthorne Road, the Bootle area office north of Liverpool.

The company was acquired by Drawlane in March 1988. In 1989, the Runcorn and Warrington depots of Crosville were acquired. Expansion saw North Western open a depot in Altrincham, though eventually rationalisation saw the operations assumed by the Bee Line Buzz Company during its independent existence as a Drawlane subsidiary.

In 1993 Bee Line was put under the same management as North Western and a few weeks later, Liverline of Bootle was acquired along with 51 vehicles. Both were maintained as separate identities under the same management. Also acquired in 1993 were the bus operations of Express

Travel, which at the time were still branded as Amberline, though this identity was not maintained.

The head office of the company later moved to Aintree depot, though a subsequent move saw the depot sold and redeveloped leaving the head office building free standing.

1995 was a busy year with two operations in the Wigan area acquired; Little White Bus and Wigan Bus Company. Also acquired in 1995 was Arrowline Travel based in Knutsford, which traded as Star Line. This brought luxury coaches on Airport related work as well as a modern fleet of mini and midi buses. The Star Line operation was later relocated to Wythenshaw, while the coaching operation was sold to Selwyns of Runcorn.

Increase in activity in the Warrington area required a new depot to be established at Haydock. The collapse of a Cheshire operator Lofty's of Mickle Trafford saw further growth in the mid Cheshire area and new Cheshire workings now take vehicles as far south as Whitchurch.

In 1997, Arriva acquired the residue of South Lancs Transport following that operator's withdrawal from Chester, and the business was put under the supervision of North Western.

In 1998, some bus operations of Timeline in the North West were purchased along with some vehicles, though the majority went to First Group. Arriva North West manages the bus and coach facilities at the Trafford Centre on behalf of the owners of this striking shopping centre which is located four miles west of Manchester. Arriva branding initially used the identity Arriva serving the North West.

In 1999, the Winsford-based Nova Scotia operation was acquired, its services being integrated into the fleet. In 2000, Arriva acquired MTL, and the bus operations were put under the control of Arriva North West, those operations being branded 'Arriva serving Merseyside' and early in 2002 the head office functions of Arriva Cymru were transferred to Aintree. Upon full integration in the later months, the company was re-titled Arriva North West and Wales.

Yorkshire Bus Group to Arriva Yorkshire

The West Riding Automobile Company and Yorkshire Woollen District Transport were put under common management by NBC and, when privatisation happened in January 1987, the management team bought both companies. Selby and District was a trading title turned into a separate company by the new owners' Caldaire Holding company. While Caldaire became involved in the North East, the core business in West Yorkshire changed very little but there was steady investment in fleet replacement and upgrade.

There was involvement in the splitting up of National Travel East leaving a residue of operations on National Express contracts, and also competitive operations in Sheffield that led to corresponding competition in Wakefield.

The South Yorkshire Road Transport Company of Pontefract was purchased in July 1994, and maintained a separate trading identity for a time. In March 1995, the Caldaire Group was acquired by British Bus. Jaronda Travel of Selby was acquired in August 1999.

The Arriva identities used were 'Arriva serving Yorkshire' and 'Arriva serving Selby' seeing a merging together of the West Riding and Yorkshire identities for the first time. Arriva Yorkshire partnered with First Leeds in the extension to the East Leeds Guided Bus Corridor along the A64 York Road. This initiative saw both operators together contributing nearly half the scheme cost of around £9.9m with the other half coming from a partnership of Leeds City Council and West Yorkshire PTE.

United, Tees and District, and Teesside Motor Services Ltd become Arriva North East

United Automobile Services Ltd was another NBC subsidiary divided up in preparation for privatisation. In 1986, the northern part of the operating area was hived off into a new company called Northumbria. United continued to trade south of the Tyne, with its head office in Darlington. The operations in Scarborough and Pickering were transferred to a subsidiary of East Yorkshire Motor Services.

In December 1987, United was bought from NBC by Caldaire Holdings, the management buyout vehicle of the West Riding management team. In 1989, the National Express coaching activities of United were sold off to a joint venture company Durham Travel Services, set up by two former United managers with National Express Ltd.

In 1990, United was split into two parts, the Durham and North Yorkshire section continuing to trade as United, the section in Cleveland trading as Tees and District. At this time, the associated businesses of Trimdon Motor Services and Teeside Motor Services were acquired, with the Trimdon business being absorbed into United and the Teeside business continuing.

In the summer of 1992, there was a demerger of the Caldaire Group, with the North East operations passing to the Westcourt Group, and Caldaire North East becoming North East Bus.

In 1994, a new head office and engineering works in Morton Road, Darlington allowed the vacation of the Grange Road site for redevelopment. Also in 1994, the Westcourt Group sold to West Midlands Travel in the November, and North East Bus became part of the National Express Group following the merger with that group in 1995.

Eden Bus Services of Bishop Auckland was acquired in October 1995 and was absorbed into the main operation.

National Express Group sold North East Bus to the Cowie Group on the last day of July 1996 and, in October, the Ripon depot operations were sold to Harrogate and District Travel.

Northumbria Motor Services Ltd into Arriva Northumbria

In 1986, the operations of United Auto were split into two parts in preparation for privatisation. The dormant Southern National Omnibus Company Ltd was renamed Northumbria and took over operations in September 1986 with a new head office in Jesmond.

In October 1987, Northumbria was acquired from NBC by its management using Proudmutual as a holding company. Proudmutual also acquired Kentish Bus in March 1988. Other acquisitions included Moor-Dale Coaches and Hunters. In 1994 the Proudmutual group was acquired by British Bus while, at the same time, Moor-Dale Coaches was sold back to former directors.

In the Arriva era, two trading identities were used: 'Arriva serving Northumbria' and 'Arriva serving the North East'.

Crosville Cymru into Arriva Cymru

Crosville Wales Ltd was, until August 1986, the Welsh and Shropshire operations of Crosville Motor Services Ltd based in Chester. In 1986, it was resolved that the Crosville company was too large to be offered for privatisation as a whole, and the then dormant Devon General Omnibus and Touring Company Ltd was revived by NBC in order to take over the assets and business of Crosville in Wales, to be renamed Crosville Wales. The management team of Crosville Wales purchased the company from NBC in December 1987.

In January 1989, the company was bought by National Express Holdings Ltd. In July of that year, it purchased a subsidiary company called Amberline, based at Speke in Liverpool, and added a bus operation to the mainly National Express coach contracts operated.

In July 1991, the National Express group was purchased by a consortium of banks led by Drawlane as explained earlier. Ultimately, this led to Crosville Wales becoming a full member of the Drawlane Group shortly before its transformation into British Bus plc. In January 1992, the Oswestry depot and its outstation at Abermule were sold to Midland Red North.

Crosville Wales took advantage of second hand vehicles from other group companies and other operators, building a fleet of Leyland Lynx and National 2s while concurrently buying further new Mercedes minibuses and Dennis Darts.

In 1995, some of the services, but no vehicles, of Alpine Travel were acquired, leading to an operation of certain services as Alpine Bus in a red and white livery. This was superseded by a

Shoreline livery of blue, white and yellow, which has been phased out and replaced by route branding. All operations were branded 'Arriva serving Wales/gwansanaethu Cymru', including those of the two acquisitions in 1998. The first was Devaway of Bretton, Chester. This brought a mixed fleet of VRTs, Nationals, and more Lynx and a depot from which to operate Chester area services. The second acquisition was Purple Motors of Bethesda. Further low floor buses arrived during 1999 to provide the Arriva share of a Quality Partnership Corridor on Deeside jointly provided with First Crosville. At the start of 2000 a large batch of low-floor Darts joined the fleet, and these displaced the last examples of the National in the fleet.

In February 2000, low-floor vehicles were introduced on low-volume rural services as north Wales authorities chose to use their share of the expanded Rural Bus Grant in improving quality rather than widening availability. One Dart MPD is equipped with a bike rack.

Arriva Cymru is now managed under the Arriva North West and Wales umbrella.

Clydeside Buses Ltd into Arriva Scotland West Ltd

Clydeside Buses and its predecessors have been serving its core area of Renfrewshire and Inverclyde since 1928. Prior to 1985, the operation had formed the northern section of Western Scottish, part of the Scottish Bus Group (SBG). In preparation for the deregulation of local bus services, Clydeside Scottish assumed responsibility for the Glasgow, Renfrewshire and Inverclyde operations of Western Scottish in 1985. Over the next six years, there was a complex series of reorganisations between Clydeside and Western until, in 1991, Clydeside became the last SBG subsidiary to be privatised when it was purchased by its employees with assistance from Luton and District Transport Group, emerging as Clydeside 2000 plc.

After 1986, there were numerous competitors in the core area and trading proved extremely difficult. When the LDT group sold to British Bus, an offer put to the shareholders of Clydeside was accepted and Clydeside joined British Bus. There was immediate effort to update the fleet against a background of tightening up of enforcement generally in the area. Some of the competitive battles had led to the Traffic Commissioner taking steps to control the number of departures and waiting times in certain town centres.

The development of services has seen Flagship Routes introduced to raise quality levels. Additionally, opportunity was taken to acquire various smaller operators in the area such as Ashton Coaches of Greenock, and a significant share in Dart Buses of Paisley. Operations from the Greenock base were restyled as GMS-Greenock Motor Services with a separate livery. McGills Bus Service Ltd of Barrhead was acquired by the group in 1997 and for a time was kept as a separate entity from Clydeside Buses. Clydeside also acquired Bridge Coaches of Paisley, being fully absorbed into Clydeside.

During 2001, the shareholding in Dart Buses was sold to Stagecoach Western and the dormant McGills company used as a vehicle to sell off all remaining Inverclyde operations which ceased trading at the end of June. The redundant depot at Greenock and subsequently former McGill's site at Barrhead were demolished with all operations spread between remaining sites at Inchinnan and Johnstone. In a final move to consolidate the business the remote head office site located in Renfrew was vacated and all employees subsequently relocated within a refurbished facility at Inchinnan depot. The Arriva serving Scotland branding covers all operations.

Expansion into Europe

September 1997	Unibus Holdings, Denmark
January 1998	Vancom Nederland
December 1998	Veonn & Hanze, Netherlands
March 1999	Bus Danmark
July 1999	Mercancias Ideal Gallego, Spain

September 1999	Transportes Finisterre, Spain
November 2000	Ami-Transportes, Portugal
December 2000	Abilio da Costa Moreira, Portugal
April 2001	Combus, Denmark
January 2002	Autocares Mallorca
June 2002	Transportes Sul ode Tejo, Portugal
July 2002	SAB Autoservizi, Italy
April 2004	Prignitzer Eisenbahn Gruppe, Germany

During 2003, Arriva completed its purchase of Transportes Sul do Tejo by acquiring the Barraqueiro Group's remaining 49%. It also began to operate its Danish rail franchises in Mid and North Jutland. In 2004, the Group enterd the German public transport market with the acquisition of Prignitzer Eisenbahn Gruppe and grew its position in the Italian public transport market with the acquisition of Società Autoservizi F.V.G. S.p.A.

These acquisitions continue the strategy of developing Arriva's mainland European transport business, which is now a major contributor to the Group's results. Arriva now has significant positions in the Netherlands, Denmark, Portugal and Italy, with smaller positions in Germany, Spain and Sweden.

Denmark

The first acquisition in mainland Europe was Unibus in Denmark, which was acquired in 1997. Unibus operated approximately 8% of the tendered market in Copenhagen and within that area is also the largest private sector provider of services for handicapped persons transport. Additionally, it had operations throughout Jutland and Zealand. Founded in 1985, Unibus grew by winning tendered bus operations for the Transport Authority for Copenhagen - HT. Unibus was the biggest coach operator in Copenhagen until in 1995, when the coaching business was sold to Lyngby Turistfart.

This involvement within the Danish bus market led to the acquisition of Bus Danmark (now Arriva Danmark) in 1999 and its wholly owned subsidiary Odakra Buss based in southern Sweden. In April 2000, Arriva Danmark acquired the former state owned Company, COMBUS. Part of the company was sold on to Connex but Arriva kept the majority of its regional and provincial bus operations throughout Denmark. Arriva Danmark operates a fleet of approximately 1150 buses, including demand responsive vehicles, and 43 train sets. During 2001 the first double-deck buses for the Danish fleet were delivered. Arriva Sverige (Odakra Buss) activities are focused in the Skane Lan region of southern Sweden operating 160 buses.

Arriva Danmark was also successful with its bid in respect of the first rail passenger franchises to be announced in Denmark. The package consists of two rail passenger franchises connecting Mid and North Jutland with Arhus. The franchises commenced operation in January 2003. Twenty-nine new Coradia Lint trains will be delivered in 2004.

The Netherlands

Arriva entered the Dutch market through the acquisition of Vancom Nederland (now Arriva Nederland) in 1998, which operated the former municipal undertaking in the city of Groningen together with demand responsive services in the region and a joint venture in the Maastricht area of Zuid Limburg.

Arriva Nederland subsequently acquired the former VSN subsidiary companies of Veonn and Hanze covering the provinces of Friesland, Groningen and Drenthe. The companies operate an extensive network of urban and interurban bus services, and demand responsive transit.

In June 1999, Arriva made its first move into rail with NoordNed, a joint venture with Dutch Rail. This joint venture, represented the first rail privatisation in the Netherlands, operates bus and train services in Friesland and train services in the Province of Groningen. Arriva took full control of Noordned in 2003.

Arriva Nederland, now operates some 1200 vehicles, 51 train sets, has 2700 employees and is the geographic hub for the Group's potential interests in the Benelux countries.

Spain

Arriva's interest in the Spanish market commenced with the acquisition of IASA and Finisterre, both located in the Galicia region. Branded Arriva Noroeste, the company operates throughout Galicia with substantial facilities at La Coruña, Lugo and Santiago de Compostela providing regular, schools and discretional services. Arriva also operates buses in Mallorca. Its combined Spanish businesses have a fleet of over 300 vehicles and 500 employees.

Sweden

Arriva first entered the Swedish bus market when it acquired the Danish company Unibus Holdings in 1997. It operates 200 vehicles and employs around 500 people in the south of Sweden.

Portugal

Arriva's presence in Iberia was further strengthened through its entry into Portuguese public transport. This was achieved through the acquisition of Ami-Transportes SA, Joao Carlos Soares and Filhos SA, Viaco Costa Lino SA and Abilio da Costa Moreira SA. Collectively, these companies operate some 250 buses, with 340 employees on regional bus services in the northern half of Portugal.

In June 2002, Arriva acquired a 51% controlling interest in Transportes Sul ode Tejo (TST), Portugal, from the Barraqueiro Group, with an option to acquire the remaining 49% by 31 December 2003. TST is the leading operator of scheduled bus and coach services in the growing commuter region south of Lisbon. The company also operates schools and works contracts. The region has a large and growing population, and much of TST's operations involve the carriage of Lisbon commuters to ferry services on the River Tejo and the new cross river railway. Arriva exercised its option to acquire the remaining 49% of TST in August 2003.

Arriva Portugal's combined business has a fleet of over 900 vehicles and 1,750 employees.

Italy

In July 2002, Arriva made its first acquisition in Italy with the purchase of SAB Autoservizi SrL, the largest private-sector bus operator in Italy, from parent company Italmobilare. The company operates mainly in the Lombardi region of northern Italy, where it has a 13% share of the bus transport market. The majority of the region's other services are operated by municipal authorities. The passenger transport market in Italy is one of the largest in Europe with both bus and rail sectors moving rapidly to a competitive tendering environment.

Arriva made a further acquisition in April 2004 when it acquired Società Autoservizi F.V.G. S.p.A. in the Udine area of the Friuli Venezia Giulia region. Arriva's combined Italian businesses operate around 1,800 vehicles and employ around 2,600 staff.

The Italian passenger market is the third largest in Europe and is evolving rapidly towards competitive tendering of all bus operations so the purchase offers significant opportunities for expansion.

Germany

Arriva entered the German public transport market - the largest in Europe - in April 2004, with the acquisition of rail company Prignitzer Eisenbahn Gruppe (PEG).

PEG runs services in the federal states of North Rhine-Westphalia, Brandenburg and Mecklenburg-West Pomerania.

With 21 train sets and 250 employees, by 2004 Arriva will be operating five franchises, two of which involve a joint venture.

Arriva Trains

In 2000, Arriva acquired two British rail franchises as part of its purchase of MTL, the Liverpool-based transport company. The refranchising process has been protracted.

Arriva failed to make the shortlist of bidders for the Merseyrail franchise although it was rated the best mainland operator in terms of punctuality and reliability in the latest figures published by the SRA.

Arriva's UK Trains division operates two rail passenger operating Companies. Arriva Trains Wales/Trenau Arriva Cymru operates interurban, commuter and rural passenger services throughout Wales and the border counties. Arriva Trains Northern which operates extensively across the north of England.

Arriva Vehicle Rental

Arriva Vehicle Rental continues to perform strongly and is expected to grow over the next five years as Govt's 'Best Value Initiative' encourages the public sector to out source vehicle fleets. The current fleet is around 11,000 vehicles based at 42 locations. Vehicle Rental has been trading with six business brands, but each is now migrating to the Arriva brand.

ARRIVA SCOTLAND

Arriva Scotland West Ltd, Old Greenock Road, Inchinnan, PA4 9PG

151	IN	M751WWR	Optare MetroRider MR31	Optare	B27F	1995	Arriva Yorkshire, 2002
152	IN	M753WWR	Optare MetroRider MR31	Optare	B27F	1995	Arriva Yorkshire, 2002
2740	u	N803BKN	Optare MetroRider MR15	Optare	B29F	1996	Arriva Southern Counties, 2004
2741	u	N804BKN	Optare MetroRider MR15	Optare	B29F	1996	Arriva Southern Counties, 2004
195	IN	P895XCU	Optare MetroRider	Optare	B31F	1996	Arriva North East, 2000
196	JO	P896XCU	Optare MetroRider	Optare	B31F	1996	Arriva North East, 2000

201-208 — Optare MetroRider MR17 — Optare — B29F — 1996

201	IN	N201NHS	203	IN	N203NHS	205	IN	N205NHS	207	IN	N207NHS
202	IN	N202NHS	204	IN	N204NHS	206	IN	N206NHS	208	IN	N208NHS

217-227 — Optare MetroRider MR17 — Optare — B29F — 1996

217	JO	P217SGB	220	JO	P220SGB	224	JO	P224SGB	226	IN	P226SGB
218	JO	P218SGB	221	JO	P221SGB	225	JO	P225SGB	227	JO	P227SGB
219	JO	P219SGB	223	JO	P223SGB						

229	w	M95EGE	Mercedes-Benz 709D	WS Wessex II	B33F	1995	Ashton Group, Greenock, 1997

239-243 — Mercedes-Benz 811D — WS Wessex II — B33F — 1995 — Ashton Group, Greenock, 1997

239	w	M278FNS	240	w	M277FNS	242	McG	M422GUS	243	w	N991KUS

245	Mc	N808PDS	Mercedes-Benz 811D	Marshall C16	B33F	1996	Ashton Group, Greenock, 1997
249	Mc	N807PDS	Mercedes-Benz 811D	Marshall C16	B33F	1996	Ashton Group, Greenock, 1997
267	JO	N81PUS	Mercedes-Benz 811D	Marshall C16	B33F	1996	Ashton Group, Greenock, 1997
268	IN	N82PUS	Mercedes-Benz 811D	Marshall C16	B33F	1996	Ashton Group, Greenock, 1997
269	JO	N26KYS	Mercedes-Benz 811D	Plaxton Beaver	B33F	1995	Ashton Group, Greenock, 1997
270	JO	N27KYS	Mercedes-Benz 811D	Plaxton Beaver	B33F	1995	Ashton Group, Greenock, 1997
271	Mc	P932YSB	Mercedes-Benz 811D	Mellor	B33F	1997	Ashton Group, Greenock, 1997
272	Mc	P936YSB	Mercedes-Benz 811D	Mellor	B33F	1997	Ashton Group, Greenock, 1997
273	JO	P937YSB	Mercedes-Benz 811D	Mellor	B33F	1997	Ashton Group, Greenock, 1997
274	Mc	P491TGA	Mercedes-Benz 711D	UVG CitiStar	B29F	1996	Ashton Group, Greenock, 1997
276	JO	P492TGA	Mercedes-Benz 711D	UVG CitiStar	B29F	1996	Ashton Group, Greenock, 1997
277	JO	P527UGA	Mercedes-Benz 711D	Marshall C19	B29F	1996	Ashton Group, Greenock, 1997
278	Mc	P526UGA	Mercedes-Benz 711D	Marshall C19	B29F	1996	Ashton Group, Greenock, 1997

280-283 — Mercedes-Benz 709D — TBP — B29F — 1995 — Ashton Group, Greenock, 1997

280	w	M792EUS	281	w	M793EUS	282	w	M794EUS	283	w	M423GUS

284	Mc	N752LUS	Mercedes-Benz 709D	UVG CitiStar	B29F	1996	Ashton Group, Greenock, 1997
285	Mc	N753LUS	Mercedes-Benz 709D	UVG CitiStar	B29F	1996	Ashton Group, Greenock, 1997

286-296 — Mercedes-Benz 709D — Marshall C19 — B29F — 1996 — Ashton Group, Greenock, 1997

286	Mc	N754LUS	289	Mc	N256PGD	292	Mc	N801PDS	295	Mc	N804PDS
287	Mc	N228MUS	290	Mc	N257PGD	293	Mc	N802PDS	296	Mc	N805PDS
288	Mc	N254PGD	291	Mc	N258PGD	294	Mc	N803PDS			

297	Mc	P930YSB	Mercedes-Benz 709D	Plaxton Beaver	B29F	1997	Ashton Group, Greenock, 1997
298	JO	P931YSB	Mercedes-Benz 709D	Plaxton Beaver	B29F	1997	Ashton Group, Greenock, 1997
299	JO	P529UGA	Mercedes-Benz 709D	Plaxton Beaver	B29F	1997	Ashton Group, Greenock, 1997
300	JO	P528UGA	Mercedes-Benz 709D	Plaxton Beaver	B29F	1997	Ashton Group, Greenock, 1997
303	Mc	M878DDS	Mercedes-Benz 709D	WS Wessex II	B29F	1994	Ashton Group, Greenock, 1997
304	Mc	N941MGG	Mercedes-Benz 709D	Marshall C19	B29F	1995	Ashton Group, Greenock, 1997
305	Mc	N942MGG	Mercedes-Benz 709D	Marshall C19	B29F	1995	Ashton Group, Greenock, 1997
306	Mc	L970VGE	Mercedes-Benz 709D	WS Wessex II	B29F	1994	Ashton Group, Greenock, 1997
401	JO	M65FDS	Dennis Dart 9.8 SDL3054	Plaxton Pointer	B41F	1995	
402	JO	M67FDS	Dennis Dart 9.8 SDL3054	Plaxton Pointer	B41F	1995	
403	IN	K538ORH	Dennis Dart 9.0 SDL3016	Plaxton Pointer	B34F	1992	Arriva London, 2002
404	IN	K539ORH	Dennis Dart 9.0 SDL3016	Plaxton Pointer	B34F	1992	Arriva London, 2002
405	IN	K540ORH	Dennis Dart 9.0 SDL3016	Plaxton Pointer	B34F	1992	Arriva London, 2002
406	IN	K541ORH	Dennis Dart 9.0 SDL3016	Plaxton Pointer	B34F	1992	Arriva London, 2002
407	JO	N681GUM	Dennis Dart 9.8 SDL3054	Plaxton Pointer	B40F	1995	Arriva London, 2002
408	JO	N684GUM	Dennis Dart 9.8 SDL3054	Plaxton Pointer	B40F	1995	Arriva London, 2002
409	IN	P822RWU	Dennis Dart 9.8m	Plaxton Pointer	B40F	1996	Arriva London, 2002
410	IN	N710GUM	Dennis Dart 9.0 SDL3053	Plaxton Pointer	B34F	1995	Arriva London, 2003
411	IN	N711GUM	Dennis Dart 9.0 SDL3053	Plaxton Pointer	B34F	1995	Arriva London, 2003

The Scottish operation is the smallest of those based in Britain and is dominated by the Dart and Mercedes-Benz minibus. In 2002 the fleet was reduced further when many minibuses were transferred to McGills, a one-time subsidiary, but now independent. However, several Mercedes mini-buses from the current Arriva Scotland fleet remain on loan to that operator and are listed here. All the Optare MetroRiders remain in the main fleet and 217, P217SGB is seen in Govan. *Mark Doggett*

412	IN	N712GUM	Dennis Dart 9.0 SDL3053	Plaxton Pointer	B34F	1995	Arriva London, 2003
413	IN	P913PWW	Dennis Dart 9m	Plaxton Pointer	B34F	1996	Arriva London, 2003
414	IN	P914PWW	Dennis Dart 9m	Plaxton Pointer	B34F	1996	Arriva London, 2003
415	IN	P915PWW	Dennis Dart 9m	Plaxton Pointer	B34F	1996	Arriva London, 2003
416	JO	P962RUL	Dennis Dart SLF 10.2m	Alexander ALX200	N36F	1997	Arriva London, 2003
417	JO	P963RUL	Dennis Dart SLF 10.2m	Alexander ALX200	N36F	1997	Arriva London, 2003
418	IN	N708GUM	Dennis Dart 9.0 SDL3053	Plaxton Pointer	B34F	1995	Arriva London, 2003
419	IN	N709GUM	Dennis Dart 9.0 SDL3053	Plaxton Pointer	B34F	1995	Arriva London, 2003

420-424

		Dennis Dart SLF 10.2m	Alexander ALX200	N36F	1997	Arriva London, 2003

420	JO	P964RUL	422	JO	P966RUL	423	JO	P967RUL	424	JO	P968RUL
421	JO	P965RUL									

425-433

		Dennis Dart 9.8SDL3054	Plaxton Pointer	B40F	1995-96	Arriva London, 2003

425	IN	N672GUM	428	IN	N683GUM	430	IN	N686GUM	432	IN	N688GUM
426	IN	N675GUM	429	IN	N685GUM	431	IN	N687GUM	433	IN	N691GUM
427	IN	N677GUM									

504	IN	M104RMS	Scania L113CRL	Alexander Strider	B51F	1995	
506	IN	M106RMS	Scania L113CRL	Alexander Strider	B51F	1995	
507	IN	M107RMS	Scania L113CRL	Alexander Strider	B51F	1995	

508-513

		Scania N113CRL	East Lancs European	N45F*	1995	*509 is N51F

508	IN	M108RMS	510	IN	M110RMS	512	IN	M112RMS	513	IN	M113RMS
509	IN	M109RMS									

514-521

		Scania L113CRL	East Lancs European	N51F	1995	

514	IN	M114RMS	516	IN	M116RMS	518	IN	M118RMS	520	IN	M120RMS
515	IN	M115RMS	517	IN	M117RMS	519	IN	M119RMS	521	IN	M121RMS

525	IN	L25LSX	Scania N113CRL	East Lancs European	N51F	1993	Scania demonstrator, 1995

633	IN	TUP572V	Leyland Leopard PSU3E/4R	Plaxton Derwent (1991)	B51F	1980	Arriva Cymru, 1999
798	JO	WSU475	Dennis Dart SLF 10.7m	Plaxton Pointer 2	N43F	1999	
799	JO	WSU476	Dennis Dart SLF 10.7m	Plaxton Pointer 2	N43F	1999	
800	JO	GSU347	Dennis Dart SLF 10.7m	Plaxton Pointer 2	N43F	1999	

801-805 — Dennis Dart SLF — Plaxton Pointer — N35F — 1996

801	JO	P801RWU	803	JO	P803RWU	804	JO	P804RWU	805	JO	P805RWU
802	JO	P802RWU									

806-815 — Dennis Dart SLF — Alexander ALX200 — N40F — 1997

806	JO	P806DBS	809	JO	P809DBS	812	JO	P812DBS	814	JO	P814DBS
807	JO	P807DBS	810	JO	P810DBS	813	JO	P813DBS	815	JO	P815DBS
808	JO	P808DBS	811	JO	P811DBS						

816-840 — Dennis Dart SLF — Plaxton Pointer — N40F — 1997

816	JO	P816GMS	823	JO	P823GMS	829	JO	P829KES	835	IN	P835KES
817	JO	P817GMS	824	JO	P824GMS	830	JO	P830KES	836	IN	P836KES
818	JO	P818GMS	825	JO	P825KES	831	JO	P831KES	837	IN	P837KES
819	JO	P819GMS	826	IN	P826KES	832	JO	P832KES	838	JO	P838KES
820	JO	P820GMS	827	IN	P827KES	833	JO	P833KES	839	JO	P839KES
821	IN	P821GMS	828	JO	P828KES	834	JO	P834KES	840	JO	P840KES
822	JO	P822GMS									

841	IN	N439GHG	Dennis Dart	Northern Counties Paladin	B39F	1995
842	IN	N440GHG	Dennis Dart	Northern Counties Paladin	B39F	1995
843	IN	N473MUS	Dennis Dart	Northern Counties Paladin	B39F	1995
844	IN	N474MUS	Dennis Dart	Northern Counties Paladin	B39F	1995
845	IN	K946SGG	Dennis Dart 9SDL3011	Plaxton Pointer	B35F	1993
846	IN	K947SGG	Dennis Dart 9SDL3011	Plaxton Pointer	B35F	1993

847-851 — Dennis Dart SLF — Alexander ALX200 — N40F — 1998

847	JO	R381JYS	849	JO	R383JYS	850	JO	R384JYS	851	JO	R385JYS
848	JO	R382JYS									

852	IN	M248SPP	Dennis Dart 9.8SDL3054	Wright Handy-bus	B40F	1994	The Shires, 1998
853	IN	M250SPP	Dennis Dart 9.8SDL3054	Wright Handy-bus	B40F	1994	The Shires, 1998
854	IN	H242MUK	Dennis Dart 9.8SDL3004	Carlyle Dartline	B40F	1991	The Shires, 1998
855	IN	M251SPP	Dennis Dart 9.8SDL3054	Wright Handy-bus	B40F	1994	The Shires, 1998
856	JO	M249SPP	Dennis Dart 9.8SDL3054	Wright Handy-bus	B40F	1994	The Shires, 1998
857	JO	H244MUK	Dennis Dart 9.8SDL3004	Carlyle Dartline	B40F	1991	The Shires, 1998
858	IN	M247SPP	Dennis Dart 9.8SDL3054	Wright Handy-bus	B40F	1994	The Shires, 1998

860-869 — Dennis Dart SLF — Alexander ALX200 — N40F — 1998-99

860	JO	S860OGB	863	JO	S863OGB	866	JO	S866OGB	868	JO	S868OGB
861	JO	S861OGB	864	JO	S864OGB	867	JO	S867OGB	869	JO	HIL2148
862	JO	S862OGB	865	JO	S865OGB						

870-878 — Volvo Citybus B10M-55 — East Lancs EL2000 — B41F — 1990-01 — Arriva London, 1999

870	w	H920XYT	876	w	H916XYT	877	w	H915XYT	878	w	H913XYT
874	w	H921XYT									

Excluding a batch of retired Volvo buses, the large single-decks operating with Arriva Scotland are Scania products. Three L113s have Alexander bodywork with 504, M104RMS illustrating the model as it heads for Erskine.
Mark Doggett

The dominant vehicle type with Arriva Scotland is the Dennis Dart. 1998 saw the arrival of five with Alexander ALX200 bodywork, represented by 850, R384JYS, which is seen in Paisley on the *Supershuttle* route linking the town with Barrhead and Auchenback. *Richard Godfrey*

880-885

										Volvo Citybus B10M-50		East Lancs		B45/31F	1990-91	London South, 1998-99

880	JO	H668GPF	882	JO	H675GPF	884	IN	H677GPF	885	IN	H670GPF
881	JO	H681GPF	883	JO	H676GPF						

889	IN	CWR519Y	Leyland Olympian ONLXB/1R	Eastern Coach Works	B45/32F	1982	Yorkshire (South), 1998
897	JO	CWR518Y	Leyland Olympian ONLXB/1R	Eastern Coach Works	B45/32F	1983	Yorkshire (South), 1998
903	JO	TPD116X	Leyland Olympian ONTL11/1R	Roe	B43/29F	1982	Kentish Bus, 1997
904	JO	CWR514Y	Leyland Olympian ONLXB/1R	Eastern Coach Works	B45/32F	1982	Yorkshire, 1998
932	JO	KYV664X	MCW Metrobus DR101/14	MCW	B43/28D	1981	Arriva London, 1999
936	JO	GYE510W	MCW Metrobus DR101/14	MCW	B43/28D	1981	Arriva London, 1999
954	IN	G154TYT	Volvo Citybus B10M-55	Alexander RV	B46/33F	1990	Arriva London (NE), 1999
956	JO	GYE507W	MCW Metrobus DR101/14	MCW	B43/28D	1981	Arriva London, 1999
957	JO	KYV751X	MCW Metrobus DR101/14	MCW	B43/28D	1982	Arriva North East, 1999
959	IN	KYV734X	MCW Metrobus DR101/14	MCW	B43/28D	1982	Arriva North East, 1999
963	IN	KYO610X	MCW Metrobus DR101/12	MCW	B43/28D	1981	Arriva London, 2000
964	JO	C404BUV	MCW Metrobus DR101/17	MCW	B43/28D	1985	Arriva The Shires, 2001
1001	JO	N750LUS	Mercedes-Benz OH1416	Wright Urbanranger	B47F	1995	

Ancillary vehicles:

701	JO	E26ECH	Scania K92CRB	Alexander PS	TV	1988	Arriva Midlands, 2003
9989	JO	G511EAJ	Leyland Lynx LX2R11C15Z4S	Leyland Lynx	TV	1990	Arriva North East, 2003
TV5	JO	LAZ5785	Mercedes-Benz L608D	Alexander AM	TV	1985	The Shires, 1998

Previous registrations:

GSU347	V313NGD	TUP572V	TUP572V, HIL2148
HIL2148	S869OGB	WSU475	V311NGD
LAZ5785	C203PCD	WSU476	V312NGD
N750LUS	N750LUS, WSU476		

Allocations:

Inchinnan (Greenock Road) - IN

MetroRider	151	152	195	201	202	203	204	205
	206	207	208	226				
Mercedes-Benz	268							
Dart	403	404	405	406	409	410	411	412
	413	414	415	418	419	425	426	427
	428	429	430	431	432	433	821	826
	827	835	836	837	841	842	843	844
	845	846	852	853	855	858		
Leopard	633							
Scania sd	504	506	507	508	509	510	512	513
	514	515	516	517	518	519	520	521
	525							
Metrobus	959	963						
Volvo Citybus	884	885	954					
Olympian	889							

Johnstone (Cochranemill Road) - JO

MetroRider	196	217	218	219	220	221	223	224
	225	227						
Mercedes-Benz	267	269	270	273	276	277	298	299
	300							
Dart	401	402	407	408	416	417	420	421
	422	423	424	798	799	800	801	802
	803	804	805	806	807	808	809	810
	811	812	813	815	816	817	818	819
	820	822	823	824	825	828	829	830
	831	832	833	834	838	839	840	847
	848	849	850	851	854	856	857	860
	861	862	863	864	865	866	867	868
	869							
MB Urbanranger	1001							
Metrobus	932	936	956	957	964			
Volvo Citybus	880	881	882	883				
Olympian	897	903	904					

On hire to McGills - Mc

Mercedes-Benz	229*	239*	240*	242	243*	245	249	271
	272	274	278	280*	281*	282*	283*	284
	285	286	287	288	289	290	291	292
	293	294	295	296	297	303	304	305
	306	(*stored for disposal)						

Unallocated - u/w

MetroRider	2740	2741		
Volvo B10M bus	874	876	877	878

ARRIVA NORTH EAST

Arriva North East Ltd, Arriva House, Admiral Way, Sunderland, SR3 3XP

141	NE	V141EJR	DAF DE33WSSB3000	Van Hool T9 Alizée	C44FT	1999	
142	NE	V142EJR	DAF DE33WSSB3000	Van Hool T9 Alizée	C44FT	1999	
143	NE	X143WNL	DAF DE33WSSB3000	Van Hool T9 Alizée	C49FT	2000	
144	NE	X144WNL	DAF DE33WSSB3000	Van Hool T9 Alizée	C49FT	2000	
145	NE	NL52XZV	DAF SB4000XF	Van Hool T9 Alizée	C49FT	2002	
146	NE	NL52XZW	DAF SB4000XF	Van Hool T9 Alizée	C49FT	2002	
147	NE	NL52XZX	DAF SB4000XF	Van Hool T9 Alizée	C49FT	2002	
148	NE	NL52XZY	DAF SB4000XF	Van Hool T9 Alizée	C49FT	2002	
214	AK	XSV691	Leyland Tiger TRCTL11/3ARZA	Plaxton Paramount 3200 III	C53F	1988	Maidstone & District, 1998
215	AK	YSU870	Leyland Tiger TRCTL11/3ARZ	Plaxton Paramount 3500 III	C53F	1988	Maidstone & District, 1998
216	AK	YSU871	Leyland Tiger TRCTL11/3ARZ	Plaxton Paramount 3500 III	C53F	1988	Maidstone & District, 1998
217	AK	F188HKK	Leyland Tiger TRCL10/3ARZA	Duple 340	C53F	1989	Maidstone & District, 1998
218	AK	F189HKK	Leyland Tiger TRCL10/3ARZA	Duple 340	C53F	1989	Maidstone & District, 1998
247	HX	B277KPF	Leyland Tiger TRCTL11/3RH	Plaxton Paramount 3200 IIE	C51F	1985	Kentish Bus, 1992

271-280

			Scania L113CRL		East Lancs European	NC45F	1996		
271	NE	P271VRG	274	AK	P274VRG	277	BL	P277VRG	279	BL	P279VRG
272	NE	P272VRG	275	BL	P275VRG	278	BL	P278VRG	280	BL	P814VTY
273	AK	P273VRG	276	BL	P276VRG					

281-290

			Scania L113CRL		East Lancs European	NC45F	1995		
281	AS	N281NCN	284	AS	N284NCN	287	BL	N287NCN	289	BL	N289NCN
282	AS	N282NCN	285	BL	N285NCN	288	BL	N288NCN	290	BL	N290NCN
283	AS	N283NCN	286	AS	N286NCN					

601	NE	BYX210V	MCW Metrobus DR101/12	MCW	B43/28F	1980	London North, 1998
604	HX	KYV646X	MCW Metrobus DR101/14	MCW	B43/28F	1982	London North, 1998
611	DU	GYE396W	MCW Metrobus DR101/12	MCW	B43/28F	1980	Arriva London, 2000
614	AS	GYE515W	MCW Metrobus DR101/14	MCW	B43/28F	1981	Arriva London, 2000

Just five Duple coaches remain operational throughout the group and a pair of 340 models new to Maidstone & District, are based at Alnwick, the location for this picture of 218, F189HKK. The pair can be found on the 57 km link between the town and the centre of Newcastle. *Richard Godfrey*

615	AS	KYV671X	MCW Metrobus DR101/14	MCW		B43/28F	1982	Arriva London, 2000
617	DU	OJD858Y	MCW Metrobus DR101/16	MCW		B43/28F	1983	Arriva London, 2000
619	w	A930SUL	MCW Metrobus DR101/16	MCW		B43/28F	1983	Arriva London, 2000
620	NE	WLT954	MCW Metrobus DR101/16	MCW		B43/28F	1984	Arriva London, 2000

621-631

			MCW Metrobus DR101/17	MCW		B43/28D*	1984-85	Arriva London, *621-5 B43/28F
621	NE	A959SYF	624	NE	B116WUL	626	NE	B86WUL	630	NE	B90WUL
622	NE	A973SYF	625	NE	C354BUV	629	NE	B89WUL	631	NE	B91WUL
623	NE	B112WUL

752	w	M752WWR	Optare MetroRider MR31	Optare		B27F	1995	Arriva Yorkshire, 2002

855-870

		Optare MetroRider		Optare MR07		BC29F	1992-95
855	w	L855WRG	866	HX	M866KCU	869	w	M869KCU	870	RD	M870KCU
863	NE	M863KCU	867	DU	M867KCU

871-876

		Optare MetroRider		Optare MR17		B31F	1995
871	BA	M871LBB	873	BL	M873LBB	875	BL	M875LBB	876	SN	M876LBB
872	BL	M872LBB	874	BL	M874LBB

877-894

		Optare MetroRider		Optare MR17		B31F	1996
877	BL	N877RTN	882	BL	N882RTN	886	AK	N886RTN	890	AK	N890RTN
878	BL	N878RTN	883	BL	N883RTN	887	NE	N887RTN	891	AS	N891RTN
879	HX	N879RTN	884	BL	N884RTN	888	NE	N192RVK	893	SN	P893XCU
880	HX	N880RTN	885	HX	N885RTN	889	AS	N889RTN	894	DU	P894XCU
881	BL	N881RTN

897-901

		Optare MetroRider		Optare MR17		B31F	1996	Arriva Scotland, 2002
897	SN	P56XTN	899	NE	P58XTN	900	NE	P59XTN	901	NE	P61XTN
898	DU	P57XTN

902-923

		Optare MetroRider MR15		Optare		B31F	1997-98
902	BL	P902DRG	908	AK	R908JNL	914	AS	R914JNL	919	AS	R919JNL
903	BL	P903DRG	909	AS	R909JNL	915	AS	R915JNL	920	BL	R920JNL
904	AS	P904DRG	910	AS	R910JNL	916	AS	R916JNL	921	NE	R921JNL
905	AS	P905JNL	911	AS	R251JNL	917	AS	R917JNL	922	HX	R922JNL
906	AS	P906JNL	912	AS	R912JNL	918	AS	R918JNL	923	HX	R923JNL
907	AS	R907JNL	913	AS	R913JNL

935	w	K726HUG	Optare MetroRider MR05	Optare		B31F	1992	Arriva Cymru, 2000
937	AS	L700BUS	Optare MetroRider MR11	Optare		B32F	1996	Arriva The Shires, 2002

1201-1205

		DAF DE33WSSB3000		Plaxton Prima Interurban		BC51F	1997
1201	HX	R291KRG	1203	MH	R293KRG	1204	HX	R294KRG	1205	HX	R295KRG
1202	HX	R292KRG

1206-1214

		DAF DE33WSSB3000		Plaxton Prima Interurban		BC51F	1999
1206	LS	V206DJR	1209	LS	V209DJR	1211	BA	V211DJR	1213	RR	V213DJR
1207	LS	V207DJR	1210	BA	V210DJR	1212	RR	V212DJR	1214	RR	V214DJR
1208	LS	V208DJR

1502	u	J620UHN	MAN 11.190 HOCL-R	Optare Vecta		B42F	1991

1504-1518

		MAN 11.190 HOCL-R		Optare Vecta		B42F	1993	*1509-13 are BC42F
1504	SN	K504BHN	1508	SN	K508BHN	1512	LS	K512BHN	1516	u	K516BHN
1505	SN	K505BHN	1509	SN	K509BHN	1513	LS	K513BHN	1517	BA	K517BHN
1506	SN	K506BHN	1510	RR	K510BHN	1514	SN	K514BHN	1518	SN	K518BHN
1507	SN	K507BHN	1511	u	K511BHN	1515	LS	K515BHN

1519-1551

		MAN 11.190 HOCL-R		Optare Vecta		B42F	1994
1519	SN	L519FHN	1527	RR	L527FHN	1535	BA	L535FHN	1544	SN	L544GHN
1520	u	L520FHN	1528	LS	L528FHN	1536	LS	L536FHN	1545	BA	L545GHN
1521	SN	L521FHN	1529	SN	L529FHN	1537	RR	L537FHN	1546	u	L546GHN
1522	u	L522FHN	1530	SN	L530FHN	1539	u	L539FHN	1547	BA	L547GHN
1523	u	L523FHN	1531	SN	L531FHN	1540	BA	L540FHN	1548	BA	L548GHN
1524	LS	L524FHN	1532	u	L532FHN	1541	BA	L541FHN	1549	BA	L549GHN
1525	SN	L525FHN	1533	SN	L533FHN	1542	SN	L542FHN	1550	BA	L550GHN
1526	SN	L526FHN	1534	LS	L534FHN	1543	BA	L543FHN	1551	RR	L551GHN

Arriva inherited with the Drawlane business several products from East Lancs coachbuilders which Drawlane had bought from the industrial conglomerate John Brown. East Lancs was based in Blackburn and had a strong customer base in the local authority sector. One of the products from that time was the European bodywork on Scania L113CRL sub frames. The North East fleet contains twenty and 281, N281NCN, illustrates the styling as it heads for Newcastle. *Tony Wilson*

1552	u	M501AJC	MAN 11.190 HOCL-R	Optare Vecta	B42F	1995	Arriva Cymru, 1998
1553	RR	M502AJC	MAN 11.190 HOCL-R	Optare Vecta	B42F	1995	Arriva Cymru, 1999
1554	u	M503AJC	MAN 11.190 HOCL-R	Optare Vecta	B42F	1995	Arriva Cymru, 1999
1555	RR	M504AJC	MAN 11.190 HOCL-R	Optare Vecta	B42F	1995	Arriva Cymru, 1999
1556	SN	UOI772	MAN 11.190 HOCL-R	Optare Vecta	BC42F	1993	Arriva Midlands North, 1999
1557	RR	L102MEH	MAN 11.190 HOCL-R	Optare Vecta	B42F	1994	Arriva Midlands North, 1999
1558	u	K140RYS	MAN 11.190 HOCL-R	Optare Vecta	BC42F	1993	Arriva Midlands North, 1999

1609-1643

		Dennis Dart SLF 10.1m			Plaxton Pointer 2	N39F	1997-99

1609	DL	R609MHN	1618	BA	S618KHN	1627	DL	S627KHN	1636	PE	S636KHN
1610	DL	S610KHN	1619	DL	S619KHN	1628	DL	S628KHN	1637	PE	S637KHN
1611	DL	S611KHN	1620	DL	S620KHN	1629	DL	S629KHN	1638	PE	S638KHN
1612	DL	S612KHN	1621	BA	S621KHN	1620	DL	S630KHN	1639	PE	S639KHN
1613	DL	S613KHN	1622	DL	S622KHN	1631	BA	S631KHN	1640	PE	S640KHN
1614	DL	S614KHN	1623	DL	S623KHN	1632	BA	S632KHN	1641	PE	S641KHN
1615	BA	S615KHN	1624	DL	S624KHN	1633	BA	S633KHN	1642	PE	S642KHN
1616	BA	S616KHN	1625	BA	S625KHN	1634	BA	S634KHN	1643	PE	S643KHN
1617	BA	S617KHN	1626	BA	S626KHN	1635	BA	S635KHN			

1701	NE	T701RCN	Dennis Dart SLF 8.8m	Plaxton Pointer MPD	N29F	1999
1702	BL	T702RCN	Dennis Dart SLF 8.8m	Plaxton Pointer MPD	N29F	1999

1703-1723

		Dennis Dart SLF 8.8m			Plaxton Pointer MPD	N29F	1999

1703	DU	V703DNL	1709	DU	V709DNL	1714	BA	V714DNL	1719	SN	V719DNL
1704	DU	V612DNL	1710	DU	V710DNL	1715	BA	V715DNL	1720	SN	V720DNL
1705	DU	V705DNL	1711	BA	V711DNL	1716	PE	V716DNL	1721	SN	V721DNL
1706	DU	V706DNL	1712	BA	V712DNL	1717	RD	V717DNL	1722	SN	V722DNL
1707	DU	V707DNL	1713	BA	V713DNL	1718	SN	V718DNL	1723	SN	V723DNL
1708	PE	V708DNL									

1724-1742 — Dennis Dart SLF 8.8m — Plaxton Pointer MPD — N29F — 1999

1724	BL	V724DNL	1729	NE	V729DNL	1734	AS	V734DNL	1739	AS	V739DNL
1725	BL	V725DNL	1730	NE	V730DNL	1735	AS	V735DNL	1740	NE	V740DNL
1726	BL	V726DNL	1731	BL	V731DNL	1736	AS	V736DNL	1741	NE	V741DNL
1727	BL	V727DNL	1732	BL	V732DNL	1737	AS	V737DNL	1742	NE	V742DNL
1728	NE	V728DNL	1733	BL	V733DNL	1738	AS	V738DNL			

1743-1749 — Dennis Dart SLF 8.8m — Plaxton Pointer MPD — N29F — 2000

1743	SN	V743ECU	1745	SN	V745ECU	1747	SN	V747ECU	1749	BL	V749ECU
1744	SN	V744ECU	1746	SN	V746ECU	1748	SN	V748ECU			

1750-1757 — Dennis Dart SLF 8.8m — Plaxton Pointer MPD — N29F — 2000

1750	NE	W751SBR	1752	NE	W753SBR	1754	RR	W756SBR	1756	LS	W758SBR
1751	NE	W752SBR	1753	RR	W754SBR	1755	LS	W757SBR	1757	SN	W759SBR

1758	BL	NK53HJA	TransBus Dart SLF 8.8m	TransBus Mini Pointer	N29F	2003
1759	SN	NK53VKA	TransBus Dart SLF 8.8m	TransBus Mini Pointer	N29F	2004
1801	BL	NK53HHX	VDL Bus DE12CSSB200	Wrightbus Commander	N44F	2003
1802	BL	NK53HHY	VDL Bus DE12CSSB200	Wrightbus Commander	N44F	2003
1803	BL	NK53HHZ	VDL Bus DE12CSSB200	Wrightbus Commander	N44F	2003

1901-1922 — DAF DE12CSSB120 — Wright Cadet — N39F — 2000

1901	SN	W301PPT	1907	SN	W309PPT	1913	SN	W317PPT	1918	RR	W78PRG
1902	SN	W302PPT	1908	SN	W311PPT	1914	SN	W319PPT	1919	RR	W79PRG
1903	SN	W303PPT	1909	SN	W312PPT	1915	RR	W69PRG	1920	RR	W81PRG
1904	SN	W304PPT	1910	SN	W313PPT	1916	RR	W72PRG	1921	RR	W82PRG
1905	SN	W307PPT	1911	SN	W314PPT	1917	RR	W76PRG	1922	RR	W83PRG
1906	SN	W308PPT	1912	SN	W315PPT						

2604	u	L604FHN	Optare MetroRider MR33	Optare	B25F	1994

2606-2645 — Optare MetroRider MR35 — Optare — B25F — 1996-97

2606	SN	P606FHN	2616	DL	P616FHN				2636	SN	P636FHN
2607	SN	P607FHN	2617	PE	P617FHN	2627	PE	P627FHN	2637	LS	P637FHN
2608	SN	P608FHN	2618	DU	P618FHN	2628	PE	P628FHN	2638	LS	P638FHN
2609	SN	P609FHN	2619	DU	P619FHN	2629	u	P629FHN	2639	LS	P639FHN
2610	DL	P610FHN	2620	w	P620FHN	2630	DL	P630FHN	2640	DL	P640FHN
2611	u	P611FHN	2621	DU	P621FHN	2631	DL	P631FHN	2641	RD	P641FHN
2612	DL	P612FHN	2622	u	P622FHN	2632	RD	P632FHN	2642	DL	P642FHN
2613	RD	P613FHN	2623	DU	P623FHN	2633	RD	P633FHN	2643	DL	P643FHN
2614	SN	P614FHN	2624	DU	P624FHN	2634	RD	P634FHN	2644	BA	P644FHN
2615	SN	P615FHN	2625	DU	P625FHN	2635	LS	P635FHN	2645	BA	P645FHN

2646-2655 — Mercedes-Benz Vario 0814 — Alexander ALX100 — B27F — 2001

2646	BL	X646WTN	2649	BL	X649WTN	2652	BL	X652WTN	2654	BL	X654WTN
2647	BL	X647WTN	2650	BL	X657WTN	2653	BL	X653WTN	2655	BL	X656WTN
2648	BL	X648WTN	2651	BL	X651WTN						

2701-2725 — Optare MetroRider MR15 — Optare — B31F — 1997-98

2701	DL	R701MHN	2708	RD	R708MHN	2714	DL	R714MHN	2720	DL	R720MHN
2702	DL	R702MHN	2709	PE	R709MHN	2715	DL	R715MHN	2721	DL	R721MHN
2703	DL	R703MHN	2710	PE	R710MHN	2716	DL	R716MHN	2722	DL	R722MHN
2704	DL	R704MHN	2711	DL	R711MHN	2717	DL	R717MHN	2723	DL	R723MHN
2705	DL	R705MHN	2712	DL	R712MHN	2718	DL	R718MHN	2724	DL	R724MHN
2706	DL	R706MHN	2713	DL	R713MHN	2719	DL	R719MHN	2725	PE	R725MHN
2707	RD	R707MHN									

2726-2737 — Optare MetroRider MR17 — Optare — B29F — 1994 — Arriva Southern Counties, 2004

2726	LS	M440HPF	2729	u	M443HPF	2732	DU	M446HPF	2735	u	M449HPF
2727	BA	M441HPF	2730	u	M444HPF	2733	DL	M447HPF	2736	DU	M452HPG
2728	LS	M442HPF	2731	u	M445HPF	2734	RD	M448HPF	2737	LS	M453HPG

2738	u	N801BKN	Optare MetroRider MR15	Optare	B29F	1996	Arriva Southern Counties, 2004
2739	u	N802BKN	Optare MetroRider MR15	Optare	B29F	1996	Arriva Southern Counties, 2004
2742	PE	P472APJ	Optare MetroRider MR17	Optare	B29F	1996	Arriva Southern Counties, 2004

2871-2879 — Volvo Citybus B10M-55 — East Lancashire EL2000 — B41F — 1990 — Arriva Scotland, 2004

2871	PE	H922XYT	2873	LS	H925XYT	2875	RR	H917XYT	2879	RR	H912XYT
2872	PE	H923XYT									

3001-3025 — Mercedes-Benz O405 — Optare Prisma — B49F — 1995

3001	RR	M301SAJ	3008	RR	N808XHN	3014	RR	N514XVN	3020	RR	N520XVN
3002	RR	M302SAJ	3009	RR	N809XHN	3015	RR	N515XVN	3021	RR	N521XVN
3003	RR	M303SAJ	3010	RR	N810XHN	3016	RR	N516XVN	3022	RR	N522XVN
3004	RR	M304SAJ	3011	RR	N511XVN	3017	RR	N517XVN	3023	RR	N523XVN
3005	RR	M305SAJ	3012	RR	N512XVN	3018	RR	N518XVN	3024	RR	N524XVN
3006	HH	N806XHN	3013	RR	N513XVN	3019	RR	N519XVN	3025	LS	N525XVN
3007	RR	N807XHN									

3026	RR	L100SBS	Mercedes-Benz O405	Wright Cityranger	B51F	1993	Arriva Midlands North, 1999

4001	u	G209HCP	DAF SB200LC550	Optare Delta	B51F	1990
4002	DU	G210HCP	DAF SB200LC550	Optare Delta	B51F	1990
4004	w	G212HCP	DAF SB200LC550	Optare Delta	B51F	1990
4005	PE	G214HCP	DAF SB200LC550	Optare Delta	B51F	1990
4006	PE	J866UPY	DAF SB200LC550	Optare Delta	B49F	1992

4008-4022 — DAF SB220LC550 — Optare Delta — B49F — 1993

4008	PE	K408BHN	4012	BA	K412BHN	4016	DU	K416BHN	4020	BA	L420FHN
4009	PE	K409BHN	4013	PE	K413BHN	4017	DU	K417BHN	4021	RD	L421FHN
4010	PE	K410BHN	4014	DU	K414BHN	4018	DU	L418FHN	4022	RD	L422FHN
4011	PE	K411BHN	4015	DU	K415BHN	4019	DU	L419FHN			

4023-4058 — DAF DE02GSSB220 — Plaxton Prestige — N45F — 1998

4023	LS	R423RPY	4032	SN	R432RPY	4041	SN	S341KHN	4050	LS	S350KHN
4024	LS	R424RPY	4033	SN	R433RPY	4042	SN	S342KHN	4051	LS	S351KHN
4025	LS	R425RPY	4034	SN	R434RPY	4043	SN	S343KHN	4052	LS	S352KHN
4026	LS	R426RPY	4035	DU	R435RPY	4044	SN	S344KHN	4053	LS	S353KHN
4027	LS	R427RPY	4036	DU	R436RPY	4045	SN	S345KHN	4054	LS	S354KHN
4028	BA	R428RPY	4037	SN	R437RPY	4046	SN	S346KHN	4055	DL	S355KHN
4029	BA	R429RPY	4038	SN	R438RPY	4047	BA	S347KHN	4056	DL	S356KHN
4030	BA	R430RPY	4039	SN	R439RPY	4048	SN	S348KHN	4057	DL	S357KHN
4031	SN	R431RPY	4040	SN	R440RPY	4049	SN	S349KHN	4058	DL	S358KHN

4059	SN	R701KCU	DAF DE02SB220GS	Northern Counties Paladin	B41F	1997

4060-4073 — DAF DE02GSSB220 — Plaxton Prestige — N41F — 1998

4060	SN	S702KFT	4064	DU	S706KFT	4068	DU	S710KFT	4071	DU	S713KRG
4061	SN	S703KFT	4065	DU	S707KFT	4069	DU	S711KFT	4072	DU	S714KRG
4062	DU	S704KFT	4066	DU	S708KFT	4070	DU	S712KRG	4073	DU	S715KRG
4063	DU	S705KFT	4067	DU	S709KFT						

Minibus operation at North East is divided between Optare MetroRider and Mercedes-Benz Vario models, though several of the latter have now moved elsewhere. The attractive town of Thirsk is the location for this view of 2707, R707MHN which was operating a morning journey from Northallerton to Ripon.
Bob Downham

4074-4082 — DAF DE02GSSB220 · Ikarus CitiBus · N43F* · 1999 · *4079-82 are N39F

4074	LS	T74AUA	4077	LS	T78AUA	4079	LS	T83AUA	4081	LS	T82AUA
4075	LS	T75AUA	4078	LS	T79AUA	4080	LS	T81AUA	4082	LS	V653LWT
4076	LS	T76AUA									

4083	w	F792DWT	DAF SB220LC550	Optare Delta	B47F	1989	Arriva Midlands North, 1999
4085	RD	J931CYL	DAF SB220LC550	Ikarus CitiBus	B48F	1992	Arriva London, 2000
4086	RD	J413NCP	DAF SB220LC550	Ikarus CitiBus	B48F	1992	Arriva London, 2000
4087	RD	J414NCP	DAF SB220LC550	Ikarus CitiBus	B48F	1992	Arriva London, 2000
4088	RD	J929CYL	DAF SB220LC550	Ikarus CitiBus	B48F	1992	Arriva London, 2000
4089	RD	J930CYL	DAF SB220LC550	Ikarus CitiBus	B48F	1992	Arriva London, 2000

4090-4097 — DAF SB220LC550 · Optare Delta · BC48F · 1989-90

4090	DU	G251SRG	4092	PE	G253SRG	4094	AK	G255UVK	4096	DL	G257UVK
4091	DU	G252SRG	4093	PE	G254SRG	4095	DL	G256UVK	4097	SN	G258UVK

4098	PE	P130RWR	DAF SB220LC550	Optare Delta	B44D	1997	Blue Bus, Bolton, 2004
4104	w	H266CFT	DAF SB220LC550	Optare Delta	BC48F	1990	
4105	PE	H267CFT	DAF SB220LC550	Optare Delta	BC48F	1990	
4106	DL	F701ECC	DAF SB220LC550	Optare Delta	BC48F	1989	Crosville Cymru, 1997
4108	SN	L532EHD	DAF SB220LC550	Ikarus CitiBus	B48F	1994	North Western, 1997
4109	SN	L533EHD	DAF SB220LC550	Ikarus CitiBus	B48F	1994	North Western, 1997

4501-4515 — Volvo B10BLE · Wright Renown · N44F · 1999

4501	NE	V501DFT	4505	NE	V505DFT	4509	NE	V509DFT	4513	NE	V513DFT
4502	NE	V502DFT	4506	NE	V506DFT	4510	NE	V510DFT	4514	NE	V514DFT
4503	NE	V503DFT	4507	NE	V507DFT	4511	NE	V511DFT	4515	NE	V515DFT
4504	NE	V504DFT	4508	NE	V508DFT	4512	NE	V512DFT			

4516-4523 — Volvo B10BLE · Alexander ALX300 · N44F · 2000

4516	NE	W292PPT	4518	NE	W294PPT	4520	NE	W296PPT	4522	NE	W298PPT
4517	NE	W293PPT	4519	NE	W295PPT	4521	NE	W297PPT	4523	NE	W299PPT

4524-4530 — Volvo B10BLE · Wright Renown · N44F · 1999 · Arriva Scotland, 2003

4524	HX	V530GDS	4526	HX	V532GDS	4528	HX	V534GDS	4530	HX	V536GDS
4525	HX	V531GDS	4527	HX	V533GDS	4529	HX	V535GDS			

5006-5018 — Leyland Lynx LX2R11C15Z4S · Leyland Lynx 2 · B49F · 1991-92

5006	w	H31PAJ	5011	BA	J651UHN	5013	BA	J653UHN	5017	BA	J657UHN
5009	BA	H253PAJ	5012	BA	J652UHN	5016	BA	J656UHN	5018	BA	J658UHN

7214	PE	WFC214Y	Leyland Olympian ONLXB/1R	Eastern Coach Works	B45/32F	1983	

7215-7222 — Leyland Olympian ONLXB/1RH · Eastern Coach Works · B42/29F · 1986-87 · Arriva London, 2003

7215	PE	D155FYM	7217	PE	D165FYM	7219	u	D216FYM	7221	PE	D157FYM
7216	NE	D160FYM	7218	NE	D189FYM	7220	u	D178FYM	7222	u	D174FYM

7241	DU	A241GHN	Leyland Olympian ONLXB/1R	Eastern Coach Works	B45/32F	1985	KentishBus, 1998
7242	PE	A242GHN	Leyland Olympian ONLXB/1R	Eastern Coach Works	B45/32F	1985	KentishBus, 1998
7244	PE	A244GHN	Leyland Olympian ONLXB/1R	Eastern Coach Works	B45/32F	1985	KentishBus, 1998

7250-7258 — Scania N113DRB · Northern Counties Palatine · B42/29F · 1994-95 · Arriva London, 2002

7250	BL	L159GYL	7253	NE	M178LYP	7255	NE	M180LYP	7257	AK	N182OYH
7251	AK	L160GYL	7254	NE	M179LYP	7256	BL	N181OYH	7258	AK	N183OYH
7252	NE	L161GYL									

7267	AK	A567NWX	Leyland Olympian ONLXB/1R	Eastern Coach Works	B45/32F	1984	Arriva Scotland, 2003
7268	DL	C268XEF	Leyland Olympian ONLXB/1R	Eastern Coach Works	B42/30F	1986	

7271-7275 — Leyland Olympian ON2R50C13Z4 · Alexander RH · B45/29F · 1993

7271	RD	L271FVN	7273	DU	L273FVN	7274	DU	L274FVN	7275	BA	L275FVN
7272	BA	L272FVN									

7276	u	G21HHG	Leyland Olympian ONCL10/1RZ	Leyland	B47/31F	1989	Atlas Bus, 1994

7279-7285 — Leyland Olympian ONCL10/1R · Northern Counties · B43/32F · 1989 · Atlas Bus, 1994

7279	RR	G756UYT	7283	RR	G760UYT	7284	NE	G761UYT	7285	BA	G762UYT
7280	RR	G757UYT									

7286	BL	UWW13X	Leyland Olympian ONLXB/1R	Roe	B47/29F	1982	Metrobus, Orpington, 1997
7292	BL	CUB66Y	Leyland Olympian ONLXB/1R	Roe	B47/29F	1983	Metrobus, Orpington, 1997
7293	NE	CUB68Y	Leyland Olympian ONLXB/1R	Roe	B47/29F	1983	Metrobus, Orpington, 1997

With the exception of two pairs of Optare Delta buses in Yorkshire and The Shires, the remaining examples of the type are now located in the North East. Pictured passing through Darlington on route 28 to Catterick Garrison, 4106 was new to Crosville Wales and is one of several in this fleet to feature high-back seating for the inter-urban route network. *Bob Downham*

| 7301 | PE | C263XEF | Leyland Olympian ONLXB/1R | Eastern Coach Works | BC42/30F | 1986 | United, 1986 |
| 7302 | AK | C264XEF | Leyland Olympian ONLXB/1R | Eastern Coach Works | BC42/30F | 1986 | United, 1986 |

7370-7377

Volvo Olympian YN2RC18Z4 — Northern Counties Palatine II — BC43/27F — 1994

| 7370 | AS | M370FTY | 7372 | AS | M372FTY | 7374 | AS | M374FTY | 7376 | AS | M376FTY |
| 7371 | AS | M371FTY | 7373 | AS | M373FTY | 7375 | AS | M375FTY | 7377 | AS | M377FTY |

7381-7393

Scania N113DRB — East Lancs Cityzen — BC43/31F — 1996

7381	BL	N381OTY	7385	BL	N385OTY	7388	BL	N388OTY	7391	BL	N391OTY
7382	BL	N382OTY	7386	BL	N386OTY	7389	BL	N389OTY	7392	BL	N392OTY
7383	BL	N383OTY	7387	BL	N387OTY	7390	BL	N390OTY	7393	BL	N393OTY
7384	BL	N384OTY									

7407	BL	C260UAJ	Leyland Olympian ONLXB/1R	Eastern Coach Works	B45/32F	1985	United, 1986
7408	BL	C261UAJ	Leyland Olympian ONLXB/1R	Eastern Coach Works	B45/32F	1985	United, 1986
7409	NE	C262UAJ	Leyland Olympian ONLXB/1R	Eastern Coach Works	B45/32F	1985	United, 1986

7410-7420

Volvo Olympian — Northern Counties Palatine II — B43/29F — 1997

7410	AS	P410CCU	7413	AS	P413CCU	7416	NE	P416CCU	7419	NE	P419CCU
7411	AS	P411CCU	7414	NE	P414CCU	7417	NE	P417CCU	7420	NE	P420CCU
7412	AS	P412CCU	7415	NE	P415CCU	7418	NE	P418CCU			

7421-7429

Volvo Olympian YN2RV16Z4 — East Lancs — B44/30F — 1994 — Arriva Southern Counties, 1998

7421	AS	M685HPF	7424	AS	M688HPF	7427	DU	M691HPF	7429	DU	M693HPF
7422	AS	M686HPF	7425	DU	M689HPF	7426	DU	M690HPF	7428	DU	M692HPF
7423	AS	M687HPF									

7430-7435

Dennis Trident — Alexander ALX400 — N51/31F — 2000

| 7430 | BL | W395RBB | 7432 | BL | W397RBB | 7434 | BL | W399RBB | 7435 | BL | W501RBB |
| 7431 | BL | W396RBB | 7433 | BL | W398RBB | | | | | | |

7436-7444

DAF DE02RSDB250 — East Lancs Lowlander — N44/29F — 2001

7436	DM	Y686EBR	7439	DM	Y689EBR	7441	DL	Y691EBR	7443	DL	Y693EBR
7437	DM	Y687EBR	7440	DM	Y685EBR	7442	DL	Y692EBR	7444	DL	Y694EBR
7438	DM	Y688EBR									

Ancillary Vehicles:-

9984	u	M734AOO	Iveco TurboDaily 59.12	Marshall C31	B25F	1995	Arriva The Shires, 2002
9986	u	G508EAJ	Leyland Lynx LX2R11C15Z4S	Leyland Lynx	TV	1990	
9987	u	G509EAJ	Leyland Lynx LX2R11C15Z4S	Leyland Lynx	TV	1990	
9988	u	G510EAJ	Leyland Lynx LX2R11C15Z4S	Leyland Lynx	TV	1990	
9990	u	G512EAJ	Leyland Lynx LX2R11C15Z4S	Leyland Lynx	TV	1990	
9991	u	H32PAJ	Leyland Lynx LX2R11C15Z4S	Leyland Lynx 2	TV	1991	

Previous Registrations:

UOI772	K141RYS	YSU870	E186XKO
WLT954	A954SUL	YSU871	E187XKO
XSV691	E91OJT		

Allocations:-

Alnwick (Lisburn Street) - AK

MetroRider	886	890	908	909		
Tiger	214	215	216	217	218	
DAF Delta	4094					
Olympian	7221	7222	7267	7302	7423	7424
Scania dd	7251	7257	7258			

Ashington (Lintonville Terrace) - AS

MetroRider	889	891	892	904	905	906	907	910
	911	912	913	914	915	916	917	918
	919	937						
Dart	1734	1735	1736	1737	1738	1739		
Scania sd	273	274	281	282	283	284	286	289
	290							
Olympian	7220	7244	7370	7371	7372	7373	7374	7375
	7376	7377	7410	7411	7412	7413	7421	7422

Bishop Auckland (Morland Street) - BA

MetroRider	871	2611	2644	2645	2727			
Dart	1615	1616	1617	1618	1621	1625	1626	1631
	1632	1633	1634	1635	1711	1712	1713	1714
	1715							
MAN Vecta	1517	1535	1540	1541	1545	1547	1548	1549
	1550							
Lynx	5009	5011	5012	5013	5016	5017	5018	
DAF Interurban	1210	1211						
DAF Delta	4012	4020						
DAF Prestige	4028	4029	4047					
Olympian	7272	7275	7285					

Blyth (Bridge Street) - BL

MetroRider	872	873	874	875	877	878	881	882
	883	884	902	903	920			
Mercedes-Benz	2646	2647	2648	2649	2650	2651	2652	2653
	2654	2655						
Dart	1702	1724	1725	1726	1727	1731	1732	1733
	1749	1758						
Scania sd	275	276	277	278	279	280	285	287
	288							
VDL Bus Commander	1801	1802	1803					
Olympian	7218	7286	7292	7407	7408			
Scania dd	7250	7256	7381	7382	7383	7384	7385	7386
	7387	7388	7389	7390	7391	7392	7393	
Trident	7430	7431	7432	7433	7434	7435		

The latest double-deck buses for North East are a batch of nine DAF DB250s with East Lancs Lowlander bodies from 2001. Seen in Barnard Castle is East Lancs Lowlander 7443, Y693EBR. The batch has been divided between Durham and Darlington. *Tony Wilson*

Darlington (Feethams) - DL - North East

Outstation: Barnard Castle

MetroRider	2610	2612	2616	2630	2631	2640	2642	2643
	2701	2702	2703	2704	2705	2706	2711	2712
	2713	2714	2715	2716	2717	2718	2719	2720
	2721	2722	2723	2724	2733			
Dart	1609	1610	1611	1612	1613	1614	1619	1620
	1622	1623	1624	1627	1628	1629	1630	1703
	1718	1719						
DAF Delta	4095	4106						
DAF Prestige	4055	4056	4057	4058				
DAF Lowlander	7441	7442	7443	7444				
Olympian	7241	7268						

Durham (Waddington Steet) - DU - North East

MetroRider	867	894	898	2618	2619	2621	2623	2624
	2625	2732	2736					
Dart	1704	1705	1706	1707	1709	1710		
DAF Delta	4002	4014	4015	4016	4017	4018	4019	4090
	4091	4096						
DAF Prestige	4030	4035	4036	4061	4062	4063	4064	4065
	4066	4067	4068	4069	4070	4071	4072	4073
Metrobus	614	617						
Olympian	7273	7274	7425	7426	7427	7428	7429	
DAF Lowlander	7436	7437	7438	7439	7440			

Hexham (Burn Lane) - HX

MetroRider	866	879	880	885	922	923	
Tiger	247						
DAF interurban	1201	1202	1203	1204	1205		
Volvo B10BLE	4524	4525	4526	4527	4528	4529	4530
Metrobus	604						

Loftus (Whitby Road) - LS

Outstation: Whitby

MetroRider	2635	2637	2638	2639	2726	2728	2737	
Dart	1755	1756						
MAN Vecta	1512	1513	1515	1524	1528	1534	1536	
Volvo Citybus	2873							
MB Prisma	3025							
DAF Prestige	4023	4024	4025	4026	4027	4050	4051	4052
	4053	4054						
DAF Ikarus	4074	4075	4076	4077	4078	4079	4080	4081
	4082							
DAF Interurban	1206	1207	1208	1209				

Newcastle (Jesmond Road) - NE

MetroRider	863	887	888	899	900	901	921	
DAF coach	141	142	143	144	145	146	147	148
Dart	1728	1729	1730	1740	1741	1742	1750	1751
	1752							
Scania sd	271	272						
Volvo B10BLE	4501	4502	4503	4504	4505	4506	4507	4508
	4509	4510	4511	4512	4513	4514	4515	4516
	4517	4518	4519	4520	4521	4522	4523	
Metrobus	601	611	620	621	622	623	624	625
	626	629	630	631				
Olympian	7216	7218	7284	7293	7409	7414	7415	7416
	7417	7418	7419	7420				
Scania dd	7252	7253	7254	7255				

Peterlee (Davey Drive) - PE

MetroRider	2617	2627	2628	2709	2710	2725	2742	
Dart	1636	1637	1638	1639	1640	1641	1642	1643
	1708	1710	1716					
Volvo B10M bus	2871	2872						
DAF Delta	4005	4006	4008	4009	4010	4011	4013	4092
	4093	4098	4105					
Olympian	7214	7215	7216	7217	7219	7242	7301	

Redcar (Ennis Road, Dormanstown) - RR

Dart	1753	1754						
MAN Vecta	1504	1510	1527	1537	1543	1551	1553	1555
	1557							
DAF Cadet	1915	1916	1917	1918	1919	1920	1921	1922
Volvo Citybus	2875	2879						
Mercedes Prisma	3001	3002	3003	3004	3005	3006	3007	3008
	3009	3010	3011	3012	3013	3014	3015	3016
	3017	3018	3019	3020	3021	3022	3023	3024
	3026							
DAF Interurban	1212	1213	1214					
Olympian	7279	7280	7283					

Richmond (Station Yard) - RD

MetroRider	870	2613	2632	2633	2634	2641	2707	2708
	2734							
Dart	1717							
DAF Delta	4021	4022						
DAF Ikarus	4085	4086	4087	4088	4089			
Olympian	7271							

Stockton (Boathouse Lane) - SN

MetroRider	876	893	897	2606	2607	2608	2609	2614
	2615	2636						
Dart	1720	1721	1722	1723	1743	1744	1745	1746
	1747	1748	1757	1759				
DAF Cadet	1901	1902	1903	1904	1905	1906	1907	1908
	1909	1910	1911	1912	1913	1914		
MAN Vecta	1505	1506	1507	1508	1509	1514	1518	1519
	1521	1525	1526	1529	1530	1531	1533	1542
	1544	1556						
MB Urbanranger	3026							
DAF Ikarus	4097	4108	4109					
DAF Prestige	4031	4032	4033	4034	4037	4038	4039	4040
	4041	4042	4043	4044	4045	4046	4048	4049
	4059							

Unallocated or stored - u/w

MetroRider	752	855	869	935	2604	2620	2622	2629
	2641	2729	2730	2731	2735	2738	2739	
MAN Vecta	1502	1511	1516	1520	1522	1523	1532	1539
	1546	1552	1554	1558				
DAF Delta	4001	4004	4083	4104				
Lynx	5006							
Olympian	7276							
Metrobus	619							

For many years assembly of the Pointer was undertaken in near-by Scarborough before transferring to Falkirk under TransBus ownership. Arriva have chosen the small 8.8 metre MPD version for many services previously operated by minibuses. Here 1740, V740DNL, illustrates the type as it returns to its home base at Newcastle.
Richard Godfrey

ARRIVA YORKSHIRE

Arriva Yorkshire Ltd; Arriva Yorkshire North Ltd,
24 Barnsley Road, Wakefield, West Yorkshire, WF1 5JX
Arriva Yorkshire West Ltd, Mill Street East, Dewsbury, West Yorkshire, WF12 9AG

11	DY	R10WAL	DAF DE02GSSB220	Ikarus CitiBus	B49F	1997	K-Line Travel, 2000
12	DY	J802KHD	DAF SB220LC550	Ikarus CitiBus	BC48F	1992	K-Line Travel, 2000
13	DY	R69GNW	DAF DE02GSSB220	Ikarus CitiBus	B49F	1998	K-Line Travel, 2000
14	DY	PIL9735	DAF SB220LC550	Ikarus CitiBus	B48F	1993	K-Line Travel, 2000
16	DY	PIL9730	DAF SB220LC550	Ikarus CitiBus	B48F	1992	K-Line Travel, 2000
17	DY	PIL9732	DAF SB220LC550	Ikarus CitiBus	B48F	1992	K-Line Travel, 2000
18	DY	PIL9733	DAF SB220LC550	Ikarus CitiBus	B48F	1993	K-Line Travel, 2000
19	DY	PIL9734	DAF SB220LC550	Ikarus CitiBus	B48F	1993	K-Line Travel, 2000
20	DY	PIL9731	DAF SB220LC550	Ikarus CitiBus	B48F	1992	K-Line Travel, 2000

21-29
DAF SB220LT550 — Ikarus CitiBus — B49F — 1994 — K-Line Travel, 2000

21	DY	M811RCP	24	DY	M814RCP	26	DY	M816RCP	28	DY	M818RCP
22	DY	M812RCP	25	DY	M815RCP	27	DY	M817RCP	29	DY	M819RCP
23	DY	M813RCP									

51	DY	H512YCX	DAF SB220LC550	Optare Delta	B48F	1991	K-Line Travel, 2000
52	DY	J23GCX	DAF SB220LC550	Optare Delta	B49F	1991	K-Line Travel, 2000

102-109
Volvo B10BLE — Wright Renown — NC44F — 2000

102	SB	W102EWU	104	SB	W104EWU	107	SB	W107EWU	109	SB	W109EWU
103	SB	W103EWU	106	SB	W106EWU	108	SB	W108EWU			

135-149
Dennis Dart 9SDL3034 — Northern Counties Paladin — B35F — 1994 — Arriva Southern Counties, 2001

135	CD	L127YVK	139	CD	L129YVK	143	CD	L159BFT	147	CD	L157YVK
136	CD	L136YVK	140	CD	L140YVK	144	CD	L114YVK	148	CD	L131YVK
137	CD	L137YVK	141	CD	L141YVK	145	CD	L149YVK	149	CD	L130YVK
138	CD	L128YVK	142	CD	L152YVK	146	CD	L146YVK			

150	CD	K601HWR	Dennis Dart 9.8SDL3012	Plaxton Pointer	B43F	1992	K-Line Travel, 2000
151	SB	G140GOL	Dennis Dart 9SDL3002	Duple Dartline	B39F	1990	K-Line Travel, 2000
152	SB	H878LOX	Dennis Dart 9SDL3002	Duple Dartline	B39F	1990	K-Line Travel, 2000
153	DY	J220HGY	Dennis Dart 9SDL3011	Plaxton Pointer	B35F	1992	Arriva Southern Counties, 2001
154	DY	J221HGY	Dennis Dart 9SDL3011	Plaxton Pointer	B35F	1992	Arriva Southern Counties, 2001
155	WF	J467OKP	Dennis Dart 9.8SDL3017	Plaxton Pointer	B40F	1992	Arriva Southern Counties, 2001
165	SB	W165HBT	Dennis Dart SLF	Alexander ALX200	N40F	2000	
166	SB	W166HBT	Dennis Dart SLF	Alexander ALX200	N40F	2000	
167	SB	TWY7	Dennis Dart SLF	Alexander ALX200	N40F	2000	

170-199
Dennis Dart SLF — Alexander ALX200 — N40F — 1997

170	DY	P170VUA	178	SB	P178VUA	186	DY	P186VUA	193	DY	P193VUA
171	DY	P171VUA	179	SB	P179VUA	187	DY	P187VUA	194	DY	P194VUA
172	DY	P172VUA	180	SB	P180VUA	188	DY	P188VUA	195	DY	P195VUA
173	DY	P173VUA	181	SB	P181VUA	189	DY	P189VUA	196	DY	P196VUA
174	DY	P174VUA	182	SB	P182VUA	190	DY	P190VUA	197	DY	P197VUA
175	DY	P175VUA	183	SB	P183VUA	191	DY	P191VUA	198	HE	P198VUA
176	DY	P176VUA	184	DY	P184VUA	192	DY	P192VUA	199	DY	P199VUA
177	SB	P177VUA	185	DY	P185VUA						

200	DY	R103GNW	Dennis Dart SLF	UVG Urbanstar	N40F	1998	Jaronda Travel, Cawood, 1999

201-229
Dennis Dart SLF — Plaxton Pointer MPD — N29F — 2000

201	WF	V201PCX	208	WF	V208PCX	215	WF	V215PCX	223	CD	V223PCX
202	WF	V202PCX	209	WF	V209PCX	216	WF	V216PCX	224	CD	V224PCX
203	WF	V203PCX	210	WF	V210PCX	217	WF	V217PCX	225	CD	V225PCX
204	WF	V204PCX	211	WF	V211PCX	218	WF	V218PCX	226	CD	V226PCX
205	WF	V205PCX	212	WF	V212PCX	219	WF	V219PCX	227	CD	V227PCX
206	WF	V206PCX	213	WF	V213PCX	220	CD	V220PCX	228	CD	V228PCX
207	WF	V207PCX	214	WF	V214PCX	221	CD	V221PCX	229	WF	V229XUB

Arriva Bus and Coach is the group's bus and coach distribution business with exclusive import rights for all VDL Bus (formerly DAF Bus International) chassis supported by a wide range of bus and coach bodywork options, from Van Hool of Belgium, Ikarus from Hungary and Plaxton from the UK, to meet new market demands. Such a vehicle which entered one of the group's fleets after operating elsewhere is 28, M818RCP. The type have proved so successful that they are being refurbished to extend their operational life. *Richard Godfrey*

333-337 — Leyland Lynx LX2R11C15Z4S — Leyland Lynx 2 — B49F — 1990

333	CD	H338TYG	335	CD	H335TYG	336	CD	H336TYG	337	CD	H337TYG

338-347 — Leyland Lynx LX2R11C15Z4S — Leyland Lynx 2 — B49F — 1990-91

338	CD	H338UWT	341	CD	H341UWT	344	CD	H344UWX	346	CD	H346UWX
339	CD	H339UWT	342	CD	H342UWT	345	CD	H345UWX	347	CD	H347UWX
340	CD	H343UWT	343	CD	H343UWX						

352-382 — Leyland Lynx LX2R11C15Z4S* — Leyland Lynx 2 — B49F — 1991 — *378 is LX2R11V18Z4S

352	CD	H755WWW	360	CD	H460WWY	368	CD	J368YWX	376	WF	J376AWT
353	CD	H756WWW	361	WF	H393WWY	369	CD	J369YWX	377	w	J377AWT
354	CD	H757WWW	362	WF	J362YWX	370	CD	J370YWX	378	w	J371AWT
355	CD	H355WWX	363	WF	J363YWX	371	CD	J371YWX	379	WF	J379BWU
356	CD	H356WWX	364	WF	J364YWX	372	CD	J372AWT	380	WF	J380BWU
357	CD	H357WWX	365	WF	J365YWX	373	CD	J373AWT	381	WF	J381BWU
358	WF	H358WWY	366	CD	J366YWX	374	CD	J374AWT	382	WF	J382BWU
359	WF	H359WWY	367	CD	J367YWX	375	WF	J375AWT			

401-405 — Volvo B10B-58 — Alexander Strider — B51F — 1993

401	CD	K401HWW	403	WF	K403HWW	404	WF	K404HWW	405	WF	K405HWX
402	WF	K402HWW									

406	WF	L406NUA	Volvo B10B-58	Wright Endeavour	BC49F	1993
407	w	L407NUA	Volvo B10B-58	Wright Endeavour	BC49F	1993
408	WF	L408NUA	Volvo B10B-58	Wright Endeavour	BC49F	1993
409	WF	L409NUA	Volvo B10B-58	Wright Endeavour	BC49F	1993

410-433 — Volvo B10B-58 — Alexander Strider — B51F — 1994

410	CD	M410UNW	416	CD	M416UNW	422	CD	M422UNW	428	CD	M428UNW
411	CD	M411UNW	417	WF	M417UNW	423	CD	M423UNW	429	CD	M429UNW
412	WF	M412UNW	418	CD	M418UNW	424	CD	M424UNW	430	CD	M430UNW
413	WF	M413UNW	419	CD	M419UNW	425	WF	M425UNW	431	CD	M431UNW
414	WF	M414UNW	420	CD	M420UNW	426	CD	M426UNW	432	CD	M432UNW
415	WF	M415UNW	421	CD	M421UNW	427	CD	M427UNW	433	CD	M433UNW

Two of the batch of Dennis Arrow buses transferred from Southern Counties in 1999 are fitted with high-back seating which is visible in this view of 509, N809TPK taken in Leeds. These are the only examples of the model with Arriva and all ten of the type are allocated to Heckmondwike. *Cliff Beeton*

440-471

			DAF DE02GSSB220			Alexander ALX300	N42F	1998	
440	WF	R440GWY	**449**	WF	R449KWT	**457**	WF	R457KWT	**465**	WF	S465GUB
441	WF	R441KWT	**450**	DY	R450KWT	**458**	DY	R458KWT	**466**	DY	S466GUB
442	WF	R442KWT	**451**	WF	R451KWT	**459**	DY	R459KWT	**467**	WF	S467GUB
443	WF	R443KWT	**452**	DY	R452KWT	**460**	WF	R460KWT	**468**	WF	S468GUB
445	WF	R445KWT	**453**	WF	R453KWT	**461**	WF	R461KWT	**469**	WF	S469GUB
446	WF	R446KWT	**454**	WF	R454KWT	**462**	WF	S462GUB	**470**	WF	S470GUB
447	WF	R447KWT	**455**	WF	R455KWT	**463**	WF	S463GUB	**471**	WF	S471GUB
448	WF	R448KWT	**456**	DY	R456KWT	**464**	WF	S464GUB			

472-491

			DAF DE02GSSB220			Alexander ALX300	N42F	1998	
472	WF	S472ANW	**477**	WF	S477ANW	**482**	DY	S482ANW	**487**	WF	S487ANW
473	WF	S473ANW	**478**	WF	S478ANW	**483**	WF	S483ANW	**488**	WF	S488ANW
474	WF	S474ANW	**479**	WF	S479ANW	**484**	WF	S484ANW	**489**	WF	S489ANW
475	WF	S475ANW	**480**	DY	S480ANW	**485**	WF	S485ANW	**490**	WF	S490ANW
476	WF	S476ANW	**481**	DY	S481ANW	**486**	WF	S486ANW	**491**	WF	S491ANW

495-499

			VDL Bus SB200			Wrightbus Commander	N44F	2004	
495	WF	YJ04HJC	**497**	WF	YJ04HJE	**498**	WF	YJ04HJF	**499**	WF	YJ04HJG
496	WF	YJ04HJD									

501-510

			Dennis Arrow			East Lancs Pyoneer	B45/35F*	1996	Arriva Southern Counties, 1999
									*509/10 are BC45/31F
501	HE	N801TPK	**504**	HE	N804TPK	**507**	HE	N807TPK	**509**	HE	N809TPK
502	HE	N802TPK	**505**	HE	N805TPK	**508**	HE	N808TPK	**510**	HE	N810TPK
503	HE	N803TPK	**506**	HE	N806TPK						

517-542

			Leyland Olympian ONLXB/1R			Eastern Coach Works	B45/33F	1982-83	
517	HE	CWR517Y	**524**	HE	CWR524Y	**530**	WF	EWX530Y	**542**	WF	EWW542Y
521	w	CWR521Y	**528**	w	EWX528Y	**541**	HE	EWW541Y			

565-612 — Leyland Olympian ONLXB/1R — Eastern Coach Works — B45/32F* — 1983-85 — *seating varies

565	CD	A565NWX	579	WF	A579NWX	589	HE	A589NWX	603	WF	B603UUM
566	WF	A566NWX	580	WF	A580NWX	590	SB	A590NWX	604	WF	B604UUM
569	HE	A569NWX	581	WF	A581NWX	591	SB	B591SWX	606	WF	B606UUM
570	HE	A570NWX	582	WF	A582NWX	594	SB	B594SWX	607	WF	B607UUM
571	HE	A571NWX	583	w	A583NWX	596	CD	B596SWX	608	WF	B608UUM
			584	WF	A584NWX	597	CD	B597SWX	609	WF	B609UUM
574	WF	A574NWX	585	HE	A585NWX	599	SB	B599SWX	610	WF	C610ANW
575	WF	A575NWX	586	HE	A586NWX	600	SB	B600UUM	611	WF	C611ANW
577	WF	A577NWX	588	HE	A588NWX	601	HE	B601UUM	612	WF	C612ANW

613	CD	E205TUB	Leyland Olympian ONTL11/1RH	Northern Counties	B43/28F	1988	South Yorkshire, Pontefract, 1995
615	CD	H106RWT	Leyland Olympian ON2R50C13Z4	Northern Counties	B43/28F	1990	South Yorkshire, Pontefract, 1995
616	CD	H108RWT	Leyland Olympian ON2R50C13Z4	Northern Counties	B43/28F	1990	South Yorkshire, Pontefract, 1995
621	SB	N621KUA	Volvo Olympian YN2RV18Z4	Northern Counties Palatine II	B43/30F	1996	
622	SB	N622KUA	Volvo Olympian YN2RV18Z4	Northern Counties Palatine II	B43/30F	1996	
623	SB	N623KUA	Volvo Olympian YN2RV18Z4	Northern Counties Palatine II	B43/30F	1996	

624-641 — DAF DE02RSDB250 — Optare Spectra — B48/29F — 1999

624	DY	T624EUB	629	DY	T629EUB	634	DY	T634EUB	638	DY	T638EUB
625	DY	T625EUB	630	DY	T630EUB	635	DY	T635EUB	639	DY	T639EUB
626	DY	T626EUB	631	DY	T631EUB	636	DY	T636EUB	640	WF	V640KVH
627	DY	T627EUB	632	DY	T632EUB	637	DY	T637EUB	641	WF	V641KVH
628	DY	T628EUB	633	WF	T633EUB						

651-674 — Volvo B7L — Alexander ALX400 — N47/28F — 2000

651	CD	W651CWX	657	CD	W657CWX	663	CD	W663CWX	669	CD	W669CWX
652	CD	W652CWX	658	CD	W658CWX	664	CD	W664CWX	671	CD	W671CWX
653	CD	W653CWX	659	CD	W659CWX	665	CD	W665CWX	672	CD	W672CWX
654	CD	W654CWX	661	CD	W661CWX	667	CD	W667CWX	673	CD	W673CWX
656	CD	W656CWX	662	CD	W662CWX	668	CD	W668CWX	674	CD	W674CWX

675-696 — Volvo B7L — Plaxton President — N47/28F — 2001

675	SB	X675YUG	681	SB	X681YUG	686	SB	X686YUG	692	HE	X692YUG
676	SB	X676YUG	682	SB	X682YUG	687	HE	X687YUG	693	HE	X693YUG
677	SB	X677YUG	683	SB	X683YUG	688	HE	X688YUG	694	HE	X694YUG
678	SB	X678YUG	684	SB	X684YUG	689	HE	X689YUG	695	HE	X695YUG
679	SB	X679YUG	685	SB	X685YUG	691	HE	X691YUG	696	HE	X696YUG

700-723 — DAF DE02PSDB250 — Optare Spectra — N47/27F — 2002

700	WF	YD02PXW	706	WF	YG52CFE	712	WF	YG52CFN	718	HE	YD02PYU
701	WF	YD02PXX	707	WF	YG52CFF	713	WF	YG52CFO	719	HE	YD02PYV
702	WF	YD02PXY	708	WF	YG52CFJ	714	WF	YG52CFP	720	HE	YD02PYW
703	WF	YD02PXZ	709	WF	YG52CFK	715	WF	YG52CFU	721	HE	YD02PYX
704	WF	YG52CFA	710	WF	YG52CFL	716	WF	YG52CFV	722	HE	YD02PYY
705	WF	YG52CFD	711	WF	YG52CFM	717	WF	YG52CFX	723	HE	YD02PYZ

746-750 — Optare MetroRider MR15 — Optare — B31F — 1995

746	DY	M746WWR	748	CD	M748WWR	749	DY	M749WWR	750	CD	M750WWR
747	u	M247WWR							

754	DY	N754LWW	Optare MetroRider MR15	Optare	B31F	1996	
755	WF	N755LWW	Optare MetroRider MR15	Optare	B31F	1996	
756	WF	N756LWW	Optare MetroRider MR15	Optare	B31F	1996	
757	DY	N757LWW	Optare MetroRider MR15	Optare	B31F	1996	
760	DY	N172WNF	Mercedes-Benz 709D	Alexander Sprint	B23F	1995	Arrive North West & Wales, 2004

761-765 — Volvo Citybus B10M-50 — East Lancs — B49/39F — 1989 — Arriva Southern Counties, 2004

761	HE	G612BPH	763	HE	G619BPH	764	HE	G620BPH	765	HE	G622BPH
762	HE	G618BPH							

766	HE	G637BPH	Volvo Citybus B10M-50	Northern Counties	B45/31F	1989	Arriva Southern Counties, 2004
767	HE	G638BPH	Volvo Citybus B10M-50	Northern Counties	B45/31F	1989	Arriva Southern Counties, 2004
768	HE	G639BPH	Volvo Citybus B10M-50	Northern Counties	B45/31F	1989	Arriva Southern Counties, 2004
769	HE	G642CHF	Volvo Citybus B10M-50	East Lancs	B49/39F	1989	Arriva Southern Counties, 2004
770	HE	G660DTJ	Volvo Citybus B10M-50	East Lancs	B49/39F	1990	Arriva Southern Counties, 2004

The only purchase of the Plaxton President for the provincial fleets was a batch of twenty delivered in 2001, though the type have been supplied to London. Illustrating the model is 685, X685YUG, which is one from Selby's allocation and it was pictured leaving York. *Bob Downham*

801-830

			Dennis Lance 11SDA3107			Alexander Strider			B47F	1993	
801	HE	K801HWW	809	HE	L809NNW	817	HE	L817NWY	824	HE	L824NWY
802	HE	K802HWW	810	HE	L810NNW	818	HE	L818NWY	825	HE	L825NWY
803	HE	K803HWW	811	HE	L811NNW	819	HE	L819NWY	826	HE	L826NYG
804	HE	K804HWW	812	HE	L812NNW	820	HE	L820NWY	827	HE	L827NYG
805	HE	K805HWX	813	HE	L813NNW	821	HE	L821NWY	828	HE	L828NYG
806	HE	L806NNW	814	HE	L814NNW	822	HE	L822NWY	829	HE	L829NYG
807	HE	L807NNW	815	HE	L815NNW	823	HE	L823NWY	830	HE	L830NYG
808	HE	L808NNW	816	HE	L816NWY						

Ancillary vehicles

252	-	C920FMP	Leyland Lynx LX1126LXCTFR1	Leyland Lynx	TV	1986	Leyland Bus, 1987
322	-	G322NNW	Leyland Lynx LX2R11C15Z4S	Leyland Lynx	TV	1990	
330	-	G330NUM	Leyland Lynx LX2R11C15Z4S	Leyland Lynx	TV	1990	
331	-	G331NUM	Leyland Lynx LX2R11C15Z4S	Leyland Lynx	TV	1990	
332	-	G332NUM	Leyland Lynx LX2R11C15Z4S	Leyland Lynx	TV	1990	

Previous Registrations:

PIL2729	J53GCX	PIL2733	K506RJX
PIL2730	J412NCP	PIL2734	K507RJX
PIL2731	K123TCP	PIL2735	L512EHD
PIL2732	J54GCX	TWY7	W167HBT

The Optare Spectra, which is the double-deck bus from the Leeds-based manufacturer, has only been built in small numbers with a total of 265 built since 1992. In 2002, Arriva Yorkshire took delivery of a batch based on the low-floor version of the DB250 chassis. Illustrating the type, and showing the enhanced tree guard, is 712, YG52CFN. *Bob Downham*

Allocations:-

Castleford (Wheldon Road) - CD

MetroRider	747	748	750					
Dart	138	139	141	142	144	145	146	150
	220	221	223	224	225	226	227	228
Lynx	333	335	336	337	338	339	340	341
	342	343	344	345	346	347	352	353
	354	355	356	357	360	366	367	368
	369	370	371	372	373	374		
Volvo B10B	401	410	411	416	418	419	420	421
	422	423	424	426	427	428	429	430
	431	432	433					
Olympian	565	596	597	613	615	616		
Volvo B7L	651	652	653	654	656	657	658	659
	661	662	663	664	665	667	668	669
	671	672	673	674				

Dewsbury (Mill Street East) - DY

MetroRider	746	749	754	757				
Mercedes-Benz	760							
Dart	135	153	154	170	171	172	173	174
	175	176	182	184	185	186	187	188
	189	190	191	192	193	194	195	196
	197	199	200					
DAF Ikarus	11	12	13	14	16	17	18	19
	20	21	22	23	24	25	26	27
	28	29						
DAF Delta	51	52						
DAF ALX 300	450	452	456	458	459	466	480	481
	482							
DAF Spectra	624	625	626	627	628	629	630	631
	632	634	635	636	637	638	639	

Heckmondwike (Beck Lane) - HE

Dart	198							
Lance	801	802	803	804	805	806	807	808
	809	810	811	812	813	814	815	816
	817	818	819	820	821	822	823	824
	825	826	827	828	829	830		
Arrow	501	502	503	504	505	506	507	508
	509	510						
Volvo Citybus	761	762	763	764	765	766	767	768
	769	770						
Olympian	517	524	541	569	570	571	585	586
	588	589	601					
Volvo B7L	687	688	689	691	692	693	694	695
	696							
DAF Spectra	718	719	720	721	722	723		

Selby (Cowie Drive, Ousegate) - SB

Dart	151	152	165	166	167	177	178	179
	180	181	183					
Volvo B10BLE	102	103	104	106	107	108	109	
Olympian	590	591	594	599	600	621	622	623
Volvo B7L	675	676	677	678	679	681	682	683
	684	685	686					

Wakefield (Belle Isle, Barnsley Road) - WF

MetroRider	755	756						
Dart	136	137	140	143	147	148	149	155
	201	202	203	204	205	206	207	208
	209	210	211	212	213	214	215	216
	217	218	219	229				
Lynx	358	359	361	362	363	364	365	375
	376	379	380	381	382			
Volvo B10B	402	403	404	405	406	408	409	412
	413	414	415	417	425			
DAF ALX300	440	441	442	443	445	446	447	448
	449	451	453	454	455	457	460	461
	462	463	464	465	467	468	469	470
	471	472	473	474	475	476	477	478
	479	483	484	485	486	487	488	489
	490	491						
VDL Bus Cmdr	495	496	497	498	499			
Olympian	530	542	566	574	575	577	579	580
	581	582	584	603	604	606	607	608
	609	610	611	612				
DAF·Spectra	633	640	641	700	701	702	703	704
	705	706	707	708	709	710	711	712
	713	714	715	716	717l			

Unallocated or stored - u/w

Lynx	377	378	
Volvo B10B	407		
Olympian	521	528	583

ARRIVA NORTH WEST & WALES

Arriva North West Ltd, Arriva Merseyside Ltd,
Arriva Cymru Ltd, Arriva Manchester Ltd, Arriva Liverpool Ltd,
73 Ormskirk Road, Aintree, Liverpool, L9 5AE

94-100		Mercedes-Benz 709D		Alexander Sprint		B25F	1996	
94	WI	P394FEA	**96**	MF	P396FEA	**98**	MF	P398FEA	**100**	MF	P401FEA
95	MF	P395FEA	**97**	MF	P397FEA	**99**	MF	P399FEA

127	WI	M127YCM	Mercedes-Benz 709D	Alexander Sprint	B29F	1995	Arriva Midlands North, 2003
129	WI	M129YCM	Mercedes-Benz 709D	Alexander Sprint	B29F	1995	Arriva Midlands North, 2003
138	WI	N468SPA	Mercedes-Benz 709D	Alexander Sprint	B27F	1995	Southern Counties(G&WS), 1998
140	WI	N470SPA	Mercedes-Benz 709D	Alexander Sprint	B27F	1995	Southern Counties(G&WS), 1998
147	CH	J3SLT	Mercedes-Benz 711D	Plaxton Beaver	B27F	1997	
148	WI	P658KEY	Mercedes-Benz 711D	Plaxton Beaver	B27F	1997	
149	CH	P473APJ	Mercedes-Benz 711D	Plaxton Beaver	B23F	1996	Arriva Southern Counties, 2001
151	WI	P688KCC	Mercedes-Benz 709D	Plaxton Beaver	B27F	1997	
153	w	N993CCC	Mercedes-Benz 709D	Alexander Sprint	B27F	1995	
154	WI	N994CCC	Mercedes-Benz 709D	Alexander Sprint	B27F	1995	
155	WI	N995CCC	Mercedes-Benz 709D	Alexander Sprint	B27F	1995	

158-163			Mercedes-Benz 709D		Alexander Sprint		B23F	1996	Timeline, Leigh, 1998
158	WY	P178FNF	**160**	CH	P180FNF	**162**	WY	P182FNF	**163**	WY	P183FNF
159	WY	P179FNF	**161**	WY	P181FNF

164	WI	P524UGA	Mercedes-Benz 709D	Plaxton Beaver	B27F	1996	Nova Scotia, Winsford, 2000
165	WI	P525UGA	Mercedes-Benz 709D	Plaxton Beaver	B27F	1996	Nova Scotia, Winsford, 2000
168	WY	M156LNC	Mercedes-Benz 811D	Alexander Sprint	B31F	1994	Timeline, Leigh, 1998
169	WY	M157LNC	Mercedes-Benz 811D	Alexander Sprint	B31F	1994	Timeline, Leigh, 1998

178-184			Mercedes-Benz 811D		Plaxton Beaver		B31F	1996	
178	WI	N178DWM	**180**	WX	P180GND	**182**	CH	P182GND	**184**	WI	P184GND
179	WI	N179DWM	**181**	WX	P181GND	**183**	CH	P183GND

The Alexander minibus body for the Mercedes-Benz Vario was the ALX100 which ceased production under TransBus ownership. This allowed all minibus production to move the Anston facility where the Beaver 2 is produced. Arriva operate 53 of the model, of which 19 are in the North West and Wales fleet. Number 361, R129GNW illustrates the type in Wrexham
Bob Downham

191	BG	N781EUA	Mercedes-Benz 811D	Plaxton Beaver	B31F	1995	Arriva Yorkshire, 2000
192	BG	N782EUA	Mercedes-Benz 811D	Plaxton Beaver	B31F	1995	Arriva Yorkshire, 2000
193	BG	N783EUA	Mercedes-Benz 811D	Plaxton Beaver	B31F	1995	Arriva Yorkshire, 2000
194	CH	N784EUA	Mercedes-Benz 811D	Plaxton Beaver	B31F	1995	Arriva Yorkshire, 2001
198	LJ	N718DJC	Mercedes-Benz 811D	Alexander Sprint	B31F	1995	
199	w	N719DJC	Mercedes-Benz 811D	Alexander Sprint	B31F	1995	

301-321

Mercedes-Benz Vario 0814   Plaxton Beaver 2   B27F   1998   320 Southern Counties, 2000

301	RH	R801YJC	307	LJ	R807YJC	312	AB	R812YJC	317	LJ	R817YJC
302	RH	R802YJC	308	LJ	R808YJC	313	AB	R813YJC	318	LJ	R818YJC
303	RH	R803YJC	309	LJ	R809YJC	314	RH	R814YJC	319	LJ	R819YJC
304	RH	R804YJC	310	BG	R810YJC	315	RH	R815YJC	320	LJ	R114TKO
305	RH	R805YJC	311	BG	R811YJC	316	RH	R816YJC	321	LJ	R821YJC

322-329

Mercedes-Benz Vario 0810   Plaxton Beaver 2   B31F   1997   Arriva Yorkshire (Y), 2000

322	LJ	R792DUB	324	LJ	R794DUB	326	LJ	R796DUB	328	WX	R798DUB
323	LJ	R793DUB	325	LJ	R795DUB	327	LJ	R797DUB	329	AB	R799DUB

331-340

Mercedes-Benz Vario 0810   Plaxton Beaver 2   B27F   1998   Arriva Southern Counties, 2000

331	RH	R101TKO	334	AB	R104TKO	337	LJ	R107TKO	339	LJ	R109TKO
332	LJ	R102TKO	335	AB	R105TKO	338	AB	R108TKO	340	RH	R110TKO
333	LJ	R103TKO									

341	AB	R341KGG	Mercedes-Benz Vario 0814	Alexander ALX100	B27F	1998	Arriva Scotland, 2001
342	AB	R112TKO	Mercedes-Benz Vario 0810	Plaxton Beaver 2	B27F	1998	Arriva Southern Counties, 2000
343	RH	R113TKO	Mercedes-Benz Vario 0810	Plaxton Beaver 2	B27F	1998	Arriva Southern Counties, 2000
344	AB	R344KGG	Mercedes-Benz Vario 0814	Alexander ALX100	B27F	1998	Arriva Scotland, 2001
345	AB	R115TKO	Mercedes-Benz Vario 0810	Plaxton Beaver 2	B27F	1998	Arriva Southern Counties, 2000
346	RH	R116TKO	Mercedes-Benz Vario 0810	Plaxton Beaver 2	B27F	1998	Arriva Southern Counties, 2000
347	LJ	R117TKO	Mercedes-Benz Vario 0810	Plaxton Beaver 2	B27F	1998	Arriva Southern Counties, 2000
350	WX	S350PGA	Mercedes-Benz Vario 0814	Plaxton Beaver 2	B27F	1998	Arriva Scotland, 2001
351	WX	S351PGA	Mercedes-Benz Vario 0814	Plaxton Beaver 2	B27F	1998	Arriva Scotland, 2001
352	WX	S352PGA	Mercedes-Benz Vario 0814	Plaxton Beaver 2	B27F	1998	Arriva Scotland, 2001
353	RH	R123TKO	Mercedes-Benz Vario 0810	Plaxton Beaver 2	B27F	1998	Arriva Southern Counties, 2001
354	LJ	R124TKO	Mercedes-Benz Vario 0810	Plaxton Beaver 2	B27F	1998	Arriva Southern Counties, 2001
355	AB	R962FYS	Mercedes-Benz Vario 0810	Mellor	C33F	1998	D & G, Rachub, 2000
356	LJ	R486UCC	Mercedes-Benz Vario 0814	Plaxton Beaver 2	B27F	1997	
357	LJ	R487UCC	Mercedes-Benz Vario 0814	Plaxton Beaver 2	B27F	1997	
358	WX	R110GNW	Mercedes-Benz Vario 0814	Plaxton Beaver 2	B27F	1998	Arriva Scotland, 2001
359	WX	R112GNW	Mercedes-Benz Vario 0814	Plaxton Beaver 2	B33F	1998	Arriva Scotland, 2001
360	WX	R113GNW	Mercedes-Benz Vario 0814	Plaxton Beaver 2	B33F	1998	Arriva Scotland, 2001
361	WX	R129GNW	Mercedes-Benz Vario 0814	Alexander ALX100	B27F	1998	Arriva Scotland, 2001
362	WX	R130GNW	Mercedes-Benz Vario 0814	Alexander ALX100	B27F	1998	Arriva Scotland, 2001
363	WX	S353PGA	Mercedes-Benz Vario 0814	Plaxton Beaver 2	B27F	1998	Arriva Scotland, 2001
364	WX	S354PGA	Mercedes-Benz Vario 0814	Plaxton Beaver 2	B27F	1998	Arriva Scotland, 2001
365	WX	S355PGA	Mercedes-Benz Vario 0814	Plaxton Beaver 2	B27F	1998	Arriva Scotland, 2001
372	BG	S822MCC	Mercedes-Benz Vario 0814	Plaxton Beaver 2	B27F	1998	
373	CW	S823MCC	Mercedes-Benz Vario 0814	Plaxton Beaver 2	B27F	1998	
374	CW	S824MCC	Mercedes-Benz Vario 0814	Plaxton Beaver 2	BC29F	1998	
375	CW	S825MCC	Mercedes-Benz Vario 0814	Plaxton Beaver 2	BC29F	1998	

380-390

Mercedes-Benz Vario 0810   Alexander ALX100   B27F   1997   Arriva Midlands North, 2003

380	CW	P61HOJ	383	CW	P53HOJ	386	CW	P56HOJ	389	CW	P59HOJ
381	CW	P51HOJ	384	CW	P54HOJ	387	CW	P57HOJ	390	AB	P260HOJ
382	CW	P52HOJ	385	CW	P255HOJ	388	CW	P58HOJ			

391	WX	W191CDN	Mercedes-Benz Vario 0814	Alexander ALX100	B27F	2000	Arriva Bus & Coach, 2000
392	WX	W192CDN	Mercedes-Benz Vario 0814	Alexander ALX100	B27F	2000	Arriva Scotland, 2001
393	BG	W193CDN	Mercedes-Benz Vario 0814	Alexander ALX100	B27F	2000	Arriva Scotland, 2001
394	BG	W194CDN	Mercedes-Benz Vario 0814	Alexander ALX100	B27F	2000	Arriva Scotland, 2001
601	SO	M301YBG	Neoplan N4009	Neoplan	N23F	1995	
602	SO	M302YBG	Neoplan N4009	Neoplan	N23F	1995	
603	SO	M303YBG	Neoplan N4009	Neoplan	N23F	1995	
611	CH	YP52JWW	Optare Alero	Optare	N12F	2003	Operated for Flintshire CC
612	CH	YP52JWO	Optare Alero	Optare	N12F	2003	Operated for Flintshire CC
613	CH	YP52JWU	Optare Alero	Optare	N12F	2003	Operated for Flintshire CC
614	CH	VU02TTF	Optare Alero	Optare	N12F	2002	Operated for Flintshire CC
615	CH	VU02TTV	Optare Alero	Optare	N12F	2002	Operated for Flintshire CC
616	CH	YO53OUH	Optare Alero	Optare	N12F	2004	Operated for Flintshire CC
617	CH	YO53OUJ	Optare Alero	Optare	N12F	2004	Operated for Flintshire CC
801	WY	R546ABA	Dennis Dart SLF 8.8m	Plaxton Pointer MPD	N28F	1997	

Arriva North West and Wales inherited several Mini Pointer Darts from Arriva Midlands North when the Cheshire operations were transferred early in 2003, bringing the total in the fleet to sixty-five. One of the type new to Arriva Wales included 839, Y539VFF, seen in Wrexham. *Bob Downham*

802-809

			Dennis Dart SLF 8.8m			Plaxton Pointer MPD		N25F	1998	
802	RU	S872SNB	804	RU	S874SNB	806	RU	S876SNB	808	RU	S878SNB
803	WY	S873SNB	805	RU	S875SNB	807	RU	S877SNB	809	RU	S879SNB

810-813

			Dennis Dart SLF 8.8m			Plaxton Pointer MPD		N29F	1999	Nova Scotia, Winsford, 2000
810	WY	T62JBA	811	WY	T63JBA	812	WY	T64JBA	813	WY	T65JBA

814-820

			Dennis Dart SLF 8.8m			Plaxton Pointer MPD		N27F	1999	
814	LJ	T564JJC	816	BG	T566JJC	818	BG	T568JJC	820	AB	T570JJC
815	LJ	T565JJC	817	BG	T567JJC	819	BG	T569JJC			

821-852

			Dennis Dart SLF 8.8m			Plaxton Pointer MPD		N27F	2000-01	
821	BG	W269NFF	831	RH	X271RFF	841	AB	Y541UJC	847	RH	Y547UJC
822	BG	W394OJC	832	RH	X272RFF	842	AB	Y542UJC	848	WX	Y548UJC
823	AB	V553ECC	833	BG	X273RFF	843	RH	Y543UJC	849	WX	Y549UJC
824	AB	V554ECC	834	AB	X274RFF	844	RH	Y544UJC	851	WX	Y551UJC
826	AB	V556ECC	838	WX	Y538VFF	846	RH	Y546UJC	852	WX	Y552UJC
827	BG	V557ECC	839	WX	Y539VFF						

856-859

			Dennis Dart SLF 8.8m			Plaxton Pointer MPD		N29F	1999	Arriva Midlands North, 2003
856	MF	T526AOB	857	MF	T527AOB	858	MF	T528AOB	859	MF	T529AOB

860-886

			Dennis Dart SLF 8.8m			Plaxton Pointer MPD		N29F	2000-01	
860	WI	X209JOF	865	WI	X215JOF	869	WI	X32KON	878	CW	Y38TDA
861	WI	X211JOF	866	WI	X216JOF	872	CW	Y32TDA	879	CW	Y39TDA
862	WI	X212JOF	867	MF	X217JOF	876	CW	Y36TDA	882	CW	Y42TDA
863	WI	X213JOF	868	MF	X218JOF	877	CW	Y37TDA	886	CW	Y46TDA
864	WI	X214JOF									

887	MF	SN03DZY	TransBus Dart SLF 8.8m	TransBus Mini Pointer	N29F	2003	Operated for Cheshire CC
888	MF	SN03DZZ	TransBus Dart SLF 8.8m	TransBus Mini Pointer	N29F	2003	Operated for Cheshire CC

1035-1040 Scania L113CRL East Lancs Flyte B47F 1996

1035	JS	P135GND	1037	JS	P137GND	1039	JS	P139GND	1040	JS	P140GND
1036	JS	P136GND	1038	JS	P138GND						

1041-1061 Scania L113CRL Northern Counties Paladin B47F 1997

1041	RU	P41MVU	1047	RU	R47XVM	1052	JS	P52MVU	1057	JS	R57XVM
1042	RU	P42MVU	1048	RU	R48XVM	1053	JS	P53MVU	1058	JS	P58MVU
1043	RU	P43MVU	1049	RU	P49MVU	1054	JS	R54XVM	1059	JS	R59XVM
1044	RU	P244NBA	1050	JS	P250NBA	1055	JS	R255WRJ	1060	JS	P260NBA
1045	RU	P45MVU	1051	JS	R51XVM	1056	JS	P56MVU	1061	JS	P61MVU
1046	RU	P46MVU									

1062	JS	M102RMS	Scania L113CRL	Northern Counties Paladin	B51F	1995	Arriva Scotland West, 2002
1063	JS	M103RMS	Scania L113CRL	Northern Counties Paladin	B51F	1995	Arriva Scotland West, 2002
1065	JS	M105RMS	Scania L113CRL	Alexander Strider	B51F	1995	Arriva Scotland West, 2002
1068	JS	L588JSG	Scania L113CRL	Northern Counties Paladin	B51F	1994	Arriva Scotland West, 2002

1101-1110 Dennis Dart 9SDL3024 Plaxton Pointer B31F 1993 Arriva London, 2001

1101	WX	L941GYL	1105	WX	L935GYL	1107	BG	L937GYL	1109	CH	L939GYL
1104	CH	L934GYL	1106	WX	L936GYL	1108	BG	L938GYL	1110	CH	L940GYL

1111	CH	J311WHJ	Dennis Dart 9SDL3002	Plaxton Pointer	B35F	1991	Arriva London, 2000
1112	BG	J312WHJ	Dennis Dart 9SDL3002	Plaxton Pointer	B35F	1991	Arriva London, 2000
1113	WX	J313WHJ	Dennis Dart 9SDL3002	Plaxton Pointer	B35F	1991	Arriva London, 2000
1114	WX	J314XVX	Dennis Dart 9SDL3011	Wright Handybus	B35F	1992	East Herts & Essex, 1998
1115	WX	J315XVX	Dennis Dart 9SDL3011	Wright Handybus	B35F	1992	East Herts & Essex, 1998
1116	AB	L150WAG	Dennis Dart 9SDL3034	Plaxton Pointer	B34F	1993	Arriva London, 2001
1117	CH	L247WAG	Dennis Dart 9SDL3024	Plaxton Pointer	B34F	1993	Arriva London, 2001
1118	BG	L148WAG	Dennis Dart 9SDL3034	Plaxton Pointer	B34F	1993	Arriva London, 2001
1119	BG	L149WAG	Dennis Dart 9SDL3034	Plaxton Pointer	B34F	1993	Arriva London, 2001

1120-1125 Dennis Dart 9SDL3034 Northern Counties Paladin B35F 1994 Arriva London, 2000

1120	MF	L120YVK	1122	MF	L126YVK	1124	MF	L123YVK	1125	MF	L121YVK
1121	MF	L125YVK	1123	MF	L151YVK						

1126	CH	N676GUM	Dennis Dart 9.8SDL3054	Plaxton Pointer	B40F	1995	Arriva London, 2001
1127	CH	N671GUM	Dennis Dart 9.8SDL3054	Plaxton Pointer	B40F	1995	Arriva London, 2001
1128	RH	N682GUM	Dennis Dart 9.8SDL3054	Plaxton Pointer	B40F	1995	Arriva London, 2001
1129	AB	N704GUM	Dennis Dart 9SDL3053	Plaxton Pointer	B34F	1995	Arriva London, 2001
1130	BG	N707GUM	Dennis Dart 9SDL3053	Plaxton Pointer	B34F	1995	Arriva London, 2001
1131	MF	H851NOC	Dennis Dart 9.8SDL3004	Carlyle Dartline	B43F	1991	Arriva Midlands North, 2003
1132	WI	G122RGT	Dennis Dart 9SDL3002	Carlyle Dartline	B33F	1990	Arriva Midlands North, 2003
1133	WI	G123RGT	Dennis Dart 9SDL3002	Carlyle Dartline	B36F	1990	Arriva Midlands North, 2003
1135	WI	G125RGT	Dennis Dart 9SDL3002	Carlyle Dartline	B36F	1990	Arriva Midlands North, 2003
1138	MF	J328VAW	Dennis Dart 9.8SDL3004	Carlyle Dartline	B40F	1991	Arriva Midlands North, 2003
1139	MF	J556GTP	Dennis Dart 9SDL3002	Wadham Stringer Portsdown	B35F	1991	Arriva Midlands North, 2003
1140	MF	H192JNF	Dennis Dart 9SDL3002	Wadham Stringer Portsdown	B35F	1990	Arriva Midlands North, 2003
1141	HU	L115YVK	Dennis Dart 9SDL3034	Northern Counties Paladin	B35F	1994	Arriva Southern Counties, 2003
1142	MF	L116YVK	Dennis Dart 9SDL3034	Northern Counties Paladin	B35F	1994	Arriva Southern Counties, 2003
1143	u	L117YVK	Dennis Dart 9SDL3034	Northern Counties Paladin	B35F	1994	Arriva Southern Counties, 2003
1146	MF	L122YVK	Dennis Dart 9SDL3034	Northern Counties Paladin	B35F	1994	Arriva Southern Counties, 2003
1148	MF	J701NHA	Dennis Dart 9.8SDL3004	East Lancs EL2000	B40F	1991	Arriva Midlands North, 2003
1149	MF	L618BNX	Dennis Dart 9SDL3034	East Lancs EL2000	B33F	1994	Arriva Midlands North, 2003
1150	BO	L150SBG	Dennis Dart 9SDL3034	East Lancs	B32F	1993	
1151	BO	L151SBG	Dennis Dart 9SDL3034	East Lancs	B32F	1993	
1152	BO	L152SBG	Dennis Dart 9SDL3034	East Lancs	B32F	1993	
1153	CH	L153UKB	Dennis Dart 9SDL3034	Plaxton Pointer	B34F	1994	
1154	BG	L154UKB	Dennis Dart 9SDL3034	Plaxton Pointer	B34F	1994	
1155	CH	L155UKB	Dennis Dart 9SDL3034	Plaxton Pointer	B34F	1994	
1156	CH	L156UKB	Dennis Dart 9SDL3034	Plaxton Pointer	B34F	1994	

1157-1170 Dennis Dart 9.8SDL3040* East Lancs B40F 1994-95 *1170 is 9.8SDL3054

1157	RU	M157WKA	1161	RU	M161WKA	1165	LJ	M165WKA	1168	RU	M168WKA
1158	RU	M158WKA	1162	RU	M162WKA	1166	RU	M166WKA	1169	RU	M169WKA
1159	RU	M159WKA	1163	RU	M163WKA	1167	RU	M167WKA	1170	RU	M170WKA
1160	RU	M160WKA	1164	BG	M164WKA						

Macclesfield's allocation includes two Dennis Darts with Wadham Stringer Portsdown bodywork, the only pair operated by Arriva, although four of its successor, the WSS Portsdown, are maintained by Southern Counties. Seen about to leave for Manchester on route 130 that also serves Wilmslow, 1140, H192JNF pauses for the camera. *Bob Downham*

1171-1187
Dennis Dart 9.8SDL3040 — Plaxton Pointer — B40F — 1995

1171	HU	M171YKA	1176	HU	M176YKA	1180	SK	M180YKA	1184 HU M184YKA
1172	BD	M172YKA	1177	HU	M177YKA	1181	BD	M181YKA	1185 BD M185YKA
1173	HU	M173YKA	1178	HU	M178YKA	1182	SK	M182YKA	1186 BD M186YKA
1174	BD	M174YKA	1179	HU	M179YKA	1183	HU	M183YKA	1187 HU M187YKA
1175	BD	M175YKA							

1188-1199
Dennis Dart 9.8SDL3054 — Plaxton Pointer — B40F — 1995

1188	WY	M188YKA	1191	HU	M191YKA	1194	HU	M194YKA	1197 BD M197YKA
1189	SK	M189YKA	1192	HU	M192YKA	1195	HU	M195YKA	1198 BD M198YKA
1190	SK	M190YKA	1193	BD	M193YKA	1196	HU	M196YKA	1199 WY M199YKA

1201-1210
Dennis Lance 11SDA3113 — Plaxton Verde — B49F — 1995

1201	BO	M201YKA	1204	BO	M204YKA	1207	BO	M207YKA	1209 BO M209YKA
1202	BO	M202YKA	1205	BO	M205YKA	1208	BO	M208YKA	1210 BO M210YKA
1203	BO	M203YKA	1206	BO	M206YKA				

1211	BD	M211YKD	Dennis Dart 9.8SDL3040	Plaxton Pointer	B40F	1995
1212	BD	M212YKD	Dennis Dart 9.8SDL3040	Plaxton Pointer	B40F	1995
1213	BD	M213YKD	Dennis Dart 9.8SDL3040	Plaxton Pointer	B40F	1995
1214	BD	M214YKD	Dennis Dart 9.8SDL3054	Plaxton Pointer	B40F	1995
1215	BD	M215YKD	Dennis Dart 9.8SDL3054	Plaxton Pointer	B40F	1995
1216	BD	M216YKD	Dennis Dart 9.8SDL3054	Plaxton Pointer	B40F	1995

1217-1264
Dennis Dart 9.8SDL3054 — East Lancs — B40F — 1995

1217	WY	M217AKB	1229	SK	M229AKB	1241	BO	N241CKA	1253 SK N253CKA
1218	WY	M218AKB	1230	SK	M230AKB	1242	BO	N242CKA	1254 MA N254CKA
1219	BG	M219AKB	1231	WY	M231AKB	1243	BO	N243CKA	1255 WY N255CKA
1220	RU	M220AKB	1232	WY	M232AKB	1244	BO	N244CKA	1256 WY N256CKA
1221	RU	M221AKB	1233	BO	N233CKA	1245	BO	N245CKA	1257 WY N257CKA
1222	RU	M322AKB	1234	BO	N234CKA	1246	BO	N246CKA	1258 SK N258CKA
1223	MA	M223AKB	1235	BO	N235CKA	1247	BO	N247CKA	1259 SK N259CKA
1224	MA	M224AKB	1236	BO	N236CKA	1248	BO	N248CKA	1260 CH N260CKA
1225	MA	M225AKB	1237	BO	N237CKA	1249	MA	N249CKA	1261 WY N261CKA
1226	MA	M226AKB	1238	BO	N238CKA	1250	MA	N250CKA	1262 WY N262CKA
1227	MA	M227AKB	1239	BO	N239CKA	1251	MA	N251CKA	1263 WY N263CKA
1228	LJ	M228AKB	1240	BO	N240CKA	1252	BG	N252CKA	1264 MA N264CKA

During the 1990s the North West operations acquired several small businesses including Star Line and South Lancashire, the latter bringing Darts with *Select* index marks into the fleet. Allocated to Huyton, 1280, L11SLT, is seen arriving in St Helens having worked route 357 from Rainford. *Bob Downham*

1265	WY	K877UDB	Dennis Dart 9.8SDL3017	Plaxton Pointer		B40F	1992	Star Line, 1995
1266	WY	M370KVR	Dennis Dart 9.8SDL3035	Northern Counties Paladin		B40F	1994	Star Line, 1995
1267	WY	M371KVR	Dennis Dart 9.8SDL3035	Northern Counties Paladin		B40F	1994	Star Line, 1995
1268	WY	M372KVR	Dennis Dart 9.8SDL3035	Northern Counties Paladin		B40F	1995	Star Line, 1995
1269	WY	M841RCP	Dennis Dart 9.8SDL3054	Northern Counties Paladin		B39F	1995	Wigan Bus Company, 1995
1270	WY	M842RCP	Dennis Dart 9.8SDL3054	Northern Counties Paladin		B39F	1995	Wigan Bus Company, 1995
1271	WY	M843RCP	Dennis Dart 9.8SDL3054	Northern Counties Paladin		B39F	1995	Wigan Bus Company, 1995
1272	SK	K911OEM	Dennis Dart 9.8SDL3017	Plaxton Pointer		B38F	1993	Blue Triangle, 1994
1273	SK	K73SRG	Dennis Dart 9.8SDL3017	Plaxton Pointer		B43F	1993	Northumbria (Hunters), 1997
1274	SK	K74SRG	Dennis Dart 9.8SDL3017	Plaxton Pointer		B43F	1993	Northumbria (Hunters), 1997
1275	SK	K75SRG	Dennis Dart 9.8SDL3017	Plaxton Pointer		B43F	1993	Northumbria (Hunters), 1997
1276	SK	J6SLT	Dennis Dart 9.8SDL3040	Plaxton Pointer		B40F	1996	South Lancashire, 1997
1277	SK	J7SLT	Dennis Dart 9.8SDL3040	Plaxton Pointer		B38F	1996	South Lancashire, 1997
1278	SK	J8SLT	Dennis Dart 9.8SDL3017	Plaxton Pointer		B38F	1992	South Lancashire, 1997
1279	SK	J9SLT	Dennis Dart 9.8SDL3017	Plaxton Pointer		B38F	1992	South Lancashire, 1997
1280	HU	L11SLT	Dennis Dart 9.8SDL3025	Plaxton Pointer		B38F	1993	South Lancashire, 1997
1281	HU	L1SLT	Dennis Dart 9SDL3011	Plaxton Pointer		B35F	1993	South Lancashire, 1997
1282	HU	L2SLT	Dennis Dart 9SDL3011	Plaxton Pointer		B35F	1993	South Lancashire, 1997
1283	SK	K817NKH	Dennis Dart 9SDL3016	Plaxton Pointer		B34F	1992	London Northern, 1994
1284	SK	K955PBG	Dennis Dart 9.8SDL3017	Plaxton Pointer		B36F	1993	Blue Triangle, 1994
1285	SK	M5SLT	Dennis Dart 9.8SDL3040	Plaxton Pointer		B40F	1994	South Lancashire, 1997
1286	HU	M950LYR	Dennis Dart 9.8SDL3040	Plaxton Pointer		B40F	1995	Arriva London, 2000
1287	WY	M20GGY	Dennis Dart 9.8SDL3040	Plaxton Pointer		B40F	1994	David Ogden, Haydock, 1995
1288	WY	M30GGY	Dennis Dart 9.8SDL3040	Plaxton Pointer		B40F	1994	David Ogden, Haydock, 1995
1289	SO	N678GUM	Dennis Dart 9.8SDL3054	Plaxton Pointer		B40F	1995	Arriva London, 2003

1290-1299

1290-1299			Dennis Lance 11SDA3113	Plaxton Verde		B49F	1994	Clydeside, 1996

1290	BO	M930EYS	1293	BO	M933EYS	1296	BO	M936EYS	1298	BO	M928EYS
1291	BO	M931EYS	1294	BO	M934EYS	1297	BO	M927EYS	1299	BO	M929EYS
1292	BO	M932EYS	1295	BO	M935EYS						

1300	SK	P3SLT	Dennis Dart	Plaxton Pointer		B40F	1996	South Lancashire, 1997

Recent changes to the single-deck fleet have seen many of the Leyland Tigers new to Shearings transferred into ancillary fleets as driver trainers. Three Tigers remain operational in the North West and Wales fleet, all at Aberystwyth. Number 1772, E52UNE, was pictured at Northwich before its recent move. *Bob Downham*

1301-1310

			Dennis Dart 9.8SDL3053			East Lancs EL2000		B30FL	1995	Arriva Southern Counties, 2001
1301	BG	M521MPF	1303	BG	M523MPF	1308	BG	N528SPA	1310	BG	N530SPA
1302	BG	M522MPF	1304	BG	M524MPF	1309	BG	N529SPA			

1323-1338

			Dennis Dart			Plaxton Pointer		B40F	1996	Arriva London, 2001-03
1323	RH	P823RWU	1327	AB	P827RWU	1330	CH	P830RWU	1333	BG	P833RWU
1325	RH	P825RWU	1328	AB	P828RWU	1331	CH	P831RWU	1334	CH	P834RWU
1326	AB	P826RWU	1329	AB	P829RWU	1332	SO	P832RWU	1338	RH	P838RWU

1340	BG	M160SKR	Dennis Dart 9SDL3053	Plaxton Pointer	B35F	1995	Arriva Southern Counties, 1999
1341	SK	M161SKR	Dennis Dart 9SDL3053	Plaxton Pointer	B35F	1995	Arriva Southern Counties, 1999
1342	SK	M162SKR	Dennis Dart 9SDL3053	Plaxton Pointer	B35F	1995	Arriva Southern Counties, 1999
1343	LJ	M163SKR	Dennis Dart 9SDL3053	Plaxton Pointer	B35F	1995	Arriva Southern Counties, 1999

1717	CW	E265WUB	Leyland Lynx LX112L10ZR1S	Leyland Lynx	B49F	1989	Arriva Midlands North, 2003
1718	CW	E268WUB	Leyland Lynx LX112L10ZR1S	Leyland Lynx	B49F	1989	Arriva Midlands North, 2003
1719	CW	E49WEM	Leyland Lynx LX112L10ZR1R	Leyland Lynx	B49F	1988	Devaway, Bretton, 1998
1727	CW	F117XTX	Leyland Lynx LX112L10ZR1R	Leyland Lynx	B51F	1988	Arriva Midlands North, 2003
1730	CW	F280AWW	Leyland Lynx LX112L10ZR1S	Leyland Lynx	B49F	1989	Arriva Midlands North, 2003
1731	CW	F301AWW	Leyland Lynx LX112L10ZR1S	Leyland Lynx	B49F	1989	Arriva Midlands North, 2003
1732	CW	F61PRE	Leyland Lynx LX112L10ZR1R	Leyland Lynx	B48F	1989	Arriva Midlands North, 2003
1741	AB	G41VME	Leyland Lynx LX2R11C15Z4S	Leyland Lynx	B49F	1989	Arriva Southern Counties, 1999
1743	CW	G49CVC	Leyland Lynx LX2R11C15Z4S	Leyland Lynx	B51F	1990	Arriva Midlands North, 2003
1746	CW	G319NNW	Leyland Lynx LX2R11C15Z4R	Leyland Lynx	B49F	1990	Arriva Midlands North, 2003
1747	CW	G327NUM	Leyland Lynx LX2R11C15Z4S	Leyland Lynx	B49F	1990	Arriva Midlands North, 2003
1748	CW	H408YMA	Leyland Lynx LX2R11C15Z4R	Leyland Lynx	B51F	1990	Arriva Midlands North, 2003
1749	CW	G329NUM	Leyland Lynx LX2R11C15Z4S	Leyland Lynx	B49F	1990	Arriva Midlands North, 2003
1750	AB	H130LPU	Leyland Lynx LX2R11C15Z4R	Leyland Lynx 2	B49F	1990	Colchester, 1994
1751	BG	H34PAJ	Leyland Lynx LX2R11C15Z4S	Leyland Lynx 2	B49F	1991	Arriva North East, 1999
1752	CW	H254PAJ	Leyland Lynx LX2R11C15Z4S	Leyland Lynx 2	B49F	1991	Arriva North East, 1999
1753	CW	H733HWK	Leyland Lynx LX2R11C15Z4R	Leyland Lynx 2	B51F	1990	Clydeside (McGills), 1997
1754	CW	J654UHN	Leyland Lynx LX2R11C15Z4S	Leyland Lynx 2	B49F	1991	Arriva North East, 1998
1755	BG	J655UHN	Leyland Lynx LX2R11C15Z4S	Leyland Lynx 2	B49F	1991	Arriva North East, 1999
1757	AB	K27EWC	Leyland Lynx LX2R11C15Z4R	Leyland Lynx 2	B49F	1992	Colchester, 1994
1772	AB	E52UNE	Leyland Tiger TRBTL11/3ARZA	Alexander N	B53F	1988	Arriva Midlands North, 2003
1776	AB	H278LEF	Leyland Tiger TRCL10/3ARZA	Alexander Q	B55F	1990	Arriva Midlands North, 2003
1777	AB	H279LEF	Leyland Tiger TRCL10/3ARZA	Alexander Q	B55F	1990	Arriva Midlands North, 2003

1993 saw the arrival of five Ikarus CitiBus-bodied DAF SB220 buses with Arriva North West. Allocated to Birkenhead, 1791, K131TCP, is seen on the other side of the Mersey in Liverpool. *Bob Downham*

1778-1788

Volvo B10M-50 Citybus — Alexander Q — B55F — 1992 — Timeline, Leigh, 1998

1778	AB	H78DVM	1785	SK	H85DVM	1787	AB	H87DVM	1788	AB	H588DVM
1779	SK	H79DVM	1786	AB	H86DVM					

1790-1794

DAF SB220LC550 — Ikarus CitiBus — B48F — 1993

1790	BD	K130TCP	1792	BD	K132TCP	1793	BD	K133TCP	1794	BD	K510RJX
1791	BD	K131TCP								

1795	AB	N25FWU	DAF SB220LC550	Northern Counties Paladin	B49F	1995	West Coast Motors, 1996
1796	AB	N24FWU	DAF SB220LC550	Northern Counties Paladin	B49F	1995	West Coast Motors, 1996
1797	AB	M847RCP	DAF SB220LC550	Northern Counties Paladin	B49F	1995	Citybus, Southampton, 1996
1799	WX	M849RCP	DAF SB220LC550	Northern Counties Paladin	B49F	1995	Citybus, Southampton, 1996

1940-1949

Dennis Lance 11SDA3113 — East Lancs — B49F — 1996 — Arriva London, 2001

1940	BO	N210TPK	1943	BO	N213TPK	1946	BO	N216TPK	1948	BO	N218TPK
1941	BO	N211TPK	1944	BO	N214TPK	1947	BO	N217TPK	1949	BO	N219TPK
1942	BO	N212TPK	1945	BO	N215TPK					

2001-2005

Scania L113CRL — Wright Axcess-ultralow — N42F — 1996

2001	JS	N101YVU	2003	JS	N103YVU	2004	JS	N104YVU	2005	JS	N105YVU
2002	GL	M2SLT								

2006-2034

Scania L113CRL — Wright Axcess-ultralow — N43F — 1996

2006	JS	N106DWM	2014	JS	N114DWM	2021	JS	N121DWM	2028	JS	N128DWM
2007	JS	N107DWM	2015	JS	N115DWM	2022	JS	N122DWM	2029	JS	N129DWM
2008	GL	N108DWM	2016	JS	N116DWM	2023	JS	N123DWM	2030	GL	N130DWM
2009	JS	N109DWM	2017	JS	N117DWM	2024	GL	N124DWM	2031	JS	N131DWM
2010	JS	N110DWM	2018	JS	N118DWM	2025	GL	N125DWM	2032	GL	N132DWM
2011	GL	N211DWM	2019	JS	N119DWM	2026	GL	N126DWM	2033	GL	N133DWM
2013	JS	N113DWM	2020	JS	N120DWM	2027	JS	N127DWM	2034	JS	N134DWM

2041-2054   Scania N113CRL   Wright Pathfinder   B37D   1994   Arriva London, 1999

2041	MA	RDZ1701	2045	RU	RDZ1705	2049	RU	RDZ1709	2052	RU	RDZ1712
2042	MA	RDZ1702	2046	MA	RDZ1706	2050	RU	RDZ1710	2053	RU	RDZ1713
2043	MA	RDZ1703	2047	RU	RDZ1707	2051	RU	RDZ1711	2054	RU	RDZ1714
2044	RU	RDZ1704	2048	RU	RDZ1708						

2201-2262   Dennis Dart SLF   Plaxton Pointer 2   N36F   2000-01

2201	HU	X201ANC	2217	BO	X217ANC	2234	BO	X234ANC	2248	MA	X248HJA
2202	HU	X202ANC	2218	BO	X218ANC	2235	BO	X235ANC	2249	MA	X249HJA
2203	HU	X203ANC	2219	BO	X219ANC	2236	BO	X236ANC	2251	MA	X251HJA
2204	HU	X204ANC	2221	BO	X221ANC	2237	BO	X237ANC	2252	MA	X252HJA
2207	HU	X207ANC	2223	BO	X223ANC	2238	MA	X238ANC	2253	MA	X253HJA
2208	HU	X208ANC	2224	BO	X224ANC	2239	MA	X239ANC	2254	MA	X254HJA
2209	HU	X209ANC	2226	BO	X226ANC	2241	MA	X241ANC	2256	MA	X256HJA
2211	HU	X211ANC	2227	BO	X227ANC	2242	MA	X242ANC	2257	BD	X257HJA
2212	HU	X212ANC	2228	BO	X228ANC	2243	MA	X243HJA	2258	BD	X258HJA
2213	HU	X213ANC	2229	BO	X229ANC	2244	MA	X244HJA	2259	BD	X259HJA
2214	HU	X214ANC	2231	BO	X231ANC	2246	MA	X246HJA	2261	BD	X261OBN
2215	BO	X215ANC	2232	BO	X232ANC	2247	MA	X247HJA	2262	BD	X262OBN
2216	BO	X216ANC	2233	BO	X233ANC						

2263-2272   Dennis Dart SLF 10.2m   Alexander ALX200   N40F   2000-01

2263	BO	X263OBN	2266	BO	X266OBN	2268	BO	X268OBN	2271	BO	X271OBN
2264	BO	X264OBN	2267	BO	X267OBN	2269	BO	X269OBN	2272	BO	X272OBN
2265	BO	X265OBN									

2273	LJ	S558MCC	Dennis Dart SLF 10.2m	Alexander ALX200	N40F	1998
2274	LJ	S559MCC	Dennis Dart SLF 10.2m	Alexander ALX200	N40F	1998

2276-2279   Dennis Dart SLF 10.2m   Alexander ALX200   N36F   1997   Arriva London, 2002-03

2276	CH	P953RUL	2277	LJ	P959RUL	2278	LJ	P960RUL	2279	LJ	P961RUL

2280-2284   Dennis Dart SLF   Plaxton Pointer   N40F   1996   Arriva Southern Counties, 2004

2280	u	P180LKL	2282	u	P182LKL	2283	u	P183LKL	2284	u	P214LKJ

2285-2288   Dennis Dart SLF   Plaxton Pointer   N39F   1996   Arriva Southern Counties, 2004

2285	u	P419HVX	2286	u	P420HVX	2287	u	P422HVX	2288	u	P430HVX

2296-2300   Dennis Dart SLF 10m   Plaxton Pointer   N34F   1997   Arriva London, 2003

2296	RH	R416COO	2298	RH	R418COO	2299	RH	R419COO	2300	RH	R420COO
2297	RH	R417COO									

2301	WR	R301PCW	Dennis Dart SLF 10.1m	Plaxton Pointer 2	N39F	1998

2302-2313   Dennis Dart SLF 10.2m   Alexander ALX200   N40F   1998

2302	WY	R302CVU	2305	WY	R305CVU	2309	WY	R309CVU	2312	WY	R312CVU
2303	WY	R303CVU	2306	WY	R606FBU	2310	WY	R310CVU	2313	WY	R313CVU
2304	WY	R304CVU	2308	WY	R308CVU	2311	WY	R311CVU			

2314-2324   Dennis Dart SLF 10.1m   Plaxton Pointer 2   N36F   1999

2314	BO	T314PNB	2317	BO	T317PNB	2320	BO	T820PNB	2323	BO	T323PNB
2315	BO	T315PNB	2318	BO	T318PNB	2321	BO	T321PNB	2324	BO	T324PNB
2316	BO	T316PNB	2319	BO	T319PNB	2322	BO	T322PNB			

2325	BG	R521UCC	Dennis Dart SLF 10.1m	Plaxton Pointer	N39F	1997	
2326	BG	R522UCC	Dennis Dart SLF 10.1m	Plaxton Pointer	N39F	1997	
2328	CH	S848RJC	Dennis Dart SLF 10.1m	Plaxton Pointer 2	N39F	1998	Ieuan Williams, Deiniolen, 1999
2330	BG	T560JJC	Dennis Dart SLF 10.1m	Plaxton Pointer 2	N39F	1999	
2331	LJ	T561JJC	Dennis Dart SLF 10.1m	Plaxton Pointer 2	N39F	1999	
2332	AB	T562JJC	Dennis Dart SLF 10.1m	Plaxton Pointer 2	N39F	1999	
2333	AB	T563JJC	Dennis Dart SLF 10.1m	Plaxton Pointer 2	N39F	1999	

2341-2361   Dennis Dart SLF   Plaxton Pointer 2   N39F*   1999-2000   *2341/2 are N33F

2341	CH	V571DJC	2347	LJ	V577DJC	2352	RH	V582DJC	2357	CH	V587DJC
2342	CH	V572DJC	2348	LJ	V578DJC	2353	RH	V583DJC	2358	CH	V588DJC
2343	LJ	V573DJC	2349	RH	V579DJC	2354	RH	V584DJC	2359	CH	V580ECC
2344	LJ	V574DJC	2350	RH	V580DJC	2355	CH	V585DJC	2360	CH	V590DJC
2345	LJ	V575DJC	2351	RH	V581DJC	2356	CH	V586DJC	2361	CH	V591DJC
2346	LJ	V576DJC									

A single batch of the DAF SB220 with East Lancs Myllennium bodywork was selected for the North West fleet shortly after the company purchased MTL. Divided between Speke and Birkenhead depots they provide an impressive sight as illustrated by 2474, Y474KNF, as it turns out of Paradise Street. *Richard Godfrey*

2391	BO	M517KPA	Dennis Lance SLF	Wright Pathfinder	N40F	1995	Arriva Southern Counties, 2002
2392	BO	M518KPA	Dennis Lance SLF	Wright Pathfinder	N40F	1995	Arriva Southern Counties, 2002
2393	BO	M519KPA	Dennis Lance SLF	Wright Pathfinder	N40F	1995	Arriva Southern Counties, 2002
2394	BO	N527SPA	Dennis Lance SLF	Wright Pathfinder	N39F	1995	Arriva Southern Counties, 2002
2395	u	M761JPA	Dennis Lance SLF 11SDA3201	Wright Pathfinder	N39F	1995	Arriva Southern Counties, 2004
2396	u	M762JPA	Dennis Lance SLF 11SDA3201	Wright Pathfinder	N39F	1995	Arriva Southern Counties, 2004
2397	u	M763JPA	Dennis Lance SLF 11SDA3201	Wright Pathfinder	N39F	1995	Arriva Southern Counties, 2004
2401	SP	R151GNW	DAF DE02GSSB220	Plaxton Prestige	N38F	1998	Arriva London, 1999
2402	SP	R152GNW	DAF DE02GSSB220	Plaxton Prestige	N38F	1998	Arriva London, 1999
2403	SP	R153GNW	DAF DE02GSSB220	Plaxton Prestige	N38F	1998	Arriva London, 1999

2404-2415

| | | DAF DE02GSSB220 | | Alexander ALX300 | N42F | 2000 | |

2404	SP	V404ENC	2407	SP	V407ENC	2410	SP	V410ENC	2413	SP	V413ENC
2405	SP	V405ENC	2408	SP	V408ENC	2411	BD	V411ENC	2414	BD	V414ENC
2406	SP	V406ENC	2409	SP	V409ENC	2412	BD	V412ENC	2415	SP	V415ENC

2416-2449

| | | DAF DE12CSSB120 | | Wright Cadet | N39F | 2000-01 | |

2416	SP	X416AJA	2426	SP	X426AJA	2434	SP	X434HJA	2442	BD	X442HJA
2417	SP	X417AJA	2427	SP	X427AJA	2435	BD	X435HJA	2443	BD	X443HJA
2418	SP	X418AJA	2428	SP	X428AJA	2436	BD	X436HJA	2445	BD	X445HJA
2419	SP	X419AJA	2429	SP	X429HJA	2437	BD	X437HJA	2446	BD	X446HJA
2421	SP	X421AJA	2431	SP	X431HJA	2438	BD	X438HJA	2447	BD	X447HJA
2422	SP	X422AJA	2432	SP	X432HJA	2439	BD	X439HJA	2448	BD	X448HJA
2423	SP	X423AJA	2433	SP	X433HJA	2441	BD	X441HJA	2449	BD	X449HJA
2424	SP	X424AJA									

2451-2474

| | | DAF DE02GSSB220 | | East Lancs Myllennium | N44F | 2001 | |

2451	BD	Y451KBU	2457	BD	Y457KBU	2463	SP	Y463KNF	2469	SP	Y469KNF
2452	BD	Y452KBU	2458	BD	Y458KBU	2464	SP	Y464KNF	2470	SP	Y733KNF
2453	BD	Y453KBU	2459	BD	Y459KBU	2465	SP	Y465KNF	2471	SP	Y471KNF
2454	BD	Y454KBU	2460	BD	Y243KBU	2466	SP	Y466KNF	2472	SP	Y472KNF
2455	BD	Y241KBU	2461	BD	Y461KNF	2467	SP	Y467KNF	2473	SP	Y473KNF
2456	BD	Y242KBU	2462	SP	Y462KNF	2468	SP	Y468KNF	2474	SP	Y744KNF

2475	u	T917KKM	DAF DE02GSSB220	Plaxton Prestige	N39F	1999	Arriva Southern Counties, 2004
2476	u	T920KKM	DAF DE02GSSB220	Plaxton Prestige	N39F	1999	Arriva Southern Counties, 2004
2477	u	T922KKM	DAF DE02GSSB220	Plaxton Prestige	N39F	1999	Arriva Southern Counties, 2004

2480-2488   VDL Bus SB120   Wrightbus Cadet   N39F   2004

2480	BG	CX04AXW	2483	BG	CX04AYA	2485	BG	CX04AYC	2487	WX	CX04EHW
2481	BG	CX04AXY	2484	BG	CX04AYB	2486	WX	CX04EHV	2400	WX	CX04EHY
2482	BG	CX04AXZ									

2601-2608   Dennis Dart SLF   Plaxton Pointer 2   N39F   1997-99   Arriva North East, 2003

| 2601 | WX | R601MHN | 2603 | WX | R603MHN | 2605 | WX | R685MHN | 2607 | WX | R607MHN |
| 2602 | WX | R602MHN | 2604 | WX | R604MHN | 2606 | WX | R606MHN | 2608 | WX | R608MHN |

2701-2730   Volvo B10BLE   Wrightbus Renown   N44F   2001

2701	JS	X701DBT	2709	JS	X709DBT	2717	SP	Y717KNF	2724	SO	Y724KNF
2702	JS	X702DBT	2710	JS	X956DBT	2718	SP	Y718KNF	2725	SO	Y475KNF
2703	JS	X703DBT	2711	JS	Y711KNF	2719	SP	Y719KNF	2726	SO	Y726KNF
2704	JS	X704DBT	2712	JS	Y712KNF	2720	SP	Y457KNF	2727	SO	Y727KNF
2705	JS	X705DBT	2713	JS	Y713KNF	2721	SP	Y721KNF	2728	SO	Y728KNF
2706	JS	X706DBT	2714	JS	Y714KNF	2722	SO	Y722KNF	2729	JS	Y729KNF
2707	JS	X707DBT	2715	JS	Y715KNF	2723	SO	Y723KNF	2730	JS	Y458KNF
2708	JS	X708DBT	2716	SP	Y716KNF						

| 2800 | JS | Y22CJW | Volvo B7L | Wrightbus Eclipse | N41F | 2001 | |

2801-2822   Volvo B6BLE   Wright Crusader 2   N39F   2000

2801	SO	X801AJA	2806	JS	X806AJA	2812	SO	X812AJA	2817	SO	X817AJA
2802	SO	X802AJA	2807	JS	X807AJA	2813	SO	X813AJA	2818	SO	X818AJA
2803	SO	X803AJA	2808	JS	X808AJA	2814	SO	X814AJA	2819	SO	X819AJA
2804	SO	X804AJA	2809	JS	X809AJA	2815	SO	X815AJA	2821	SO	X821AJA
2805	JS	X805AJA	2811	JS	X811AJA	2816	SO	X816AJA	2822	SO	X822AJA

3022	MF	A152UDM	Leyland Olympian ONLXB/1R	Eastern Coach Works	B45/32F	1984	Arriva Midlands North, 2003
3037	WI	B197DTU	Leyland Olympian ONLXB/1R	Eastern Coach Works	B45/32F	1985	Arriva Midlands North, 2003
3038	MF	B198DTU	Leyland Olympian ONLXB/1R	Eastern Coach Works	B45/32F	1985	Arriva Midlands North, 2003
3039	MF	A139MRN	Leyland Olympian ONLXB/1R	Eastern Coach Works	B45/32F	1984	Arriva Midlands North, 2003
3041	MF	A141MRN	Leyland Olympian ONLXB/1R	Eastern Coach Works	B45/32F	1984	Arriva Midlands North, 2003

3047-3069   Leyland Olympian ONLXB/1R   Eastern Coach Works   B45/32F   1983-85   3048/9/64 AMN, 2003

3047	AB	A147OFR	3051	AB	B151TRN	3063	CH	B963WRN	3065	AB	B965WRN
3048	WI	B148TRN	3054	WI	B154TRN	3064	MF	B964WRN	3069	AB	B967WRN
3049	WI	B149TRN	3062	WI	B962WRN						

3071	BG	B251NVN	Leyland Olympian ONLXB/1R	Eastern Coach Works	B45/32F	1985	Arriva North East, 2000
3073	BG	B513LFP	Leyland Olympian ONLXB/1R	Eastern Coach Works	B45/32F	1984	Fox County, 1998
3094	CH	B194BLG	Leyland Olympian ONLXB/1R	Eastern Coach Works	B45/32F	1985	Crosville, 1986

3101-3115   Leyland Olympian ON2R50C13Z4   Northern Counties   B47/30F   1990   Arriva London, 2000

3101	WX	H101GEV	3105	BD	H105GEV	3109	MA	H109GEV	3113	BD	H113GEV
3102	MA	H102GEV	3106	MA	H106GEV	3110	MA	H110GEV	3114	BD	H114GEV
3103	MA	H103GEV	3107	MA	H107GEV	3112	BD	H112GEV	3115	BD	H115GEV
3104	MA	H104GEV	3108	MA	H108GEV						

3122	BG	C212GTU	Leyland Olympian ONLXB/1R	Eastern Coach Works	B42/27F	1985	Crosville, 1986
3131	AB	F991UME	Leyland Olympian ONLXB/1RH	Optare	B47/29F	1989	Arriva Southern Counties, 1999
3135	AB	F455BKF	Leyland Olympian ONCL10/2RZ	Northern Counties	B51/34F	1989	
3137	AB	F457BKF	Leyland Olympian ONCL10/2RZ	Northern Counties	B51/34F	1989	
3139	AB	F459BKF	Leyland Olympian ONCL10/2RZ	Northern Counties	B51/34F	1989	
3146	WI	G916LHA	Leyland Olympian ON2R50G16ZA	East Lancs	B45/29F	1989	Arriva Midlands North, 2003
3147	WI	G917LHA	Leyland Olympian ON2R50G16ZA	East Lancs	B45/29F	1989	Arriva Midlands North, 2003
3148	WI	G918LHA	Leyland Olympian ON2R50G16ZA	East Lancs	B45/29F	1989	Arriva Midlands North, 2003
3149	WI	G919LHA	Leyland Olympian ON2R50G16ZA	East Lancs	B45/29F	1989	Arriva Midlands North, 2003

3206-3213   Leyland Olympian ONCL10/1RZ   Northern Counties   B47/30F   1989   Arriva Fox County, 1999

| 3206 | SP | G506SFT | 3209 | SP | G509SFT | 3212 | BG | G512SFT | 3213 | SP | G513SFT |
| 3208 | BD | G508SFT | | | | | | | | | |

3214	BG	G754UYT	Leyland Olympian ONCL10/1R	Northern Counties	B43/32F	1989	Arriva Midlands North, 2003
3215	BG	G755UYT	Leyland Olympian ONCL10/1R	Northern Counties	B43/32F	1989	Arriva Midlands North, 2003
3218	BG	G758UYT	Leyland Olympian ONCL10/1R	Northern Counties	B43/32F	1989	Arriva Midlands North, 2003
3219	BG	G759UYT	Leyland Olympian ONCL10/1R	Northern Counties	B43/32F	1989	Arriva Midlands North, 2003

3221-3225

Leyland Olympian ONLXB/1RZ — Alexander RL — B45/30F — 1989 — Arriva Fox County, 1999

3221	SP	G521WJF	3223	SP	G523WJF	3224	SP	G524WJF	3225	SP	G525WJF
3222	SP	G522WJF									

3226	BG	F96PRE	Leyland Olympian ONCL10/1RZ	Alexander RL	B47/32F	1988	Arriva Midlands North, 2003
3227	BG	F97PRE	Leyland Olympian ONCL10/1RZ	Alexander RL	B47/32F	1988	Arriva Midlands North, 2003

3251-3270

Leyland Olympian ONCL10/1RZ — Northern Counties — B45/30F — 1989

3251	BD	F251YTJ	3256	SP	F256YTJ	3261	SP	F261YTJ	3266	RX	F266YTJ
3252	SP	F252YTJ	3257	SP	F257YTJ	3262	BD	F262YTJ	3268	RX	F268YTJ
3253	BD	F253YTJ	3258	SP	F258YTJ	3263	BD	F263YTJ	3269	RX	F269YTJ
3254	SP	F254YTJ	3259	SP	F259YTJ	3264	BD	F264YTJ	3270	RX	F270YTJ
3255	SP	F255YTJ	3260	SP	F260YTJ						

3271-3308

Volvo Olympian YN2RV18Z4 — Northern Counties Palatine II — B47/30F — 1995-96

3271	BD	N271CKB	3281	BD	N281CKB	3290	BD	N290CKB	3299	BD	N299CKB
3272	BD	N272CKB	3282	BD	N282CKB	3291	BD	N291CKB	3301	BD	N301CKB
3273	BD	N273CKB	3283	BD	N283CKB	3292	BD	N292CKB	3302	BD	N302CKB
3274	BD	N274CKB	3284	BD	N284CKB	3293	BD	N293CKB	3303	BD	N303CLV
3275	BD	N275CKB	3285	BD	N285CKB	3294	BD	N294CKB	3304	BD	N304CLV
3276	BD	N276CKB	3286	BD	N286CKB	3295	BD	N295CKB	3305	BD	N305CLV
3277	BD	N277CKB	3287	BD	N287CKB	3296	BD	N296CKB	3306	BD	N306CLV
3278	BD	N278CKB	3288	BD	N288CKB	3297	BD	N297CKB	3307	BD	N307CLV
3279	BD	N279CKB	3289	BD	N289CKB	3298	BD	N298CKB	3308	BD	N308CLV

3309-3337

Volvo Olympian YN2RV18Z4 — Northern Counties Palatine II — B47/30F — 1998

3309	GL	R309WVR	3315	GL	R315WVR	3326	SP	R326WVR	3332	SP	R332WVR
3310	GL	R310WVR	3317	GL	R317WVR	3327	SP	R327WVR	3334	SP	R334WVR
3311	GL	R311WVR	3319	GL	R319WVR	3329	SP	R329WVR	3335	SP	R335WVR
3312	GL	R312WVR	3321	GL	R321WVR	3330	SP	R330WVR	3336	SP	R336WVR
3313	GL	R313WVR	3322	GL	R322WVR	3331	SP	R331WVR	3337	SP	R337WVR
3314	GL	R314WVR	3324	GL	R324WVR						

3338	SP	M218YKC	Volvo Olympian YN2RV18Z4	Northern Counties Palatine II	B47/29F	1995
3339	SP	M219YKC	Volvo Olympian YN2RV18Z4	Northern Counties Palatine II	B47/29F	1995
3340	u	M921PKN	Volvo Olympian YN2R50C16Z4	Northern Counties Palatine	B47/30F	1994
3341	SP	L211SBG	Volvo Olympian YN2RV18Z4	Northern Counties Palatine II	B47/29F	1993

3343-3349

Volvo Olympian — Northern Counties Palatine I — B47/29F — 1998

3343	WX	R233AEY	3345	WX	R235AEY	3347	SP	R237AEY	3349	BD	R239AEY
3344	SP	R234AEY	3346	SP	R236AEY	3348	BD	R238AEY			

3350-3354

Volvo Olympian YN2RV18Z4 — Northern Counties Palatine — B47/30F — 1996 — Arriva Southern Counties, 2004

3350	u	N705TPK	3352	u	N707TPK	3353	u	N708TPK	3354	u	N709TPK
3351	u	N706TPK									

3355-3360

Volvo Olympian — Northern Counties Palatine — B45/30F — 1997 — Arriva Southern Counties, 2004

3355	u	P938MKL	3357	u	P940MKL	3359	u	P942MKL	3360	u	P943MKL
3356	u	P939MKL	3358	u	P941MKL						

3601-3613

DAF DB250RS505* — Northern Counties Palatine II — B47/30F — 1995 — *3611-13 are DE02RSSB250
Arriva London, 2001

3601	SP	N601DWY	3605	SP	N605DWY	3608	SP	N608DWY	3611	SP	N611DWY
3602	SP	N602DWY	3606	SP	N606DWY	3609	SP	N609DWY	3612	SP	N612DWY
3603	SP	N603DWY	3607	SP	N607DWY	3610	SP	N610DWY	3613	SP	N613DWY
3604	SP	N604DWY									

3614-3618

DAF DE23RSDB250 — Northern Counties Palatine 2 — B43/24D — 1998 — Arriva London/SC, 2003/04

3614	RX	R213CKO	3616	GI	R201CKO	3617	GI	R202CKO	3618	GI	R203CKO
3615	RX	V715LWT									

3646	JS	G661DTJ	Volvo Citybus B10M-50	East Lancs	B49/39F	1990	Arriva Southern Counties, 1998
3647	JS	G647EKA	Volvo Citybus B10M-50	East Lancs	B49/39F	1990	Arriva Southern Counties, 1998
3650	JS	G650EKA	Volvo Citybus B10M-50	East Lancs	B49/39F	1990	
3651	JS	G651EKA	Volvo Citybus B10M-50	East Lancs	B49/39F	1990	
3652	JS	G652EKA	Volvo Citybus B10M-50	East Lancs	B49/39F	1990	
3653	JS	G653EKA	Volvo Citybus B10M-50	East Lancs	B49/39F	1990	

New to Fox County, Olympian 3224, G524WJF is a Leyland Olympian with Alexander RL bodywork. As we go to press the last of the Bristol VRs have been withdrawn from open-top service on the north Wales coast, leaving the service in the hands of open-top Olympians and transferred Metrobuses. *Bob Downham*

3674-3682

Volvo Citybus B10M-50 — Alexander RV — B47/32F — 1989 — Arriva London, 2000

3674	SO	F104TML	3677	SO	F107TML	3679	SO	F109TML	3682	SO	F112TML
3676	SO	F106TML	3678	SO	F108TML	3680	SO	F110TML			

3690-3699

Volvo Citybus B10M-50 — East Lancs — B45/34F — 1991 — London South, 1998

3690	BO	H660GPF	3692	JS	H662GPF	3697	SK	H667GPF	3699	BD	H679GPF
3691	BO	H661GPF	3695	BD	H665GPF						

3831-3836

Dennis Dominator DDA1032* — East Lancs — B47/29F — 1990 — *3833-6 are DDA1031

3831	CH	G801THA	3833	CH	H803AHA	3835	CH	H805AHA	3836	CH	H806AHA
3832	CH	G802THA	3834	CH	H804AHA						

3837	u	N716TPK	Dennis Dominator DDA2006	East Lancs	B45/31F	1996
3975	u	GYE365W	MCW Metrobus DR101/12	MCW	O43/28D	1980	Original Sightseeing Tour, 2004
3976	u	GYE456W	MCW Metrobus DR101/12	MCW	O43/28D	1980	Original Sightseeing Tour, 2004
3977	u	KYV663X	MCW Metrobus DR101/14	MCW	PO43/28D	1981	Original Sightseeing Tour, 2004
3978	u	KYV689X	MCW Metrobus DR101/14	MCW	O43/28D	1981	Original Sightseeing Tour, 2004
3980	SO	GKA449L	Leyland Atlantean AN68/1R	Alexander AL	O43/32F	1973
3981	SO	OLV551M	Leyland Atlantean AN68/1R	Alexander AL	O43/32F	1974
3984	RH	E224WBG	Leyland Olympian ONCL10/1RZ	Alexander RL	O43/30F	1988
3987	RH	E227WBG	Leyland Olympian ONCL10/1RZ	Alexander RL	O43/30F	1988
3995	RH	G35HKY	Scania N113DRB	Northern Counties	O47/33F	1990	Arriva Fox County, 2002
5003	AB	M945LYR	DAF SB3000WS601	Van Hool Alizée	C49FT	1995	London North East, 1998
5004	AB	NEY819	DAF SB3000WS601	Van Hool Alizée	C49FT	1995	London North East, 1998

5301-5320

Scania L113CRL — Wright Axcess-ultralow — N40F — 1996

5301	GL	P301HEM	5307	GL	P307HEM	5312	GL	P312HEM	5317	GL	P317HEM
5302	GL	P302HEM	5308	GL	P308HEM	5313	GL	P313HEM	5318	GL	P318HEM
5303	GL	P303HEM	5309	GL	P309HEM	5314	GL	P314HEM	5319	GL	P319HEM
5305	GL	P305HEM	5310	GL	P310HEM	5315	GL	P315HEM	5320	GL	P320HEM
5306	GL	P306HEM	5311	GL	P311HEM	5316	GL	P316HEM			

6248-6251

Dennis Dart SLF CNG — Plaxton Pointer — N41F — 19996

6248	SO	S248UVR	6249	SO	S249UVR	6250	SO	S250UVR	6251	SO	S251UVR

6301	SP	L301TEM	Volvo B10B			Alexander Strider		B49F	1994		
6302	SP	L302TEM	Volvo B10B			Alexander Strider		B49F	1994		
6303	SP	L303TEM	Volvo B10B			Alexander Strider		B49F	1994		

6402-6413 Neoplan N4016 Neoplan N39F 1994

6402	GL	L402TKB	6405	GL	L405TKB	6408	GL	L408TKB	6411	GL	L411UFY
6403	GL	L403TKB	6406	GL	L406TKB	6409	GL	L409TKB	6412	GL	L412UFY
6404	GL	L404TKB	6407	GL	L407TKB	6410	GL	L410TKB	6413	GL	L413TKB

6501-6543 Volvo B10B Wright Endurance BC49F 1994

6501	JS	L501TKA	6512	JS	L512TKA	6523	BO	M523WHF	6533	SP	M533WHF
6502	JS	L502TKA	6513	JS	L513TKA	6524	SP	M524WHF	6534	SP	M534WHF
6503	JS	L503TKA	6514	SO	M514WHF	6525	BO	M525WHF	6535	SP	M535WHF
6504	JS	L504TKA	6515	SO	M515WHF	6526	BO	M526WHF	6536	SP	M536WHF
6505	JS	L505TKA	6516	SO	M516WHF	6527	SO	M527WHF	6537	SP	M537WHF
6506	JS	L506TKA	6517	BO	M517WHF	6528	SO	M528WHF	6538	SP	M538WHF
6507	SO	L507TKA	6518	BO	M518WHF	6529	BO	M529WHF	6540	SP	M540WHF
6508	JS	L508TKA	6519	BO	M519WHF	6530	JS	M530WHF	6541	SP	M541WHF
6509	JS	L509TKA	6520	BO	M520WHF	6531	BO	M531WHF	6542	SP	M542WHF
6510	JS	L510TKA	6521	BO	M521WHF	6532	JS	M532WHF	6543	SP	M543WHF
6511	JS	L511TKA	6522	BO	M522WHF						

6544-6623 Volvo B10B Wright Endurance BC49F 1994-96

6544	SO	M544WTJ	6565	BO	M565YEM	6584	GL	N584CKA	6605	JS	N605CKA
6545	SO	M545WTJ	6566	GL	M566YEM	6585	GL	N585CKA	6606	JS	N606CKA
6546	SO	M546WTJ	6567	GL	M567YEM	6586	SP	N586CKA	6607	JS	N607CKA
6547	SP	M547WTJ	6568	GL	M568YEM	6587	HU	N587CKA	6608	JS	N608CKA
6548	SP	M548WTJ	6569	GL	M569YEM	6588	SP	N588CKA	6609	JS	N609CKA
6549	SP	M549WTJ	6570	GL	M570YEM	6589	SP	N589CKA	6610	JS	N610CKA
6550	SP	M550WTJ	6571	GL	M571YEM	6590	SP	N590CKA	6611	JS	N611CKA
6551	SP	M551WTJ	6572	GL	M572YEM	6591	SP	N591CKA	6612	JS	N612CKA
6552	HU	M552WTJ	6573	GL	M573YEM	6592	SP	N592CKA	6613	SP	N613CKA
6553	SP	M553WTJ	6574	SP	M574YEM	6593	SP	N593CKA	6614	SP	N614CKA
6554	SP	M554WTJ	6575	GL	M575YEM	6594	SP	N594CKA	6615	SP	N615CKA
6556	HU	M556WTJ	6576	GL	N576CKA	6595	SP	N595CKA	6616	SP	N616CKA
6557	HU	M557WTJ	6577	GL	N577CKA	6596	SP	N596CKA	6617	SP	N617CKA
6558	SO	M558WTJ	6578	GL	N578CKA	6597	SP	N597CKA	6618	SP	N618CKA
6559	SO	M559WTJ	6579	GL	N579CKA	6598	SP	N598CKA	6619	SP	N619CKA
6561	BO	M561WTJ	6580	GL	N580CKA	6599	GL	N599CKA	6620	SP	N620CKA
6562	BO	M562WTJ	6581	GL	N581CKA	6601	GL	N601CKA	6621	SP	N621CKA
6563	BO	M563WTJ	6582	GL	N582CKA	6603	GL	N603CKA	6622	SP	N622CKA
6564	BO	M564YEM	6583	GL	N583CKA	6604	JS	N604CKA	6623	HU	N623CKA

6901-6913 Volvo B10B-58 Northern Counties Paladin B51F 1993-95 Liverbus, 1995

6901	HU	K101OHF	6904	HU	K104OHF	6907	HU	K107OHF	6910	HU	M110XKC
6902	HU	K102OHF	6905	HU	K105OHF	6908	HU	K108OHF	6912	HU	M112XKC
6903	HU	K103OHF	6906	HU	K106OHF	6909	HU	M109XKC	6913	HU	M113XKC

7201-7244 Volvo B6 9.9M Plaxton Pointer B38F 1994

7201	JS	L201TKA	7213	JS	L213TKA	7224	JS	L224TKA	7235	JS	L235TKA
7202	JS	L202TKA	7214	JS	L214TKA	7225	JS	L225TKA	7236	JS	L236TKA
7203	JS	L203TKA	7215	JS	L215TKA	7226	JS	L226TKA	7237	JS	L237TKA
7204	JS	L204TKA	7216	JS	L216TKA	7227	JS	L227TKA	7238	SK	L238TKA
7205	JS	L205TKA	7217	JS	L217TKA	7228	JS	L228TKA	7239	SK	L239TKA
7206	JS	L206TKA	7218	JS	L218TKA	7229	JS	L229TKA	7240	SK	L240TKA
7208	JS	L208TKA	7219	JS	L219TKA	7230	JS	L230TKA	7241	SK	L241TKA
7209	JS	L209TKA	7220	JS	L220TKA	7231	JS	L231TKA	7242	SK	L242TKA
7210	JS	L210TKA	7221	JS	L221TKA	7232	JS	L232TKA	7243	SK	L243TKA
7211	JS	L211TKA	7222	JS	L222TKA	7233	JS	L233TKA	7244	SK	L244TKA
7212	JS	L212TKA	7223	JS	L223TKA	7234	JS	L234TKA			

7531-7545 Dennis Dart SLF 9.8m Plaxton Pointer N38F 1996-97

7531	RU	N531DWM	7535	RU	P535MBU	7539	RU	P539MBU	7543	RU	P543MBU
7532	RU	N532DWM	7536	HU	P536MBU	7540	RU	P540MBU	7544	RU	P544MBU
7533	RU	P533MBU	7537	HU	P537MBU	7541	RU	P541MBU	7545	RU	P545MBU
7534	RU	P534MBU	7538	HU	P538MBU	7542	RU	P542MBU			

Prior to its sale to Arriva, MTL took delivery of sixty-four Darts with Marshall Capital bodywork. Most are still allocated to the Merseyside depots though 7621, T621PNC, is one of a trio now at Wythenshawe. It is seen in the town's bus station while heading for Altrincham. *Mark Doggett*

7547-7571

			Dennis Dart	SLF 9.8m		Plaxton Pointer			N38F		1998
7547	BO	R547ABA	7553	WX	R553ABA	7560	LJ	R560ABA	7566	LJ	R566ABA
7548	BO	R548ABA	7554	BD	R554ABA	7561	HU	R561ABA	7567	HU	R567ABA
7549	BO	R549ABA	7556	BD	R556ABA	7562	LJ	R562ABA	7568	HU	R568ABA
7550	BD	R550ABA	7557	BD	R557ABA	7563	LJ	R563ABA	7569	HU	R569ABA
7551	BD	R551ABA	7558	BD	R558ABA	7564	LJ	R564ABA	7570	HU	R570ABA
7552	BD	R552ABA	7559	BD	R559ABA	7565	LJ	R565ABA	7571	HU	R571ABA

7612-7623

			Dennis Dart SLF 10.5m			Marshall Capital			N38F		1999
7612	SK	T612PNC	7615	JS	T615PNC	7618	JS	T618PNC	7621	WY	T621PNC
7613	SK	T613PNC	7616	JS	T616PNC	7619	JS	T619PNC	7622	WY	T622PNC
7614	SK	T614PNC	7617	JS	T617PNC	7620	JS	T620PNC	7623	SO	T623PNC

7624-7676

			Dennis Dart SLF 10.5m			Marshall Capital			N38F		1999-2000
7624	SO	V624DBN	7637	SK	V637DVU	7650	SK	V650DVU	7663	GL	V663DVU
7625	SO	V625DVU	7638	SK	V638DVU	7651	SO	V651DVU	7664	GL	V664DVU
7626	SO	V626DVU	7639	SK	V639DVU	7652	SO	V652DVU	7665	GL	V665DVU
7627	SO	V627DVU	7640	SK	V640DVU	7653	SO	V653DVU	7667	SK	V667DVU
7628	SO	V628DVU	7641	SK	V641DVU	7654	SO	V654DVU	7668	GL	V668DVU
7629	SO	V629DVU	7642	SK	V642DVU	7655	SO	V655DVU	7669	GL	V669DVU
7630	SO	V630DVU	7643	SK	V643DVU	7656	SO	V656DVU	7670	GL	V670DVU
7631	SO	V631DVU	7644	SK	V644DVU	7657	SO	V657DVU	7671	GL	V671DVU
7632	SO	V632DVU	7645	SK	V645DVU	7658	SO	V658DVU	7672	GL	V672DVU
7633	JS	V633DVU	7646	SK	V646DVU	7659	GL	V659DVU	7673	SK	V673DVU
7634	SK	V634DVU	7647	SK	V647DVU	7660	GL	V660DVU	7674	SK	V674DVU
7635	SK	V635DVU	7648	SK	V648DVU	7661	GL	V661DVU	7675	SK	V675DVU
7636	SK	V636DVU	7649	SK	V649DVU	7662	GL	V662DVU	7676	WY	V676DVU

Ancillary vehicles:-

8166	DOC26V	Leyland National 2 NL116L11/1R		TV	1980	West Midlands Travel, 1996
8167	DOC37V	Leyland National 2 NL116L11/1R		TV	1980	West Midlands Travel, 1996
8168	124YTW	Volvo B58-61	Plaxton Supreme IV	TV	1980	G M Buses, 1986
8169	C324LDT	Volvo B9M	Plaxton Paramount 3200 II	TV	1986	D&G ,Rachub, 2000
8172	PFY72J	Leyland Panther	Marshall	TV	1971	
8173	D443UHC	Mercedes-Benz L608D	Reeve Burgess	RV	1986	Hastings & District, 1987
8174	JTL804V	Bedford YLQ	Plaxton Supreme IV Express	TV	1979	Lewis, Llanrhystud, 1995
8175	TNR812X	Bedford YMQ	Duple Dominant IV	TV	1981	Purple, Bethesda, 1998
8176	GEY389Y	Bedford YNT	Duple Dominant IV	TV	1982	Purple, Bethesda, 1998
8180	K946OEM	Mercedes-Benz 811D	Marshall C16	TV	1993	Fareway, 1997
8181	VBG101V	Leyland National 2 NL116L11/1R		TV	1980	
8183	VBG106V	Leyland National 2 NL116L11/1R		TV	1980	
8184	H28MJN	Leyland Lynx LX2R11G15Z4R	Leyland Lynx	TV	1991	Colchester, 1994
8185	G149CHP	Leyland Lynx LX112L10ZR1S	Leyland Lynx	TV	1989	Arriva Midlands North, 2003
8186	E642VFY	Leyland Lynx LX112L10ZR1R	Leyland Lynx	TV	1988	Devaway, Bretton, 1998
8187	G324NWW	Leyland Lynx LX2R11C15Z4S	Leyland Lynx	TV	1990	Arriva Yorkshire, 1999
8189	WWM914W	Leyland National 2 NL116L11/1R		TV	1980	
8190	BCW824V	Leyland National 2 NL106L11/1R		TV	1980	Liverbus, 1999
8192	E641VFY	Leyland Lynx LX112L10ZR1R	Leyland Lynx	TV	1988	Devaway, Bretton, 1998
8193	D634BBV	Leyland Lynx LX112L10ZR1	Leyland Lynx	TV	1987	Nova Scotia, Winsford, 2000
8194	D108NDW	Leyland Lynx LX112TL11ZR1R	Leyland Lynx	TV	1987	Arriva Southern Counties, 2000
8195	D155HML	Leyland Lynx LX112TL11ZR1S	Leyland Lynx	TV	1987	Arriva Southern Counties, 2000
8196	D157HML	Leyland Lynx LX112TL11ZR1S	Leyland Lynx	TV	1987	Arriva Southern Counties, 2000
8197	PUK637R	Leyland National 11351A/1R	East Lancs Greenway (1994)	TV	1977	Arriva Midlands North, 2003
8198	PUK652R	Leyland National 11351A/1R	East Lancs Greenway (1994)	TV	1977	Arriva Midlands North, 2003
8199	TPD106X	Leyland Olympian ONTL11/1R	Roe	Publicity	1982	Arriva Southern Counties, 1998
8200	F267YTJ	Leyland Olympian ONCL10/1RZ	Northern Counties	Road Safety	1989	

Previous Registrations:

124YTW	DEN247W	M2SLT	N102YVU
J6SLT	N192BNB	M5SLT	M20CLA
L411UFY	L175THF	NEY819	M944LYR
L412UFY	L176THF		

Allocations:-

Aberystwyth (Park Avenue) - AB

Outstations: Dolgellau, Machynlleth and New Quay

Mercedes-Benz	171	312	313	329	334	335	338	341
	342	344	345	355	390			
Dart	820	823	824	826	834	841	842	1116
	1129	1326	1327	1328	1329	2332	2333	
Tiger bus	1772	1776	1777					
Lynx	1739	1741	1750	1757				
Volvo B10M bus	1778	1786	1787	1788				
DAF Paladin	1795	1796	1797					
DAF coach	5003	5004						
Olympian	3047	3051	3065	3067	3131	3135	3137	3139

Bangor (Beach Road) - BG

Outstations: Amlwch; Caernarfon; Holyhead and Pwllheli

Mercedes-Benz	191	192	193	310	311	372	393	394
Dart	816	817	818	819	821	822	827	833
	1107	1108	1112	1118	1119	1130	1154	1164
	1219	1252	1301	1302	1303	1304	1308	1309
	1310	1333	1340	2325	2326	2330		
VDL Bus Cadet	2480	2481	2482	2483	2484	2485		
Lynx	1751	1755						
Olympian	3071	3073	3122	3212	3214	3215	3218	3219
	3226							
	3227							

Vehicles used on the Manchester Airport services carry *Skyline* branding which was aimed at encouraging staff to leave their cars away from the airport and travel there by bus. Seen heading for the airport on route 19 that also incorporates the cargo area and enthusiast's viewing zone is 2313, R313CVU. *Mark Doggett*

Birkenhead (Laird Street) - BD

Dart	1172	1174	1175	1181	1185	1186	1193	1197
	1198	1211	1212	1213	1214	1215	1216	2257
	2258	2259	2261	2262	7550	7551	7552	7554
	7556	7557	7558	7559				
Volvo B10M bus	3695	3699						
DAF Cadet	2435	2436	2437	2438	2439	2441	2442	2443
	2445	2446	2447	2448	2449			
DAF Ikarus	1790	1791	1792	1793	1794			
DAF ALX300	2411	2412	2414					
DAF Myllennium	2451	2452	2453	2454	2455	2456	2457	2458
	2459	2460	2461					
Olympian	3105	3112	3113	3114	3115	3208	3251	3253
	3262	3263	3264	3271	3272	3273	3274	3275
	3276	3277	3278	3279	3281	3282	3283	3284
	3285	3286	3287	3288	3289	3290	3291	3292
	3293	3294	3295	3296	3297	3298	3299	3301
	3302	3303	3304	3305	3306	3307	3308	3348
	3349							

Bootle (Hawthorne Road) - BO

Dart	1150	1151	1152	1233	1234	1235		
	1236	1237	1238	1239	1240	1241	1242	1243
	1244	1245	1246	1247	1248	2215	2216	2217
	2218	2219	2221	2223	2224	2226	2227	2228
	2229	2231	2232	2233	2234	2235	2236	2237
	2263	2264	2265	2266	2267	2268	2269	2271
	2272	2314	2315	2316	2317	2318	2319	2320
	2321	2322	2323	2324	7547	7548	7549	

Lance	1201	1202	1203	1204	1205	1206	1207	1208
	1209	1210	1290	1291	1292	1293	1294	1295
	1296	1297	1298	1299	1940	1941	1942	1943
	1944	1945	1946	1947	1948	1949	2391	2392
	2393	2394						
Volvo B10B	6517	6518	6519	6520	6521	6522	6523	6525
	6526	6529	6531	6561	6562	6563	6564	6565
Volvo Citybus	3690	3691						

Chester (Manor Lane, Hawarden) - CH

Alero	611	612	613	614	615	616	617	
Mercedes-Benz	147	149	160	182	183	194		
Dart	1104	1109	1110	1111	1117	1126	1127	1153
	1155	1156	1260	1330	1331	1334	2276	2328
	2341	2342	2355	2356	2357	2358	2359	2360
	2361							
Dominator	3831	3832	3833	3834	3835	3836		
Olympian	3063	3094						

Crewe (Delamere Street) - CW

Mercedes-Benz	373	374	375	380	381	382	383	384
	385	386	387	388	389			
Dart	872	876	877	878	879	882	886	
Lynx	1717	1718	1719	1727	1730	1731	1732	1743
	1746	1747	1749	1752	1753	1754		

Huyton (Wilson Road) - HU

Dart	1141	1171	1173	1176	1177	1178	1179	1183
	1184	1187	1191	1192	1194	1195	1196	1280
	1281	1282	1286	2201	2202	2203	2204	2207
	2208	2209	2211	2212	2213	2214	7536	7537
	7538	7561	7567	7568	7569	7570	7571	
Volvo B10B	6552	6556	6557	6587	6623	6901	6902	6903
	6904	6095	6906	6907	6908	6909	6910	6912
	6913							

Liverpool (Green Lane) - GL

Dart	7659	7660	7661	7662	7663	7664	7665	7668
	7669	7670	7671	7672				
Neoplan	6402	6403	6404	6405	6406	6407	6408	6409
	6410	6411	6412	6413				
Volvo B10B	6566	6567	6568	6569	6570	6571	6572	6573
	6575	6576	6577	6578	6579	6580	6581	6582
	6583	6584	6585	6599	6601	6603		
Scania sd	2002	2008	2011	2024	2025	2026	2030	2032
	2033	5301	5302	5303	5305	5306	5307	5308
	5309	5310	5311	5312	5313	5314	5315	5316
	5317	5318	5319	5320				
Olympian	3309	3310	3311	3312	3313	3314	3315	3317
	3319	3321	3322	3324				

Liverpool (Shaw Road, Speke) - SP

DAF Cadet	2416	2417	2418	2419	2421	2422	2423	2424
	2426	2427	2428	2429	2431	2432	2433	2434
Volvo B10BLE	2716	2717	2718	2719	2720	2721	6301	6302
	6303	6524	6533	6534	6535	6536	6537	6538
	6540	6541	6542	6543	6547	6548	6549	6550
	6551	6553	6554	6574	6586	6588	6589	6590
	6591	6592	6593	6594	6595	6596	6597	6598
	6613	6614	6615	6616	6617	6618	6619	6620
	6621	6622						
DAF Prestige	2401	2402	2403					
DAF ALX300	2404	2405	2406	2407	2408	2409	2410	2413
	2415							
DAF Myllennium	2462	2463	2464	2465	2466	2467	2468	2469
	2470	2471	2472	2473	2474			
DAF Palatine	3601	3602	3603	3604	3605	3606	3607	3608
	3609	3610	3611	3612	3613			
Olympian	3206	3209	3213	3221	3222	3223	3224	3225
	3252	3254	3255	3256	3257	3258	3259	3260
	3261	3326	3327	3329	3330	3331	3332	3334
	3335	3336	3337	3338	3339	3341	3344	3346
	3348							

Llandudno Junction (Glan-y-mor Road) - LJ

Mercedes-Benz	0198	0307	0308	0309	0317	0318	0319	0320
	0321	0322	0323	0324	0325	0326	0327	0332
	0333	0337	0339	0347	0354	0356	0357	
Dart	0814	0815	1165	1228	1343	2273	2274	2277
	2278	2279	2301	2331	2343	2344	2345	2346
	2347	2348	7560	7562	7563	7564	7565	7566

Manchester (St Andrew's Square, Piccadilly) - MA

Dart	1223	1224	1225	1226	1227	1249	1250	1251
	1254	1264	2238	2239	2241	2242	2243	2244
	2246	2247	2248	2249	2251	2252	2253	2254
	2256							
Scania sd	2041	2042	2043	2046				
Olympian	3102	3103	3104	3106	3107	3108	3109	3110

Macclesfield (Sunderland Street) - MF

Mercedes-Benz	0095	0096	0097	0098	0099	0100		
Dart	0856	0857	0858	0859	0867	0868	0887	0888
	1120	1121	1122	1123	1124	1125	1131	1138
	1139	1140	1142	1146	1148	1149		
Scania sd	1048							
Olympian	3022	3038	3039	3041	3064			

Rhyl (Ffynnongroew Road) - RH

Mercedes-Benz	0301	0302	0303	0304	0305	0314	0315	0316
	0331	0340	0343	0346	0353			
Dart	0831	0832	0843	0844	0846	0847	1128	1323
	1325	1338	2296	2297	2298	2299	2300	2349
	2350	2351	2352	2353	2354			
Open top	3984	3987	3995					

Transferred from Arriva Scotland, 1062, M102RMS is a Scania L113 with Northern Counties Paladin bodywork. It is seen on a journey on route 362 in St Helens, having returned from Wigan, where it was built. Since its construction in 1995 the then Northern Counties facility - which itself was built on the site of Massey Bros bodyworks, became part of the Henley Group's Plaxtons facility; then TransBus' double-deck assembly line, and in May 2004 part of Alexander Dennis. *Bob Downham*

Runcorn (Beechwood) - RU

Dart	802	804	805	806	807	808	809	1157
	1158	1159	1160	1161	1162	1163	1166	1167
	1168	1169	1170	1220	1221	1222	7531	7532
	7533	7534	7535	7539	7541	7542	7543	7544
	7545							
Scania sd	1041	1042	1043	1044	1045	1046	1047	1048
	1049	2044	2045	2047	2048	2049	2050	2051
	2052	2053	2054					

St Helens (Jackson Street) - JS

Dart	7615	7616	7617	7618	7619	7620	7633	
Volvo B6	2805	2806	2807	2808	2809	2811	2812	7201
	7202	7203	7204	7205	7206	7208	7209	7210
	7211	7212	7213	7214	7215	7216	7217	7218
	7219	7220	7221	7222	7223	7224	7225	7226
	7227	7228	7229	7230	7231	7232	7233	7234
	7235	7236	7237					
Scania sd	1035	1036	1037	1038	1039	1040	1050	1051
	1052	1053	1054	1055	1056	1057	1058	1059
	1060	1061	1062	1063	1065	1068	2001	2003
	2004	2005	2006	2007	2009	2010	2013	2014
	2015	2016	2017	2018	2019	2020	2021	2022
	2023	2027	2028	2029	2031	2034		
Volvo B10B	2701	2702	2703	2704	2705	2706	2707	2708
	2709	2710	2711	2712	2713	2714	2715	2729
	2730	6501	6502	6503	6504	6505	6506	6508
	6509	6510	6511	6512	6513	6530	6532	6604
	6605	6606	6607	6608	6609	6610	6611	6612
Volvo B7	2800							
Volvo Citybus	3646	3647	3650	3651	3652	3653	3692	

The number of Lynx continues to decline with just twenty remaining with Arriva North West and Wales. One of seven Mark 2 Lynx is 1753, H733HWK which joined Arriva when McGills of Barrhead was acquired by the Scottish operation. It is seen in Macclesfield, where the bus station is adjacent to the depot. *Bob Downham*

Skelmersdale (Neverstitch Road) - SK

Dart	1180	1182	1189	1190	1229	1230	1253	1258
	1259	1272	1273	1274	1275	1276	1277	1278
	1279	1283	1284	1285	1300	1341	1342	7612
	7613	7614	7634	7635	7636	7637	7638	7639
	7640	7641	7642	7643	7644	7645	7646	7647
	7648	7649	7650	7667	7673	7674	7675	
Volvo B6	7238	7239	7240	7241	7242	7243	7244	
Volvo B10M bus	1779	1785						
Volvo Citybus	3697							

Southport (Canning Road) - SO

Neoplan N4009	601	602	603					
Dart	1289	1332	6248	6249	6250	6251	7623	7624
	7625	7626	7627	7628	7629	7630	7631	7632
	7651	7652	7653	7654	7655	7656	7657	7658
Volvo B6	2801	2802	2803	2804	2813	2814	2815	2816
	2817	2818	2819	2821	2822			
Volvo B10B	2722	2723	2724	2725	2726	2727	2728	6507
	6514	6515	6516	6527	6528	6544	6545	6546
	6558	6559						
Volvo Citybus	3674	3676	3677	3678	3679	3680	3682	
Open-top	3980	3981						

Winsford (Winsford Industrial Estate) - WI

Mercedes-Benz	94	127	129	138	140			
	148	151	154	155	164	165	178	179
	184							
Dart	860	861	862	863	864	865	866	869
	1132	1133	1135					
Lynx	1724							
DAF SB220	1799							
Olympian	3037	3048	3049	3054	3062	3146	3147	3148
	3149							

Wrexham (Berse Road, Caego) - WX

Mercedes-Benz	180	181	328	350	351	352	358	
	359	360	361	362	363	364	365	391
	392							
Dart	838	839	848	849	851	852	1101	1105
	1106	1113	1114	1115	2301	2601	2602	2603
	2604	2605	2606	2607	2608	7553		
VDL Bus Cadet	2486	2487	2488					
Olympian	3101	3343	3345					

Wythenshawe (Greeba Road) - WY

Mercedes-Benz	158	159	161	162	163	168	169	
Dart	801	803	810	811	812	813	1188	1199
	1217	1218	1231	1232	1255	1256	1257	1261
	1262	1263	1265	1266	1267	1268	1269	1270
	1271	1287	1288	2302	2303	2304	2305	2306
	2307	2308	2309	2310	2311	2312	2313	2601
	2602	2603	2604	2605	2606	2607	2608	7621
	7622	7676						

Rail reserve - RX

Olympian	3266	3268	3269	3270
DAF Palatine	3614	3615		

Unallocated or stored - u/w

Mercedes-Benz	153	199						
Dart	1143	1332	2280	2281	2282	2283	2284	2285
	2286	2287	2288	7540				
Lance	2395	2396	2397					
Lynx	1750	1751	1755					
DAF Prestige	2475	2476	2477					
Dominator	3837							
Olympian	3266	3268	3269	3270	3340	3350	3351	3352
	3353	3354	3355	3356	3357	3358	3359	3360
DAF Palatine	3616	3617	3618					

ARRIVA MIDLANDS

Arriva Midlands North Ltd, Arriva Derby Ltd; Stevensons of Uttoxeter Ltd;
Arriva Fox County Ltd, PO Box 613, Melton Road, Thurmaston, Leicester, LE4 8ZN

127	SD	Y207RJU	Vauxhall Zafira	Vauxhall	M6	2001	
129	SD	Y189RJU	Vauxhall Zafira	Vauxhall	M6	2001	
1001	MH	BU53AWP	Mercedes-Benz Sprinter 412	Koch	N15	2003	
1002	MH	BU53AWR	Mercedes-Benz Sprinter 412	Koch	N15	2003	

1127-1146 Mercedes-Benz Vario 0814 Plaxton Beaver 2 B27F 1997

1127	SD	R127LNR	1132	HY	R132LNR	1137	SD	R137LNR	1142	HY	R142LNR
1128	W	R128LNR	1133	HY	R133LNR	1138	SD	R138LNR	1143	HY	R143LNR
1129	HY	R129LNR	1134	HY	R134LNR	1139	SD	R139LNR	1144	HY	R144LNR
1130	HY	R130LNR	1135	HY	R135LNR	1140	W	R140LNR	1145	HY	R145LNR
1131	HY	R131LNR	1136	W	R136LNR	1141	HY	R141LNR	1146	HY	R146LNR

1147-1170 Mercedes-Benz Vario 0814 Alexander ALX100 B27F 1998

1147	HY	R147UAL	1153	CV	R153UAL	1159	WG	R159UAL	1165	WG	R165UAL
1148	CK	R148UAL	1154	CV	R154UAL	1160	SS	R160UAL	1166	WG	R166UAL
1149	WG	R149UAL	1155	CV	R155UAL	1161	CV	R161UAL	1167	WG	R167UAL
1150	CV	R150UAL	1156	CV	R156UAL	1162	WG	R162UAL	1168	TA	R168UAL
1151	CV	R151UAL	1157	CV	R157UAL	1163	DE	R163UAL	1169	TA	R169UAL
1152	CV	R152UAL	1158	WG	R158UAL	1164	WG	R164UAL	1170	TA	R170UUT

1171-1180 Mercedes-Benz Vario 0814 Plaxton Beaver 2 B27F 1997 Arriva Yorkshire, 1999

1171	HY	R765DUB	1174	WG	R770DUB	1177	CK	R788DUB	1179	WG	R790DUB
1172	WG	R768DUB	1175	WG	R785DUB	1178	WG	R789DUB	1180	CK	R791DUB
1173	SS	R769DUB	1176	WG	R787DUB						

Arriva Midlands operate a pair of Mercedes-Benz Sprinter 412 into the Peak District. Seen at Tur Langton, 1001, BU53AWP, illustrates the Koch conversion that is one of the first low-floor van-derived minibuses for the British market. *Richard Godfrey*

Pictured in Stafford, 2032, M802MOJ is one of four Darts supplied in 1994 for Shrewsbury. Only two remain in the fleet in this condition as 2031 has been withdrawn and 2034 re-bodied after fire damage. *Cliff Beeton*

1243-1252

					Mercedes-Benz 811D		Alexander Sprint		B31F	1995	

1243	SY	N463EHA	1246	SE	N466EHA	1249	CK	N469EHA	1251	BT	N471EHA
1244	CK	N464EHA	1247	SY	N467EHA	1250	BT	N470EHA	1252	BT	N472EHA
1245	SE	N465EHA	1248	CK	N468EHA						

1253	CK	L773RWW	Mercedes-Benz 811D	Plaxton Beaver	B31F	1994	Arriva Yorkshire, 1999
1260	SH	P438HKN	Mercedes-Benz 811D	Plaxton Beaver	B31F	1994	Arriva North West, 2000
1268	TF	N168WNF	Mercedes-Benz 709D	Alexander Sprint	B23F	1994	Timeline, Leigh, 1998
1269	TF	N169WNF	Mercedes-Benz 709D	Alexander Sprint	B23F	1994	Timeline, Leigh, 1998
1270	SH	N170WNF	Mercedes-Benz 709D	Alexander Sprint	B23F	1994	Timeline, Leigh, 1998
1356	CK	N356OBC	Mercedes-Benz 709D	Alexander Sprint	B27F	1996	Arriva Fox County, 2002
1357	CK	N357OBC	Mercedes-Benz 709D	Alexander Sprint	B27F	1996	Arriva Fox County, 2002
1358	SY	N358OBC	Mercedes-Benz 709D	Alexander Sprint	B27F	1996	Arriva Fox County, 2002
1359	SY	P608JJU	Mercedes-Benz 709D	Reeve Burgess Beaver	B27F	1996	
1360	SY	P296OOA	Mercedes-Benz 709D	Alexander Sprint	B27F	1995	?, 2003
1370	w	N170WNF	Mercedes-Benz 709D	Alexander Sprint	B23F	1995	Timeline, Leigh, 1998
1372	CK	N472XRC	Mercedes-Benz 709D	Alexander Sprint	B27F	1996	

1373-1381

					Mercedes-Benz 709D		Alexander Sprint		B27F	1996	

1373	DE	N473XRC	1376	DE	N476XRC	1378	DE	N478XRC	1380	DE	N480XRC
1374	DE	N474XRC	1377	DE	N477XRC	1379	DE	N479XRC	1381	DE	N481XRC
1375	DE	N475XRC									

1382-1392

					Mercedes-Benz 709D		Plaxton Beaver		B27F	1996	

1382	DE	P482CAL	1385	BT	P485CAL	1388	DE	P488CAL	1391	DE	P491CAL
1383	DE	P483CAL	1386	SY	P486CAL	1390	SH	P490CAL	1392	TF	P492CAL
1384	DE	P484CAL	1387	DE	P487CAL						

1931	SE	J31SFA	Leyland Swift ST2R44C97A4	Wright Handybus	B39F	1992
1932	SE	J32SFA	Leyland Swift ST2R44C97A4	Wright Handybus	B39F	1992
1934	SE	J34SRF	Leyland Swift ST2R44C97A4	Wright Handybus	B39F	1992

The 2004 Arriva Bus Handbook

Delivered in 1991 Dart 2001, H501GHA, spent much of its time at Telford before transferring to Oswestry. It is shown in Welshpool. *Bob Downham*

2001	OS	H501GHA	Dennis Dart 8.5SDL3003	East Lancs EL2000	B35F	1991	

2002-2023   Dennis Dart 9SDL3034   East Lancs EL2000   B33F   1994

2002	SE	L502BNX	2008	BT	L508BNX	2013	SY	L513BNX	2019	CK	L519BNX
2003	SE	L503BNX	2009	BT	L509BNX	2014	SY	L514BNX	2020	CK	L620BNX
2004	SE	L504BNX	2010	CK	L510BNX	2015	SY	L515BNX	2021	SH	L521BNX
2005	SE	L605BNX	2011	TF	L511BNX	2016	SY	L516BNX	2022	CK	L522BNX
2006	SE	L506BNX	2012	TF	L512BNX	2017	BT	L517BNX	2023	CK	L523BNX
2007	BT	L507BNX									

2024	LE	P824RWU	Dennis Dart	Plaxton Pointer	B40F	1996	Arriva London, 2001
2025	SD	N680GUM	Dennis Dart 9.8SDL3054	Plaxton Pointer	B40F	1995	Arriva London, 2002
2026	SD	N673GUM	Dennis Dart 9.8SDL3054	Plaxton Pointer	B40F	1995	Arriva London, 2002
2027	SD	N674GUM	Dennis Dart 9.8SDL3054	Plaxton Pointer	B40F	1995	Arriva London, 2002
2028	TF	N679GUM	Dennis Dart 9.8SDL3054	Plaxton Pointer	B40F	1995	Arriva London, 2002
2029	BT	L300SBS	Dennis Dart 9.8SDL3035	Plaxton Pointer	B40F	1994	
2030	CK	J327VAW	Dennis Dart 9.8SDL3004	Carlyle Dartline	B40F	1991	Williamsons, Shrewsbury, 1998
2032	SD	M802MOJ	Dennis Dart 9.8SDL3040	Marshall C37	B40F	1994	
2033	SD	M803MOJ	Dennis Dart 9.8SDL3040	Marshall C37	B40F	1994	
2034	BT	M804MOJ	Dennis Dart 9.8SDL3040	Marshall (2001)	B35F	1994	
2035	CV	P835RWU	Dennis Dart	Plaxton Pointer	B40F	1996	Arriva London, 2001
2036	CV	P836RWU	Dennis Dart	Plaxton Pointer	B40F	1996	Arriva London, 2001
2037	LE	P837RWU	Dennis Dart	Plaxton Pointer	B40F	1996	Arriva London, 2001
2038	OS	M30MPS	Dennis Dart 9.8SDL3054	Marshall C37	BC40F	1995	Arriva Southern Counties, 1999

2039-2055   Dennis Dart   Plaxton Pointer   B40F   1996   Arriva London, 2001-02

2039	LE	P839RWU	2044	MH	P844PWW	2048	SS	P848PWW	2052	LE	P852PWW
2040	CV	P840PWW	2045	MH	P845PWW	2049	SS	P849PWW	2053	LE	P853PWW
2041	LE	P841PWW	2046	LE	P846PWW	2050	SS	P850PWW	2054	LE	P854PWW
2042	CV	P842PWW	2047	SS	P847PWW	2051	LE	P851PWW	2055	LE	P855PWW
2043	SS	P843PWW									

2058	CK	G218LGK	Dennis Dart 9SDL3002	Duple Dartline	B36F	1990	Arriva Southern Counties, 1999
2060	TA	M20MPS	Dennis Dart 9.8SDL3054	Marshall C37	B40F	1994	Arriva Southern Counties, 1999
2061	CK	G141GOL	Dennis Dart 9SDL3002	Duple Dartline	B39F	1990	Arrowline, Knutsford, 1992

During 2002, eight 9metre Dennis Darts with Plaxton Pointer bodywork were transferred to the Midlands North fleet from London. Six are allocated to Shrewsbury, where 2070, K550ORH, is seen on local cross-town route 25 from Bayston Hill. *Bob Downham*

2062-2070

Dennis Dart 9SDL3016 · Plaxton Pointer · B34F · 1992 · Arriva London, 2002

2062	BT	K542ORH	**2064**	SY	K544ORH	**2067**	SY	K547ORH	**2069**	SY	K549ORH
2063	BT	K543ORH	**2065**	SY	K545ORH	**2068**	SY	K548ORH	**2070**	SY	K550ORH

2072	TF	H459UGO	Dennis Dart 8.5SDL3003	Carlyle Dartline	B28F	1990	Arriva London, 2000
2076	w	H470UGO	Dennis Dart 8.5SDL3003	Carlyle Dartline	B28F	1990	Arriva London, 2000
2079	TF	H91MOB	Dennis Dart 8.5SDL3003	Carlyle Dartline	B28F	1990	Arriva North West, 2001
2081	SY	K551ORH	Dennis Dart 9SDL3016	Plaxton Pointer	B34F	1992	Arriva London, 2001
2082	SY	K552ORH	Dennis Dart 9SDL3016	Plaxton Pointer	B34F	1992	Arriva London, 2001
2085	CK	L139YVK	Dennis Dart 9SDL3034	Northern Counties Paladin	B35F	1994	Arriva The Shires, 2002
2086	CK	L142YVK	Dennis Dart 9SDL3034	Northern Counties Paladin	B35F	1994	Arriva The Shires, 2002
2087	CK	L144YVK	Dennis Dart 9SDL3034	Northern Counties Paladin	B35F	1994	Arriva The Shires, 2002
2089	SS	N689GUM	Dennis Dart 9.8SDL3054	Plaxton Pointer	B40F	1995	Arriva London, 2002
2090	SS	N690GUM	Dennis Dart 9.8SDL3054	Plaxton Pointer	B40F	1995	Arriva London, 2002

2091-2095

Dennis Dart 9.8SDL3035 · Plaxton Pointer · B40F · 1994

2091	BT	L301NFA	**2093**	BT	L303NFA	**2094**	BT	L304NFA	**2095**	BT	L305NFA
2092	BT	L302NFA									

2096	OS	N806EHA	Dennis Dart 9.8SDL3054	East Lancs	B40F	1995	
2097	OS	N807EHA	Dennis Dart 9.8SDL3054	East Lancs	B40F	1995	
2098	OS	N808EHA	Dennis Dart 9.8SDL3054	East Lancs	B40F	1995	
2099	SD	M805MOJ	Dennis Dart 9.8SDL3054	Marshall C37	B40F	1994	
2100	BT	L766DPE	Dennis Dart 9.8SDL3034	Wadham Stringer Winchester	C39F	1993	Arriva Southern Counties, 1999

2194-2198

Dennis Dart 9.8SDL3040 · East Lancs EL2000 · B40F · 1994

2194	DE	L34PNN	**2196**	DE	L36PNN	**2197**	DE	L37PNN	**2198**	DE	L38PNN
2195	DE	L35PNN									

2201-2206

Dennis Dart SLF · Plaxton Pointer · N39F · 1997

2201	SS	P201HRY	**2203**	SS	P203HRY	**2205**	CV	P205HRY	**2206**	CV	P206HRY
2202	SS	P202HRY	**2204**	LE	P204HRY						

2207	TA	S207DTO	Dennis Dart SLF	Plaxton Pointer 2	N39F	1998
2208	HY	S208DTO	Dennis Dart SLF	Plaxton Pointer 2	N39F	1998

Pictured in Corby, Mini Pointer Dart 2274, FL52MML carries Midland Mainline colours. One of two in this scheme the pair also have MML suffix letters to their index marks. *Richard Godfrey*

2209-2212			TransBus Dart SLF 8.8m		TransBus Mini Pointer	N29F	2003		
2209	SS	SN03LGC	**2210**	SS	SN03LGD	**2211**	SS	SN03LGE	**2212** SS SN03LGF

2214	HY	P954RUL	Dennis Dart SLF 10.2m	Alexander ALX200	N36F	1997	Arriva London, 2002
2215	DE	R45VJF	Dennis Dart SLF 10.2m	Alexander ALX200	N40F	1997	
2216	DE	R46VJF	Dennis Dart SLF 10.2m	Alexander ALX200	N40F	1997	

2217-2224			Dennis Dart SLF 9.8m		Plaxton Pointer 2	N33F	1999		
2217	DE	T47WUT	**2219**	TA	T49JJF	**2222**	DE	T52JJF	**2224** DE T54JJF
2218	DE	T48WUT	**2221**	DE	T51JJF	**2223**	DE	T53JJF	

2226-2238			Dennis Dart SLF 10.2m		Alexander ALX200	N40F	2000		
2226	DE	W226SNR	**2229**	DE	W229SNR	**2233**	DE	W233SNR	**2236** DE W236SNR
2227	DE	W227SNR	**2231**	DE	W231SNR	**2234**	DE	W234SNR	**2237** DE W237SNR
2228	DE	W228SNR	**2232**	DE	W232SNR	**2235**	DE	W235SNR	**2238** DE W238SNR

2239-2251			Dennis Dart SLF 8.8m		Plaxton Pointer MPD	N29F	2000		
2239	HY	W239SNR	**2243**	MH	W243SNR	**2247**	LE	W247SNR	**2249** HY W249SNR
2241	LE	W241SNR	**2244**	LE	W244SNR	**2248**	LE	W248SNR	**2251** CV W251SNR
2242	HY	W242SNR	**2246**	LE	W246SNR				

2252	DE	X252HBC	Dennis Dart SLF 10.2m	Alexander ALX200	N40F	2000	

2253-2267			Dennis Dart SLF 8.8m		Plaxton Pointer MPD	N29F	2001		
2253	LE	Y253YBC	**2258**	LE	Y258YBC	**2262**	LE	Y262YBC	**2265** LE Y265YBC
2254	LE	Y254YBC	**2259**	LE	Y259YBC	**2263**	LE	Y263YBC	**2266** LE Y266YBC
2256	LE	Y256YBC	**2261**	LE	Y261YBC	**2264**	LE	Y264YBC	**2267** LE Y267YBC
2257	LE	Y257YBC							

2268-2275			Dennis Dart SLF 8.8m		Plaxton Pointer MPD	N29F	2002		
2268	LE	SK52MLE	**2270**	LE	SK52MLJ	**2272**	LE	SK52MLN	**2274** MH FK52MML
2269	LE	SK52MLF	**2271**	LE	SK52MLL	**2273**	LE	SK52MLO	**2275** MH FL52MML

Route 404 is one of the local town services for Oswestry with the current vehicle type being the Mini Pointer Dart. Number 2297, BF52NZP is one of a trio from 2002. *Bob Downham*

2276-2280

TransBus Dart SLF 8.8m — TransBus Mini Pointer — N29F — 2003

2276	DE	SN53ESG	2277	DE	SN53ESO	2279	TF	SN03LDV	2280	TF	SN03LDX

2281-2288

Dennis Dart SLF — Plaxton Pointer MPD — N29F — 1999

| 2281 | SD | V201KDA | 2283 | SD | V203KDA | 2285 | SD | V205KDA | 2287 | CK | V207KDA |
| 2282 | SD | V202KDA | 2284 | SD | V204KDA | 2286 | CK | V206KDA | 2288 | CK | V208KDA |

2289-2297

Dennis Dart SLF — Plaxton Pointer MPD — N29F — 2001-02

2289	CK	BU51KWJ	2292	CK	BU51KWL	2294	CK	Y184TUK	2296	OS	BF52NZO
2290	CK	BU51KWN	2293	CK	BU51KWK	2295	OS	BF52NZN	2297	OS	BF52NZP
2291	CK	BU51KWM									

| 2299 | TF | T61JBA | Dennis Dart SLF | Marshall Capital | N37F | 1999 | Arriva North West, 2000 |

2301-2305

Dennis Dart SLF 10.6m — Plaxton Pointer — N37F — 1996

| 2301 | SY | N301ENX | 2303 | SY | N303ENX | 2304 | SY | N304ENX | 2305 | SY | N305ENX |
| 2302 | SY | N302ENX | | | | | | | | | |

2306-2310

Dennis Dart SLF 10.6m — Plaxton Pointer — NC37F — 1996

| 2306 | SY | P306FEA | 2308 | SY | P308FEA | 2309 | SY | P309FEA | 2310 | SY | P310FEA |
| 2307 | SY | P307FEA | | | | | | | | | |

2311-2315

Dennis Dart SLF 10.6m — East Lancs Spryte — N41F — 1996

| 2311 | SD | P311FEA | 2313 | SD | P313FEA | 2314 | SD | P314FEA | 2315 | SD | P315FEA |
| 2312 | SD | P312FEA | | | | | | | | | |

2316-2327

Dennis Dart SLF 10.6m — Plaxton Pointer — NC39F — 1997

2316	BT	P316FEA	2319	BT	P319HOJ	2322	SE	P322HOJ	2325	CK	P325HOJ
2317	BT	P317FEA	2320	BT	P320HOJ	2323	CK	P323HOJ	2326	SE	P326HOJ
2318	CK	P318FEA	2321	SE	P321HOJ	2324	SE	P324HOJ	2327	SE	P327HOJ

Thirty Volvo B6BLEs with Wright Crusader 2 bodies were supplied to the north Midlands fleet for routes in Tamworth and The Wrekin, though subsequent transfers see them over a wider area. Pictured in Leegomery, 2628, V228KDA, is one of those allocated to Wellington depot and is seen on the Wrekin supported redLine route 44. *Bill Potter*

2329-2344

Dennis Dart SLF 10.6m — Plaxton Pointer 2 — NC39F — 1997-98

2329	SD	R329TJW	2334	SD	R334TJW	2338	SY	R338TJW	2342	SY	R342TJW
2330	SD	R330TJW	2335	SD	R335TJW	2339	SY	R339TJW	2343	SY	R343TJW
2331	SD	R331TJW	2336	SD	R336TJW	2340	SY	R340TJW	2344	SY	R344TJW
2332	SD	R332TJW	2337	SD	R337TJW	2341	SY	R341TJW			

2345-2353

Dennis Dart SLF 10.6m — Plaxton Pointer 2 — NC44F — 1999

2345	SY	S345YOG	2348	OS	S348YOG	2350	OS	S350YOG	2352	OS	S352YOG
2346	SY	S346YOG	2349	OS	S349YOG	2351	OS	S351YOG	2353	OS	S353YOG
2347	OS	S347YOG									

2354-2358

Dennis Dart SLF 10.2m — Alexander ALX200 — N36F — 1997 — Arriva London, 2002

2354	CK	P952RUL	2356	CK	P956RUL	2357	CK	P957RUL	2358	CK	P958RUL
2355	CK	P955RUL									

2359-2366

Dennis Dart SLF 9.5m — East Lancs Spryte — N31F — 1996 — Arriva Southern Counties, 2002

2359	TF	N238VPH	2361	TF	N241VPH	2363	TF	N243VPH	2365	TF	N248VPH
2360	TF	N240VPH	2362	TF	N242VPH	2364	TF	N244VPH	2366	TF	N249VPH

2613-2642

Volvo B6BLE — Wright Crusader 2 — N40F — 1999-2000

2613	TA	V213KDA	2621	TA	V221KDA	2629	TA	V229KDA	2636	TF	V236KDA
2614	TA	V214KDA	2622	TA	V212KDA	2630	TF	V230KDA	2637	TF	V237KDA
2615	TA	V215KDA	2623	TA	V223KDA	2631	SH	V231KDA	2638	SH	V238KDA
2616	TA	V216KDA	2624	TA	V224KDA	2632	SH	V232KDA	2639	SH	V239KDA
2617	TA	V217KDA	2625	TA	V225KDA	2633	TF	V233KDA	2640	TA	V210KDA
2618	TA	V218KDA	2626	TA	V226KDA	2634	TF	V234KDA	2641	TA	V211KDA
2619	TA	V219KDA	2627	TA	V227KDA	2635	TF	V235KDA	2642	TA	V209KDA
2620	TA	V220KDA	2628	TA	V228KDA						

2703-2707

DAF DE12CSSB120 — Wrightbus Cadet — N39F — 2002

2703	SY	BU02URX	2705	SY	BU02URZ	2706	SY	BU02USB	2707	SY	BU02USC
2704	SY	BU02URY									

2708-2727   DAF DE12CSSB120   Wrightbus Cadet   N39F   2001

2708	SD	Y348UON	2715	TF	Y365UON	2720	SH	Y347UON	2724	SH	Y364UON
2711	TF	Y351UON	2716	TF	Y356UON	2721	SH	Y361UON	2725	SH	Y346UON
2712	TF	Y352UON	2717	TF	Y357UON	2722	SH	Y362UON	2726	SH	Y366UON
2713	TF	Y353UON	2718	TF	Y358UON	2723	SH	Y363UON	2727	SH	Y367UON
2714	TF	Y354UON	2719	TF	Y349UON						

2728-2736   DAF DE12CSSB120   Wrightbus Cadet   N39F   2002-03

2728	SH	BF52OAG	2731	SD	BU03HRD	2733	SD	BU03HRF	2735	SD	BU03HRJ
2729	SY	BF52NZM	2732	SD	BU03HRE	2734	SD	BU03HRG	2736	SD	BU03HRK
2730	SD	BU03HRC									

2737	OS	CX04EHZ	DAF DE12CSSB120	Wrightbus Cadet	N39F	2004	Arriva North West & Wales, 2004
2998	SE	P315FAW	Optare L1150	Optare Excel	N40F	1997	Williamsons, Shrewsbury, 1998
2999	SE	P316FAW	Optare L1150	Optare Excel	N40F	1997	Williamsons, Shrewsbury, 1998
3037	SY	TPC103X	Leyland Tiger TRCTL11/2R	East Lancs (1989)	BC49F	1982	London & Country, 1989
3038	OS	C141SPB	Leyland Tiger TRCTL11/3RH	East Lancs (1991)	B59F	1986	London & Country, 1991
3039	CK	49XBF	Leyland Tiger TRBTL11/2RP	Plaxton Derwent 2	B54F	1988	Arriva North West, 2000
3053	BT	F33ENF	Leyland Tiger TRBL10/3ARZA	Alexander N	B53F	1989	Timeline, 1994

3071-3080   Dennis Falcon HC SDA421   East Lancs EL2000   B48F   1990   London & Country, 1991

3071	BT	G301DPA	3074	TF	G304DPA	3077	OS	G307DPA	3079	BT	G309DPA
3072	TF	G302DPA	3075	TF	G305DPA	3078	OS	G308DPA	3080	w	G310DPA
3073	TA	G303DPA	3076	BT	G306DPA						

3081-3089   Dennis Falcon HC SDA423   East Lancs EL2000   B48F   1992-93

3081	TF	K211UHA	3084	SE	K214UHA	3086	SH	K216UHA	3088	SY	K218UHA
3082	TF	K212UHA	3085	TF	K215UHA	3087	TF	K217UHA	3089	OS	K219UHA
3083	TF	K213UHA									

3091-3098   Dennis Falcon SDA421   East Lancs EL2000   B48F   1990

3091	SH	G381EKA	3093	OS	G383EKA	3095	TF	G385EKA	3097	TF	G387EKA
3092	SH	G382EKA	3094	TF	G384EKA	3096	SY	G386EKA	3098	TF	G388EKA

3101	CK	F258GWJ	Leyland Lynx LX112L10ZR1R	Leyland Lynx	B51F	1989	The Wright Company, 1993
3102	CK	E72KBF	Leyland Lynx LX112L10ZR1	Leyland Lynx	B51F	1988	
3103	CK	F284AWW	Leyland Lynx LX112L10ZR1S	Leyland Lynx	B49F	1989	Arriva Yorkshire (W), 1999
3104	BT	G110OUG	Leyland Lynx LX2R11C15Z4S	Leyland Lynx	B49F	1990	Arriva Yorkshire (W), 2000
3105	BT	G324NUM	Leyland Lynx LX2R11C15Z4S	Leyland Lynx	B51F	1990	Arriva Yorkshire (W), 2000
3106	BT	F281AWW	Leyland Lynx LX112L10ZR1S	Leyland Lynx	B49F	1989	Arriva Yorkshire (W), 1999
3107	BT	G108OUG	Leyland Lynx LX2R11C15Z4S	Leyland Lynx	B49F	1990	Arriva Yorkshire (W), 2000
3108	BT	G38YHJ	Leyland Lynx LX2R11C15Z4R	Leyland Lynx	B49F	1989	Arriva The Shires, 2002
3109	BT	G40YHJ	Leyland Lynx LX2R11C15Z4R	Leyland Lynx	B49F	1989	Arriva The Shires, 2002
3148	SD	JIL5367	Leyland 11351A/1R(Volvo)	East Lancs Greenway(1994)	B49F	1977	Arriva Southern Counties, 1998
3149	DE	SJI5569	Leyland 11351A/1R(Volvo)	East Lancs Greenway(1994)	B49F	1977	Arriva Southern Counties, 1998
3201	SS	P201RWR	DAF DE33WSSB3000	Van Hool Alizée	C51FT	1997	First Edinburgh, 2001
3203	SS	YJ53VFY	DAF DE40XSSB4000	Van Hool T9 Alizée	C49FT	2003	
3204	SS	YJ03PFX	DAF DE40XSSB4000	Van Hool T9 Alizée	C49FT	2003	
3205	SS	P205RWR	DAF DE33WSSB3000	Van Hool Alizée	C51FT	1997	Arriva Yorkshire, 2000
3206	SS	YJ04BKF	VDL Bus SB4000	Van Hool T9 Alizée	C49FT	2004	
3209	SS	T209XVO	DAF DE33WSSB3000	Van Hool Alizée	C51FT	1999	
3210	SS	T119AUA	DAF DE33WSSB3000	Van Hool T9 Alizée	C51FT	1999	
3211	SS	662NKR	Volvo B10M-62	Plaxton Expressliner 2	C49FT	1996	
3215	SY	803HOM	Volvo B10M-61	Plaxton Paramount 3200 III	C53F	1987	Blue Bus Services, 1995
3236	WG	F406DUG	Volvo B10M-60	Plaxton Paramount 3200 III	BC50F	1989	Wallace Arnold, 1992
3301	SD	H914XYT	Volvo Citybus B10M-55	East Lancs EL2000	B41F	1990	Arriva London (NE), 1999
3302	SD	H918XYT	Volvo Citybus B10M-55	East Lancs EL2000	B41F	1990	Arriva London (NE), 1999
3303	SD	H919XYT	Volvo Citybus B10M-55	East Lancs EL2000	B41F	1990	Arriva London (NE), 1999

3304-3313   Volvo Citybus B10M-50   Alexander Q   B55F   1991   Timeline, Leigh, 1998

3304	SY	H73DVM	3307	SD	H76DVM	3310	SY	H81DVM	3312	SD	H83DVM
3305	SY	H74DVM	3308	SD	H577DVM	3311	SD	H82DVM	3313	SD	H84DVM
3306	SD	H575DVM	3309	SY	H580DVM						

3401	DE	E23ECH	Scania K92CRB	Alexander PS	B51F	1988
3402	DE	F28JRC	Scania K93CRB	Alexander PS	B51F	1989

Carrying a silver park and ride livery for a Leicester scheme are four Wrightbus Commanders based at Thurmaston depot. Number 3702, FD52GGP, is seen in the city. A further batch of the type has entered service in Telford where they have displaced smaller Cadets from some of the new routes. *Tony Wilson*

3415-3429
Scania L113CRL | Plaxton Paladin | NC45F* | 1998 | *3415-19 are NC47F

3415	TA	R415TJW	3419	TA	R419TJW	3423	TA	R423TJW	3427	SY	R427TJW
3416	TA	R416TJW	3420	TA	R420TJW	3424	TA	R424TJW	3428	SY	R428TJW
3417	TA	R417TJW	3421	TA	R421TJW	3425	TA	R425TJW	3429	SY	R429TJW
3418	TA	R418TJW	3422	TA	R422TJW	3426	TA	R426TJW			

3466-3479
Scania L113CRL | East Lancs European | NC51F* | 1996 | *3476-9 are NC49F

3466	SS	N166PUT	3470	SS	N170PUT	3474	SS	N174PUT	3477	CV	N177PUT
3467	SS	N167PUT	3471	SS	N171PUT	3475	SS	N175PUT	3478	CV	N178PUT
3468	SS	N168PUT	3472	SS	N172PUT	3476	CV	N176PUT	3479	CV	N179PUT
3469	SS	N169PUT	3473	SS	N173PUT						

3489-3493
Scania L113CRL | East Lancs European | N51F | 1996

| 3489 | SS | N429XRC | 3491 | SS | N431XRC | 3492 | DE | N432XRC | 3493 | DE | N433XRC |
| 3490 | CV | N430XRC | | | | | | | | | |

3501-3504
Scania N113CRL | East Lancs European | B42F | 1995

| 3501 | SY | M401EFD | 3502 | SY | M402EFD | 3503 | SY | M403EFD | 3504 | SY | M404EFD |

3601-3612
Volvo B10BLE | Alexander ALX300 | N44F | 2000

3601	HY	V601DBC	3604	DE	V604DBC	3607	SS	V607DBC	3610	CV	V610DBC
3602	HY	V602DBC	3605	DE	V605DBC	3608	SS	V608DBC	3611	CV	V611DBC
3603	HY	V603DBC	3606	DE	V606DBC	3609	CV	V609DBC	3612	CV	V612DBC

3701-3704
DAF DE02GSSB200 | Wrightbus Commander | N44F | 2003

| 3701 | LE | FD52GGO | 3702 | LE | FD52GGP | 3703 | LE | FD52GGU | 3704 | LE | FD52GGV |

3705-3718
DAF DE02CSSB200 | Wrightbus Commander | N44F | 2002

3705	TF	BF52NZR	3709	TF	BF52NZV	3713	TF	BF52NZZ	3716	TF	BF52OAC
3706	TF	BF52NZS	3710	TF	BF52NZW	3714	TF	BF52OAA	3717	TF	BF52OAD
3707	TF	BF52NZT	3711	TF	BF52NZX	3715	TF	BF52OAB	3718	TF	BF52OAE
3708	TF	BF52NZU	3712	TF	BF52NZY						

| 4001 | MH | L94HRF | DAF DB250RS200505 | Optare Spectra | B48/29F | 1993 | Midland (Stevensons), 1998 |
| 4002 | MH | L95HRF | DAF DB250RS200505 | Optare Spectra | B48/29F | 1993 | Midland (Stevensons), 1998 |

4134-4145 — Scania N113DRB — Northern Counties — B47/33F — 1990-91 — Arriva North West, 1999

4134	WG	G34HKY	4138	WG	G38HKY	4142	WG	G714LKW	4144	WG	H804RWJ
4136	WG	G36HKY	4141	WG	G711LKW	4143	WG	H803RWJ	4145	WG	H805RWJ
4137	WG	G37HKY									

4153-4158 — Scania N113DRB — Alexander RH — B47/33F — 1989 — BTS, Borehamwood, 1993

| 4153 | WG | F153DET | 4155 | WG | F155DET | 4157 | WG | F157DET | 4158 | WG | F158DET |
| 4154 | WG | F154DET | | | | | | | | | |

4159-4178 — Scania N113DRB — East Lancs — B47/33F — 1994-95

4159	WG	M159GRY	4165	WG	M165GRY	4171	SS	M171GRY	4175	SS	M175GRY
4160	WG	M160GRY	4166	WG	M166GRY	4172	SS	M172GRY	4176	SS	M176GRY
4161	WG	M161GRY	4168	WG	M168GRY	4173	SS	M173GRY	4177	SS	M177GRY
4162	MH	M162GRY	4169	SS	M169GRY	4174	SS	M174GRY	4178	SS	M178GRY
4163	WG	M163GRY	4170	SS	M170GRY						

4180-4184 — Scania N113DRB — East Lancs — B45/33F — 1995

| 4180 | SS | N160VVO | 4182 | SS | N162VVO | 4183 | SS | N163VVO | 4184 | SS | N164VVO |
| 4181 | SS | N161VVO | | | | | | | | | |

4191-4195 — Scania N113DRB — East Lancs — BC43/29F* — 1995 — 4194/5 are B45/33F

| 4191 | LE | M831SDA | 4193 | LE | M833SDA | 4194 | LE | M834SDA | 4195 | LE | M835SDA |
| 4192 | LE | M832SDA | | | | | | | | | |

| 4301 | DE | GTO301V | Leyland Fleetline FE30AGR | Northern Counties | B43/30F | 1980 | |

4320-4334 — Volvo Citybus B10M-50 — East Lancs — B45/33F — 1990-91 — London South, 1998

4320	DE	H650GPF	4324	DE	H655GPF	4328	DE	H669GPF	4332	DE	H680GPF
4321	WG	H652GPF	4325	DE	H659GPF	4329	DE	H671GPF	4333	DE	H682GPF
4322	DE	H653GPF	4326	DE	H663GPF	4330	DE	H672GPF	4334	DE	H684GPF
4323	DE	H654GPF	4327	DE	H664GPF	4331	DE	H674GPF			

4335-4343 — Volvo Citybus B10M-50 — Marshall — B45/33F — 1984

4335	DE	B135GAU	4338	DE	B138GAU	4340	DE	B140GAU	4342	DE	B142GAU
4336	DE	B136GAU	4339	DE	B139GAU	4341	DE	B141GAU	4343	DE	B143GAU
4337	DE	B137GAU									

4344-4353 — Volvo Citybus B10M-50 — Northern Counties — B42/33F — 1986/88

4344	DE	C144NRR	4347	DE	C147NRR	4350	DE	E150BTO	4352	DE	E152BTO
4345	DE	C145NRR	4348	DE	C148NRR	4351	DE	E151BTO	4353	DE	E153BTO
4346	DE	C146NRR	4349	DE	E149BTO						

4354	DE	F114TML	Volvo Citybus B10M-50	Alexander RV	B47/31F	1989	Arriva London, 1999
4355	DE	F111TML	Volvo Citybus B10M-50	Alexander RV	B47/31F	1989	Arriva London, 1999
4376	DE	YAU126Y	Volvo Citybus B10M-50	Marshall	B45/33F	1983	

4379-4383 — Volvo Citybus B10M-50 — East Lancs — B45/31F — 1984

| 4379 | DE | A129DTO | 4381 | DE | A131DTO | 4382 | w | A132DTO | 4383 | DE | A133DTO |
| 4380 | w | A130DTO | | | | | | | | | |

| 4384 | DE | B134GAU | Volvo Citybus B10M-50 | Marshall | B45/33F | 1984 | |

4389-4393 — Volvo Citybus B10M-50 — East Lancs — B45/34F — 1990 — London South, 1998

| 4389 | TA | H649GPF | 4390 | CK | H651GPF | 4391 | TA | H656GPF | 4393 | TA | H658GPF |

| 4396 | CK | G646BPH | Volvo Citybus B10M-50 | Northern Counties Palatine | B45/35F | 1989 | Bee Line Buzz, 1993 |
| 4397 | CK | G647BPH | Volvo Citybus B10M-50 | Northern Counties Palatine | B45/35F | 1989 | Bee Line Buzz, 1993 |

4501-4514 — Leyland Olympian ONLXB/1R — Eastern Coach Works — B45/33F — 1983-84 — *4514 is O45/32F

| 4501 | CV | A501EJF | 4503 | SS | A503EJF | 4508 | w | A508EJF | 4512 | LE | A512EJF |
| 4502 | CV | A502EJF | 4504 | LE | A504EJF | 4509 | LE | A509EJF | 4514 | WG | B514LFP |

4516	SS	A132SMA	Leyland Olympian ONLXB/1R	Eastern Coach Works	B45/32F	1983	
4518	WG	A134SMA	Leyland Olympian ONLXB/1R	Eastern Coach Works	O45/32F	1983	
4527	CV	B187BLG	Leyland Olympian ONLXB/1RZ	Eastern Coach Works	B45/32F	1984	Crosville Cymru, 1990
4528	LE	B190BLG	Leyland Olympian ONLXB/1RZ	Eastern Coach Works	B45/32F	1984	Crosville Cymru, 1990

While the Olympian dominates the Arriva Midlands' double-deck fleet the Scania double-decks are shared between the North East and Midlands. Transferred from North West, to where the open-top example has since returned, is 4144, H804RWJ. *Richard Godfrey*

4531-4534 — Leyland Olympian ONCL10/1RZ — Northern Counties Palatine — B47/30F — 1989 — Arriva Southern Counties, 2000

4531	SE	G501SFT	4532	SE	G502SFT	4533	BT	G503SFT	4534	BT	G504SFT

4535-4541 — Leyland Olympian ONCL10/1RZ — Northern Counties Palatine — B47/30F — 1989 — Bee Line Buzz, 1993

4535	BT	G505SFT	4537	BT	G507SFT	4540	BT	G510SFT	4541	BT	G511SFT

4545	SE	B274LPH	Leyland Olympian ONTL11/1R	Eastern Coach Works	B43/29F	1985	Arriva Southern Counties, 1998
4546	SE	B275LPH	Leyland Olympian ONTL11/1R	Eastern Coach Works	B43/29F	1985	Arriva Southern Counties, 1998

4558-4561 — Leyland Olympian ONLXB/1RH — Optare — B47/29F — 1989 — Arriva Southern Counties, 2001

4558	HY	E158OMD	4559	HY	E159OMD	4560	HY	E160OMD	4561	SS	E161OMD

4569	TF	D190FYM	Leyland Olympian ONLXB/1RH	Eastern Coach Works	B42/30F	1986	Arriva London, 2003
4570	TF	D170FYM	Leyland Olympian ONLXB/1RH	Eastern Coach Works	B42/30F	1986	Arriva London, 2003
4571	CK	D171FYM	Leyland Olympian ONLXB/1RH	Eastern Coach Works	B42/30F	1986	Arriva London, 2003

4601-4613 — Volvo Olympian YN2RV18Z4 — Northern Counties Palatine — B47/29F — 1996

4601	LE	P601CAY	4605	LE	P605CAY	4608	LE	P608CAY	4611	WG	P611CAY
4602	LE	P602CAY	4606	WG	P606CAY	4609	WG	P609CAY	4612	WG	P612CAY
4603	LE	P603CAY	4607	WG	P607CAY	4610	WG	P610CAY	4613	SS	P613CAY
4604	LE	P604CAY									

4614-4643 — Volvo Olympian — Northern Counties Palatine — B47/29F — 1998

4614	CV	R614MNU	4621	CV	R621MNU	4629	DE	R629MNU	4637	LE	R637MNU
4615	CV	R615MNU	4622	CV	R622MNU	4630	DE	R630MNU	4638	LE	R638MNU
4616	LE	R616MNU	4623	CV	R623MNU	4631	DE	R631MNU	4639	DE	R639MNU
4617	LE	R617MNU	4624	LE	R624MNU	4632	LE	R632MNU	4640	DE	R640MNU
4618	LE	R618MNU	4625	DE	R625MNU	4633	LE	R633MNU	4641	DE	R641MNU
4619	LE	R619MNU	4626	DE	R626MNU	4634	LE	R634MNU	4642	DE	R642MNU
4620	CV	R620MNU	4627	DE	R627MNU	4636	LE	R636MNU	4643	DE	R643MNU

Several rural services around Shrewsbury are operated by Arriva Midlands using a fleet of Optare Solo buses provided by the County Council. These carry Shropshire Bus colours, shown here on 6002, BU03HPX.
Bob Downham

4644-4653   Volvo Olympian   Northern Counties Palatine   B47/29F   1998

4644	SS	S644KJU	4647	SS	S647KJU	4650	SS	S650KJU	4652	SS	S652KJU
4645	LE	S645KJU	4648	SS	S648KJU	4651	SS	S651KJU	4653	SS	S653KJU
4646	SS	S646KJU	4649	SS	S649KJU						

4665-4669   Volvo Olympian YN2RV18Z4   Northern Counties Palatine   B47/30F   1996

4665	DE	N165XVO	4667	DE	P167BTV	4668	LE	P168BTV	4669	LE	P169BTV
4666	DE	N166XVO									

4701-4716   DAF DE02RSDB250   East Lancs Lowlander   N44/29F   2001

4701	WG	Y701XJF	4705	WG	Y705XJF	4709	WG	Y709XJF	4714	WG	FE51YWM
4702	WG	Y702XJF	4706	WG	Y706XJF	4711	WG	FE51YWJ	4715	WG	FE51WSU
4703	WG	Y703XJF	4707	WG	Y707XJF	4712	WG	FE51YWK	4716	WG	FE51WSV
4704	WG	Y704XJF	4708	WG	FE51YWH	4713	WG	FE51YWL			

4717-4733   DAF DE02PSDB250   East Lancs Lowlander   N44/29F   2002

4717	WG	FD02UKB	4722	SS	FN52XBG	4726	SS	PN52XBF	4730	SS	FD02UKR
4718	WG	FD02UKC	4723	SS	FD02UKJ	4727	SS	FD02UKN	4731	SS	FD02UKS
4719	SS	FD02UKE	4724	SS	FD02UKK	4728	SS	FD02UKO	4732	SS	FD02UKT
4720	SS	PN52XBH	4725	SS	FD02UKL	4729	SS	FD02UKP	4733	SS	FD02UKU
4721	SS	FD02UKG									

4734-4745   DAF DE02PSDB250   East Lancs Lowlander   N44/29F   2003

4734	DE	PN52XRJ	4737	DE	PN52XRM	4740	WG	PN52XRR	4743	DE	PN52XRU
4735	WG	PN52XRK	4738	WG	PN52XRO	4741	WG	PN52XRS	4744	DE	PN52XRV
4736	DE	PN52XRL	4739	DE	PN52XRP	4742	DE	PN52XRT	4745	DE	PN52XRW

6000-6006   Optare Solo M850   Optare   N24F   2003   Operated for Shropshire CC

6000	SY	BU03HRL	6002	SY	BU03HPX	6004	SY	BU03HPZ	6006	SY	FJ04PFX
6001	SY	BU03HPV	6003	SY	BU03HPY	6005	SY	BU03HRA			

6007   SH   FN04AFJ   Optare Solo M920   Optare   N33F   2004

Arriva Midlands now operate forty-five low-floor DAF DB250s with East Lancs Lowlander bodies, all based at eastern depots. Seen in Leicester, 4723, FD02UKJ illustrates the styling. Visible is the seating installed in the batch, which have a higher-backed version of the standard bus unit. *Richard Godfrey*

Ancillary vehicles

3213	HY	FIL3451	Volvo B10M-60	Van Hool Alizée H	TV	1989	Tellings Golden Miller, 1992
3235	SE	GIL6949	Volvo B10M-61	Plaxton Paramount 3500	TV	1987	Arriva The Shires, 1997
3236	SW	F406DUG	Volvo B10M-60	Plaxton Paramount 3500	TV	1989	Wallace Arnold, 1992
3403	WS	E25ECH	Scania K92CRB	Alexander PS	TV	1988	
3404	WS	F27JRC	Scania K93CRB	Alexander PS	TV	1989	
9501	TH	F51ENF	Leyland Lynx LX112L10ZR1R	Leyland Lynx	TV	1988	
9505	TF	614WEH	Volvo B58-61	Plaxton P 3200 II (1986)	TV	1976	Shearings, 1991
9507	TH	HIL3652	Volvo B10M-61	Duple 340	TV	1987	Coliseum, Southampton, 1985
							Crosville Cymru, 1995

9504-9509			Leyland Tiger TRBL10/3ARZA	Alexander N	B53F	1989	Timeline, 1994
9504	SE	F34ENF	**9506**	BT	F40ENF	**9508**	BT	F36ENF	**9509**	CK	F39ENF

Previous registrations:

49XBF	F603CET, A19RBL, F603CET	FIL3451	F803TMD
614WEH	LOT777R	HIL3652	E472BTN
662NKR	N211TBC	JIL5367	NOE598R
803HOM	D264HFX	P608JJU	P111MML
D170FYM	D170FYM, 7CLT	SJI5569	NPJ471R
D190FYM	D190FYM, 319CLT		

Allocations

Burton-on-Trent (Wetmore Road) - BT

Mercedes-Benz	1250	1251	1252	1385				
Dart	2007	2008	2009	2017	2029	2034	2057	2062
	2063	2091	2092	2093	2094	2095	2100	2316
	2317	2319	2320					
Lynx	3104	3105	3106	3107	3108	3109		
Tiger	3053							
Falcon	3071	3076	3079					
Olympian	4533	4534	4535	4537	4540	4541		

Purchased by Shearings, and brought into the Arriva Midlands fleet through Timeline, 3312, H83DVM is a Volvo Citybus with Alexander Q-type bodywork. It was pictured while working from Shifnal before moving to Stafford where it is currently based. *Bill Potter*

Cannock (Delta Way) - CK

Mercedes-Benz	1148	1177	1180	1244	1248	1249	1253	1356
	1357	1372						
Dart	2010	2019	2020	2022	2023	2030	2058	2061
	2073	2074	2078	2085	2086	2087	2286	2287
	2288	2289	2290	2291	2292	2293	2294	2318
	2323	2325	2354	2355	2356	2357	2358	
Tiger	3039							
Lynx	3101	3102	3103					
Citybus	4390	4396	4397					
Olympian	4571							

Coalville (Ashby Road) - CV

Mercedes-Benz	1150	1151	1152	1153	1154	1155	1156	1157
	1161							
Dart	2035	2036	2040	2042	2205	2206	2251	
Volvo B10BLE	3609	3610	3611	3612				
Scania	3476	3477	3478	3479	3490			
Olympian	4501	4502	4527	4614	4615	4620	4621	4622
	4623							

Arriva operate a pair of Optare Excel buses. These were acquired with the operations of Williamsons who used them on Shropshire Bus services. They have now been relocated to Swadlincote and carry corporate colours as shown by 2998, P315FAW, seen leaving Leicester on a return journey of route 118. *Tony Wilson*

Derby (London Road) - DE

Mercedes-Benz	1163	1373	1374	1375	1376	1377	1378	1379
	1380	1381	1382	1383	1384	1387	1391	
Dart	2194	2195	2196	2197	2198	2215	2216	2217
	2218	2221	2222	2223	2224	2226	2227	2228
	2229	2231	2232	2233	2234	2235	2236	2237
	2238	2252	2276	2277				
Greenway	3149							
Scania sd	3401	3402	3492	3493				
Volvo B10BLE	3604	3605	3606					
Fleetline	4301							
Volvo Citybus	4320	4322	4323	4324	4325	4326	4327	4328
	4329	4330	4331	4332	4333	4334	4335	4336
	4337	4338	4339	4340	4341	4342	4343	4344
	4345	4346	4347	4348	4349	4350	4351	4352
	4353	4354	4355	4376	4379	4381	4383	4384
Olympian	4625	4626	4627	4629	4630	4631	4639	4640
	4641	4642	4643	4665	4666	4667		
DAF Lowlander	4734	4736	4737	4739	4742	4743	4744	4745

Hinckley (Jacknell Road, Dodwells Bridge) - HY

Mercedes-Benz	1129	1130	1131	1132	1133	1134	1135	1141
	1142	1143	1144	1145	1146	1147	1171	
Dart	2208	2214	2239	2242	2249			
Volvo B10M coach	3213							
Volvo B10BLE	3601	3602	3603					
Olympian	4558	4559	4560					

Leicester (Melton Road, Thurmaston) - LE

Mercedes-Benz	1149	1168	1169	1170				
Dart	2024	2037	2039	2041	2046	2051	2052	2053
	2054	2204	2207	2219	2241	2244	2246	2247
	2248	2253	2254	2256	2257	2258	2259	2261
	2262	2263	2264	2265	2266	2267	2268	2269
	2270	2271	2272	2273				
DAF Commander	3701	3702	3703	3704				
Volvo Citybus	4389	4391	4393					
Olympian	4504	4509	4512	4528	4601	4602	4603	4604
	4605	4608	4616	4617	4618	4619	4624	4632
	4633	4634	4636	4637	4638	4645	4668	4669

Leicester (Peacock Lane, Southgates) - SS

Mercedes-Benz	1160	1173						
Dart	2043	2047	2048	2049	2050	2089	2090	2201
	2202	2203	2209	2210	2211	2212		
DAF coach	3201	3203	3204	3205	3206	3209	3210	
Volvo B10M coach	3211							
Scania SD	3466	3467	3468	3469	3470	3471	3472	3473
	3474	3475	3489	3491				
Volvo B10BLE	3607	3608						
Scania DD	4169	4170	4171	4172	4173	4174	4175	4176
	4177	4178	4180	4181	4182	4183	4184	
Olympian	4503	4516	4561	4613	4644	4646	4647	4648
	4649	4650	4651	4652	4653			
DAF Lowlander	4719	4720	4721	4722	4723	4724	4725	4726
	4727	4728	4729	4730	4731	4732	4733	

Market Harborough - MH

Mercedes-Benz	1001	1002	1179		
Dart	2044	2045	2243	2274	2275
DAF Spectra	4001	4002			
Scania DD	4162				

Oswestry (Oswald Road) - OS

Dart	2001	2038	2096	2097	2098	2295	2296	2297
	2347	2348	2349	2350	2351	2352	2353	
Tiger	3038							
Falcon	3077	3078	3080	3089	3093			

Shifnal (Railway Yard) - SH

Mercedes-Benz	1260	1270	1371					
Solo	6007							
Dart	2021							
Volvo B6	2631	2632	2638	2639				
DAF Cadet	2720	2721	2722	2723	2724	2725	2726	2727
	2728							
Falcon	3084	3086	3091	3092	3093			

The batch of five East Lancs Spryte-bodied Darts were supplied to Midlands North in 1996 and these are used at Stafford. A batch that is similar, but shorter was supplied to Southern Counties, and several of these have now transferred north. Showing this attractive styling is 2313, P313FEA. *Cliff Beeton*

Shrewsbury (Spring Gardens) - SY

Mercedes-Benz	1243	1247	1358	1359	1360	1386	1390
Solo	6000	6001	6002	6003	6004	6005	6006
Dart	2013	2014	2015	2016	2070	2064	2065	2067
	2068	2069	2081	2082	2301	2302	2303	2304
	2305	2306	2307	2308	2309	2310	2338	2339
	2340	2341	2342	2343	2344	2345	2346
DAF SB120 Cadet	2703	2704	2705	2706	2707	2729
Falcon	3096
Tiger	3037
Volvo B10M bus	3215	3304	3305	3309	3310
Scania sd	3427	3428	3429	3501	3502	3503	3504

Stafford (Dorrington Park Industrial Estate, Common Road) - SD

Zafira	127	129
Mercedes-Benz	1127	1137	1138	1139
Dart	2025	2026	2027	2032	2033	2099	2281	2282
	2283	2284	2285	2311	2312	2313	2314	2315
	2329	2330	2331	2332	2334	2335	2336	2337
DAF Cadet	2708	2730	2731	2732	2733	2734	2735	2736
Greenway	3148
Volvo B10M bus	3301	3302	3303	3306	3307	3308	3311	3312
	3313

Swadlincote (Midland Road) - SC

Mercedes-Benz	1245	1246						
Swift	1931	1932	1934					
Dart	2002	2003	2004	2005	2006	2321	2322	2324
	2326	2327						
Optare Excel	2998	2999						
Falcon	3084							
Olympian	4531	4532	4545	4546				

Tamworth (Aldergate) - TA

Dart	2060							
Volvo B6	2613	2614	2615	2616	2617	2618	2619	2620
	2621	2622	2623	2624	2625	2626	2627	2628
	2629	2640	2641	2642				
Falcon	3073							
Scania sd	3415	3416	3417	3418	3419	3420	3421	3422
	3423	3424	3425	3426				
Scania dd	4191	4192	4193	4194	4195			

Telford (Charlton Street, Wellington) - TF

Mercedes-Benz	1268	1269	1392					
Dart	2011	2012	2028	2072	2079	2279	2280	2299
	2359	2360	2361	2362	2363	2364	2365	2366
Volvo B6	2630	2633	2634	2635	2636	2637		
DAF Cadet	2711	2712	2713	2714	2715	2716	2717	2718
	2719							
Falcon	3072	3074	3075	3081	3082	3083	3085	3087
	3088	3094	3095	3097	3098			
DAF Commander	3705	3706	3707	3708	3709	3710	3711	3712
	3713	3714	3715	3716	3717	3718		
Volvo Olympian	4569	4570						

Wigston (Station Street, South Wigston) - WG

Mercedes Benz	1158	1159	1162	1164	1165	1166	1167	1172
	1174	1175	1176	1178				
Volvo B10M coach	3236							
Scania dd	4134	4136	4137	4138	4141	4142	4143	4144
	4145	4153	4154	4155	4157	4158	4159	4160
	4161	4163	4165	4166	4168			
Volvo Citybus	4321							
Olympian open top	4514	4518						
Olympian	4606	4607	4609	4610	4611	4612		
DAF Lowlander	4701	4702	4703	4704	4705	4706	4707	4708
	4709	4711	4712	4713	4714	4715	4716	4717
	4718	4735	4738	4740	4741			

Unallocated and withdrawn - u/w

Mercedes-Benz	1128	1136	1140	1231	1238	1770
Dart	2056	2076	2083			
Falcom	3080					
Olympian	4508					
Volvo Citybus	4380					

ARRIVA THE SHIRES & ESSEX

Arriva The Shires Ltd; Arriva East Herts & Essex Ltd
487 Dunstable Road, Luton, LU4 8DS

218-268		Mercedes-Benz 308D		Leicester Carriage		M7L	1992-98	Op'd for Hertfordshire CC
218	GR	K668PLH	**256**	GR	N106EVS	**259**	GR	N109EVS	**264**	GR	P404MLD
230	GR	K390RLR	**257**	GR	N107EVS	**262**	GR	P402MLD	**265**	GR	P405MLD
245	GR	M425BLU	**258**	GR	N108EVS	**263**	GR	P403MLD	**268**	GR	N248GBM
246	GR	M426BLU									

442	HW	Y42HBT	Optare Solo M850	Optare	N23F	2001	Op'd for Buckinghamshire CC
443	HA	YS02UBX	Optare Alero	Optare	N14F	2002	
444	HA	YS02UBY	Optare Alero	Optare	N14F	2002	
446	AY	Y46HBT	Optare Solo M850	Optare	N23F	2001	Op'd for Buckinghamshire CC
447	AY	Y47HBT	Optare Solo M850	Optare	N23F	2001	Op'd for Buckinghamshire CC
448	AY	Y48HBT	Optare Solo M850	Optare	N23F	2001	Op'd for Buckinghamshire CC
449	AY	Y49HBT	Optare Solo M850	Optare	N23F	2001	Op'd for Buckinghamshire CC
454	AY	YN04LXF	Optare Alero	Optare	N17F	2004	Op'd for Buckinghamshire CC
455	AY	YN04LXG	Optare Alero	Optare	N17F	2004	Op'd for Buckinghamshire CC
456	AY	YN04LXH	Optare Alero	Optare	N17F	2004	Op'd for Buckinghamshire CC
1257	HA	T557UOX	Mercedes-Benz Vito 110CDi	Traveliner	M6	1999	
2105	HI	M45WUR	Mercedes-Benz 709D	Plaxton Beaver	B27F	1995	
2106	HI	M46WUR	Mercedes-Benz 709D	Plaxton Beaver	B27F	1995	
2107	HI	M47WUR	Mercedes-Benz 709D	Plaxton Beaver	B27F	1995	
2108	HI	M38WUR	Mercedes-Benz 811D	Plaxton Beaver	BC31F	1995	
2113	HI	M43WUR	Mercedes-Benz 709D	Plaxton Beaver	B27F	1995	
2114	AY	N918ETM	Mercedes-Benz 709D	Plaxton Beaver	B27F	1995	

2116-2136		Mercedes-Benz 709D		Plaxton Beaver		B27F*	1995	*2116 is BC27F
2116	HA	N186EMJ	**2121**	HA	N191EMJ	**2126**	HA	N196EMJ	**2131**	LU	N911ETM
2117	u	N187EMJ	**2122**	HA	N192EMJ	**2127**	AY	N907ETM	**2132**	LU	N912ETM
2118	HA	N188EMJ	**2123**	HA	N193EMJ	**2128**	LU	N908ETM	**2133**	LU	N913ETM
2119	HA	N189EMJ	**2124**	HA	N194EMJ	**2129**	LU	N909ETM	**2136**	LU	N916ETM
2120	HA	N190EMJ	**2125**	HA	N195EMJ						

Stevenage is the location for this view of Mercedes-Benz 2148, N378JGS, a 709 model with Plaxton Beaver bodywork.
Richard Godfrey

2138-2162 Mercedes-Benz 709D Plaxton Beaver B27F 1996

2138	HA	N368JGS	2145	HA	N375JGS	2151	HA	N381JGS	2157	HI	N387JGS
2139	HA	N369JGS	2146	HI	N376JGS	2152	HI	N382JGS	2158	HA	N366JGS
2140	HA	N370JGS	2147	HI	N377JGS	2153	HI	N383JGS	2159	HA	N367JGS
2141	HI	N371JGS	2148	HI	N378JGS	2154	HI	N384JGS	2160	HI	P670PNM
2142	HI	N372JGS	2149	HI	N379JGS	2155	HI	N385JGS	2161	HI	P671PNM
2143	HA	N373JGS	2150	HI	N380JGS	2156	HI	N386JGS	2162	HI	P669PNM
2144	HI	N374JGS									

2166	GR	J465UFS	Mercedes-Benz 609D	Crystals	BC24F	1992	Checker, Garston, 1997

2171-2195 Mercedes-Benz Vario 0810 Plaxton Beaver 2 B27F 1997-98

2171	HW	R171VBM	2177	HI	R177VBM	2182	HH	R182DNM	2189	HA	R189DNM
2172	HA	R172VBM	2178	HH	R178VBM	2183	HH	R183DNM	2190	HA	R190DNM
2173	GR	R173VBM	2179	HH	R179VBM	2184	HH	R184DNM	2194	HA	R194DNM
2175	HA	R175VBM	2180	HH	R180VBM	2185	HH	R185DNM	2195	HA	R195DNM
2176	AY	R176VBM	2181	HH	R181DNM						

2196	HA	R196DNM	Mercedes-Benz Vario 0814	Plaxton Beaver 2	B31F	1998	
2197	HA	R197DNM	Mercedes-Benz Vario 0814	Plaxton Beaver 2	B31F	1998	
2198	HA	R198DNM	Mercedes-Benz Vario 0814	Plaxton Beaver 2	B31F	1998	
2224	LU	L424CPB	Mercedes-Benz 709D	Dormobile Routemaker	B25F	1993	Arriva Southern Counties, 1999

2240-2249 Mercedes-Benz Vario 0810 Plaxton Beaver 2 B27F 1997 Arriva Yorkshire, 1999-2003

2240	AY	R760DUB	2242	u	R762DUB	2246	HH	R766DUB	2248	HA	R758DUB
2241	HH	R761DUB	2244	AY	R764DUB	2247	AY	R767DUB	2249	HH	R759DUB

2370-2377 Mercedes-Benz Vario 0810 Plaxton Beaver 2 B25F* 1998 *2373 is BC25F

2370	WR	R940VPU	2373	WR	R943VPU	2375	WR	R945VPU	2377	WR	R947VPU
2371	HA	R941VPU	2374	WR	R944VPU	2376	WR	R946VPU			

2410	u	N780EUA	Mercedes-Benz 811D	Plaxton Beaver	B32F	1995	Arriva North West, 2001
2415	LU	N175DWM	Mercedes-Benz 811D	Plaxton Beaver	B31F	1996	Arriva North West, 2002
2416	AY	N176DWM	Mercedes-Benz 811D	Plaxton Beaver	B31F	1996	Arriva North West, 2002
2417	AY	N177DWM	Mercedes-Benz 811D	Plaxton Beaver	B31F	1996	Arriva North West, 2002
3068	u	H408ERO	Leyland Lynx LX2R11C15Z4S	Leyland Lynx	BC45F	1990	
3069	u	H409ERO	Leyland Lynx LX2R11C15Z4S	Leyland Lynx	BC45F	1990	
3070	u	H410ERO	Leyland Lynx LX2R11C15Z4S	Leyland Lynx	B45F	1990	
3079	GR	F151KGS	Volvo B10M-56	Plaxton Derwent II	B54F	1988	Buffalo, Flitwick, 1995
3080	AY	F152KGS	Volvo B10M-56	Plaxton Derwent II	B54F	1988	Buffalo, Flitwick, 1995
3081	GR	F153KGS	Volvo B10M-56	Plaxton Derwent II	B54F	1988	Buffalo, Flitwick, 1995
3089	HI	L133HVS	Volvo B10B-58	Alexander Strider	B51F	1993	Buffalo, Flitwick, 1995

3091-3098 Dennis Dart 9.8SDL3004 Carlyle Dartline B40F 1991 London Country NW, 1991

3091	HA	H922LOX	3094	HA	H926LOX	3096	HA	H243MUK	3098	HA	H245MUK
3093	AY	H925LOX									

3099	AY	K447XPA	Dennis Dart 9.8SDL3017	Plaxton Pointer	B40F	1992	Buffalo, Flitwick, 1995
3100	HA	K448XPA	Dennis Dart 9.8SDL3017	Plaxton Pointer	B40F	1992	Buffalo, Flitwick, 1995
3101	AY	L460NMJ	Dennis Dart 9.8SDL3035	Plaxton Pointer	B40F	1994	Lucky Bus, Watford, 1997
3102	GR	L200BUS	Dennis Dart 9.8SDL3035	Plaxton Pointer	B40F	1994	Lucky Bus, Watford, 1997
3103	HA	L300BUS	Dennis Dart 9SDL3031	Marshall C36	B34F	1994	Lucky Bus, Watford, 1997
3104	AY	L400BUS	Dennis Dart 9SDL3031	Marshall C36	B34F	1994	Lucky Bus, Watford, 1997

3105-3136 Volvo B6-9.9M Northern Counties Paladin N40F 1994

3105	HI	L305HPP	3113	HI	L313HPP	3121	LU	M721OMJ	3129	HI	M729OMJ
3106	HI	L306HPP	3114	HI	L314HPP	3122	LU	M722OMJ	3130	HI	M730OMJ
3107	HI	L307HPP	3115	HW	L315HPP	3123	u	M723OMJ	3131	HI	M711OMJ
3108	HI	L308HPP	3116	HW	L316HPP	3124	HI	M724OMJ	3132	HI	M712OMJ
3109	HI	L309HPP	3117	AY	M717OMJ	3125	HI	M725OMJ	3133	HI	M713OMJ
3110	HW	L310HPP	3118	AY	M718OMJ	3126	HI	M726OMJ	3134	HI	M714OMJ
3111	HI	L311HPP	3119	AY	M719OMJ	3127	HI	M727OMJ	3135	HI	M715OMJ
3112	HI	L312HPP	3120	LU	M720OMJ	3128	HI	M728OMJ	3136	HI	M716OMJ

3137	AY	L43MEH	Volvo B6-9.9M	Plaxton Pointer	B40F	1994	Stevensons, 1994
3138	HW	L922LJO	Volvo B6-9.9M	Northern Counties Paladin	B40F	1994	Yellow Bus, Stoke Mandeville
3139	HW	L923LJO	Volvo B6-9.9M	Northern Counties Paladin	B40F	1994	Yellow Bus, Stoke Mandeville

New to Lucky Bus, Dennis Dart 3104, L400BUS features the Marshall C36 body. When photographed, it was operating the service from Aylesbury where the vehicle is based. *Richard Godfrey*

3143-3149 Scania L113CRL East Lancs European N51F 1995

3143	LU	N693EUR	3145	HW	N695EUR	3147	LU	N697EUR	3149	LU	N699EUR
3144	HW	N694EUR	3146	HW	N696EUR	3148	LU	N698EUR			

3151-3166 Scania L113CRL East Lancs European NC47F 1995

3151	HH	N701EUR	3155	HH	N705EUR	3159	HH	N709EUR	3163	HW	N713EUR
3152	HH	N702EUR	3156	HH	N706EUR	3160	HH	N710EUR	3164	AY	N714EUR
3153	HH	N703EUR	3157	HH	N707EUR	3161	HH	N711EUR	3165	AY	N715EUR
3154	HH	N704EUR	3158	HW	N708EUR	3162	HH	N712EUR	3166	AY	N716EUR

3167	LU	N28KGS	Scania L113CRL	East Lancs European	N51F	1996
3168	LU	N29KGS	Scania L113CRL	East Lancs European	N51F	1996
3169	HW	N31KGS	Scania L113CRL	East Lancs European	N51F	1996
3170	LU	N32KGS	Scania L113CRL	East Lancs European	N51F	1996
3171	HH	P671OPP	Dennis Dart SLF	East Lancs Flyte	N41F	1996
3172	AY	P672OPP	Dennis Dart SLF	East Lancs Flyte	N41F	1996
3173	HH	P673OPP	Dennis Dart SLF	East Lancs Flyte	N41F	1996
3174	HA	P674OPP	Dennis Dart SLF	East Lancs Flyte	N41F	1996

3175-3190 Dennis Dart SLF Plaxton Pointer N39F* 1997 *3175-8 are N41F

3175	HH	P175SRO	3179	GR	P179SRO	3183	GR	P183SRO	3187	GR	P187SRO
3176	HH	P176SRO	3180	GR	P180SRO	3184	GR	P184SRO	3188	GR	P188SRO
3177	HH	P177SRO	3181	GR	P181SRO	3185	GR	P185SRO	3189	GR	P189SRO
3178	AY	P178SRO	3182	GR	P182SRO	3186	GR	P186SRO	3190	GR	P190SRO

3191-3205 Scania L113CRL Northern Counties Paladin N51F* 1997 *3196-9,3201-5 are NC47F

3191	LU	R191RBM	3195	LU	R195RBM	3199	LU	R199RBM	3203	AY	R203RBM
3192	LU	R192RBM	3196	HI	R196RBM	3201	HI	R201RBM	3204	AY	R204RBM
3193	LU	R193RBM	3197	HI	R197RBM	3202	HI	R202RBM	3205	AY	R205RBM
3194	LU	R194RBM	3198	LU	R198RBM						

Arriva operate just five Alexander Dash buses, all ordered for Scotland fleet and based on the Volvo B6. Three are now with The Shires, the remaining pair with Southern Counties. Pictured passing through Chesham, 3243, M843DDS highlights the 'v' windscreen treatment of the model. *Richard Godfrey*

3206-3215 — Dennis Dart SLF — Plaxton Pointer — N31F — 1997-98

3206	GR	R206GMJ	3209	GR	R209GMJ	3212	GR	R212GMJ	3214	GR	R214GMJ
3207	GR	R207GMJ	3210	GR	R210GMJ	3213	GR	R213GMJ	3215	HH	R215GMJ
3208	GR	R208GMJ	3211	GR	R211GMJ						

3216-3229 — Dennis Dart SLF — Plaxton Pointer 2 — N39F* — 1998-98 — *seating varies

3216	HH	S216XPP	3219	HI	T219NMJ	3228	HH	T828NMJ	3229	HH	T829NMJ
3217	HH	S217XPP	3227	HI	T827NMJ						

3230-3239 — Dennis Dart SLF — Plaxton Pointer MPD — N29F — 1999-2000

3230	HA	V230HBH	3233	HH	V233HBH	3236	HH	V236HBH	3238	HH	V238HBH
3231	HA	V231HBH	3234	HH	V234HBH	3237	HH	V237HBH	3239	HH	V239HBH
3232	HH	V232HBH	3235	HH	V235HBH						

3242	HW	M842DDS	Volvo B6-9.9	Alexander Dash	B45F	1993	Scotland West, 1998
3243	HW	M843DDS	Volvo B6-9.9	Alexander Dash	B45F	1993	Scotland West, 1998
3244	HW	M844DDS	Volvo B6-9.9	Alexander Dash	B45F	1993	Scotland West, 1998

3250-3260 — Volvo B6BLE — Wright Crusader 2 — N40F* — 1999 — *3258-60 are N33D

3250	HA	V250HBH	3253	HA	V253HBH	3256	HA	V256HBH	3259	GR	V259HBH
3251	HA	V251HBH	3254	HA	V254HBH	3257	HA	V257HBH	3260	GR	V260HBH
3252	HA	V252HBH	3255	HA	V255HBH	3258	GR	V258HBH			

3261-3268 — Volvo B10BLE — Wright Renown — N44F — 1999

3261	LU	V261HBH	3263	LU	V263HBH	3265	LU	V265HBH	3267	LU	V267HBH
3262	LU	V262HBH	3264	LU	V264HBH	3266	LU	V266HBH	3268	LU	V268HBH

3269	GR	T493KGB	DAF DE02GCSB220 LPG	Plaxton Prestige	N42F	1999	Arriva Scotland West, 2000

3270-3276 — DAF DE02GCSB220 LPG — Plaxton Prestige — N39F — 1999

3270	GR	V270HBH	3272	GR	V272HBH	3274	GR	V274HBH	3276	GR	V276HBH
3271	GR	V271HBH	3273	GR	V273HBH	3275	GR	V275HBH			

As new low-floor buses arrive, many well-known models of bus are now heading for extinction from the major fleets. As we go to press just one Leyland National and one Lynx remain with The Shires. High Wycombe is the location for this view of the last Lynx, 3345, H255GEV. *Richard Godfrey*

3277	GR	T491KGB	DAF DE02GSSB220 LPG	Plaxton Prestige	N42F	1999	Arriva Scotland West, 2000
3278	GR	T492KGB	DAF DE02GSSB220 LPG	Plaxton Prestige	N42F	1999	Arriva Scotland West, 2000
3279	GR	T495KGB	DAF DE02GSSB220 LPG	Plaxton Prestige	N42F	1999	Arriva Scotland West, 2000

3280-3297   Dennis Dart SLF   Plaxton Pointer MPD   N29F   1999-2000

3280	LU	V280HBH	3285	LU	V285HBH	3290	LU	V290HBH	3294	HI	V294HBH
3281	LU	V281HBH	3286	LU	V286HBH	3291	LU	V291HBH	3295	GR	X295MBH
3282	LU	V282HBH	3287	LU	V287HBH	3292	LU	V292HBH	3296	GR	X296MBH
3283	LU	V283HBH	3288	LU	V288HBH	3293	HI	V293HBH	3297	GR	X297MBH
3284	LU	V284HBH	3289	LU	V289HBH						

3324	GR	E564BNK	Volvo B10M-56	Plaxton Derwent II	B54F	1988	Sampsons, Hoddesdon, 1989
3329	u	K760JVX	DAF SB220LC550	Optare Delta	B49F	1992	West's, Woodford Green, 1997
3334	HA	L124YVK	Dennis Dart 9SDL3034	Northern Counties Paladin	B35F	1994	Arriva London, 2003
3345	HW	H255GEV	Leyland Lynx LX2R11C15Z4S	Leyland Lynx	B49F	1990	
3352	HA	J402XVX	Dennis Dart 9.8SDL3012	Wright Handybus	B40F	1992	
3353	HA	J403XVX	Dennis Dart 9.8SDL3012	Wright Handybus	B40F	1992	
3354	AY	J404XVX	Dennis Dart 9.8SDL3012	Wright Handybus	B40F	1992	

3355-3364   Dennis Dart 9.8SDL3017   Plaxton Pointer   B40F   1993

3355	u	K405FHJ	3358	HA	K408FHJ	3361	GR	K411FHJ	3363	HA	K413FHJ
3356	HA	K406FHJ	3359	HA	K409FHJ	3362	HA	K412FHJ	3364	HA	K414FHJ
3357	HA	K407FHJ	3360	HA	K410FHJ						

3365	HW	L415NHJ	Dennis Dart 9.8SDL3025	Wright Handybus	B40F	1994	
3366	HA	J64BJN	Dennis Dart 9SDL3012	Wright Handybus	BC40F	1992	West's, Woodford Green, 1997
3367	HA	J65BJN	Dennis Dart 9SDL3011	Wright Handybus	B35F	1992	West's, Woodford Green, 1997

3368-3372   Dennis Dart 9SDL3011   Plaxton Pointer   B35F   1992

3368	HA	K318CVX	3369	HA	K319CVX	3371	HA	K321CVX	3372	HA	K322CVX

3374	AY	K761JVX	Dennis Dart 9SDL3017	Wright Handybus	B40F	1992	West's, Woodford Green, 1997
3375	AY	K762JVX	Dennis Dart 9SDL3017	Wright Handybus	B40F	1992	West's, Woodford Green, 1997
3376	AY	M266VPU	Dennis Lance SLF	Wright Pathfinder	N40F	1994	

3377	AY	M267VPU	Dennis Lance SLF	Wright Pathfinder	N40F	1994	
3378	u	M268VPU	Dennis Lance SLF	Wright Pathfinder	N40F	1994	
3385	GR	M951LYR	Dennis Dart 9.8SDL3040	Plaxton Pointer	B40F	1995	Grey Green, 1996
3386	HI	P256FPK	Dennis Dart SLF	Plaxton Pointer	N39F	1997	
3398	WR	L118YVK	Dennis Dart 9SDL3034	Northern Counties Paladin	B35F	1994	Arriva London, 2003
3399	WR	L119YVK	Dennis Dart 9SDL3034	Northern Counties Paladin	B35F	1994	Arriva London, 2003
3413	WR	P833HVX	Dennis Dart	Plaxton Pointer	B34F	1996	
3414	HA	P334HVX	Dennis Dart	Plaxton Pointer	B34F	1996	
3416	WR	R416HVX	Dennis Dart SLF	Wright Crusader	N41F	1998	
3417	WR	R417HVX	Dennis Dart SLF	Wright Crusader	N41F	1998	
3418	WR	R418HVX	Dennis Dart SLF	Wright Crusader	N41F	1998	
3435	HA	R165GNW	Dennis Dart SLF	Wright Crusader	N36F	1997	
3439	HA	R169GNW	Dennis Dart SLF	Wright Crusader	N36F	1997	
3440	HA	R170GNW	Dennis Dart SLF	Wright Crusader	N36F	1997	

3441-3449

DAF DE02GSSB220 — Plaxton Prestige — NC37F — 1997

3441	WR	R201VPU	**3444**	WR	R204VPU	**3446**	HA	R206VPU	**3448**	HA	R208VPU
3442	WR	R202VPU	**3445**	HA	R205VPU	**3447**	HA	R207VPU	**3449**	HA	R209VPU
3443	WR	R203VPU									

3452-3459

Volvo B10BLE — Alexander ALX300 — N44F — 2000

| 3452 | HI | W452XKX | **3454** | HI | W454XKX | **3458** | HI | W458XKX | **3459** | HI | W459XKX |
| 3453 | HI | W453XKX | **3457** | HI | W457XKX | | | | | | |

3461-3481

Dennis Dart SLF — Alexander ALX200 — N26D — 2000

3461	HA	W461XKX	**3466**	HA	W466XKX	**3472**	HA	W472XKX	**3477**	HA	W477XKX
3462	HA	W462XKX	**3467**	HA	W467XKX	**3473**	HA	W473XKX	**3478**	HA	W478XKX
3463	HA	W463XKX	**3468**	HA	W468XKX	**3474**	HA	W474XKX	**3479**	HA	W479XKX
3464	HA	W464XKX	**3469**	HA	W469XKX	**3475**	HA	W475XKX	**3481**	HA	W481XKX
3465	HA	W465XKX	**3471**	HA	W471XKX	**3476**	HA	W476XKX			

3482-3498

Dennis Dart SLF — Plaxton Pointer MPD — N39F — 2000

3482	HW	W482XKX	**3486**	AY	W486XKX	**3491**	HI	W491YGS	**3495**	HI	W495YGS
3483	WR	W483XKX	**3487**	AY	W487XKX	**3492**	AY	W492YGS	**3496**	HI	W496YGS
3484	AY	W484XKX	**3488**	LU	W488XKX	**3493**	HI	W493YGS	**3497**	AY	W497YGS
3485	AY	W485XKX	**3489**	LU	W489XKX	**3494**	HI	W494YGS	**3498**	HI	W498YGS

3500	GR	KE51PSZ	Dennis Dart SLF 8.8m	Alexander Pointer MPD	N28F	2001	
3501	GR	KE51PTO	Dennis Dart SLF 8.8m	Alexander Pointer MPD	N28F	2001	
3502	GR	KE51PTU	Dennis Dart SLF 8.8m	Alexander Pointer MPD	N28F	2001	
3503	GR	KS51KOH	Peugeot Expert	Crystals	M8	2001	Operated for Hertfordshire CC
3504	GR	KS51KOE	Peugeot Expert	Crystals	M8	2001	Operated for Hertfordshire CC
3505	GR	KS51KPG	Peugeot Expert	Crystals	M8	2001	Operated for Hertfordshire CC
3509	GR	KE51PTX	Dennis Dart SLF 8.8m	Alexander Pointer MPD	N28F	2001	

3811-3815

Dennis Dart 8.5SDL3003 — Wright Handybus — B30F — 1991 — Wycombe Bus, 2000

| 3811 | HW | G554SGT | **3813** | HW | G560SGT | **3814** | HW | G570SGT | **3815** | HW | JDZ2353 |
| 3812 | u | G552SGT | | | | | | | | | |

3816-3820

Dennis Dart 8.5SDL3003 — Wright Handybus — B29F — 1991 — Wycombe Bus, 2000

| 3816 | u | H881BGN | **3818** | HA | H368XGC | **3819** | AY | H369XGC | **3820** | AY | H370XGC |
| 3817 | HA | H367XGC | | | | | | | | | |

3821-3827

Dennis Dart SLF — Plaxton Pointer 2 — N36F — 1996 — Wycombe Bus, 2000

| 3821 | HW | N521MJO | **3823** | AY | N523MJO | **3825** | HW | P525YJO | **3827** | HW | P527YJO |
| 3822 | HW | N522MJO | **3824** | HW | N524MJO | **3826** | HW | P526YJO | | | |

3830	WR	KE04CZF	VDL Bus SB120	Wrightbus Cadet	N35F	2004	
3831	WR	KE04CZG	VDL Bus SB120	Wrightbus Cadet	N35F	2004	
3832	WR	KE04CZH	VDL Bus SB120	Wrightbus Cadet	N35F	2004	
3833	AY	M503VJO	Dennis Dart 9SDL3054	Marshall C37	B38F	1995	Wycombe Bus, 2000
3834	AY	M504VJO	Dennis Dart 9SDL3054	Marshall C37	B38F	1995	Wycombe Bus, 2000
3837	HW	KE53NEU	TransBus Dart 8.8m	TransBus Mini Pointer	N29F	2004	
3838	HW	KE53NFA	TransBus Dart 8.8m	TransBus Mini Pointer	N29F	2004	
3839	HW	KE53NFC	TransBus Dart 8.8m	TransBus Mini Pointer	N29F	2004	

3841-3855

Volvo B10B — Plaxton Verde — B51F — 1995-96 — Wycombe Bus, 2000

| 3841 | HW | N621FJO | **3843** | HW | N623FJO | **3853** | HW | N415NRG | **3855** | HW | N415NRG |
| 3842 | HW | N622FJO | **3844** | HW | N624FJO | **3854** | HW | N414NRG | | | |

| 4015 | GR | HIL7595 | Volvo B10M-61 | Plaxton Paramount 3500 III | C53F | 1988 | Moor-Dale, 1994 |
| 4016 | GR | SIB4846 | Leyland Tiger TRCTL11/3ARZA | Plaxton Paramount 3200 III | C53F | 1988 | London Country NW, 1990 |

During 2002 The Shires' Colchester and Southend operations were transferred to Southern Counties management. During the change a batch of DAF SB120s with 9.4m Wrightbus Cadet bodies was in build. Pictured at Stevenage, 4518, KL52CWK is seen heading for Hertford. In the Autumn of 2003, a reorganisation within VDL saw a name change, with DAF Bus chassis now being known as VDL Bus; and the bodybuilders Berkhof and Jonckheere now known as VDL Berkhof and VDL Jonckheere. *Richard Godfrey*

4020	GR	SIB7480	Leyland Tiger TRCTL11/3ARZA	Plaxton Paramount 3200 III	C51F	1988	London Country NW, 1990
4023	GR	E323OMG	Leyland Tiger TRCTL11/3ARZA	Plaxton Paramount 3200 III	C53F	1988	London Country NW, 1990
4025	GR	SIB8529	Leyland Tiger TRCTL11/3ARZA	Plaxton Paramount 3500 III	C51FT	1988	London Country NW, 1990
4026	GR	SIB7481	Leyland Tiger TRCTL11/3ARZA	Plaxton Paramount 3500 III	C51FT	1988	London Country NW, 1990
4028	GR	MIL2350	Dennis Javelin 12SDA1919	Duple 320	C57F	1990	Lucky Bus, Watford, 1997
4035	GR	H199AOD	Volvo B10M-60	Plaxton Expressliner	C46FT	1996	Trathens, Plymouth, 1996
4037	GR	P100LOW	Dennis Javelin	UVG Unistar	C55FTL	1996	Lucky Bus, Watford, 1997
4040	GR	YIB2396	Volvo B10M-61	Plaxton Paramount 3200 II	C53F	1986	Checker, Garston, 1997
4043	u	YIB2397	Leyland Tiger TRCTL11/3RZ	Duple 320	C57F	1987	Checker, Garston, 1997

4047-4054

			DAF DE33WSSB3000	Plaxton Prima Interurban	C53F	1997	
4047	HH	R447SKX	4049 HH R449SKX	4051 LU R451SKX	4053 LU R453SKX		
4048	HH	R448SKX	4050 LU R450SKX	4052 LU R452SKX	4054 LU R454SKX		

4057-4063

			DAF SB3000WS601	Van Hool Alizée HE	C53F*	1994-95	London North East, 1998
							*4057/8 are C51F
4057	HH	M947LYR	4059 HH M942LYR	4061 HH M949LYR	4063 HH M943LYR		
4058	HH	M946LYR	4060 HH M948LYR				

4325-4333

			Volvo B10M-60	Plaxton Paramount 3200 III	C53F	1989-91	Express Travel, 1995
4325	GR	F425UVW	4327 GR F467UVW	4332 GR H567MPD	4333 GR H845AHS		

4359-4369

			DAF DE33WSSB3000	Plaxton Prima Interurban	C53F	2000	
4359	LU	W359XKX	4363 LU W363XKX	4366 LU W366XKX	4368 LU W368XKX		
4361	LU	W361XKX	4364 LU W364XKX	4367 LU W367XKX	4369 LU W369XKX		
4362	LU	W362XKX	4365 LU W365XKX				

4370	u	D196WJC	Leyland Tiger TRCTL11/3RZ	Plaxton Paramount 3200 II	C49F	1987	Arriva North West & Wales, 2004
4371	GR	J26UNY	Leyland Tiger TRCL10/3ARZM	Plaxton 321	C53F	1992	Arriva Southern Counties, 2004
4400	GR	H616UWR	Volvo B10M-60	Plaxton Paramount 3500 III	C50F	1991	Arrive Southern Counties, 2002
4426	GR	S426MCC	DAF DE02GSSN220	Plaxton Prestige	N42F	1999	Arriva North West, 2003
4427	GR	S427MCC	DAF DE02GSSN220	Plaxton Prestige	N42F	1999	Arriva North West, 2003
4429	GR	S429MCC	DAF DE02GSSN220	Plaxton Prestige	N42F	1999	Arriva North West, 2003
4490	GR	T490KGB	DAF DE02GSSB220	Plaxton Prestige	N42F	1999	Arriva Scotland, 2002
4491	GR	T494KGB	DAF DE02GSSB220	Plaxton Prestige	N42F	1999	Arriva Scotland, 2002

4514-4518 — DAF DE12CSSB120 9.4m — Wrightbus Cadet — N35F — 2002

4514	GR	KE51PVF	4516	HI	KE51PVK	4517	HI	KL52CWJ	4518	HI	KL52CWK
4515	GR	KE51PVZ									

4519-4525 — VDL Bus DE12CSSB120 9.4m — Wrightbus Cadet — N35F — 2003

4519	HI	KE03OUN	4521	WR	KE03OUS	4523	HH	KE03OUK	4525	HI	KE03OUM
4520	HI	KE03OUP	4522	WR	KE03OUU	4524	HH	KE03OUL			

5000	LU	BKE847T	Bristol VRT/SL3/6LXB	Eastern Coach Works	B43/31F	1979	Maidstone & District, 1997
5033	LU	SNV933W	Bristol VRT/SL3/6LXB	Eastern Coach Works	B43/31F	1980	United Counties, 1986

5084-5094 — Leyland Olympian ONCL10/1RZ — Alexander RL — B47/32F* — 1988 — *5091 is BC47/29F

5084	LU	F634LMJ	5089	LU	F639LMJ	5091	LU	F641LMJ	5093	LU	F643LMJ
5086	LU	F636LMJ	5090	LU	F640LMJ	5092	LU	F642LMJ	5094	LU	F644LMJ
5087	LU	F637LMJ									

5095-5107 — Leyland Olympian ON2R50C13Z4 — Alexander RL — B47/32F — 1989-90 — *5104 is BC47/29F
5099-5103 are B47/34F

5095	LU	G645UPP	5099	AY	G649UPP	5102	AY	G652UPP	5105	LU	G655UPP
5096	LU	G646UPP	5100	AY	G650UPP	5103	AY	G653UPP	5106	LU	G656UPP
5097	AY	G647UPP	5101	AY	G651UPP	5104	AY	G654UPP	5107	LU	G657UPP
5098	LU	G648UPP									

5108	AY	F506OYW	Leyland Olympian ONTL11/1RH	Northern Counties	B47/30F	1988	Yellow Bus, Stoke Mandeville
5109	HW	G129YEV	Leyland Olympian ONCL10/2RZ	Northern Counties	B49/33F	1989	London Country NW, 1990
5110	HW	G130YEV	Leyland Olympian ONCL10/2RZ	Northern Counties	B49/33F	1989	London Country NW, 1990

5113-5125 — Leyland Olympian ONCL10/1RZ — Leyland — B47/31F — 1989-90 — London Country NW, 1990

5113	GR	G283UMJ	5118	GR	G288UMJ	5121	GR	G291UMJ	5123	GR	G293UMJ
5116	GR	G286UMJ	5120	HW	G290UMJ	5122	HW	G292UMJ	5124	HW	G294UMJ
5117	GR	G287UMJ									

5126-5129 — Leyland Olympian ON2R50C13Z4 — Leyland — B47/31F — 1991

5126	HW	H196GRO	5127	HW	H197GRO	5128	HW	H198GRO	5129	HW	H199GRO

5130	HW	F747XCS	Leyland Olympian ONCL10/1RZ	Alexander RL	B47/32F	1989	A1 Service (McMenemy), 1995
5132	HW	H202GRO	Leyland Olympian ON2R50C13Z4	Leyland	B47/31F	1991	
5133	HW	H203GRO	Leyland Olympian ON2R50C13Z4	Leyland	B47/31F	1991	
5134	HW	G131YWC	Leyland Olympian ONCL10/2RZ	Northern Counties	B49/33F	1989	Ensign, Purfleet, 1991
5135	HW	G132YWC	Leyland Olympian ONCL10/2RZ	Northern Counties	B49/33F	1989	London Country NW, 1990

5136-5145 — Volvo Olympian YN2RV18Z4 — Northern Counties Palatine — B47/30F — 1996

5136	LU	N36JPP	5139	LU	N39JPP	5142	LU	N42JPP	5144	LU	N35JPP
5137	LU	N37JPP	5140	LU	N46JPP	5143	LU	N43JPP	5145	LU	N45JPP
5138	LU	N38JPP	5141	LU	N41JPP						

5146-5161 — Volvo Olympian — Northern Counties Palatine II — BC39/29F — 1998

5146	GR	S146KNK	5150	GR	S150KNK	5154	GR	S154KNK	5159	AY	S159KNK
5147	HH	S147KNK	5151	GR	S151KNK	5156	AY	S156KNK	5160	AY	S160KNK
5148	HH	S148KNK	5152	HH	S152KNK	5157	u	S157KNK	5161	AY	S161KNK
5149	GR	S149KNK	5153	GR	S153KNK	5158	AY	S158KNK			

5165	LU	EWW544Y	Leyland Olympian ONLXB/1R	Eastern Coach Works	B45/32F	1983	Yorkshire, 1998
5170	LU	B605UUM	Leyland Olympian ONLXB/1R	Eastern Coach Works	B45/32F	1983	Yorkshire, 1998
5381	LU	MUH281X	Leyland Olympian ONLXB/1R	Eastern Coach Works	B45/32F	1982	Rhondda, 1992

5421-5433 — Dennis Trident — Alexander ALX400 — N47/31F — 2000

5421	LU	W421XKX	5424	LU	W424XKX	5427	LU	W427XKX	5431	LU	W431XKX
5422	LU	W422XKX	5425	LU	W425XKX	5428	LU	W428XKX	5432	LU	W432XKX
5423	LU	W423XKX	5426	LU	W426XKX	5429	LU	W429XKX	5433	LU	W433XKX

5825-5829 — Leyland Olympian ONLXB/1RH — Alexander RH — B47/26D — 1988 — Wycombe Bus, 2000

5825	HW	E225CFC	5826	u	E226CFC	5828	HW	E228CFC	5829	HW	E229CFC

5830-5835 — Leyland Olympian ON2R50G16Z4 — Alexander RH — B47/29F — 1990 — Wycombe Bus, 2000

5830	AY	G230VWL	5832	AY	G232VWL	5834	HW	G234VWL	5835	LU	G235VWL
5831	HW	G231VWL									

Route branding for the Oxford to Aylesbury service 280 is shown on Olympian 5160, S160KNK. This carries a Northern Counties Palatine II body and is one of six allocated to the route. *Mark Lyons*

5836-5856

Leyland Olympian ONLXB/1RH   Eastern Coach Works   B42/26D   1986-87   Arriva London, 2003

5836	WR	WLT916	5842	WR	D146FYM	5847	WR	D224FYM	5852	u	-	
5837	WR	D187FYM	5843	WR	D242FYM	5848	u	-	5853	HW	D166FYM	
5838	WR	C38CHM	5844	WR	D211FYM	5849	WR	C31CHM	5854	HW	D167FYM	
5839	WR	D181FYM	5845	WR	D231FYM	5850	WR	C59CHM	5855	HW	D168FYM	
5840	WR	815DYE	5846	WR	D240FYM	5851	WR	C36CHM	5856	HW	D169FYM	
5841	WR	D203FYM										

5866	LU	FKM866V	Bristol VRT/SL3/6LXB	Eastern Coach Works	B43/31F	1979	Maidstone & District, 1997

6000-6024

DAF DE02PSDB250   Alexander ALX400   N45/20D   2002-03

6000	GR	KL52CWN	6007	GR	KL52CWW	6013	GR	KL52CXE	6019	GR	KL52CXM
6001	GR	KL52CWO	6008	GR	KL52CWZ	6014	GR	KL52CXF	6020	GR	KL52CXN
6002	GR	KL52CWP	6009	GR	KL52CXA	6015	GR	KL52CXG	6021	GR	KL52CXO
6003	GR	KL52CWR	6010	GR	KL52CXB	6016	GR	KL52CXH	6022	GR	KL52CXP
6004	GR	KL52CWT	6011	GR	KL52CXC	6017	GR	KL52CXJ	6023	GR	KL52CXR
6005	GR	KL52CWU	6012	GR	KL52CXD	6018	GR	KL52CXK	6024	GR	KL52CXS
6006	GR	KL52CWV									

Special event vehicle:

5301	LU	JHK495N	Leyland Atlantean AN68/1R	Eastern Coach Works	O43/31F	1975	

Ancillary vehicles:

1171	R823CNB	Ford Transit	Ford	M12	1997	
1251	P137MTU	LDV Convoy	LDV	M16	1996	
1252	P697UFR	LDV Convoy	LDV	M16	1996	
2235	N935ETU	Iveco TurboDaily 59-12	Mellor	TV	1995	Cymru, 1998
2236	N936ETU	Iveco TurboDaily 59-12	Mellor	TV	1995	Cymru, 1998
2346	M726UTW	Iveco TurboDaily 59.12	Marshall C31	TV	1994	
3067	H407ERO	Leyland Lynx LX2R11C15Z4S	Leyland Lynx	TV	1990	
3072	F402PUR	Leyland Lynx LX112L10ZR1R	Leyland Lynx	B51F	1989	
3074	F404PUR	Leyland Lynx LX112L10ZR1R	Leyland Lynx	B51F	1989	
3087	G97VMM	Leyland Swift LBM6T/2RS	Wadham Stringer Vanguard II	TV	1989	London Country NW, 199

Arriva The Shires operate a batch of DAF DB250s with Alexander ALX400 bodywork on Transport for London (TfL) routes. Number 6006, KL52CWV was photographed outside Bushey Hall School while operating route 142. *Richard Godfrey*

3315	A855UYM	Volvo B10M-61	East Lancs (1992)	TV	1984	Grey Green, 1997
3316	A856UYM	Volvo B10M-61	East Lancs (1992)	TV	1984	Grey Green, 1997
3321	B861XYR	Volvo B10M-61	East Lancs (1992)	TV	1985	Grey Green, 1997
3325	E565BNK	Volvo B10M-56	Plaxton Derwent II	TV	1988	Sampsons, Hoddesdon, 1989
3328	G621YMG	DAF SB220LC550	Optare Delta	TV	1989	West's, Woodford Green, 1997
3335	H350PNO	Leyland Swift LBM6T/2RS	Wadham Stringer Vanguard	TV	1991	West's, Woodford Green, 1997
3344	H254GEV	Leyland Lynx LX2R11C15Z4S	Leyland Lynx	B49F	1990	
4036	L500BUS	Iveco 480-10-21	Wadham Stringer	TV	1995	Lucky Bus, Watford, 1997
4038	ADZ4731	Volvo B10M-56	Plaxton Viewmaster IV Exp	TV	1982	
4039	WIB1113	Volvo B10M-61	Plaxton Paramount 3200 II	TV	1985	Checker, Garston, 1997
4310	A250SVW	Leyland Tiger TRCTL11/3RP	Duple Caribbean	C57F	1984	Arriva Southern Counties, 2004

Previous Registrations:

ADZ4731	KNP3X		
D196WJC	D900STU, NEY819	L500BUS	M289OUR
F425UVW	F449PSL, NXI9004	MIL2350	G171BLH
F467UVW	F450PSL, NXI9005	SIB4846	E321OMG
H350PNO	H550AMT, A19BUS, H20BUS	SIB7480	E325OMG
H567MPD	H842AHS, NXI9001	SIB7481	E326OMG
HIL7595	E663UNE	SIB8529	E324OMG
J64BJN	J9BUS	WIB1113	B504CGP
J65BJN	J6BUS	YIB2396	C510LGH
J65UNA	J59MHF, J6SLT	YIB2397	D296RKW

Allocations

Aylesbury (Smeaton Close, Brunel Park) - AY

Outstation - Leighton Buzzard

Alero	454	455	456					
Mercedes-Benz	2114	2127	2176	2240	2244	2247	2416	2417
Optare Solo	446	447	448	449				
Dart	3093	3099	3101	3104	3172	3178	3354	3374
	3375	3484	3485	3486	3487	3492	3497	3819
	3820	3823	3829	3833	3834			
Volvo B6	3117	3118	3119	3137				
Volvo B10M bus	3080							
Lance	3376	3377						
Scania sd	3164	3165	3166	3203	3204	3205		
Olympian	5097	5099	5100	5101	5102	5103	5104	5108
	5156	5158	5159	5160	5161	5828	5829	5830
	5832							

Harlow (Fourth Avenue) - HA

Outstation - Langston Road, Debden

Mercedes-Benz Vito	1257							
Optare Alero	0443	0444						
Mercedes-Benz	2116	2118	2119	2120	2121	2122	2123	2124
	2125	2126	2138	2139	2140	2143	2145	2151
	2158	2159	2172	2175	2189	2190	2194	2195
	2248	2370	2371					
Dart	3091	3094	3096	3098	3100	3103	3174	3230
	3231	3334	3352	3353	3356	3357	3358	3359
	3360	3362	3363	3364	3366	3367	3368	3369
	3371	3372	3413	3414	3435	3439	3440	3461
	3462	3463	3464	3465	3466	3467	3468	3469
	3471	3472	3473	3474	3475	3476	3477	3478
	3479	3481	3817	3818				
Volvo B6	3250	3251	3252	3253	3254	3255	3256	3257
DAF Prestige	3445	3446	3447	3448	3449			

Hemel Hempstead (Whiteleaf Road) - HH

Mercedes-Benz	2178	2179	2180	2181	2182	2183	2184	2185
	2241	2246	2249					
Dart	3171	3173	3175	3176	3177	3215	3216	3217
	3228	3229	3232	3233	3234	3235	3236	3237
	3238	3239	3835	3836				
DAF Cadet	4523	4524						
Scania sd	3151	3152	3153	3154	3155	3156	3157	3159
	3160	3161	3162					
DAF coach	4057	4058	4059	4060	4061	4063		
DAF Prima	4047	4048	4049					
Olympian	5126	5127	5128	5147	5148	5152		

Henley-on-Thames is the location for this view of Volvo B10B 3842, N622FJO. One of seven acquired with the Wycombe Bus business from Go-Ahead, they are the only examples of the Verde on Volvo chassis with the group. *John Marsh*

High Wycombe (Newlands bus station) - HW

Outstation: Old Amersham

Mercedes-Benz	2171	2196	2197	2198				
Solo	0442							
Dart	3365	3482	3811	3813	3814	3815	3821	3822
	3824	3825	3826	3827	3837	3838	3839	
Volvo B6	3110	3115	3116	3126	3127	3138	3139	3242
	3243	3244						
Lynx	3345							
Volvo B10B	3841	3842	3843	3844	3853	3854	3855	
Scania sd	3144	3145	3146	3158	3163	3169		
Olympian	5109	5110	5120	5122	5124	5129	5130	5132
	5133	5134	5135	5825	5831	5834	5853	5854
	5855	5856						

Hitchin (Fishponds Road) - HI

Outstation: Norton Green Road, Stevenage

Mercedes-Benz	2105	2106	2107	2113	2141	2142	2144	2146
	2147	2148	2149	2150	2152	2153	2154	2155
	2156	2157	2160	2161	2162	2177		
Dart	3219	3227	3293	3294	3386	3491	3493	3494
	3495	3496	3498					
Volvo B6	3105	3106	3107	3108	3109	3111	3112	3113
	3114	3128	3129					
DAF Cadet	4516	4517	4518	4519	4520	4525		
Volvo B10B	3089	3452	3453	3454	3457	3458	3459	
Scania sd	3196	3197	3201	3202				

Luton (Dunstable Road) - LU

Mercedes-Benz	2128	2129	2131	2132	2133	2136	2224	2415
Dart	3280	3281	3282	3283	3284	3285	3286	3287
	3288	3289	3290	3291	3292	3488	3489	
Volvo B6	3120	3121	3122	3124	3125	3130	3131	3132
	3133	3134	3135	3136				
DAF suburban	4050	4051	4052	4053	4054	4359	4361	4362
	4363	4364	4365	4366	4367	4368	4369	
Scania sd	3143	3147	3148	3149	3167	3168	3170	3191
	3192	3193	3194	3195	3198	3199		
Volvo B10BLE	3261	3262	3263	3264	3265	3266	3267	3268
Bristol VR	5000	5033	5866					
Olympian	5084	5086	5087	5089	5090	5091	5092	5093
	5094	5095	5096	5098	5105	5106	5107	5136
	5137	5138	5139	5140	5141	5142	5143	5144
	5145	5165	5170	5381	5835			
Trident	5421	5422	5423	5424	5425	5426	5427	5428
	5429	5431	5432	5433				

Ware (Marsh Lane) - WR

Outstation - Pindar Road, Hoddesdon

Mercedes-Benz	2373	2374	2375	2376	2377			
Dart	3334	3352	3398	3399	3413	3416	3417	3418
	3428	3441	3442	3443	3444	3483	3828	
DAF Cadet	3830	3831	3832	4521	4522			
Olympian	5836	5837	5838	5839	5840	5841	5842	5843
	5844	5845	5846	5847	5849	5850	5851	

Watford (St Albans Road, Garston) - GR - includes private hire fleet and Dial a Ride

Peugeot Expert	3503	3504	3505					
Mercedes-Benz	0218	0230	0245	0246	0256	0257	0258	0259
	0262	0263	0264	0265	0268	2166	2173	
Dart	3102	3179	3180	3181	3182	3183	3184	
	3185	3186	3187	3188	3189	3190	3206	3207
	3208	3209	3210	3211	3212	3213	3214	3295
	3296	3297	3361	3385	3500	3501	3502	3509
Volvo B6	3258	3259	3260					
DAF Cadet	4514	4515						
Volvo B10M bus	3079	3081	3324					
DAF Prestige	3269	3270	3271	3272	3273	3274	3275	3276
	3277	3278	3279	4426	4427	4428	4429	4490
	4491							
Volvo B10M coach	4015	4035	4040	4400	4325	4327	4332	4333
Tiger coach	4016	4020	4023	4025	4026	4371		
Javelin coach	4028	4037						
Olympian	5113	5116	5117	5118	5121	5123	5146	5149
	5150	5151	5153	5154				
DAF President	6000	6001	6002	6003	6004	6005	6006	6007
	6008	6009	6010	6011	6012	6013	6014	6015
	6016	6017	6018	6019	6020	6021	6022	6023
	6024							

Unallocated

Mercedes-Benz	2187	2242	2410	
Dart	3011	3355	3816	
Volvo B6	3123			
Tiger coach	4043	4370		
Lance	3378			
Lynx	3068	3069	3070	
DAF Delta	3329			
Olympian	5157	5826	5848	5852

ARRIVA LONDON

Arriva London North Ltd, 16 Watsons Road, Wood Green, London, N22 4TZ
Arriva London South Ltd, Croydon Bus Garage, Brighton Road, South Croydon, CR2 6EL

ADL1	BK	V701LWT	Dennis Dart SLF 10.2m			Alexander ALX200		N27D	1999		

ADL2-8			Dennis Dart SLF 10.2m			Alexander ALX200		N30D	2000		
2	EM	W602VGJ	4	EM	W604VGJ	6	EM	W606VGJ	8	EM	W608VGJ
3	EM	W603VGJ	5	EM	W605VGJ	7	EM	W607VGJ			

ADL9-23			Dennis Dart SLF 10.8m			Alexander ALX200		N33D	1999		
9	TC	V609LGC	13	TC	V613LGC	17	TC	V617LGC	21	TC	V621LGC
10	TC	V610LGC	14	TC	V614LGC	18	TC	V618LGC	22	TC	V622LGC
11	TC	V611LGC	15	TC	V615LGC	19	TC	V619LGC	23	TC	V623LGC
12	TC	V612LGC	16	TC	V616LGC	20	TC	V620LGC			

ADL969-983			Dennis Dart SLF 10.2m			Alexander ALX200		N27D	1998		
969	BK	S169JUA	973	BK	S173JUA	977	BK	S177JUA	981	BK	S181JUA
970	BK	S170JUA	974	BK	S174JUA	978	BK	S178JUA	982	BK	S182JUA
971	BK	S171JUA	975	BK	S175JUA	979	BK	S179JUA	983	BK	S183JUA
972	BK	S172JUA	976	BK	S176JUA	980	BK	S180JUA			

CW1	WN	W218CDN	DAF DE12CSSB120			Wright Cadet		N31D	2000		

For their London routes, Arriva conform to the 85% red rule with the adaptation of the corporate livery to red with a reduced area of cream. Alexander ALX200-bodied Dart V613LGC illustrates the scheme in Croydon as it heads for Caterham rail station. *Mark Doggett*

During the 1990s overall advertisements were particularly common on British buses, though their popularity in London declined following a requirement that they should not pass the Palace of Westminster. During London Fashion Week in 2004 several buses emerged with overall displays, including Arriva's DLA167, W367VGJ which carries the colours of Zandra Rhodes. *Richard Godfrey*

DDL1-18

Dennis Dart SLF 10.1m Plaxton Pointer 2 N26D 1998

1	TH	S301JUA	6	TH	S306JUA	11	TH	S311JUA	15	TH	S315JUA
2	TH	S302JUA	7	TH	S307JUA	12	TH	S312JUA	16	BK	S316JUA
3	TH	S303JUA	8	TH	S308JUA	13	TH	S313JUA	17	BK	S317JUA
4	TH	S304JUA	9	TH	S309JUA	14	TH	S314JUA	18	BK	S318JUA
5	TH	S305JUA	10	TH	S310JUA						

DI4	EC	P754RWU	DAF DE33WSSB3000	Ikarus Blue Danube 396	C53F	1997	Arriva E Herts & Essex, 1998
DI7	u	T110AUA	DAF DE33WSSB3000	Ikarus Blue Danube 350	C53F	1999	Teamdeck, Honley, 2004

DLA1-64

DAF DE02RSDB250 10.6m Alexander ALX400 N45/21D 1998-99

1	WN	R101GNW	17	CT	S217JUA	33	WN	S233JUA	49	TH	S249JUA
2	TH	S202JUA	18	CT	S218JUA	34	WN	S234JUA	50	TH	S250JUA
3	TH	S203JUA	19	CT	S219JUA	35	WN	S235JUA	51	TH	S251JUA
4	TH	S204JUA	20	CT	S220JUA	36	WN	S236JUA	52	TH	S252JUA
5	TH	S205JUA	21	CT	S221JUA	37	WN	S237JUA	53	TH	S253JUA
6	TH	S206JUA	22	WN	S322JUA	38	SF	S238JUA	54	TH	S254JUA
7	TH	S207JUA	23	WN	S223JUA	39	TH	S239JUA	55	TH	S255JUA
8	TH	S208JUA	24	WN	S224JUA	40	TH	S240JUA	56	TH	S256JUA
9	TH	S209JUA	25	WN	S225JUA	41	TH	S241JUA	57	TH	S257JUA
10	TH	S210JUA	26	WN	S226JUA	42	TH	S242JUA	58	TH	S258JUA
11	CT	S211JUA	27	WN	S227JUA	43	TH	S243JUA	59	TH	S259JUA
12	CT	S212JUA	28	WN	S228JUA	44	TH	S244JUA	60	TH	S260JUA
13	CT	S213JUA	29	WN	S229JUA	45	WN	S245JUA	61	TH	S261JUA
14	CT	S214JUA	30	WN	S230JUA	46	WN	S246JUA	62	TH	S262JUA
15	CT	S215JUA	31	WN	S231JUA	47	WN	S247JUA	63	TH	S263JUA
16	CT	S216JUA	32	WN	S232JUA	48	TH	S248JUA	64	TH	S264JUA

DLA65-92

DAF DE02RSDB250 10.6m Alexander ALX400 N45/19D 1999

65	WN	S265JUA	72	WN	S272JUA	79	WN	S279JUA	86	WN	S286JUA
66	WN	S266JUA	73	WN	S273JUA	80	WN	S280JUA	87	WN	S287JUA
67	WN	S267JUA	74	WN	S274JUA	81	WN	S281JUA	88	WN	S288JUA
68	WN	S268JUA	75	WN	S275JUA	82	WN	S282JUA	89	WN	S289JUA
69	WN	S269JUA	76	WN	S276JUA	83	WN	S283JUA	90	WN	S290JUA
70	WN	S270JUA	77	WN	S277JUA	84	WN	S284JUA	91	WN	S291JUA
71	WN	S271JUA	78	WN	S278JUA	85	WN	S285JUA	92	WN	S292JUA

DLA93-125

DAF DE02RSDB250 10.6m Alexander ALX400 N45/19D* 1999 *DLA124/5 are N45/17D

93	E	T293FGN	102	SF	T302FGN	110	SF	T310FGN	118	E	T318FGN
94	E	T294FGN	103	SF	T303FGN	111	SF	T311FGN	119	E	T319FGN
95	E	T295FGN	104	SF	T304FGN	112	SF	T312FGN	120	E	T320FGN
96	SF	T296FGN	105	SF	T305FGN	113	SF	T313FGN	121	E	T421GGO
97	SF	T297FGN	106	SF	T306FGN	114	SF	T314FGN	122	E	T322FGN
98	SF	T298FGN	107	SF	T307FGN	115	SF	T315FGN	123	E	T323FGN
99	SF	T299FGN	108	SF	T308FGN	116	E	T316FGN	124	WN	T324FGN
100	SF	T110GGO	109	SF	T309FGN	117	E	T317FGN	125	WN	T325FGN
101	SF	T301FGN									

DLA126-189

DAF DE02RSDB250 10.2m Alexander ALX400 N43/21D 2000

126	TH	V326DGT	142	BN	V342DGT	159	BN	V359DGT	175	TC	W432WGJ
127	TH	V327DGT	143	BN	V343DGT	160	BN	V660LGC	176	TC	W376VGJ
128	TH	V628LGC	144	BN	V344DGT	161	BN	V361DGT	177	TC	W377VGJ
129	TH	V329DGT	145	BN	V345DGT	162	BN	V362DGT	178	TC	W378VGJ
130	TH	V330DGT	146	BN	V346DGT	163	BN	V363DGT	179	TC	W379VGJ
131	TH	V331DGT	147	BN	V347DGT	164	BN	V364DGT	180	TC	W433WGJ
132	TH	V332DGT	148	BN	V348DGT	165	BN	V365DGT	181	TC	W381VGJ
133	TC	V633LGC	149	BN	V349DGT	166	N	W366VGJ	182	TC	W382VGJ
134	TC	V334DGT	150	BN	V650LGC	167	N	W367VGJ	183	TC	W383VGJ
135	TC	V335DGT	151	BN	V351DGT	168	N	W368VGJ	184	TC	W384VGJ
136	TC	V336DGT	152	BN	V352DGT	169	N	W369VGJ	185	TC	W385VGJ
137	N	V337DGT	153	BN	V353DGT	170	N	W431WGJ	186	TC	W386VGJ
138	N	V338DGT	154	BN	V354DGT	171	TC	W371VGJ	187	TC	W387VGJ
139	N	V339DGT	155	TC	V355DGT	172	TC	W372VGJ	188	TC	W388VGJ
140	N	V640LGC	156	TC	V356DGT	173	TC	W373VGJ	189	TC	W389VGJ
141	N	V341DGT	158	TC	V358DGT	174	TC	W374VGJ			

DLA190-223

DAF DE02RSDB250 10.2m Alexander ALX400 N43/21D 2000

190	E	W434WGJ	199	E	W399VGJ	208	SF	W408VGJ	216	TC	X416FGP
191	E	W391VGJ	200	E	W435WGJ	209	SF	W409VGJ	217	TC	X417FGP
192	E	W392VGJ	201	CT	W401VGJ	210	E	W438WGJ	218	TC	X418FGP
193	E	W393VGJ	202	CT	W402VGJ	211	E	W411VGJ	219	TC	X419FGP
194	E	W394VGJ	203	CT	W403VGJ	212	E	W412VGJ	220	TC	X501GGO
195	E	W395VGJ	204	SF	W404VGJ	213	WN	W413VGJ	221	TC	X421FGP
196	E	W396VGJ	205	SF	W436WGJ	214	WN	W414VGJ	222	TC	X422FGP
197	E	W397VGJ	206	SF	W437WGJ	215	TC	X415FGP	223	TC	X423FGP
198	E	W398VGJ	207	SF	W407VGJ						

DLA224-321

DAF DE02RSDB250 10.2m Alexander ALX400 N43/20D 2000-01

224	SF	X424FGP	249	CT	X449FGP	274	SF	Y474UGC	298	CT	Y498UGC
225	E	X425FGP	250	TC	X506GGO	275	SF	Y475UGC	299	CT	Y499UGC
226	E	X426FGP	251	TC	X451FGP	276	E	Y476UGC	300	CT	Y524UGC
227	E	X427FGP	252	TC	X452FGP	277	AR	Y477UGC	301	CT	Y501UGC
228	WN	X428FGP	253	TC	X453FGP	278	AR	Y478UGC	302	CT	Y502UGC
229	WN	X429FGP	254	TC	X454FGP	279	AR	Y479UGC	303	CT	Y503UGC
230	AR	X502GGO	255	TC	X507GGO	280	AR	Y522UGC	304	CT	Y504UGC
231	AR	X431FGP	256	TC	X508GGO	281	AR	Y481UGC	305	CT	Y526UGC
232	AR	X432FGP	257	TC	X457FGP	282	AR	Y482UGC	306	CT	Y506UGC
233	TC	X433FGP	258	TC	X458FGP	283	AR	Y483UGC	307	CT	Y507UGC
234	TC	X434FGP	259	TC	X459FGP	284	AR	Y484UGC	308	CT	Y508UGC
235	TC	X435FGP	260	TC	Y451UGC	285	AR	Y485UGC	309	CT	Y509UGC
236	TC	X436FGP	261	TC	Y461UGC	286	AR	Y486UGC	310	CT	Y527UGC
237	TC	X437FGP	262	TC	Y462UGC	287	AR	Y487UGC	311	N	Y511UGC
238	TC	X438FGP	263	TC	Y463UGC	288	AR	Y488UGC	312	N	Y512UGC
239	AR	X439FGP	264	TC	Y464UGC	289	AR	Y489UGC	313	N	Y513UGC
240	AR	X503GGO	265	TC	Y465UGC	290	EM	Y523UGC	314	N	Y514UGC
241	AR	X441FGP	266	TC	Y466UGC	291	CT	Y491UGC	315	N	Y529UGC
242	AR	X442FGP	267	TC	Y467UGC	292	CT	Y492UGC	316	N	Y516UGC
243	AR	X443FGP	268	TC	Y468UGC	293	CT	Y493UGC	317	N	Y517UGC
244	AR	X504GGO	269	TC	Y469UGC	294	CT	Y494UGC	318	N	Y518UGC
245	AR	X445FGP	270	CT	Y452UGC	295	CT	Y495UGC	319	N	Y519UGC
246	AR	X446FGP	271	CT	Y471UGC	296	CT	Y496UGC	320	N	Y531UGC
247	AR	X447FGP	272	SF	Y472UGC	297	CT	Y497UGC	321	N	Y521UGC
248	CT	X448FGP	273	SF	Y473UGC						

Arriva London have found the DAF DB250 chassis to meet its needs with almost 400 supplied with ALX400 bodies; 110 with President styling and a further 93 with Wrightbus bodywork. Pictured in Oxford Street, DLA301, Y501UGC is seen operating the 73 to Tottenham. *Mark Lyons*

DLA322-336

DAF DE02RSDB250 10.2m Alexander ALX400 N45/20D 2003

322	TH	LG52DAO	326	TH	LG52DBV	330	TH	LG52DCF	334	TH	LG52DCX
323	TH	LG52DAU	327	TH	LG52DBY	331	TH	LG52DCO	335	TH	LG52DCY
324	TH	LG52DBO	328	TH	LG52DBZ	332	TH	LG52DCU	336	TH	LG52DCZ
325	TH	LG52DBU	329	TH	LG52DCE	333	TH	LG52DCV			

DLA337-389

DAF DE02RSDB250 10.2m TransBus ALX400 N45/20D 2003

337	TH	LJ03MFX	351	EM	LJ03MKZ	364	EM	LJ03MKL	377	CT	LJ03MTK
338	TH	LJ03MFY	352	EM	LJ03MLE	365	EM	LJ03MWE	378	CT	LJ03MTU
339	TH	LJ03MFZ	353	EM	LJ03MLF	366	EM	LJ03MWF	379	CT	LJ03MTV
340	TH	LJ03MGE	354	EM	LJ03MLK	367	EM	LJ03MWG	380	CT	LJ03MTY
341	TH	LJ03MGU	355	EM	LJ03MJX	368	EM	LJ03MWK	381	CT	LJ03MTZ
342	TH	LJ03MGV	356	EM	LJ03MJY	369	EM	LJ03MWL	382	CT	LJ03MUA
343	TH	LJ03MDV	357	EM	LJ03MKA	370	CT	LJ03MUY	383	CT	LJ03MUB
344	TH	LJ03MDX	358	EM	LJ03MKC	371	CT	LJ03MVC	384	CT	LJ03MYU
345	TH	LJ03MDY	359	EM	LJ03MKD	372	CT	LJ03MVD	385	CT	LJ03MYV
346	TH	LJ03MDZ	360	EM	LJ03MKE	373	CT	LJ03MVE	386	CT	LJ03MYX
347	TH	LJ03MEU	361	EM	LJ03MKF	374	CT	LJ03MSY	387	CT	LJ03MYY
348	EM	LJ03MKU	362	EM	LJ03MKG	375	CT	LJ03MTE	388	CT	LJ03MYZ
349	EM	LJ03MKV	363	EM	LJ03MKK	376	CT	LJ03MTF	389	CT	LJ03MZD
350	EM	LJ03MKX									

DLP1-20

DAF DE02RSDB250 10.6m Plaxton President N45/19D 1999

1	E	V601LGC	6	E	T206XBV	11	E	T211XBV	16	E	T216XBV
2	E	T202XBV	7	E	T207XBV	12	E	T212XBV	17	E	T217XBV
3	E	T203XBV	8	E	T208XBV	13	E	T213XBV	18	E	T218XBV
4	E	T204XBV	9	E	T209XBV	14	E	T214XBV	19	E	T219XBV
5	E	T205XBV	10	E	T210XBV	15	E	T215XBV	20	E	T220XBV

Plaxton President bodywork has been supplied in 10.6m and 10.2metre lengths to Arriva London. From the 2001 delivery the longer DLP54, LJ51DJZ, was photographed in Wood Green while operating Route 29 from the local former-trolleybus depot. *Richard Godfrey*

DLP40-75

DAF DE02RSDB250 10.6m   Plaxton President   N45/24D   2001

40	WN	Y532UGC	49	WN	Y549UGC	58	WN	LJ51DKF	67	WN	LJ51DLD
41	WN	Y541UGC	50	WN	LJ51DJU	59	WN	LJ51DKK	68	WN	LJ51DLF
42	WN	Y542UGC	51	WN	LJ51DJV	60	WN	LJ51DKL	69	WN	LJ51DLK
43	WN	Y543UGC	52	WN	LJ51DJX	61	WN	LJ51DKN	70	WN	LJ51DLN
44	WN	Y544UGC	53	WN	LJ51DJY	62	WN	LJ51DKO	71	WN	LJ51DLU
45	WN	Y533UGC	54	WN	LJ51DJZ	63	WN	LJ51DKU	72	WN	LJ51DLV
46	WN	Y546UGC	55	WN	LJ51DKA	64	WN	LJ51DKV	73	WN	LJ51DLX
47	WN	Y547UGC	56	WN	LJ51DKD	65	WN	LJ51DKX	74	WN	LJ51DLY
48	WN	Y548UGC	57	WN	LJ51DKE	66	WN	LJ51DKY	75	WN	LJ51DLZ

DLP76-90

DAF DE02RSDB250 10.2m   Plaxton President   N43/20D   2002

76	E	LJ51OSX	80	E	LJ51ORC	84	E	LJ51ORK	88	E	LF02PKD
77	E	LJ51OSY	81	E	LJ51ORF	85	E	LJ51ORL	89	E	LF02PKE
78	E	LJ51OSZ	82	E	LJ51ORG	86	E	LF02PKA	90	E	LF02PKJ
79	E	LJ51ORA	83	E	LJ51ORH	87	E	LF02PKC			

DLP91-110

DAF DE02RSDB250 10.6m   Plaxton President   N45/20D   2002

91	E	LF52URS	96	E	LF52URX	101	E	LF52URG	106	E	LF52URM
92	E	LF52URT	97	E	LF52URB	102	E	LF52URH	107	E	LF52UPP
93	E	LF52URU	98	E	LF52URC	103	E	LF52URJ	108	E	LF52UPR
94	E	LF52URV	99	E	LF52URD	104	E	LF52URK	109	E	LF52UPS
95	E	LF52URW	100	E	LF52URE	105	E	LF52URL	110	E	LF52UPT

DPL1	EC	N551LUA	DAF DE33WSSB3000	Plaxton Première 350	C49FT	1996	Arriva East Herts & Essex, 1998
DPL2	EC	398CLT	DAF DE33WSSB3000	Plaxton Première 350	C49FT	1996	Arriva East Herts & Essex, 1998
DP3	EC	P753RWU	DAF DE33WSSB3000	Plaxton Première 350	C53F	1997	Arriva East Herts & Essex, 1998
DP5	EC	R162GNW	DAF DE33WSSB3000	Plaxton Excalibur	C53F	1998	Westbus, Hounslow, 2002
DP6	EC	T56AUA	DAF DE33WSSB3000	Plaxton Première 350	C53F	1999	On Time, Wandsworth, 2002

DPP421-431

Dennis Dart SLF 10m   Plaxton Pointer   N34F   1997   Arriva East Herts & Essex, 1998

421	TC	R421COO	424	TC	R424COO	427	TC	R427COO	430	TC	R430COO
422	TC	R422COO	425	TC	R425COO	428	TC	R428COO	431	TC	R431COO
423	TC	R423COO	426	TC	R426COO	429	TC	R429COO			

First of the Wrightbus Pulsar Gemini DW class, DW1, LJ03MWM, illustrates the type as it heads along Godstone Road in Kenley towards Caterham station. Recent arrivals take the type total to 93 and have allowed older buses to be displaced to provincial fleets. *Richard Godfrey*

DRL151-158

			Dennis Dart 9SDL3024		Plaxton Pointer			B34F	1993	London Buses, 1995
151	BF	L151WAG		153	BF	L153WAG	155	EM	L155WAG	157	EM	L157WAG
152	BF	L152WAG		154	EM	L154WAG	156	EM	L156WAG	158	EM	L158WAG

DRL201-206

			Dennis Dart 9SDL3053	Plaxton Pointer	B34F	1995
201	EM	N701GUM	203	EM	N703GUM	205	TH	N705GUM	206	EM	N706GUM
202	EM	N702GUM

DRL216	EM	P916PWW	Dennis Dart 9m	Plaxton Pointer	B34F	1996	
DRL217	EM	P917PWW	Dennis Dart 9m	Plaxton Pointer	B34F	1996	
DRL218	EM	P918PWW	Dennis Dart 9m	Plaxton Pointer	B34F	1996	
DRN117	EM	L117YVK	Dennis Dart 9SDL3034	Northern Counties Paladin	B35F	1994	Arriva Southern Counties, 1998
DVH6	EC	G906TYR	DAF MB230LB615	Van Hool Alizée H	C53F	1990	Arriva East Herts & Essex, 1998
DVH8	EC	G908TYR	DAF MB230LB615	Van Hool Alizée H	C49FT	1990	Arriva East Herts & Essex, 1998

DW1-50

			DAF DB250RSLF 10.3m	Wrightbus Pulsar Gemini	N43/22D	2003
1	TC	LJ03MWM	14	TC	LJ03MWC	27	TC	LJ53BGK	39	BF	LJ53NHF
2	TC	LJ03MWN	15	TC	LJ03MWD	28	TC	LJ53BGO	40	BF	LJ53NHG
3	TC	LJ03MWP	16	TC	LJ03MVF	29	TC	LJ53BGU	41	BF	LJ53NHH
4	TC	LJ03MWU	17	TC	LJ03MVG	30	TC	LJ53NHV	42	BF	LJ53NHK
5	TC	LJ03MWV	18	TC	LJ53NHT	31	TC	LJ53NHX	43	BF	LJ53NHL
6	TC	LJ03MVT	19	TC	LJ53NHU	32	TC	LJ53NHY	44	BF	LJ53NHM
7	TC	LJ03MVU	20	TC	LJ53BFP	33	TC	LJ53NHZ	45	BF	LJ53NHN
8	TC	LJ03MVV	21	TC	LJ53BFU	34	TC	LJ53NJE	46	BF	LJ53NHO
9	TC	LJ03MVW	22	TC	LJ53BFV	35	BF	LJ53NJF	47	BF	LJ53NHP
10	TC	LJ03MVX	23	TC	LJ53BFX	36	BF	LJ53NJK	48	BF	LJ53NGO
11	TC	LJ03MVY	24	TC	LJ53BFY	37	BF	LJ53NJN	49	BF	LJ53NGU
12	TC	LJ03MVZ	25	TC	LJ53BGE	38	BF	LJ53NHE	50	BF	LJ53NGV
13	TC	LJ03MWA	26	TC	LJ53BGF						

DW51-93 — VDL Bus DB250 10.3m — Wrightbus Pulsar Gemini — N43/22D — 2004

No	Code	Reg	No	Code	Reg	No	Code	Reg	No	Code	Reg
51	TC	LJ04LDX	62	OLST	LJ04LDC	73	BN	LJ04LGK	84	BN	LJ04LFX
52	TC	LJ04LDY	63	OLST	LJ04LDD	74	BN	LJ04LGL	85	BN	LJ04LFY
53	BN	LJ04LDZ	64	OLST	LJ04LDE	75	BN	LJ04LGN	86	BN	LJ04LFZ
54	BN	LJ04LEF	65	OLST	LJ04LDF	76	BN	LJ04LGU	87	BN	LJ04LGA
55	BN	LJ04LEU	66	OLST	LJ04LDK	77	BN	LJ04LGV	88	BN	LJ04LGC
56	OLST	LJ04LFA	67	BN	LJ04LDL	78	BN	LJ04LGW	89	BN	LJ04LGD
57	OLST	LJ04LFB	68	BN	LJ04LDN	79	BN	LJ04LGX	90	BN	LJ04LGE
58	OLST	LJ04LFD	69	BN	LJ04LDU	80	BN	LJ04LGY	91	BN	LJ04LGF
59	OLST	LJ04LFE	70	BN	LJ04LDV	81	BN	LJ04LFU	92	BN	LJ04LFH
60	OLST	LJ04LFF	71	BN	LJ04LGF	82	BN	LJ04LFV	93	BN	LJ04LFK
61	OLST	LJ04LDA	72	BN	LJ04LGG	83	BN	LJ04LFW			

DWL1-22 — DAF DE12CSSB120 10.2m — Wrightbus Cadet — N31D — 2001

No	Code	Reg	No	Code	Reg	No	Code	Reg	No	Code	Reg
1	BN	Y801DGT	7	BN	LJ51DDK	13	BN	LJ51DDX	18	BN	LJ51DFC
2	BN	Y802DGT	8	BN	LJ51DDL	14	BN	LJ51DDY	19	BN	LJ51DFD
3	BN	Y803DGT	9	BN	LJ51DDN	15	BN	LJ51DDZ	20	BN	LJ51DFE
4	BN	Y804DGT	10	BN	LJ51DDO	16	BN	LJ51DEU	21	BN	LJ51DFF
5	BN	Y805DGT	11	BN	LJ51DDU	17	BN	LJ51DFA	22	BN	LJ51DFG
6	BN	Y806DGT	12	BN	LJ51DDV						

DWL23-29 — DAF DE12CSSB120 10.8m — Wrightbus Cadet — N34D — 2002

No	Code	Reg	No	Code	Reg	No	Code	Reg	No	Code	Reg
23	E	LF02PLU	25	E	LF02PLX	27	E	LF02PMO	29	E	LF02PMV
24	E	LF02PLV	26	E	LF02PLZ						

DWL30-55 — DAF DE12CSSB120 10.2m — Wrightbus Cadet — N30D — 2002-03

No	Code	Reg	No	Code	Reg	No	Code	Reg	No	Code	Reg
30	WN	LF02PMX	37	WN	LF02PNO	44	WN	LF52UTB	50	WN	LF52UOB
31	WN	LF02PMY	38	WN	LF02PNU	45	WN	LF52UNW	51	WN	LF52UOC
32	WN	LF02PNE	39	WN	LF02PNV	46	WN	LF52UNX	52	WN	LF52UOD
33	WN	LF02PNJ	40	WN	LF02PNX	47	WN	LF52UNY	53	WN	LF52UOE
34	WN	LF02PNK	41	WN	LF02PNY	48	WN	LF52UNZ	54	WN	LF52USZ
35	WN	LF02PNL	42	WN	LF02POA	49	WN	LF52UOA	55	WN	LF52UTA
36	WN	LF02PNN	43	WN	LF02POH						

DWL56-67 — DAF DE12CSSB120 10.2m — Wrightbus Cadet — N30D — 2003

No	Code	Reg	No	Code	Reg	No	Code	Reg	No	Code	Reg
56	E	LJ03MUW	59	BF	LJ03MZG	62	BF	LJ03MYH	65	BF	LJ03MYM
57	BF	LJ03MZE	60	BF	LJ03MZL	63	BF	LJ03MYK	66	BF	LJ53NGX
58	BF	LJ03MZF	61	BF	LJ03MYG	64	BF.	LJ03MYL	67	BF	LJ53NGY

DWS1-18 — VDL Bus SB120 — Wrightbus Cadet — N — 2003

No	Code	Reg	No	Code	Reg	No	Code	Reg	No	Code	Reg
1	BF	LJ53NGZ	6	BF	LJ53NFT	11	BF	LJ53NFZ	15	BF	LJ53NGN
2	BF	LJ53NHA	7	BF	LJ53NFU	12	BF	LJ53NGE	16	BF	LJ53NFE
3	BF	LJ53NHB	8	BF	LJ53NFV	13	BF	LJ53NGF	17	BF	LJ53NFF
4	BF	LJ53NHC	9	BF	LJ53NFX	14	BF	LJ53NGG	18	BF	LJ53NFG
5	BF	LJ53NHD	10	BF	LJ53NFY						

L4-102 — Leyland Olympian ONLXB/1RH — Eastern Coach Works — B42/26D — 1986 — London Buses, 1994

No	Code	Reg	No	Code	Reg	No	Code	Reg	No	Code	Reg
5	BN	C805BYY	25	N	C25CHM	46	BN	C46CHM	58	N	C58CHM
8	N	WLT807	35	N	C35CHM	49	N	C49CHM	65	N	C65CHM
21	N	C21CHM	37	N	C37CHM	50	N	C50CHM	66	N	C66CHM
22	N	C22CHM	45	N	C45CHM	56	N	C56CHM	102	N	C102CHM
24	N	C24CHM									

L135-258 — Leyland Olympian ONLXB/1RH — Eastern Coach Works — B42/26D — 1986-87 — London Buses, 1994-95

No	Code	Reg	No	Code	Reg	No	Code	Reg	No	Code	Reg
135	N	D135FYM	180	N	480CLT	198	N	D198FYM	230	N	D230FYM
143	N	D143FYM	185	N	D185FYM	201	N	D201FYM	232	N	D232FYM
147	N	D147FYM	186	N	D186FYM	214	N	D214FYM	237	N	D237FYM
150	N	D150FYM	188	N	D188FYM	217	N	217CLT	244	TH	VLT244
159	N	D159FYM	191	N	D191FYM	218	N	D218FYM	246	N	D246FYM
161	N	D161FYM	192	N	D192FYM	223	N	D223FYM	251	N	D251FYM
162	N	D162FYM	194	N	D194FYM	226	N	D226FYM	257	N	D257FYM
164	N	D164FYM	196	N	D196FYM	228	N	D228FYM	258	N	D258FYM
179	N	D179FYM	197	N	D197FYM						

New to Kentish Bus, L530, G530VBB is a Leyland Olympian with Northern Counties bodywork. In 1995, the former London Buses South company was purchased, becoming Cowie South London, thus making Cowie the largest single operator in the London Buses area. As the London operations were tidied up, the former Kentish Bus and Londonlinks operations at Cambridge Heath, Battersea and Walworth, and the East Herts & Essex operations from Edmonton were incorporated into the London operation. *Richard Godfrey*

L315-354

Leyland Olympian ON2R50C13Z4 Alexander RH   B43/25D   1992   London Buses, 1994

315	BK	J315BSH	323	BK	J323BSH	334	BK	J334BSH	350	BK	J350BSH
316	BK	J316BSH	324	BK	J324BSH	337	BK	J337BSH	351	PH	J351BSH
317	BK	J317BSH	328	PH	J328BSH	339	BK	J339BSH	352	PH	J352BSH
318	BK	J318BSH	331	BK	J331BSH	340	w	J340BSH	353	PH	J353BSH
319	BK	J319BSH	332	BK	J332BSH	346	BK	J346BSH	354	PH	J354BSH
322	BK	J322BSH									

L514-556

Leyland Olympian ON2R50C13Z4* Northern Counties   B47/27D   1990   Kentish Bus, 1996
*514/ 541/3/4/6-8/50-4 are type ONCL10/1RZA

514	CT	G514VBB	525	CT	G525VBB	536	CT	G536VBB	547	DX	G547VBB
515	CT	G515VBB	526	DX	G526VBB	537	TH	G537VBB	548	DX	G548VBB
516	CT	G516VBB	527	DX	G527VBB	538	CT	G538VBB	549	DX	G549VBB
517	CT	G517VBB	528	DX	G528VBB	539	u	G539VBB	550	N	G550VBB
518	CT	G518VBB	529	DX	G529VBB	540	u	G540VBB	551	N	G551VBB
519	CT	G519VBB	530	DX	G530VBB	541	u	G541VBB	552	N	G552VBB
520	TH	G520VBB	531	DX	G531VBB	542	u	G542VBB	553	N	G553VBB
521	CT	G521VBB	532	DX	G532VBB	543	DX	G543VBB	554	N	G554VBB
522	DX	G522VBB	533	DX	G533VBB	544	DX	G544VBB	555	N	G555VBB
523	DX	G523VBB	534	DX	G534VBB	545	DX	G545VBB	556	N	G556VBB
524	DX	G524VBB	535	DX	G535VBB	546	DX	G546VBB			

L694-704

Volvo Olympian YN2RV16Z4   East Lancs   B44/30F   1994   Southern Counties, 1999

694	CN	M694HPF	697	CN	M697HPF	700	CN	M700HPF	703	CN	M703HPF
695	CN	M695HPF	698	CN	M698HPF	701	CN	M701HPF	704	CN	M704HPF
696	CN	M696HPF	699	CN	M699HPF	702	CN	M702HPF			

M537	EC	GYE537W	MCW Metrobus DR101/14	MCW	B43/28D	1981	London Buses, 1994
M573	EC	GYE575W	MCW Metrobus DR101/14	MCW	B43/28D	1981	London Buses, 1994

M617-798

MCW Metrobus DR101/14   MCW   B43/28D   1981   London Buses, 1994

617	EC	KYO617X	665	w	KYV665X	770	SF	KYV770X	777	EC	KYV777X
652	SF	KYV652X	718	EM	KYV718X	772	EM	KYV772X	798	SF	KYV798X

The first of Arriva's articulated buses for London entered service in the spring of 2004. Seen on at the NOrth Weald rally in July is new arrival MA30, BX04MYY.

M1075-1303 MCW Metrobus DR101/17 MCW B43/28D 1984-85

1075	EC	B75WUL	1136	EC	B136WUL	1253	EC	B253WUL	1300	EM	B300WUL
1126	EC	B126WUL	1231	EC	B231WUL	1254	EC	B254WUL	1303	EC	B303WUL
1130	EC	B130WUL	1248	EC	B248WUL						

M1310-1406 MCW Metrobus DR101/17 MCW B43/28D 1985

1312	EC	C312BUV	1320	EC	C320BUV	1327	EM	C327BUV	1398	EC	C398BUV
1313	EC	C313BUV	1322	w	C322BUV	1332	EC	C332BUV	1402	AR	C402BUV
1314	EC	C314BUV	1324	w	C324BUV	1367	EC	C367BUV	1405	AR	C405BUV
1318	EC	C318BUV	1326	EC	C326BUV	1379	EC	VLT88	1406	AR	C406BUV
1319	w	C319BUV									

| M1437 | EC | VLT12 | MCW Metrobus DR102/17 | MCW | | BC43/24F | 1985 | Arriva East Herts & Essex, 1998 |

MA1-76 Mercedes-Benz O530G Mercedes-Benz Citaro AB49T 2004

1	EC	BX04MWW	20	EC	BX04MXU	39	-	-	58	-	-
2	EC	BX04MWY	21	EC	BX04MXV	40	-	-	59	-	-
3	EC	BX04MWZ	22	EC	BX04MXW	41	-	-	60	-	-
4	EC	BX04MXA	23	EC	BX04MXY	42	-	-	61	-	-
5	EC	BX04MXB	24	EC	BX04MXZ	43	-	-	62	-	-
6	EC	BX04MXC	25	EC	BX04MYA	44	-	-	63	-	-
7	EC	BX04MXD	26	EC	BX04MYB	45	-	-	64	-	-
8	EC	BX04MXE	27	EC	BX04MYC	46	-	-	65	-	-
9	EC	BX04MXG	28	EC	BX04MYD	47	-	-	66	-	-
10	EC	BX04MXH	29	EC	BX04MYF	48	-	-	67	-	-
11	EC	BX04MXJ	30	TM	BX04MYY	49	-	-	68	-	-
12	EC	BX04MXK	31	-	-	50	-	-	69	-	-
13	EC	BX04MXL	32	TM	BX04NDD	51	-	-	70	-	-
14	EC	BX04MXM	33	TM	BX04NDG	52	-	-	71	-	-
15	EC	BX04MXN	34	-	-	53	-	-	72	-	-
16	EC	BX04MXP	35	TM	BX04NDV	54	-	-	73	-	-
17	EC	BX04MXR	36	-	-	55	-	-	74	-	-
18	EC	BX04MXS	37	-	-	56	-	-	75	-	-
19	EC	BX04MXT	38	-	-	57	-	-	76	-	-

Mini Pointer Darts operated by Arriva London have a more provincial style single-door layout, as shown on PDL56, LJ51DBX, as it operates route 450 in West Croydon. *Tony Wilson*

PDL1-18

Dennis Dart SLF 8.8m   Plaxton Pointer MPD   N29F*   2000   *16-18 are N21F

1	EM	V421DGT	6	EM	V426DGT	11	EM	V431DGT	15	EM	V435DGT
2	EM	V422DGT	7	EM	V427DGT	12	EM	V432DGT	16	CT	W136VGJ
3	EM	V423DGT	8	EM	V428DGT	13	EM	V433DGT	17	CT	W137VGJ
4	EM	V424DGT	9	EM	V429DGT	14	EM	V434DGT	18	CT	W138VGJ
5	EM	V425DGT	10	EM	V430DGT						

PDL19-38

Dennis Dart SLF 10.7m   Plaxton Pointer 2   N31D   2000

19	BF	X519GGO	24	BF	X524GGO	29	BK	X529GGO	34	BK	X534GGO
20	BF	X471GGO	25	BF	X475GGO	30	BK	X481GGO	35	BK	X485GGO
21	BF	X521GGO	26	BF	X526GGO	31	BK	X531GGO	36	BK	X536GGO
22	BF	X522GGO	27	BF	X527GGO	32	BK	X532GGO	37	BK	X537GGO
23	BF	X523GGO	28	BF	X478GGO	33	BK	X533GGO	38	BK	X538GGO

PDL39-49

Dennis Dart SLF 8.8m   Plaxton Pointer MPD   N29F   2001

39	AR	X239PGT	42	AR	X242PGT	45	AR	X546GGO	48	AR	X248PGT
40	AR	X541GGO	43	AR	X243PGT	46	AR	X246PGT	49	AR	X249PGT
41	AR	X241PGT	44	AR	X244PGT	47	AR	X247PGT			

PDL50-69

Dennis Dart SLF 8.8m   Plaxton Pointer MPD   N29F   2001-02

50	TH	LJ51DAA	55	TH	LJ51DBV	60	EM	LJ51DCF	65	E	LJ51DCY
51	TH	LJ51DAO	56	TH	LJ51DBX	61	EM	LJ51DCO	66	E	LJ51DCZ
52	TH	LJ51DAU	57	TH	LJ51DBY	62	EM	LJ51DCU	67	E	LJ51DDA
53	TH	LJ51DBO	58	TH	LJ51DBZ	63	EM	LJ51DCV	68	E	LJ51DDE
54	TH	LJ51DBU	59	TH	LJ51DCE	64	E	LJ51DCX	69	E	LJ51DDF

PDL70-94

Dennis Dart SLF 8.8m   Plaxton Pointer MPD   N29F   2002

70	EM	LF02PTZ	77	EM	LF52UON	83	E	LF52URZ	89	E	LF52USJ
71	EM	LF52UOG	78	EM	LF52UOO	84	E	LF52USB	90	u	LF52USL
72	EM	LF52UOH	79	EM	LF52UOP	85	E	LF52USC	91	E	LF52URN
73	EM	LF52UOJ	80	EM	LF52UOR	86	E	LF52USD	92	E	LF52URO
74	EM	LF52UOK	81	EM	LF52UNV	87	E	LF52USG	93	E	LF52URP
75	EM	LF52UOL	82	E	LF52URY	88	E	LF52USH	94	E	LF52URR
76	EM	LF52UOM									

During 2004 several of the remaining Routemaster-operated routes will be converted to modern buses. Arriva have already re-classed some examples as specials. Carrying Leaside Travel names and suitably dressed for a wedding private hire is RMC1453, 453CLT. *Phillip Stephenson*

RM5-736

			AEC Routemaster R2RH			Park Royal			B36/28R	1959-61	London Buses, 1994-97
											RM54 ex preservation 2003

5	AR	VLT5	275	BN	VLT275	432	BN	SVS617	664	BN	WLT664
6	BN	VLT6	295	BN	VLT295	467	BN	XVS851	676	BN	WLT676
25	BN	VLT25	311	BN	KGJ142A	531	BN	WLT531	719	BN	WLT719
29	BN	OYM453A	348	BN	WLT348	548	BN	SVS618	736	BN	XYJ418
54	BN	LDS279A	385	BN	WLT385	652	CT	WLT652			

RM838	BN	WLT838	AEC Routemaster R2RH	Park Royal	B36/28R	1961
RM871	BN	WLT871	AEC Routemaster R2RH	Park Royal	B36/28R	1961
RM875	BN	WLT875	AEC Routemaster R2RH	Park Royal	B36/28R	1961

RML882-901

			AEC Routemaster R2RH/1			Park Royal			B40/32R	1961	London Buses, 1994
882	CT	WLT882	888	CT	WLT888	895	BN	WLT895	897	CT	WLT897
884	CT	WLT884	892	BN	WLT892	896	CT	WLT896	901	CT	WLT901

RM909	BN	WLT909	AEC Routemaster R2RH	Park Royal	B36/28R	1961	preservation, 2002

RM970-1398

			AEC Routemaster R2RH			Park Royal			B36/28R	1961-65	London Buses, 1995
970	BN	WLT970	1124	BN	VYJ806	1164	CT	NSG636A	1330	BN	KGH975A
997	BN	WLT997	1125	BN	KGH858A	1185	u	XYJ427	1361	BN	VYJ808
1003	BN	3CLT	1145	CT	LDS402A	1324	BN	324CLT	1398	BN	KGJ118A

RMC1453	EC	453CLT	AEC Routemaster R2RH	Park Royal	B36/28R	1962	Arriva East Herts & Essex, 1998
RMC1464	EC	464CLT	AEC Routemaster R2RH	Park Royal	O36/28R	1962	Arriva East Herts & Essex, 1998

RM1593-2217

			AEC Routemaster R2RH			Park Royal			B36/28R	1961-65	London Buses, 1995
1593	BN	593CLT	1801	BN	801DYE	1968	CT	ALD968B	2122	CT	CUV122C
1640	CT	640CLT	1811	BN	EGF220B	1975	BN	ALD975B	2179	BN	CUV179C
1725	BN	725DYE	1822	BN	822DYE	1978	BN	ALD978B	2185	BN	CUV185C
1734	BN	734DYE	1872	BN	ALD872B	2050	CT	ALM50B	2217	BN	CUV217C
1776	CT	776DYE	1941	CT	ALD941B	2060	CT	ALM60B			

Representing the standard RML class is 2538, JJD538D from Brixton depot. It is seen passing through Trafalgar Square in February 2004. *Richard Godfrey*

RML2261-2359   AEC Routemaster R2RH/1   Park Royal   B40/32R   1965

2261	AR	CUV261C	2294	AR	CUV294C	2326	CT	CUV326C	2344	CT	CUV344C
2264	BN	CUV264C	2301	BN	CUV301C	2328	CT	CUV328C	2346	AR	CUV346C
2265	AR	CUV265C	2304	CT	CUV304C	2329	CT	CUV329C	2347	BN	CUV347C
2266	BN	CUV266C	2307	BN	CUV307C	2330	AR	CUV330C	2350	AR	CUV350C
2267	AR	CUV267C	2315	AR	CUV315C	2333	BN	CUV333C	2351	BN	CUV351C
2277	AR	CUV277C	2322	AR	CUV322C	2334	CT	CUV334C	2354	CT	CUV354C
2280	CT	CUV280C	2323	AR	CUV323C	2340	AR	CUV340C	2355	CT	CUV355C
2287	CT	CUV287C	2324	BN	CUV324C	2341	AR	CUV341C	2356	CT	CUV356C
2292	AR	CUV292C	2325	CT	CUV325C	2343	BN	CUV343C	2359	CT	CUV359C

RML2366-2598   AEC Routemaster R2RH/1   Park Royal   B40/32R   1966

2366	BN	JJD366D	2418	CT	JJD418D	2523	BN	JJD523D	2562	AR	JJD562D
2370	CT	JJD370D	2434	AR	JJD434D	2524	BN	JJD524D	2563	AR	JJD563D
2372	AR	JJD372D	2452	BN	JJD452D	2525	AR	JJD525D	2567	CT	JJD567D
2373	AR	JJD373D	2457	CT	JJD457D	2526	CT	JJD526D	2569	AR	JJD569D
2375	BN	JJD375D	2468	AR	JJD468D	2527	AR	JJD527D	2571	CT	JJD571D
2380	AR	JJD380D	2477	BN	JJD477D	2528	AR	JJD528D	2572	BN	JJD572D
2382	BN	JJD382D	2483	CT	JJD483D	2531	BN	JJD531D	2573	BN	JJD573D
2383	BN	JJD383D	2491	BN	JJD491D	2533	BN	JJD533D	2574	BN	JJD574D
2386	CT	JJD386D	2492	CT	JJD492D	2534	CT	JJD534D	2577	BN	JJD577D
2387	BN	JJD387D	2494	CT	JJD494D	2536	BN	JJD536D	2582	AR	JJD582D
2391	AR	JJD391D	2503	AR	JJD503D	2538	BN	JJD538D	2586	BN	JJD586D
2394	AR	JJD394D	2504	AR	JJD504D	2544	AR	JJD544D	2588	AR	JJD588D
2401	CT	JJD401D	2505	BN	JJD505D	2545	BN	JJD545D	2589	AR	JJD589D
2406	CT	JJD406D	2510	AR	JJD510D	2546	AR	JJD546D	2591	BN	JJD591D
2407	BN	JJD407D	2512	BN	JJD512D	2548	BN	JJD548D	2595	AR	JJD595D
2408	AR	JJD408D	2514	BN	JJD514D	2549	BN	JJD549D	2597	CT	JJD597D
2409	CT	JJD409D	2518	AR	JJD518D	2552	CT	JJD552D	2598	BN	JJD598D
2416	CT	JJD416D	2521	BN	JJD521D						

While the Dennis Trident had a head start as the only low-floor double-deck then available, the Volvo B7TL has caught up. Arriva operate seventy-three with ALX400 bodies including VLA12, LJ03MYC, seen here operating route176 to Penge. *Richard Godfrey*

RML2608-2655 — AEC Routemaster R2RH/1 — Park Royal — B40/32R — 1967

2608	CT	NML608E	2625	AR	NML625E	2635	AR	NML635E	2648	BN	NML648E
2611	AR	NML611E	2627	BN	NML627E	2636	BN	NML636E	2653	BN	NML653E
2617	AR	NML617E	2628	AR	NML628E	2638	AR	NML638E	2655	AR	NML655E
2619	BN	NML619E	2632	AR	NML632E	2643	AR	NML643E			

RML2658-2759 — AEC Routemaster R2RH/1 — Park Royal — B40/32R — 1968

2658	AR	SMK658F	2684	AR	SMK684F	2716	CT	SMK716F	2747	AR	SMK747F
2660	AR	SMK660F	2685	CT	SMK685F	2718	BN	SMK718F	2750	CT	SMK750F
2663	AR	SMK663F	2686	AR	SMK686F	2719	AR	SMK719F	2752	CT	SMK752F
2666	AR	SMK666F	2688	CT	SMK688F	2726	BN	SMK726F	2753	BN	SMK753F
2674	BN	SMK674F	2692	BN	SMK692F	2730	BN	SMK730F	2754	CT	SMK754F
2675	CT	SMK675F	2694	AR	SMK694F	2741	BN	SMK741F	2756	AR	SMK756F
2678	AR	SMK678F	2708	AR	SMK708F	2742	CT	SMK742F	2759	BN	SMK759F
2682	CT	SMK682F	2715	BN	SMK715F	2746	AR	SMK746F			

TPL1	EC	124CLT	Leyland Tiger TRCTL11/3ARZM	Plaxton Paramount 3200 III	C53F	1989	Arriva East Herts & Essex, 1998
TPL2	EC	361CLT	Leyland Tiger TRCTL11/3ARZM	Plaxton Paramount 3200 III	C53F	1989	Arriva East Herts & Essex, 1998
TPL8	EC	70CLT	Leyland Tiger TRCT10/3ARZA	Plaxton Paramount 3200 III	C53F	1991	Arriva East Herts & Essex, 1998
TPL518	EC	530MUY	Leyland Tiger TRCTL11/3ARZ(Vo)	Plaxton Paramount 3500 III	C51FT	1988	Arriva East Herts & Essex, 1998

VLA1-55 — Volvo B7TL 10.6m — TransBus ALX400 4.4m — N49/22D — 2003

1	N	LJ03MYP	15	N	LJ03MXH	29	N	LJ53BDO	43	N	LJ53BCV
2	N	LJ03MYR	16	N	LJ03MXK	30	N	LJ53BDU	44	N	LJ53BCX
3	N	LJ03MYS	17	N	LJ03MXL	31	N	LJ53BDV	45	N	LJ53BCY
4	N	LJ03MYT	18	N	LJ03MXM	32	N	LJ53BDX	46	N	LJ53BAA
5	N	LJ03MXV	19	N	LJ03MXN	33	N	LJ53BDY	47	N	LJ53BAO
6	N	LJ03MXW	20	N	LJ03MXP	34	N	LJ53BDZ	48	N	LJ53BAU
7	N	LJ03MXX	21	N	LJ53BFK	35	N	LJ53BEO	49	N	LJ53BAV
8	N	LJ03MXY	22	N	LJ53BFL	36	N	LJ53BBV	50	N	LJ53BBE
9	N	LJ03MXZ	23	N	LJ53BFM	37	N	LJ53BBX	51	N	LJ53BBF
10	N	LJ03MYA	24	N	LJ53BFN	38	N	LJ53BBZ	52	N	LJ53BBK
11	N	LJ03MYB	25	N	LJ53BFO	39	N	LJ53BCF	53	N	LJ53BBN
12	N	LJ03MYC	26	N	LJ53BCZ	40	N	LJ53BCK	54	N	LJ53BBO
13	N	LJ03MYD	27	N	LJ53BDE	41	N	LJ53BCO	55	N	LJ53BBU
14	N	LJ03MYF	28	N	LJ53BDF	42	N	LJ53BCU			

VLA56-73 Volvo B7TL 10.6m TransBus ALX400 4.4m N49/22D 2004

56	N	LJ04LFL	61	SS	LJ04LFS	66	SS	LJ04YWV	70	SS	LJ04YWZ
57	N	LJ04LFM	62	SS	LJ04LFT	67	SS	LJ04YWW	71	SS	LJ04YXA
58	N	LJ04LFN	63	SS	LJ04YWS	68	SS	LJ04YWX	72	SS	LJ04YXB
59	N	LJ04LFP	64	SS	LJ04YWT	69	SS	LJ04YWY	73	SS	LJ04YWE
60	SS	LJ04LFR	65	SS	LJ04YWU						

VLW1-41 Volvo B7TL Wrightbus Eclipse Gemini N41/22D 2001-02

1	WN	Y581UGC	12	WN	LJ51DFV	22	WN	LJ51DGY	32	WN	LJ51DHN
2	WN	Y102TGH	13	WN	LJ51DFX	23	WN	LJ51DGZ	33	WN	LJ51DHO
3	WN	LJ51DJF	14	WN	LJ51DFY	24	WN	LJ51DHA	34	WN	LJ51DHP
4	WN	LJ51DJK	15	WN	LJ51DFZ	25	WN	LJ51DHC	35	WN	LJ51DHV
5	WN	LJ51DJO	16	WN	LJ51DGE	26	WN	LJ51DHD	36	WN	LJ51DHX
6	WN	LJ51DFK	17	WN	LJ51DGF	27	WN	LJ51DHE	37	WN	LJ51DHY
7	WN	LJ51DFL	18	WN	LJ51DGO	28	WN	LJ51DHF	38	WN	LJ51DHZ
8	WN	LJ51DFN	19	WN	LJ51DGU	29	WN	LJ51DHG	39	WN	LJ51DJD
9	WN	LJ51DFO	20	WN	LJ51DGV	30	WN	LJ51DHK	40	WN	LJ51DJE
10	WN	LJ51DFP	21	WN	LJ51DGX	31	WN	LJ51DHL	41	WN	LJ51OSK
11	WN	LJ51DFU									

VLW42-104 Volvo B7TL Wrightbus Eclipse Gemini N41/22D 2002-03

42	WN	LF02PKO	58	WN	LF02PTU	74	WN	LF52UTM	90	AR	LF52URA
43	WN	LF02PKU	59	WN	LF02PTX	75	WN	LF52USM	91	AR	LF52UPD
44	WN	LF02PKV	60	WN	LF02PTY	76	WN	LF52USN	92	AR	LF52UPE
45	WN	LF02PKX	61	WN	LF02PVE	77	WN	LF52USO	93	AR	LF52UPG
46	WN	LF02PKY	62	WN	LF02PVJ	78	WN	LF52USS	94	AR	LF52UPH
47	WN	LF02PKZ	63	WN	LF02PVK	79	WN	LF52UST	95	AR	LF52UPJ
48	WN	LF02PLJ	64	WN	LF02PVL	80	WN	LF52USU	96	AR	LF52UPK
49	WN	LF02PLN	65	WN	LF02PVN	81	WN	LF52USV	97	AR	LF52UPL
50	WN	LF02PLO	66	WN	LF02PVO	82	WN	LF52USW	98	AR	LF52UPM
51	WN	LF02PRZ	67	WN	LF52UTC	83	WN	LF52USX	99	AR	LG52DDA
52	WN	LF02PSO	68	WN	LF52UTE	84	WN	LF52USY	100	AR	LG52DDE
53	WN	LF02PSU	69	EC	LF52USE	85	AR	LF52UPV	101	AR	LG52DDF
54	WN	LF02PSX	70	WN	LF52UTG	86	AR	LF52UPW	102	AR	LG52DDJ
55	WN	LF02PSY	71	WN	LF52UTH	87	AR	LF52UPX	103	AR	LG52DDK
56	WN	LF02PSZ	72	WN	LF52UTJ	88	AR	LF52UPY	104	AR	LG52DDL
57	WN	LF02PTO	73	WN	LF52UTL	89	AR	LF52UPZ			

VLW105-179 Volvo B7TL Wrightbus Eclipse Gemini N41/22D 2003

105	BK	LJ03MHU	124	AR	LF52UOX	143	SF	LG03MFA	162	SF	LG03MRX
106	BK	LJ03MHV	125	AR	LF52UOY	144	SF	LG03MFE	163	SF	LG03MRY
107	BK	LJ03MHX	126	AR	LF52UPA	145	SF	LG03MFF	164	SF	LG03MSU
108	BK	LJ03MHY	127	AR	LF52UPB	146	SF	LG03MFK	165	SF	LG03MSV
109	BK	LJ03MHZ	128	AR	LF52UPC	147	SF	LG03MBF	166	SF	LG03MSX
110	BK	LJ03MJE	129	AR	LG52DAA	148	SF	LG03MBU	167	SF	LG03MMU
111	BK	LJ03MJF	130	AR	LJ03MGZ	149	SF	LG03MBV	168	SF	LG03MMV
112	BK	LJ03MJK	131	AR	LJ03MHA	150	SF	LG03MBX	169	AR	LG03MMX
113	BK	LJ03MJU	132	AR	LJ03MHE	151	SF	LG03MBY	170	AR	LG03MOA
114	BK	LJ03MJV	133	AR	LJ03MHF	152	SF	LG03MDE	171	AR	LG03MOF
115	BK	LJ03MGX	134	AR	LJ03MHK	153	SF	LG03MDF	172	AR	LG03MOV
116	BK	LJ03MGY	135	AR	LJ03MHL	154	SF	LG03MDK	173	AR	LG03MPE
117	AR	LF52UPN	136	AR	LJ03MHM	155	SF	LG03MDN	174	AR	LG03MPF
118	AR	LF52UPO	137	AR	LJ03MHN	156	SF	LG03MDU	175	AR	LG03MPU
119	AR	LF52UOS	138	AR	LJ03MFN	157	SF	LG03MPX	176	AR	LG03MPV
120	AR	LF52UOT	139	AR	LJ03MFP	158	SF	LG03MPY	177	AR	LG03MLL
121	AR	LF52UOU	140	SF	LJ03MFU	159	SF	LG03MPZ	178	AR	LG03MLN
122	AR	LF52UOV	141	SF	LJ03MFV	160	SF	LG03MRU	179	AR	LG03MLV
123	AR	LF52UOW	142	SF	LG03MEV	161	SF	LG03MRV			

VLW180-199 Volvo B7TL Wrightbus Eclipse Gemini N45/24D 2003

180	AR	LJ03MLX	185	AR	LJ03MMF	190	AR	LJ03MXR	195	AR	LJ53BEU
181	AR	LJ03MLY	186	AR	LJ03MMK	191	AR	LJ03MXS	196	AR	LJ53BEY
182	AR	LJ03MLZ	187	AR	LJ03MKM	192	AR	LJ03MXT	197	AR	LJ53BFA
183	AR	LJ03MMA	188	AR	LJ03MKN	193	AR	LJ03MXU	198	AR	LJ53BFE
184	AR	LJ03MME	189	AR	LJ03MYN	194	AR	LJ03MWX	199	AR	LJ53BFF

VPL3	EC	185CLT	Volvo B10M-61	Plaxton Paramount 3200 II	C53F	1986	Arriva East Herts & Essex, 1998
VPL4	EC	205CLT	Volvo B10M-61	Plaxton Paramount 3200 II	C53F	1986	Arriva East Herts & Essex, 1998
VPL503	EC	VLT32	Volvo B10M-60	Plaxton Paramount 3500 III	C49FT	1991	Arriva East Herts & Essex, 1998

Special Event Vehicle:

RV1	EC	GJG750D	AEC Regent V 2D3RA	Park Royal	B40/32F	1966	Arriva East Herts & Essex, 1998

Ancillary Vehicles:

M469	GYE469W	MCW Metrobus DR101/12	MCW	TV	1981	London Buses, 1994
M537	GYE537W	MCW Metrobus DR101/14	MCW	TV	1981	London Buses, 1994

M569-798

MCW Metrobus DR101/14 — MCW — TV — 1981 — London Buses, 1994

569	GYE569W	721	KYV721X	752	KYV752X	778	KYV778X
591	GYE591W	732	KYV732X	762	KYV762X	787	KYV787X
699	KYV699X	733	KYV733X	765	KYV765X	798	KYV798X
715	KYV715X	747	KYV747X	773	KYV773X		

M903	A903SUL	MCW Metrobus DR101/16	MCW	TV	1983	London Buses, 1994
M984	A984SYF	MCW Metrobus DR101/17	MCW	TV	1983	London Buses, 1994
M1000	A700THV	MCW Metrobus DR101/17	MCW	TV	1984	London Buses, 1994

M1084-1105

MCW Metrobus DR134/1 — MCW — TV — 1984 — London Buses, 1994

1084	B84WUL	1095	B95WUL	1098	B98WUL	1103	B103WUL
1092	B92WUL	1096	B96WUL	1100	B100WUL	1104	B104WUL
1094	B94WUL	1097	B97WUL	1101	B101WUL	1105	B105WUL

M1121-1399

MCW Metrobus DR101/17 — MCW — TV — 1984 — London Buses, 1994

1121	B121WUL	1129	B129WUL	1170	B170WUL	1214	B214WUL
1123	B123WUL	1140	B140WUL	1179	B179WUL	1399	C399BVU
1124	B124WUL						

Previous Registrations:

7CLT	D170FYM	KGH975A	330CLT	VLT32	H903AHS
70CLT	H643GRO	KGJ118A	398CLT	VLT47	C47CHM
124CLT	G661WMD	KGJ142A	WLT311	VLT88	C379BUV
185CLT	C874CYX	LDS279A	VLT54	VLT173	D173FYM
205CLT	C876CYX	LDS402A	145CLT	VLT244	D244FYM
217CLT	D217FYM	NSG636A	164CLT	VYJ806	124CLT
319CLT	D190FYM	NVS485	292CLT	VYJ808	361CLT
324CLT	324CLT, VYJ807	OYM453A	VLT29	WLT372	D172FYM
330CLT	-	SVS615	WLT346	WLT554	D154FYM
361CLT	G662WMD	SVS617	WLT432	WLT751	D151FYM
398CLT	N552LUA	SVS618	WLT548	WLT807	C808BYY
480CLT	D180FYM	TSK270	WLT713	WLT909	WLT909, WTS418A
519CLT	D219FYM	T324FGN	T324FGN, 99D53451	WLT916	C816BYY
530MUY	E118KFV	T325FGN	T325FGN, 99D53440	WSJ739	WLT313
656DYE	D156FYM	V423DGT	V435DGT	XVS851	WLT467
815DYE	D215FYM	V435DGT	V423DGT	XYJ418	WLT736
EGF220B	811DYE	VLT12	C437BUV	XYJ427	185CLT
J354BSH	J354BSH, VLT32	VLT13	C813BYY	WTS418A	WLT909
KGH858A	125CLT	VLT27	C27CHM		

Allocations

Barking (638 Ripple Road) - DX

Dart	ADL1	DDL16	DDL17	DDL18	PDL29	PDL30	PDL31	PDL32
	PDL33	PDL34	PDL35	PDL36	PDL37	PDL38	ADL969	ADL970
	ADL971	ADL972	ADL973	ADL974	ADL975	ADL976	ADL977	ADL978
	ADL979	ADL980	ADL981	ADL982	ADL983			
Metrobus	M1129							
Olympian	L315	L316	L317	L318	L319	L322	L323	L324
	L331	L332	L334	L337	L339	L346	L350	L522
	L523	L524	L526	L527	L528	L529	L530	L531
	L532	L533	L534	L535	L544	L545	L546	
B7 Gemini	VLW105	VLW106	VLW107	VLW108	VLW109	VLW110	VLW111	VLW112
	VLW113	VLW114	VLW115	VLW116				

DAF Cadet	DWL1	DWL2	DWL3	DWL4	DWL5	DWL6	DWL7	DWL8
	DWL9	DWL10	DWL11	DWL12	DWL13	DWL14	DWL15	DWL16
	DWL17	DWL18	DWL19	DWL20	DWL21	DWL22		
Routemaster	RM6	RM25	RM29	RM54	RM275	RM295	RM311	RM348
	RM385	RM432	RM467	RM531	RM548	RM664	RM676	RM719
	RM736	RM838	RM871	RM875	RML892	RML895	RM970	RM997
	RM1003	RM1124	RM1125	RM1280	RM1292	RM1324	RM1330	RM1361
	RM1398	RM1593	RM1725	RM1734	RM1801	RM1811	RM1822	RM1872
	RM1975	RM1978	RM2179	RM2185	RM2217	RML2264	RML2266	RML2301
	RML2307	RML2324	RML2333	RML2343	RML2347	RML2351	RML2366	RML2375
	RML2382	RML2383	RML2387	RML2407	RML2452	RML2477	RML2491	RML2505
	RML2512	RML2514	RML2521	RML2523	RML2524	RML2531	RML2533	RML2536
	RML2538	RML2545	RML2548	RML2549	RML2572	RML2573	RML2574	RML2577
	RML2586	RML2591	RML2598	RML2619	RML2627	RML2636	RML2648	RML2653
	RML2674	RML2692	RML2715	RML2718	RML2726	RML2730	RML2741	RML2753
	RML2759							
DAF ALX400	DLA142	DLA143	DLA144	DLA145	DLA146	DLA147	DLA148	DLA149
	DLA150	DLA151	DLA152	DLA153	DLA154	DLA159	DLA160	DLA161
	DLA162	DLA163	DLA164	DLA165				

Dart	PDL16	PDL17	PDL18					
Routemaster	RM652	RM909	RML882	RML884	RML888	RML896	RML897	RML901
	RM1145	RM1164	RM1185	RM1312	RM1640	RM1776	RM1941	RM1968
	RM2050	RM2060	RM2122	RML2280	RML2287	RML2304	RML2325	RML2326
	RML2328	RML2329	RML2334	RML2344	RML2354	RML2355	RML2356	RML2359
	RML2370	RML2386	RML2401	RML2406	RML2409	RML2416	RML2418	RML2457
	RML2483	RML2492	RML2494	RML2526	RML2534	RML2552	RML2567	RML2571
	RML2597	RML2608	RML2675	RML2682	RML2685	RML2688	RML2716	RML2742
	RML2750	RML2752	RML2754					
DAF ALX400	DLA11	DLA12	DLA13	DLA14	DLA15	DLA16	DLA17	DLA18
	DLA19	DLA20	DLA21	DLA201	DLA202	DLA203	DLA248	DLA249
	DLA270	DLA271	DLA291	DLA292	DLA293	DLA294	DLA295	DLA296
	DLA297	DLA298	DLA299	DLA300	DLA301	DLA302	DLA303	DLA304
	DLA305	DLA306	DLA307	DLA308	DLA309	DLA310	DLA370	DLA371
	DLA372	DLA373	DLA374	DLA375	DLA376	DLA377	DLA378	DLA379
	DLA380	DLA381	DLA382	DLA383	DLA384	DLA385	DLA386	DLA387
	DLA388	DLA389						

Preparing to leave from Arnos Grove Underground station is DWL53, LF52UOE, a Wrightbus Cadet-bodied SB120. As well as those supplied to Arriva's British operations the model can be found with Arriva Netherlands in left-hand drive form.
Tony Wilson

Croydon (Brighton Road, South Croydon) - TC

Dart	ADL9	ADL10	ADL11	ADL12	ADL13	ADL14	ADL15	ADL16
	ADL17	ADL18	ADL19	ADL20	ADL21	ADL22	ADL23	DPP421
	DPP422	DPP423	DPP424	DPP425	DPP426	DPP427	DPP428	DPP429
	DPP430	DPP431						
DAF ALX400	DLA133	DLA134	DLA135	DLA136	DLA155	DLA156	DLA158	DLA171
	DLA172	DLA173	DLA174	DLA175	DLA176	DLA177	DLA178	DLA179
	DLA180	DLA181	DLA182	DLA183	DLA184	DLA185	DLA186	DLA187
	DLA188	DLA189	DLA215	DLA216	DLA217	DLA218	DLA219	DLA220
	DLA221	DLA222	DLA223	DLA233	DLA234	DLA235	DLA236	DLA237
	DLA238	DLA250	DLA251	DLA252	DLA253	DLA254	DLA255	DLA256
	DLA257	DLA258	DLA259	DLA260	DLA261	DLA262	DLA263	DLA264
	DLA265	DLA266	DLA267	DLA268	DLA269			
DAF Pulsar	DW1	DW2	DW3	DW4	DW5	DW6	DW7	DW8
	DW9	DW10	DW11	DW12	DW13	DW14	DW15	DW16
	DW17	DW18	DW19	DW20	DW21	DW22	DW23	DW24
	DW25	DW26	DW27	DW28	DW29	DW30	DW31	DW32
	DW33	DW34						

Edmonton (1e Towpath Road, Stonehill Business Park) - EC

Dart	ADL2	ADL3	ADL4	ADL5	ADL6	ADL7	ADL8	PDL1
	PDL2	PDL3	PDL4	PDL5	PDL6	PDL7	PDL8	PDL9
	PDL10	PDL11	PDL12	PDL13	PDL14	PDL15	PDL60	PDL61
	PDL62	PDL63	PDL70	PDL71	PDL72	PDL73	PDL74	PDL75
	PDL76	PDL77	PDL78	PDL79	PDL80	PDL81	DRN117	DRL154
	DRL155	DRL156	DRL157	DRL158	DRL201	DRL203	DRL206	DRL216
	DRL217	DRL218						
Volvo B10M	VPL3	VPL4	VPL503					
Tiger	TPL1	TPL2	TPL8	TPL518				
DAF	DPL1	DPL2	DPL3	DI4	DP5	DP6	DVH6	DVH8
AEC Regent V	RV1							
Routemaster	RMC1453	RMC1464						
Metrobus	M537	M573	M617	M777	M1075	M1124	M1126	M1130
	M1136	M1231	M1248	M1253	M1254	M1303	M1312	M1313
	M1314	M1318	M1320	M1326	M1327	M1332	M1362	M1367
	M1379	M1398	M1437					
Olympian	L328	L351	L352	L353	L354			
Volvo B7 Gemini	VLW69							
DAF DB250	DLA348	DLA349	DLA350	DLA351	DLA352	DLA353	DLA354	DLA355
	DLA356	DLA357	DLA358	DLA359	DLA360	DLA361	DLA362	DLA363
	DLA364	DLA365	DLA366	DLA367	DLA368	DLA369		

Enfield (Southbury Road, Ponders End) - E

Dart	PDL64	PDL65	PDL66	PDL67	PDL68	PDL69	PDL82	PDL83
	PDL84	PDL85	PDL86	PDL87	PDL88	PDL89	PDL91	PDL92
	PDL93	PDL94						
Cadet	DWL23	DWL24	DWL25	DWL26	DWL27	DWL29	DWL56	
DAF President	DLP1	DLP2	DLP3	DLP4	DLP5	DLP6	DLP7	DLP8
	DLP9	DLP10	DLP11	DLP12	DLP13	DLP14	DLP15	DLP16
	DLP17	DLP18	DLP19	DLP20	DLP76	DLP77	DLP78	DLP79
	DLP80	DLP81	DLP82	DLP83	DLP84	DLP85	DLP86	DLP87
	DLP88	DLP89	DLP90	DLP91	DLP92	DLP93	DLP94	DLP95
	DLP96	DLP97	DLP98	DLP99	DLP100	DLP101	DLP102	DLP103
	DLP104	DLP105	DLP106	DLP107	DLP108	DLP109	DLP110	
DAF ALX400	DLA93	DLA94	DLA95	DLA116	DLA117	DLA118	DLA119	DLA120
	DLA121	DLA122	DLA123	DLA190	DLA191	DLA192	DLA193	DLA194
	DLA195	DLA196	DLA197	DLA198	DLA199	DLA200	DLA210	DLA211
	DLA212	DLA225	DLA226	DLA227	DLA276			

Norwood (Knights Hill, West Norwood) (N)

Olympian	L5	L8	L21	L22	L24	L25	L35	L37
	L45	L46	L49	L50	L56	L58	L65	L66
	L102	L135	L143	L147	L150	L159	L161	L162
	L164	L179	L180	L185	L186	L188	L191	L192
	L194	L196	L197	L198	L201	L207	L214	L217
	L218	L223	L226	L228	L230	L232	L237	L246
	L251	L257	L258					
DAF ALX400	DLA137	DLA138	DLA139	DLA140	DLA141	DLA166	DLA167	DLA168
	DLA169	DLA170	DLA311	DLA312	DLA313	DLA314	DLA315	DLA316
	DLA317	DLA318	DLA319	DLA320	DLA321			
Volvo B7TL ALX400	VLA1	VLA2	VLA3	VLA4	VLA5	VLA6	VLA7	VLA8
	VLA9	VLA10	VLA11	VLA12	VLA13	VLA14	VLA15	VLA16
	VLA17	VLA18	VLA19	VLA20	VLA21	VLA22	VLA23	VLA24
	VLA25	VLA26	VLA27	VLA28	VLA29	VLA30	VLA31	VLA32
	VLA33	VLA34	VLA35	VLA36	VLA37	VLA38	VLA39	VLA40
	VLA41	VLA42	VLA43	VLA44	VLA45	VLA46	VLA47	VLA48
	VLA49	VLA50	VLA51	VLA52	VLA53	VLA54	VLA55	

Stamford Hill (Rookwood Road) - SF

Metrobus	M469	M652	M721	M732	M733	M747	M752	M762
	M765	M770	M773	M798	M903	M1000	M1121	M1123
	M1140	M1170	M1179	M1214				
Olympian	L525	L536	L547	L548	L549			
DAF ALX400	DLA38	DLA96	DLA97	DLA98	DLA99	DLA101	DLA102	DLA103
	DLA104	DLA105	DLA106	DLA107	DLA108	DLA109	DLA111	DLA112
	DLA113	DLA114	DLA115	DLA204	DLA205	DLA206	DLA207	DLA208
	DLA209	DLA224	DLA272	DLA273	DLA274	DLA275		
Volvo B7 Gemini	VLW140	VLW141	VLW142	VLW143	VLW144	VLW145	VLW146	VLW147
	VLW148	VLW149	VLW150	VLW151	VLW152	VLW153	VLW154	VLW155
	VLW156	VLW157	VLW158	VLW159	VLW160	VLW161	VLW162	VLW163
	VLW164	VLW165	VLW166	VLW167	VLW168			

Thornton Heath (719 London Road) - TH

Dart	DDL1	DDL2	DDL4	DDL6	DDL7	DDL8	DDL9	DDL10
	DDL11	DDL12	DDL13	DDL14	DDL15	PDL50	PDL51	PDL52
	PDL53	PDL54	PDL55	PDL56	PDL57	PDL58	PDL59	DRL205
Olympian	L244							
DAF ALX400	DLA2	DLA3	DLA4	DLA5	DLA6	DLA7	DLA8	DLA9
	DLA10	DLA39	DLA40	DLA41	DLA42	DLA43	DLA44	DLA48
	DLA49	DLA50	DLA51	DLA52	DLA53	DLA54	DLA55	DLA56
	DLA57	DLA58	DLA59	DLA60	DLA61	DLA62	DLA63	DLA64
	DLA126	DLA127	DLA128	DLA129	DLA130	DLA131	DLA132	DLA322
	DLA323	DLA324	DLA325	DLA326	DLA327	DLA328	DLA329	DLA330
	DLA331	DLA332	DLA333	DLA334	DLA335	DLA336	DLA337	DLA338
	DLA339	DLA340	DLA341	DLA342	DLA343	DLA344	DLA345	DLA346
	DLA347							

Tottenham (Philip Lane) - AR

Dart	PDL39	PDL40	PDL41	PDL42	PDL43	PDL44	PDL45	PDL46
	PDL47	PDL48	PDL49					
Routemaster	RM5	RML2261	RML2265	RML2267	RML2277	RML2292	RML2294	RML2315
	RML2322	RML2323	RML2330	RML2340	RML2341	RML2346	RML2350	RML2372
	RML2373	RML2380	RML2391	RML2394	RML2408	RML2434	RML2468	RML2503
	RML2504	RML2510	RML2518	RML2525	RML2527	RML2528	RML2544	RML2546
	RML2562	RML2563	RML2569	RML2582	RML2588	RML2589	RML2595	RML2611
	RML2625	RML2628	RML2632	RML2635	RML2638	RML2643	RML2655	RML2658
	RML2660	RML2663	RML2666	RML2678	RML2684	RML2686	RML2694	RML2708
	RML2719	RML2746	RML2747	RML2756				
Metrobus	M1402	M1405	M1406					

DAF ALX400	DLA230	DLA231	DLA232	DLA239	DLA240	DLA241	DLA242	DLA243
	DLA244	DLA245	DLA246	DLA247	DLA277	DLA278	DLA279	DLA280
	DLA281	DLA282	DLA283	DLA284	DLA285	DLA286	DLA287	DLA288
	DLA289							
Volvo B7 Gemini	VLW85	VLW86	VLW87	VLW88	VLW89	VLW90	VLW91	VLW92
	VLW93	VLW94	VLW95	VLW96	VLW97	VLW98	VLW99	VLW100
	VLW101	VLW102	VLW103	VLW104	VLW105	VLW117	VLW118	VLW119
	VLW120	VLW121	VLW122	VLW123	VLW124	VLW125	VLW126	VLW127
	VLW128	VLW129	VLW130	VLW131	VLW132	VLW133	VLW134	VLW135
	VLW136	VLW137	VLW138	VLW139	VLW169	VLW170	VLW171	VLW172
	VLW173	VLW174	VLW175	VLW176	VLW177	VLW178	VLW179	VLW180
	VLW181	VLW182	VLW183	VLW184	VLW185	VLW186	VLW187	VLW188
	VLW189	VLW190	VLW191	VLW192	VLW193	VLW194	VLW195	VLW196
	VLW197	VLW198	VLW199					

Wood Green (High Road) - WN (sub depot at Regent's Avenue, Palmers Green - AD)

DAF Cadet	CW1	DWL30	DWL31	DWL32	DWL33	DWL34	DWL35	DWL36
	DWL37	DWL38	DWL39	DWL40	DWL41	DWL42	DWL43	DWL44
	DWL45	DWL46	DWL47	DWL48	DWL49	DWL50	DWL51	DWL52
	DWL53	DWL54	DWL55					
DAF ALX400	DLA1	DLA22	DLA23	DLA24	DLA25	DAL26	DLA27	DLA28
	DLA29	DLA30	DLA31	DLA32	DLA33	DLA34	DLA35	DLA36
	DLA37	DLA45	DLA46	DLA47	DLA65	DLA66	DLA67	DLA68
	DLA69	DLA70	DLA71	DLA72	DLA73	DLA74	DLA75	DLA76
	DLA77	DLA78	DLA79	DLA80	DLA81	DLA82	DLA83	DLA84
	DLA85	DLA86	DLA87	DLA88	DLA89	DLA90	DLA91	DLA92
	DLA124	DLA125	DLA213	DLA214	DLA228	DLA229		
DAF President	DLP40	DLP41	DLP42	DLP43	DLP44	DLP45	DLP46	DLP47
	DLP48	DLP49	DLP50	DLP51	DLP52	DLP53	DLP54	DLP55
	DLP56	DLP57	DLP58	DLP59	DLP60	DLP61	DLP62	DLP63
	DLP64	DLP65	DLP66	DLP67	DLP68	DLP69	DLP70	DLP71
	DLP72	DLP73	DLP74	DLP75				
Volvo B7 Gemini	VLW1	VLW2	VLW3	VLW4	VLW5	VLW6	VLW7	VLW8
	VLW9	VLW10	VLW11	VLW12	VLW13	VLW14	VLW15	VLW16
	VLW17	VLW18	VLW19	VLW20	VLW21	VLW22	VLW23	VLW24
	VLW25	VLW26	VLW27	VLW28	VLW29	VLW30	VLW31	VLW32
	VLW33	VLW34	VLW35	VLW36	VLW37	VLW38	VLW39	VLW40
	VLW41	VLW42	VLW43	VLW44	VLW45	VLW46	VLW47	VLW48
	VLW49	VLW50	VLW51	VLW52	VLW53	VLW54	VLW55	VLW56
	VLW57	VLW58	VLW59	VLW60	VLW61	VLW62	VLW63	VLW64
	VLW65	VLW66	VLW67	VLW68	VLW70	VLW71	VLW72	VLW73
	VLW74	VLW75	VLW76	VLW77	VLW78	VLW79	VLW80	VLW81
	VLW82	VLW83	VLW84					

On loan to Original London Sightseeing Tour (OLST)

| VDL Bus Pulsar | DW61 | DW62 | DW63 | DW64 | DW65 | DW66 | DW67 | DW68 |
| | DW69 | DW70 | DW71 | DW72 | DW73 | | | |

Unallocated

Dart	PDL90						
DAF coach	DI7						
Mercedes-Benz Citaro	MA30	MA31	MA32	MA33	MA34	MA35	MA36
Metrobus	M665	M1319	M1322	M1324			
Olympian	L340	L539	L540	L541	L542		
DAF ALX400	DLA157						

ORIGINAL LONDON SIGHTSEEING TOUR

The Original London Sightseeing Tour Ltd, Jews Road, Wandsworth, SW18 1TB

DD202	VVN202Y	Dennis Dominator DDA149	Northern Counties	PO43/31D	1983	London Pride, 2001
DD203	VVN203Y	Dennis Dominator DDA149	Northern Counties	PO43/31D	1983	London Pride, 2001
EMB763	D553YNO	MCW Metrobus DR115/4	MCW	PO61/35D	1987	New World FirstBus, 2001
EMB764	E964JAR	MCW Metrobus DR115/4	MCW	PO61/35D	1987	New World FirstBus, 2001
EMB765	E965JAR	MCW Metrobus DR115/4	MCW	PO61/35D	1987	New World FirstBus, 2001
EMB766	E966JAR	MCW Metrobus DR115/4	MCW	PO61/35D	1987	New World FirstBus, 2001
EMB767	E767JAR	MCW Metrobus DR115/4	MCW	PO61/35D	1987	New World FirstBus, 2001
EMB768	E768JAR	MCW Metrobus DR115/4	MCW	PO61/35D	1987	New World FirstBus, 2001
EMB769	E769JAR	MCW Metrobus DR115/4	MCW	PO61/35D	1987	New World FirstBus, 2001
EMB770	E770JAR	MCW Metrobus DR115/4	MCW	PO61/35D	1987	New World FirstBus, 2001
EMB771	E771JAR	MCW Metrobus DR115/4	MCW	PO61/35D	1987	New World FirstBus, 2001
EMB772	E772JAR	MCW Metrobus DR115/4	MCW	PO61/35D	1987	New World FirstBus, 2001
EMB773	E773JAR	MCW Metrobus DR115/4	MCW	PO61/35D	1987	New World FirstBus, 2001
MB24w	WYW24T	MCW Metrobus DR101/8	MCW	PO43/28D	1979	Cowie Leaside, 1995
MB51w	WYW51T	MCW Metrobus DR101/8	MCW	PO43/28D	1979	Arriva London, 1999
MB121	BYX121V	MCW Metrobus DR101/9	MCW	PO43/28D	1979	Cowie South London, 1996
MB123w	BYX123V	MCW Metrobus DR101/9	MCW	PO43/28D	1979	Cowie Leaside, 1995
MB143	BYX143V	MCW Metrobus DR101/9	MCW	CPO43/28D	1979	Cowie Leaside, 1996
MB185w	BYX185V	MCW Metrobus DR101/9	MCW	PO43/28D	1979	Cowie South London, 1996
MB245w	BYX245V	MCW Metrobus DR101/12	MCW	PO43/28D	1980	Cowie Leaside, 1996
MB251	BYX251V	MCW Metrobus DR101/12	MCW	PO43/28D	1980	Arriva London, 2000
MB296	BYX296V	MCW Metrobus DR101/12	MCW	PO43/28D	1980	London South, 1998
MB304	BYX304V	MCW Metrobus DR101/12	MCW	CPO43/28D	1980	Cowie South London, 1996
MB310w	BYX310V	MCW Metrobus DR101/12	MCW	PO43/28F	1980	Arriva London, 1996
MB314	BYX314V	MCW Metrobus DR101/12	MCW	PO43/28D	1979	London South, 1998
MB346w	GYE346W	MCW Metrobus DR101/12	MCW	PO43/28D	1980	Arriva London, 1996
MB351	GYE351W	MCW Metrobus DR101/12	MCW	O43/28D	1980	London General, 1998
MB353	GYE353W	MCW Metrobus DR101/12	MCW	PO43/28D	1980	London General, 1997
MB389	GYE389W	MCW Metrobus DR101/12	MCW	PO43/28D	1980	Arriva London, 1999
MB399	GYE399W	MCW Metrobus DR101/12	MCW	B43/28D	1980	Arriva London, 2000
MB495	GYE495W	MCW Metrobus DR101/14	MCW	PO43/28D	1980	Cowie South London, 1996
MB500	GYE500W	MCW Metrobus DR101/14	MCW	PO43/28D	1980	Arriva London, 1999
MB509	GYE509W	MCW Metrobus DR101/14	MCW	PO43/28D	1980	Arriva London, 1998
MB525	GYE525W	MCW Metrobus DR101/14	MCW	PO43/28D	1981	London South, 1998
MB530	GYE530W	MCW Metrobus DR101/14	MCW	B43/28D	1981	Arriva London, 2000
MB533	GYE533W	MCW Metrobus DR101/14	MCW	PO43/28D	1981	London South, 1998
MB539	GYE539W	MCW Metrobus DR101/14	MCW	PO43/28D	1981	Cowie South London, 1996

The Original Tour operate two dual-doored Dominators with Northern Counties bodywork. These feature off-side doors as illustrated by DD203, VVN203Y, seen with City Sightseeing London Vinyls.
Paul Stokes

119

Recent arrivals for The Original Tour are Alexander-bodied Olympians transferred from Arriva London during 2003. Fourteen are now in use, including OA333, J433BSH, which had quite a load in Parliament Square during a February duty. *Richard Godfrey*

MB553	GYE553W	MCW Metrobus DR101/14	MCW	PO43/28D	1981	Cowie South London, 1996
MB555	GYE555W	MCW Metrobus DR101/14	MCW	PO31/14F	1981	Arriva London, 2000
MB558	GYE558W	MCW Metrobus DR101/14	MCW	PO43/28D	1981	Cowie South London, 1996
MB603	GYE603W	MCW Metrobus DR101/14	MCW	PO43/28D	1981	Arriva London, 2000
MB609	KYO609X	MCW Metrobus DR101/14	MCW	B43/28D	1981	Arriva London, 2000
MB646	KYV646X	MCW Metrobus DR101/14	MCW	B43/28D	1981	Arriva London, 1998
MB659	KYV659X	MCW Metrobus DR101/14	MCW	B43/28D	1981	Arriva London, 1999
MB672	KYV672X	MCW Metrobus DR101/14	MCW	PO43/28D	1981	London North, 1998
MB682	KYV682X	MCW Metrobus DR101/14	MCW	B43/28D	1981	Arriva London, 2000
MB707	KYV707X	MCW Metrobus DR101/14	MCW	PO43/28D	1981	London North, 1998
MB710	KYV710X	MCW Metrobus DR101/14	MCW	B43/28D	1981	Arriva London, 2000
MB724	KYV724X	MCW Metrobus DR101/14	MCW	B43/28D	1981	Arriva London, 2002
MB729	KYV729X	MCW Metrobus DR101/14	MCW	B43/28D	1981	Arriva London, 2000
MB746	KYV746X	MCW Metrobus DR101/14	MCW	B43/28D	1982	Arriva London, 1999
MB748	KYV748X	MCW Metrobus DR101/14	MCW	PO43/28D	1982	London North, 1998
MB754	KYV754X	MCW Metrobus DR101/14	MCW	PO43/28D	1982	Arriva London, 1998
MB799	KYV799X	MCW Metrobus DR101/14	MCW	PO43/28D	1982	Arriva London, 2000
MB840	OJD840Y	MCW Metrobus DR101/16	MCW	PO43/28D	1983	Cowie South London, 1996
MB863	OJD863Y	MCW Metrobus DR101/16	MCW	B43/28D	1983	Arriva London, 2000
MB895	A895SUL	MCW Metrobus DR101/16	MCW	PO43/28D	1983	Arriva London, 2000
MB927	A927SUL	MCW Metrobus DR101/16	MCW	PO43/28D	1983	London South, 1998
MB1152	B152WUL	MCW Metrobus DR101/17	MCW	PO43/28D	1983	Arriva London, 1999
MB1227	B227WUL	MCW Metrobus DR101/17	MCW	PO43/28D	1983	Arriva London, 1999
MB1239	B239WUL	MCW Metrobus DR101/17	MCW	B43/28D	1983	Arriva London, 2002
MB1265	B265WUL	MCW Metrobus DR101/17	MCW	B43/28D	1983	Arriva London, 2002
MB1310	C310BUV	MCW Metrobus DR101/17	MCW	B43/28D	1983	Arriva London, 2002
MB1401	C401BUV	MCW Metrobus DR101/17	MCW	B43/28D	1983	Arriva London, 2002
ML10	B240LRA	MCW Metroliner DR130/7	MCW	O63/23F	1986	Dunn Line, Nottingham, 1994
ML12	A112KFX	MCW Metroliner DR130/5	MCW	O67/22F	1984	London Pride, 2001
ML13	A113KFX	MCW Metroliner DR130/5	MCW	O67/20F	1984	London Pride, 2001
ML14	A114KFX	MCW Metroliner DR130/5	MCW	O67/20F	1984	London Pride, 2001
ML15	B115ORU	MCW Metroliner DR130/7	MCW	O63/20F	1984	London Pride, 2001
ML16	C906GUD	MCW Metroliner DR130/21	MCW	O63/23F	1985	London Pride, 2001
ML17	C907GUD	MCW Metroliner DR130/21	MCW	O63/17F	1985	London Pride, 2001
ML18	C118FKH	MCW Metroliner DR130/24	MCW	O63/20F	1986	London Pride, 2001
ML19	IIL7269	MCW Metroliner DR130/3	MCW	O63/20F	1984	London Pride, 2001
ML20	B224VHW	MCW Metroliner DR130/3	MCW	O63/20F	1984	London Pride, 2001

Re-imported from Hong Kong, a batch of tri-axle Metroliners were latterly used by New World First Bus. They were built for CMB as 108 seaters in a 3+2 arrangement and used mostly on Hong Kong island. Eleven have been re-built as partial open-top for use on The Original Tour with EMB765, E965JAR, shown here. *Dave Heath*

ML21	B121ORU	MCW Metroliner DR130/3	MCW	063/20F	1984	London Pride, 2001
ML22	B222VHW	MCW Metroliner DR130/3	MCW	063/16F	1984	London Pride, 2001
ML25	B225VHW	MCW Metroliner DR130/3	MCW	063/18F	1984	London Pride, 2001
ML27	A667XDA	MCW Metroliner DR130/6	MCW	063/23F	1984	London Pride, 2001
ML28	B824AAT	MCW Metroliner DR130/3	MCW	063/16F	1984	London Pride, 2001
ML29	B825AAT	MCW Metroliner DR130/3	MCW	063/16F	1984	London Pride, 2001
ML32	C52VJU	MCW Metroliner DR130/22	MCW	063/23F	1985	London Pride, 2001
ML33	C133CFB	MCW Metroliner DR130/24	MCW	063/18F	1986	London Pride, 2001

OA320-349			Leyland Olympian ON2R50C13Z4	Alexander RH		PO43/25D* 1992	Arriva London, 2003
						*320 is PO42/25D, 321 is 042/25D.	

320	J320BSH	336	J336BSH	343	J343BSH	347	J347BSH
321	J321BSH	338	J338BSH	344	J344BSH	348	J348BSH
333	J433BSH	341	J341BSH	345	J345BSH	349	J349BSH
335	J335BSH	342	J342BSH				

Previous Registrations:

B240LRA	B901XJO, A5BOB		E772JAR	DV2896 (HK)
D553YNO	DV471 (HK)		E773JAR	DU3481 (HK)
E767JAR	DU3460 (HK)		E964JAR	DT4549 (HK)
E768JAR	DU8346 (HK)		E965JAR	DV4883 (HK)
E769JAR	DT7256 (HK)		E966JAR	DV3433 (HK)
E770JAR	DU8506 (HK)		IIL7269	B117ORU
E771JAR	DT9187 (HK)		C118KFH	C593JAT

Depots: Jews Road, Wandsworth

ARRIVA SOUTHERN COUNTIES

Arriva Southern Counties Ltd, Arriva West Sussex Ltd,
Arriva Kent Thameside Ltd; Arriva Kent & Sussex Ltd; New Enterprise Ltd
Arriva Medway Towns Ltd, Arriva Guildford & West Surrey Ltd;
Arriva Colchester Ltd; Arriva Southend Ltd
Invicta House, Armstrong Road, Maidstone, Kent, ME15 6TX

Minibuses

1118-1122			Mercedes-Benz 0810 Vario	Plaxton Beaver 2	B27F	1998	
1118	GI	R118TKO	**1120**	GI	R120TKO	**1121**	GI	R121TKO	**1122**	GI	R122TKO
1119	GI	R119TKO									

1450	TW	M450HPF	Optare MetroRider MR17	Optare	B29F	1994	Londonlinks, 1997
1451	TW	M451HPF	Optare MetroRider MR17	Optare	B29F	1994	Londonlinks, 1997
1475	SI	P475DPE	Mercedes-Benz 711D	Plaxton Beaver	B27F	1997	
1476	TW	P476DPE	Mercedes-Benz 711D	Plaxton Beaver	B27F	1997	
1477	TW	P477DPE	Mercedes-Benz 711D	Plaxton Beaver	B27F	1997	
1479	TW	P479DPE	Mercedes-Benz 711D	Plaxton Beaver	B27F	1997	
1480	HK	P480DPE	Mercedes-Benz 711D	Plaxton Beaver	B27F	1997	

1601-1605			Dennis Dart SLF	Plaxton Pointer MPD	N29F	2000	
1601	TW	W601YKN	**1603**	TW	W603YKN	**1604**	TW	W604YKN	**1605**	TW	W605YKN
1602	TW	W602YKN									

1606-1617			TransBus Dart 8.8m	TransBus Mini Pointer	N29F	2004	
1606	GI	GN04UCW	**1609**	GI	GN04UCZ	**1612**	GI	GN04UDE	**1615**	GI	GN04UDJ
1607	GI	GN04UCX	**1610**	GI	GN04UDB	**1613**	GI	GN04UDG	**1616**	GI	GN04UDK
1608	GI	GN04UCY	**1611**	GI	GN04UDD	**1614**	GI	GN04UDH	**1617**	GI	GN04UDL

1751-1756			Mercedes-Benz Sprinter 411CDi	Mercedes-Benz	N15F	2002	
1751	SE	DE52OKV	**1753**	SE	DE52OKX	**1755**	SE	DE52OLM	**1756**	SE	DE52OLN
1752	SE	DE52OKW	**1754**	SE	DE52OKZ						

1805-1808			Optare MetroRider MR15	Optare	B29F	1996	
1805	NF	N805BKN	**1806**	NF	N806BKN	**1807**	NF	N807BKN	**1808**	NF	N808BKN

1809-1814			Optare MetroRider MR	Optare	B29F	1998	
1809	NF	R809TKO	**1811**	NF	R811TKO	**1813**	NF	R813TKO	**1814**	NF	R814TKO
1810	NF	R810TKO	**1812**	NF	R812TKO						

1850	DA	L600BUS	Optare MetroRider MR11	Optare	B31F	1995	Arriva The Shires, 2001
1851	DA	L800BUS	Optare MetroRider MR11	Optare	B31F	1996	Arriva The Shires, 2001
1852	DA	N852YKE	Optare MetroRider MR13	Optare	B25F	1995	Londonlinks, 1995

E2115	GI	N919ETM	Mercedes-Benz 709D	Plaxton Beaver	B27F	1995	
E2134	GI	N914ETM	Mercedes-Benz 709D	Plaxton Beaver	B27F	1995	

E2174-2193			Mercedes-Benz Vario 0810	Plaxton Beaver 2	B27F	1997-98	
E2174	CO	R174VBM	**E2187**	GI	R187DNM	**E2191**	SE	R191DNM	**E2193**	SE	R193DNM
E2186	SI	R186DNM	**E2188**	SE	R188DNM	**E2192**	SE	R192DNM			

E2243	CO	R763DUB	Mercedes-Benz Vario 0810	Plaxton Beaver 2	B27F	1997	Arriva Yorkshire, 2000

E2372-2384			Mercedes-Benz Vario 0810	Plaxton Beaver 2	B25F	1998	
E2372	CO	R942VPU	**E2379**	GI	R949VPU	**E2381**	GI	R951VPU	**E2383**	SI	R953VPU
E2378	GI	R948VPU	**E2380**	GI	R950VPU	**E2382**	CO	R952VPU	**E2384**	w	R954VPU

E2388	SI	P478DPE	Mercedes-Benz 711D	Plaxton Beaver 2	B27F	1997	
E2391	SI	P481DPE	Mercedes-Benz 711D	Plaxton Beaver 2	B27F	1997	
E2392	GI	P482DPE	Mercedes-Benz 711D	Plaxton Beaver 2	B27F	1997	

Shortly before we went to press, Arriva Southern Counties accepted delivery of a large number of new buses with twelve Pointers and forty-nine Volvo double-decks for Gillingham and Cadets and Commanders for Maidstone. Seen in Dartford with lettering for the 480/490 is Scania 3257, N257BKK. *Richard Godfrey*

Coaches

2031	TO	UJI2338	Scania K113CRB	Plaxton Paramount 3500 III	C49FT	1990	Happy Days, Woodseaves, 1994
2051	TO	M51AWW	Scania K113CRB	Van Hool Alizée	C51F	1995	Arriva Yorkshire (W), 1999
2054	TO	M54AWW	Scania K113CRB	Van Hool Alizée	C49FT	1995	Arriva Yorkshire (W), 1999
2194	TO	J25UNY	Leyland Tiger TRCL10/3ARZM	Plaxton 321	C53F	1992	Bebb, Llantwit Fardre, 1993
2196	CO	J27UNY	Leyland Tiger TRCL10/3ARZM	Plaxton 321	C53F	1992	Bebb, Llantwit Fardre, 1993
2830	TO	TIB5903	Volvo B10M-61	Van Hool Alizée H	C53F	1988	Jason, St Mary Cray, 1996
2831	TO	TIB5904	Volvo B10M-61	Van Hool Alizée H	C53F	1988	Jason, St Mary Cray, 1996
2835	TO	A11GTA	Volvo B10M-60	Plaxton Paramount 3500 III	C53F	1991	Kentish Bus, 1997
2846	ME	H846AHS	Volvo B10M-60	Plaxton Paramount 3500 III	C49FT	1991	Express Travel, Liverpool, 1995
2851	TO	G801BPG	Volvo B10M-60	Plaxton Paramount 3500 III	C37FT	1989	Speedlink, 1997
2894	TO	W183CDN	DAF DE33WSSB3000	Van Hool T9 Alizée	C52F	2000	
2895	TO	SCZ9651	DAF DE33WSSB3000	Van Hool T9 Alizée	C49F	1999	Eirebus, Dublin, 2003
2896	TO	SCZ9652	DAF DE33WSSB3000	Van Hool T9 Alizée	C49F	1999	Eirebus, Dublin, 2003
2897	TO	R157GNW	DAF DE33WSSB3000	Ikarus Blue Danube 396	C49F	1998	
2898	TO	W198CDN	DAF DE33WSSB3000	Ikarus Blue Danube 396	C53F	2000	
2899	TO	F899GUM	DAF MB230LB615	Plaxton Paramount 3500 III	C53F	1989	O'Sullivan, Killarney, 1997
2900	TO	F621HGO	DAF MB230LT615	Van Hool Alizée H	C53FT	1989	London Coaches (Kent), 1997
2901	TO	F901GUM	DAF MB230LB615	Plaxton Paramount 3500 III	C53F	1989	O'Sullivan, Killarney, 1996
2902	TO	J36GCX	DAF SB2305DHS585	Duple 320	C57F	1992	Eagle, Bristol, 1997

2903-2910 | | DAF DE33WSSB3000 | Plaxton Première 320 | C53F | 1998

2903	ME	R903BKO	2905	ME	R905BKO	2907	ME	R907BKO	2909	ME	R909BKO
2904	ME	R904BKO	2906	ME	R906BKO	2908	ME	R908BKO	2910	ME	R910BKO

2911	ME	R455SKX	DAF DE33WSSB3000	Plaxton Prima	C53F	1997	Arriva The Shires, 2003
2912	ME	R456SKX	DAF DE33WSSB3000	Plaxton Prima	C53F	1997	Arriva The Shires, 2003
E4305	CO	BAZ7384	Leyland Tiger TRCTL11/3RH	Plaxton Paramount 3500 II	C51F	1985	London & Country (G&WS), 1992
E4352	CO	M52AWW	Scania K113CRB	Van Hool Alizée	C44FT	1995	Arriva Yorkshire (W), 1999
E4353	CO	M53AWW	Scania K113CRB	Van Hool Alizée	C51F	1995	Arriva Yorkshire (W), 1999

Single-deck Buses

3041	TW	E885KYW	Leyland Lynx LX112TL11ZR1S	Leyland Lynx	B49F	1987	London Coaches (Kent), 1996
3043	u	E887KYW	Leyland Lynx LX112TL11ZR1S	Leyland Lynx	B47F	1987	London Coaches (Kent), 1996
3044	u	E890KYW	Leyland Lynx LX1126LXCTZR1S	Leyland Lynx	B47F	1987	London Coaches (Kent), 1996
3045	TW	F45ENF	Leyland Lynx LX112L10ZR1R	Leyland Lynx	B49F	1988	Shearings, 1991
3046	ME	F46ENF	Leyland Lynx LX112L10ZR1R	Leyland Lynx	B49F	1988	Shearings, 1991
3049	ME	H256YLG	Leyland Lynx LX2R11V18Z4R	Leyland Lynx 2	B49F	1990	Aintree Coachline, 1995
3051	NF	H814EKJ	Leyland Lynx LX2R11C15Z4S	Leyland Lynx 2	B49F	1991	Kentish Bus, 1997
3052	ME	H816EKJ	Leyland Lynx LX2R11C15Z4S	Leyland Lynx 2	B49F	1991	Kentish Bus, 1997
3054	ME	H815EKJ	Leyland Lynx LX2R11C15Z4S	Leyland Lynx 2	B49F	1991	Boro'line, Maidstone, 1992
3065	HK	G45VME	Leyland Lynx LX2R11C15Z4S	Leyland Lynx 2	B49F	1989	Boro'line, Maidstone, 1992
3103	HK	L500DKT	Dennis Dart 9SDL3032	WSC Portsdown	B43F	1994	Wealden Beeline, 1997
3104	HK	M501PKJ	Dennis Dart 9SDL3032	WSC Portsdown	B43F	1994	Wealden Beeline, 1997
3105	HK	M502RKO	Dennis Dart 9SDL3032	WSC Portsdown	B43F	1995	Wealden Beeline, 1997
3106	HK	L503HKM	Dennis Dart 9SDL3032	WSC Portsdown	B43F	1994	Wealden Beeline, 1997

3112-3158

Dennis Dart 9SDL3034 — Northern Counties Paladin — B35F — 1994

3112	DA	L112YVK	3134	NF	L134YVK	3145	GI	L145YVK	3155	NF	L155YVK
3113	NF	L113YVK	3135	NF	L135YVK	3150	DA	L150YVK	3156	NF	L156YVK
3132	NF	L132YVK	3138	GI	L138YVK	3153	GI	L153YVK	3158	NF	L158BFT
3133	NF	L133YVK	3143	NF	L143YVK	3154	GI	L154YVK			

3165	SI	J465MKL	Dennis Dart 9.8SDL3012	Plaxton Pointer	B40F	1991
3166	SI	J466OKP	Dennis Dart 9.8SDL3017	Plaxton Pointer	B40F	1992
3168	CO	J468OKP	Dennis Dart 9.8SDL3017	Plaxton Pointer	B40F	1992
3170	HO	J470SKO	Dennis Dart 9.8SDL3017	Plaxton Pointer (1995)	B40F	1992
3171	SI	J471SKO	Dennis Dart 9.8SDL3017	Plaxton Pointer	B40F	1992
3172	ME	N234TPK	Dennis Dart SLF	Plaxton Pointer 2	N35F	1996
3174	SI	M100CBB	Dennis Dart 9.8SDL3040	Plaxton Pointer	B40F	1995	Cardiff Bluebird, 1996
3175	SR	M200CBB	Dennis Dart 9.8SDL3040	Plaxton Pointer	B40F	1995	Cardiff Bluebird, 1996

3176-3183

Dennis Dart SLF — Plaxton Pointer — N40F — 1996

3176	ME	P176LKL	3178	GI	P178LKL	3179	DA	P179LKL	3181	ME	P181LKL
3177	ME	P177LKL									

3184	TW	P184LKL	Dennis Dart SLF	Plaxton Pointer	N37F	1997
3185	TW	P185LKL	Dennis Dart SLF	Plaxton Pointer	N37F	1997

3186-3191

Dennis Dart SLF — Plaxton Pointer — N40F — 1997

3186	NF	P186LKJ	3188	NF	P188LKJ	3190	NF	P190LKJ	3191	NF	P191LKJ
3187	NF	P187LKJ	3189	NF	P189LKJ						

3192-3247

Dennis Dart SLF — Plaxton Pointer 2 — N40F — 1997

3192	ME	P192LKJ	3207	ME	P207LKJ	3221	GI	P221MKL	3235	GI	P235MKN
3193	ME	P193LKJ	3208	ME	P208LKJ	3223	GI	P223MKL	3236	GI	P236MKN
3194	ME	P194LKJ	3209	ME	P209LKJ	3224	GI	P224MKL	3237	GI	P237MKN
3195	ME	P195LKJ	3210	HK	P210LKJ	3225	GI	P225MKL	3238	GI	P238MKN
3196	ME	P196LKJ	3211	HK	P211LKJ	3226	GI	P226MKL	3239	GI	P239MKN
3197	GU	P197LKJ	3212	HK	P212LKJ	3227	GI	P227MKL	3240	GI	P240MKN
3198	GU	P198LKJ	3213	HK	P213LKJ	3228	GI	P228MKL	3241	GI	P241MKN
3199	SI	P199LKJ				3229	GI	P229MKL	3242	GI	P242MKN
3201	ME	P201LKJ	3215	ME	P215LKJ	3230	GI	P230MKL	3243	GI	P243MKN
3202	ME	P202LKJ	3216	GI	P216LKJ	3231	GI	P231MKL	3244	GI	P244MKN
3203	ME	P203LKJ	3217	u	P217MKL	3232	GI	P232MKL	3245	GI	P245MKN
3204	ME	P204LKJ	3218	DA	P218MKL	3233	GI	P233MKN	3246	ME	P246MKN
3205	ME	P205LKJ	3219	GI	P219MKL	3234	GI	P234MKN	3247	ME	P247MKN
3206	ME	P206LKJ	3220	GI	P220MKL						

Dart 3176, P176LKL has been repainted in the colours of Maidstone corporation to celebrate the centenary of buses in the town. It was photographed in Maidstone's Park Wood Parade in March 2004. *Martin Smith*

3248	HO	P278FPK	Dennis Dart SLF			Plaxton Pointer 2		N40F	1997		
3249	ME	P279FPK	Dennis Dart SLF			Plaxton Pointer 2		N40F	1997		

3250-3259 — Scania L113CRL, Wright Axcess-ultralow, N43F, 1995

3250	NF	N250BKK	3253	NF	N253BKK	3256	NF	N256BKK	3258	NF	N258BKK
3251	NF	N251BKK	3254	NF	N254BKK	3257	NF	N257BKK	3259	NF	N259BKK
3252	NF	N252BKK	3255	NF	N255BKK						

3261-3272 — Dennis Dart SLF, Plaxton Pointer 2, N39F, 1998

3261	DA	R261EKO	3264	DA	R264EKO	3267	DA	R267EKO	3270	DA	R270EKO
3262	DA	R262EKO	3265	DA	R265EKO	3268	DA	R268EKO	3271	DA	R271EKO
3263	DA	R263EKO	3266	DA	R266EKO	3269	DA	R269EKO	3272	DA	R272EKO

3273-3289 — Dennis Dart SLF, Plaxton Pointer 2, N39F*, 1999 — *3276-81 are N37F

3273	NF	T273JKM	3278	DA	T278JKM	3282	DA	T282JKM	3286	DA	T286JKM
3274	NF	T274JKM	3279	DA	T279JKM	3283	DA	T283JKM	3287	DA	T287JKM
3275	NF	T275JKM	3280	DA	T280JKM	3284	DA	T284JKM	3288	DA	T288JKM
3276	DA	T276JKM	3281	DA	T281JKM	3285	DA	T285JKM	3289	NF	T289JKM
3277	DA	T277JKM									

3291-3303 — Dennis Dart SLF, Plaxton Pointer 2, N34D, 2001

3291	DA	Y291TKJ	3294	DA	Y294TKJ	3297	DA	Y297TKJ	3301	DA	Y302TKJ
3292	DA	Y292TKJ	3295	DA	Y295TKJ	3298	DA	Y298TKJ	3302	DA	Y301TKJ
3293	DA	Y293TKJ	3296	DA	Y296TKJ	3299	DA	Y299TKJ	3303	DA	Y303TKJ

3307	ME	R307CMV	Dennis Dart SLF			Plaxton Pointer 2		N39F	1997		
3308	ME	R308CMV	Dennis Dart SLF			Plaxton Pointer 2		N39F	1997		

3601-3619 — Volvo B6-9.9M, Plaxton Pointer, B40F, 1994-95

3601	GI	L601EKM	3606	SR	L606EKM	3611	TW	M611PKP	3615	TO	M615PKP
3602	GI	L602EKM	3607	GI	L607EKM	3612	TW	M612PKP	3616	TW	M616PKP
3603	GI	L603EKM	3608	TW	L608EKM	3613	TW	M613PKP	3617	TW	M617PKP
3604	GI	L604EKM	3609	TW	L609EKM	3614	ME	M614PKP	3619	TO	M619PKP
3605	GI	L605EKM	3610	TW	L610EKM						

In common with other Arriva fleets the DAF, now VDL Bus, SB120 with Wrightbus Cadet bodywork has been selected for single-deck buses. Pictured in Guildford, 3928, GK51SZF is one of the 2002 intake. *Dave Heath*

3701-3706 — Dennis Dart SLF — Plaxton Pointer SPD — N44F — 1998

3701	ME	S701VKM	3703	ME	S703VKM	3705	ME	S705VKM	3706	ME	S706VKM
3702	ME	S702VKM	3704	ME	S704VKM					

3911-3921 — DAF DE02GSSB220 — Plaxton Prestige — N39F — 1999

3911	NF	T911KKM	3914	NF	T914KKM	3916	NF	T916KKM	3919	TW	T919KKM
3912	NF	T912KKM	3915	NF	T915KKM	3918	TW	T918KKM	3921	NF	T921KKM
3913	NF	T913KKM								

3923-3932 — DAF DE12CSSB120 — Wrightbus Cadet — N39F — 2002

3923	CR	GK51SYY	3926	GU	GK51SZD	3929	GU	GK51SZG	3931	GU	GK51SZL
3924	CR	GK51SYZ	3927	GU	GK51SZE	3930	GU	GK51SZJ	3932	GU	GK51SZN
3925	GU	GK51SZC	3928	GU	GK51SZF					

3933-3944 — DAF DE12CSSB120 — Wrightbus Cadet — N39F — 2002

3933	GU	GK52YUW	3936	u	GK52YVA	3939	GU	GK52YVD	3942	GU	GK52YVG
3934	GU	GK52YUX	3937	GU	GK52YVB	3940	GU	GK52YVE	3943	GU	GK52YVJ
3935	GU	GK52YUY	3938	GU	GK52YVC	3941	GU	GK52YVF	3944	GU	GK52YVL

3945-3960 — VDL Bus SB120 — Wrightbus Cadet — N29F — 2004

3945	DA	GK53AOH	3949	DA	GK53AOO	3953	DA	GK53AOU	3957	DA	GK53AOY
3946	DA	GK53AOJ	3950	DA	GK53AOP	3954	DA	GK53AOV	3958	DA	GK53AOZ
3947	DA	GK53AOL	3951	DA	GK53AOR	3955	DA	GK53AOW	3959	ME	GN04UFW
3948	DA	GK53AON	3952	DA	GK53AOT	3956	DA	GK53AOX	3960	ME	GN04UFX

3961-3969 — VDL Bus SB200 — Wrightbus Commander — N44F — 2004

3961	ME	GN04UFY	3964	ME	GN04UGB	3966	ME	GN04UGD	3968	ME	GN04UGF
3962	ME	GN04UFZ	3965	ME	GN04UGC	3967	ME	GN04UGE	3969	ME	GN04UGG
3963	ME	GN04UGA								

Arriva Southern Counties supply buses for eight operations. Generally fleet numbers have remained unchanged since the fleets of Maidstone and District and London and Country were placed under a single management. In 2002 part of The Shires fleet was transferred and these carry an 'E' prefix. Subsequent transfers have resulted in a mix of number styles at depots. Here, DSL45, N245VPH, is seen in Maidstone. *Martin Smith*

DS2-9
Dennis Dart 9.8SDL3035   East Lancs EL2000   B40F   1993

2	HK	L502CPJ	**5**	HK	L505CPJ	**7**	SE	L509CPJ	**9**	SE	L511CPJ
4	CO	L506CPJ	**6**	CO	L508CPJ	**8**	SE	L510CPJ			

DS14-24
Dennis Dart 9.8SDL3054   East Lancs EL2000   B40F   1995-96

14	SE	M525MPM	**19**	HO	N539TPF	**21**	CO	N541TPF	**23**	CO	N543TPK
15	CO	M526MPM	**20**	CO	N540TPF	**22**	GU	N542TPK	**24**	GI	N544TPK

DSL25-36
Dennis Dart SLF   Plaxton Pointer 2   N35F   1996   North Western (Beeline), 1998

25	CR	N225TPK	**28**	CR	N228TPK	**31**	CR	N231TPK	**35**	CR	N235TPK
26	CR	N226TPK	**29**	GU	N229TPK	**32**	HO	N232TPK	**36**	CR	N236TPK
27	GU	N227TPK	**30**	CR	N230TPK	**33**	CR	N233TPK			

DSL37-55
Dennis Dart SLF   East Lancs Spryte   N31F   1996-97

37	HO	N237VPH	**46**	ME	N246VPH	**51**	GU	P251APM	**54**	SI	P254APM
39	GI	N239VPH	**47**	GU	N247VPH	**53**	GU	P253APM	**55**	SI	P255APM
45	ME	N245VPH	**50**	GU	P250APM						

DSL68-96
Dennis Dart SLF   Plaxton Pointer 2   N39F   1997

68	HO	P268FPK	**75**	GI	P275FPK	**84**	GU	P284FPK	**91**	GU	P291FPK
69	HO	P269FPK	**76**	GI	P276FPK	**85**	HO	P285FPK	**92**	GU	P292FPK
70	GI	P270FPK	**77**	GI	P277FPK	**86**	GU	P286FPK	**93**	GU	P293FPK
71	GI	P271FPK	**80**	HO	P380FPK	**87**	GU	P287FPK	**94**	GU	P294FPK
72	GI	P272FPK	**81**	HO	P281FPK	**88**	GU	P288FPK	**95**	GU	P295FPK
73	GI	P273FPK	**82**	HO	P282FPK	**89**	GU	P289FPK	**96**	GU	P296FPK
74	HO	P274FPK	**83**	HO	P283FPK	**90**	GU	P290FPK			

DSL97-106
Dennis Dart SLF   Plaxton Pointer 2   N39F   1997

97	GU	R297CMV	**100**	GU	R310CMV	**103**	GU	R303CMV	**106**	GU	R296CMV
98	GU	R298CMV	**101**	GU	R301CMV	**104**	GU	R304CMV			
99	GU	R299CMV	**102**	GU	R302CMV	**105**	GU	R305CMV			

DSL109	GU	T109LKK	Dennis Dart SLF	Plaxton Pointer 2	N39F	1999	
DSL110	GU	T110LKK	Dennis Dart SLF	Plaxton Pointer 2	N39F	1999	
DSL591	CR	T591CGT	Dennis Dart SLF	Plaxton Pointer 2	N39F	1999	
DSL592	CR	T592CGT	Dennis Dart SLF	Plaxton Pointer 2	N39F	1999	
LSL008	CR	M520KPA	Dennis Lance SLF	Wright Pathfinder	N40F	1995	

LS20-24
Dennis Lance 11SDA3113 — East Lancs — N49F — 1996

20	HO	N220TPK	22	TW	N322TPK	23	GU	N223TPK	24	GU	N224TPK
21	GU	N221TPK								

V201-204
Volvo B6-9.9M — Northern Counties Paladin — B39F — 1994 — Londonlinks, 1997

201	CO	L201YCU	202	u	L202YCU	203	NF	L203YCU	204	NF	L204YCU

512	GU	L512CPJ	Volvo B6-9.9M	Plaxton Pointer	B41F	1994	
513	ME	L513CPJ	Volvo B6-9.9M	Plaxton Pointer	B41F	1994	
516	ME	L516CPJ	Volvo B6-9.9M	Plaxton Pointer	B41F	1994	
E3092	SE	H923LOX	Dennis Dart 9.8SDL3004	Carlyle Dartline	B40F	1991	London Country NW, 1991

E3218-E3226
Dennis Dart SLF — Plaxton Pointer 2 — N33F* — 1998 — * E3224-6 are N39F

E3218	SE	T218NMJ	E3221	SE	T821NMJ	E3223	SE	T823NMJ	E3225	SE	T825NMJ
E3220	SE	T820NMJ	E3222	SE	T822NMJ	E3224	SE	T824NMJ	E3226	SE	T826NMJ

E3241	CO	M841DDS	Volvo B6-9.9	Alexander Dash	B45F	1993	Scotland West, 1998
E3246	CO	M846DDS	Volvo B6-9.9	Alexander Dash	B45F	1993	Scotland West, 1998

E3341-E3347
Leyland Lynx LX2R11C15Z4S — Leyland Lynx — B49F — 1990

E3341	CO	H251GEV	E3343	CO	H253GEV	E3346	CO	H256GEV	E3347	CO	H257GEV
E3342	CO	H252GEV								

E3349	SE	J316XVX	Dennis Dart 9SDL3011	Wright Handybus	B35F	1992	
E3350	SE	J317XVX	Dennis Dart 9SDL3011	Wright Handybus	B35F	1992	
E3370	SE	K320CVX	Dennis Dart 9SDL3011	Plaxton Pointer	B35F	1992	
E3373	SE	K323CVX	Dennis Dart 9SDL3011	Plaxton Pointer	B35F	1992	
E3379	SE	M269VPU	Dennis Lance SLF	Wright Pathfinder	N40F	1994	
E3384	SE	M764JPA	Dennis Lance SLF 11SDA3201	Wright Pathfinder	N39F	1995	

E3387-E3397
Dennis Dart SLF — Plaxton Pointer — N39F — 1997

E3387	SE	P257FPK	E3390	GY	P259FPK	E3393	SE	P263FPK	E3396	SE	P266FPK
E3388	GY	P258FPK	E3391	SE	P261FPK	E3394	SE	P264FPK	E3397	SE	P267FPK
E3389	GY	P259FPK	E3392	SE	P262FPK	E3395	SE	P265FPK			

E3400	GY	R310NGM	Dennis Dart SLF	Plaxton Pointer 2	N33F	1997	Town & Country, Corringham, '00
E3401	GY	R311NGM	Dennis Dart SLF	Plaxton Pointer 2	N33F	1997	Town & Country, Corringham, '00
E3402	GY	R312NGM	Dennis Dart SLF	Plaxton Pointer 2	N33F	1997	Town & Country, Corringham, '00
E3403	GY	R313NGM	Dennis Dart SLF	Plaxton Pointer 2	N33F	1997	Town & Country, Corringham, '00

E3404-3412
Dennis Dart — Plaxton Pointer — B34F — 1996

E3404	SE	P324HVX	E3407	GY	P327HVX	E3409	TW	P329HVX	E3411	TW	P331HVX
E3405	GY	P325HVX	E3408	TW	P328HVX	E3410	TW	P330HVX	E3412	TW	P332HVX
E3406	CO	P326HVX								

E3421-3431
Dennis Dart SLF — Plaxton Pointer — N39F — 1996

E3421	GY	P421HVX	E3425	GY	P425HVX	E3427	GY	P427HVX	E3429	GY	P429HVX
E3423	GY	P423HVX	E3426	GY	P426HVX	E3428	GY	P428HVX	E3431	GY	P431HVX
E3424	GY	P424HVX								

E4335	CO	J56GCX	DAF SB220LC550	Ikarus CitiBus	B48F	1992	South London, 1997
E4336	CO	J926CYL	DAF SB220LC550	Ikarus CitiBus	B48F	1992	Grey Green, 1997
E4337	CO	J927CYL	DAF SB220LC550	Ikarus CitiBus	B48F	1992	Grey Green, 1997
E4339	CO	K124TCP	DAF SB220LC550	Ikarus CitiBus	B48F	1992	Cowie South London, 1997

E4500-4510
DAF DE12CSSB120 10.2m — Wrightbus Cadet — N31D — 2002

E4500	GY	KE51PTY	E4503	GY	KE51PUF	E4506	GY	KE51PUK	E4509	GY	KE51PUV
E4501	GY	KE51PTZ	E4504	GY	KE51PUH	E4507	GY	KE51PUO	E4510	GY	KC51NFO
E4502	GY	KE51PUA	E4505	GY	KE51PUJ	E4508	GY	KE51PUU			

E4511	GY	KE51PUY	DAF DE12CSSB120 9.4m	Wrightbus Cadet	N27F	2002	
E4512	GY	KC51PUX	DAF DE12CSSB120 9.4m	Wrightbus Cadet	N27F	2002	
E4513	GY	KE51PVA	DAF DE12CSSB120 9.4m	Wrightbus Cadet	N27F	2002	

A batch of forty-nine Volvo B7TLs with TransBus ALX400 bodies have arrived for operation in Gillingham. An early sighting shows the use of colours for routes including the Green Line name, which is owned by Arriva. Number 6426, GN04UET, called in at Birkenhead for viewing by the guests at the new depot which was opened by the Secretary of State for Transport, Rt Hon Alistair Darling MP, on 11th May 2004. *Bill Potter*

Double-deck buses

901	HO	F571SMG	Leyland Olympian ONLXB/1RZ	Alexander RL		B47/32F	1988	Alder Valley, 1990
907	HO	F577SMG	Leyland Olympian ONLXB/1RZ	Alexander RL		B47/32F	1988	Alder Valley, 1990
908	HO	F578SMG	Leyland Olympian ONLXB/1RZ	Alexander RL		B47/32F	1988	Alder Valley, 1990

5557-5565			Volvo Olympian YN2RC16Z4*	Northern Counties Palatine II	B47/30F	1994	*5565 is YN2RV18Z4
5557	NF	L557YCU	5559	NF	L559YCU	5562	SR	L562YCU	5564	ME	L564YCU
5558	NF	L558YCU	5561	ME	L561YCU	5563	ME	L563YCU	5565	SR	L565YCU

5765-5770			Leyland Olympian ON2R50C13Z4	Northern Counties		B47/30F	1991	Boro'line, Maidstone, 1992
5765	SR	H765EKJ	5767	SR	H767EKJ	5769	SR	H769EKJ	5770	GI	H770EKJ
5766	SR	H766EKJ	5768	SR	H768EKJ						

5887	SR	F580SMG	Leyland Olympian ONLXB/1RZ	Alexander RL		B47/32F	1988	Alder Valley, 1990

5891-5900			Leyland Olympian ONLXB/1RH	Northern Counties		B45/30F	1988	
5891	HK	E891AKN	5894	HK	F894BKK	5897	HK	F897DKK	5899	HK	F899DKK
5892	HK	F892BKK	5895	HK	F895BKK	5898	HK	F898DKK	5900	HK	F900DKK
5893	HK	F893BKK	5896	TW	F896DKK						

5901-5905			Leyland Olympian ON2R50G13Z4	Northern Counties Palatine	B45/30F	1990	
5901	ME	G901SKP	5903	HK	G903SKP	5904	TW	G904SKP	5905	TO	G905SKP
5902	HK	G902SKP									

5906-5910			Leyland Olympian ON2R50C13Z4	Northern Counties Palatine	B45/30F	1993	
5906	TW	K906SKR	5908	TW	K908SKR	5909	ME	K909SKR	5910	HK	K910SKR
5907	TW	K907SKR									

5911-5925			Volvo Olympian YN2R50C16Z4	Northern Counties Palatine	B47/30F	1994-95	5913 rebodied 1995
5911	HK	M911MKM	5915	ME	M915MKM	5919	ME	M919MKM	5923	HK	M923PKN
5912	ME	M912MKM	5916	ME	M916MKM	5920	ME	M920MKM	5924	HK	M924PKN
5913	ME	M913MKM	5917	ME	M917MKM	5922	HK	M922PKN	5925	HK	M925PKN
5914	ME	M914MKM	5918	SR	M918MKM						

5926-5937   Volvo Olympian   Northern Counties Palatine   B47/30F   1997

5926	ME	P926MKL	5929	ME	P929MKL	5932	ME	P932MKL	5935	ME	P935MKL
5927	ME	P927MKL	5930	ME	P930MKL	5933	ME	P933MKL	5936	ME	P936MKL
5928	ME	P928MKL	5931	ME	P931MKL	5934	ME	P934MKL	5937	ME	P937MKL

6200	GU	LF02PVA	Volvo B7L	Wrightbus Eclipse	N41F	2002	On extended loan

6204-6212   DAF DE23RSDB250*   Northern Counties Palatine 2   B43/24D   1998   *6212 is DE02RSDB250

6204	TW	R204CKO	6207	TW	R207CKO	6209	TW	R209CKO	6211	TW	R211CKO
6205	TW	R205CKO	6208	TW	R208CKO	6210	TW	R210CKO	6212	TW	R212CKO
6206	TW	R206CKO									

6213-6219   DAF DE20RSDB250   Wrightbus Pulsar Gemini   N41/24D   2004

6213	DA	GK53AOA	6215	DA	GK53AOC	6217	DA	GK53AOE	6219	DA	GK53AOG
6214	DA	GK53AOB	6216	DA	GK53AOD	6218	DA	GK53AOF			

6401-6449   Volvo B7TL   TransBus ALX400   N--/--F   2004

6401	GI	GN04UDM	6414	GI	GN04UED	6426	GI	GN04UET	6438	GI	GN04UFG
6402	GI	GN04UDP	6415	GI	GN04UEE	6427	GI	GN04UEU	6439	GI	GN04UFH
6403	GI	GN04UDS	6416	GI	GN04UEF	6428	GI	GN04UEV	6440	GI	GN04UFJ
6404	GI	GN04UDT	6417	GI	GN04UEG	6429	GI	GN04UEW	6441	GI	GN04UFK
6405	GI	GN04UDU	6418	GI	GN04UEH	6430	GI	GN04UEX	6442	GI	GN04UFL
6406	GI	GN04UDV	6419	GI	GN04UEJ	6431	GI	GN04UEY	6443	GI	GN04UFM
6407	GI	GN04UDW	6420	GI	GN04UEK	6432	GI	GN04UEZ	6444	GI	GN04UFP
6408	GI	GN04UDX	6421	GI	GN04UEL	6433	GI	GN04UFA	6445	GI	GN04UFR
6409	GI	GN04UDY	6422	GI	GN04UEM	6434	GI	GN04UFB	6446	GI	GN04UFS
6410	GI	GN04UDZ	6423	GI	GN04UEP	6435	GI	GN04UFC	6447	GI	GN04UFT
6411	GI	GN04UEA	6424	GI	GN04UER	6436	GI	GN04UFD	6448	GI	GN04UFU
6412	GI	GN04UEB	6425	GI	GN04UES	6437	GI	GN04UFE	6449	GI	GN04UFV
6413	GI	GN04UEC									

7613-7622   Volvo Citybus B10M-50   East Lancs   B49/39F   1989

613	CO	G613BPH	7615	CO	G615BPH	7616	NF	G616BPH	617	CO	G617BPH
614	CO	G614BPH									

7624-7643   Volvo Citybus B10M-50   Northern Counties   B45/31F   1989   Londonlinks, 1997

7624	GI	G624BPH	7629	GI	G629BPH	7633	GI	G633BPH	7640	GI	G640BPH
7625	GI	G625BPH	7630	GI	G630BPH	7634	GI	G634BPH	7641	GI	G641BPH
7626	GI	G626BPH	7631	GI	G631BPH	7635	GI	G635BPH	7642	GI	G642BPH
7627	GI	G627BPH	7632	GI	G632BPH	7636	GI	G636BPH	7643	GI	G643BPH

7702	u	G641CHF	Volvo Citybus B10M-50	East Lancs	B49/39F	1989	North Western, 1996
7706	NF	G648CHF	Volvo Citybus B10M-50	East Lancs	B49/39F	1989	North Western, 1996
7708	u	G659DTJ	Volvo Citybus B10M-50	East Lancs	B49/39F	1990	North Western, 1996
DD13	GU	N713TPK	Dennis Dominator DDA2006	East Lancs	B45/31F	1996	
DD14	GU	N714TPK	Dennis Dominator DDA2006	East Lancs	B45/31F	1996	
DD15	GU	N715TPK	Dennis Dominator DDA2006	East Lancs	B45/31F	1996	
M586	TO	GYE586W	MCW Metrobus DR101/14	MCW	B43/30D	1981	Arriva London, 1999
M615	u	KYO615X	MCW Metrobus DR101/14	MCW	B43/30D	1982	Arriva London, 1999
M1263	TO	B263WUL	MCW Metrobus DR101/17	MCW	B43/28D	1985	Arriva London, 1999
M1275	TO	B275WUL	MCW Metrobus DR101/17	MCW	B43/28D	1985	Arriva London, 1999
M1280	TO	B280WUL	MCW Metrobus DR101/17	MCW	B43/28D	1985	Arriva London, 1999

E5273-5278   Dennis Dominator DDA1031   East Lancs   B43/25F   1989-90   Arriva Southern Counties, 1999

E5273	SE	G663FKA	E5275	SE	G665FKA	E5276	SE	G626EKA	E5278	SE	G628EKA
E5274	SE	G664FKA									

E5286	SE	K36XNE	Dennis Dominator DDA2005	East Lancs	B45/31F	1993	Arriva Southern Counties, 1999
E5287	SE	K37XNE	Dennis Dominator DDA2005	East Lancs	B45/31F	1993	Arriva Southern Counties, 1999
E5288	SE	K38YVM	Dennis Dominator DDA2005	East Lancs	B45/31F	1993	Arriva Southern Counties, 1999
E5386	SE	C32CHM	Leyland Olympian ONLXB/1RH	Eastern Coach Works	B42/26D	1986	Arriva London, 2003
E5387	SE	D172FYM	Leyland Olympian ONLXB/1RH	Eastern Coach Works	B42/26D	1986	Arriva London, 2003
E5388	GY	D234FYM	Leyland Olympian ONLXB/1RH	Eastern Coach Works	B42/26D	1986	Arriva London, 2003
E5389	CO	C41HHJ	Leyland Olympian ONLXCT/1RH	Eastern Coach Works	B47/31F	1985	

E5392-5396   Leyland Olympian ONLXB/1RZ   Alexander RL   B47/32F   1988   London & Country (GWS), 1996

E5392	SE	F572SMG	E5394	SE	F574SMG	E5395	SE	F575SMG	E5396	SE	F576SMG
E5393	SE	F573SMG									

Now carrying a yellow livery for school duties, 7636, G636BPH, is a Volvo Citybus with an underfloor engine. It was new to Grey-Green for London duties and was pictured in Chatham in May 2004. Following the arrival of the new buses many of the mid-life examples are being transferred as we go press. *Gerry Mead*

E5397	CO	F245MTW	Leyland Olympian ONCL10/1RZ	Leyland	BC43/29F	1988	
E5398	CO	F246MTW	Leyland Olympian ONCL10/1RZ	Leyland	BC43/29F	1988	Southend, 1996
E5399	SE	F579SMG	Leyland Olympian ONLXB/1RZ	Alexander RL	B47/32F	1988	London & Country (GWS), 1996
E5402	GY	H262GEV	Leyland Olympian ON2R50G13Z4	Leyland	B47/31F	1990	
E5403	SR	H263GEV	Leyland Olympian ON2R50G13Z4	Leyland	B47/31F	1990	
E5404	CO	H264GEV	Leyland Olympian ON2R50G13Z4	Leyland	BC43/29F	1990	
E5405	GY	H265GEV	Leyland Olympian ON2R50G13Z4	Leyland	BC43/29F	1990	
E5407	CO	H47MJN	Leyland Olympian ON2R50C13Z4	Leyland	BC43/29F	1991	Southend, 1996
E5408	CO	H48MJN	Leyland Olympian ON2R50C13Z4	Leyland	B47/31F	1991	
E5409	CO	H49MJN	Leyland Olympian ON2R50C13Z4	Leyland	B47/31F	1991	

E5434-5451			Dennis Trident		Alexander ALX400	N47/31F	2000
E5434	SE	W434XKX	**E5438** SE W438XKX		**E5442** SE W442XKX	**E5446** SE W446XKX	
E5435	SE	W435XKX	**E5439** SE W439XKX		**E5443** SE W443XKX	**E5447** SE W447XKX	
E5436	SE	W436XKX	**E5441** SE W441XKX		**E5445** SE W445XKX	**E5451** SE W451XKX	
E5437	SE	W437XKX					

Ancillary vehicles:

YDT47	CO	F47ENF	Leyland Lynx LX112L10ZR1R	Leyland Lynx	TV	1988	Shearings, 1991
YDT48	ME	F48ENF	Leyland Lynx LX112L10ZR1R	Leyland Lynx	TV	1988	Shearings, 1991
YFB70	DA	G70PKR	Mercedes-Benz 609D	Reeve Burgess	Staff	1989	
YDT148	NF	L148YVK	Dennis Dart 9SDL3034	Northern Counties Paladin	TV	1994	
YDT154	DA	J154NKN	Mercedes-Benz 814D	Dormobile Routemaker	TV	1992	Crossways, Swanley, 1996

YDT205-212			Volvo B6-9.9M		Northern Counties Paladin	TV	1994	Londonlinks, 1997
205	GI	L205YCU	**208**	GI L207YCU	**210**	GI L210YCU	**212**	GI L212YCU
206	GI	L206YCU	**209**	ME L207YCU	**211**	CH L211YCU		

YDT307	u	J307WHJ	Dennis Dart 9SDL3002	Plaxton Pointer	TV	1991	Arriva London, 2004
YDT310	ME	J310WHJ	Dennis Dart 9SDL3002	Plaxton Pointer	TV	1991	Arriva London, 2004
ZDT339	CH	SIB6709	Leyland NL106AL11/1R (6HLXB)		TV	1982	
ZDT341	w	SIB6711	Leyland 10351A/1R	East Lancs Greenway (1992)	TV	1979	
YDT375	w	PDZ6275	Leyland 11351A/2R	East Lancs Greenway (1994)	TV	1977	Panther, Crawley, 1991

YDT379	HO	RDZ4279	Leyland 11351/1R	East Lancs Greenway (1995)	TV	1975	Alder Valley, 1990
YFB437	DA	L437CPJ	Mercedes-Benz 811D	Plaxton Beaver	Staff	1994	Londonlinks, 1997
YDT463	DA	J463MKL	Dennis Dart 9.8SDL3012	Plaxton Pointer	TV	1991	
YDT469	DA	J469OKP	Dennis Dart 9.8SDL3017	Plaxton Pointer	TV	1992	
YFB474	GU	P474APJ	Mercedes-Benz 811D	Plaxton Beaver	Staff	1996	
YDT505	NF	L505CPJ	Dennis Dart 9.8SDL3035	East Lancs EL2000	TV	1993	
YDT514	ME	L514CPJ	Volvo B6-9.9M	Plaxton Pointer	TV	1994	
YDT515	ME	L515CPJ	Volvo B6-9.9M	Plaxton Pointer	TV	1994	
YFB698	w	P698PRJ	LDV Convoy	LDV	Staff	1996	Cart, Oldham, 1998
YFB833	ME	?	LDV Convoy	LDV	Staff	19	?
YDT888	w	E888KYW	Leyland Lynx LX1126LXCTZR1S	Leyland Lynx	TV	1987	Arriva The Shires, 2002
YDT965	SE	E965PME	Leyland Lynx LX112TL11ZR1R	Leyland Lynx	TV	1988	Yellow Bus, Stoke M'ville, 1995
YDT966	SE	E966PME	Leyland Lynx LX112TL11ZR1R	Leyland Lynx	TV	1988	Yellow Bus, Stoke M'ville, 1995

Previous Registrations:

A11GTA	H832AHS	SCZ9652	99D81498, T179AUA
BAZ7384	C210PPE	SIB6709	LFR865X
L503HKM	L10FUG	SIB6711	HPF310N
PDZ6275	UFG54S	TIB5903	E316OPR
RDZ4279	KPA380P	TIB5904	E319OPR
SCZ9651	99D81499, T178AUA	UJI2338	G897DEH

Allocations

Colchester (Magdalen Street) - CO - Colchester

Mercedes-Benz	E2174	E2243	E2372	E2382			
Tiger	2196	E4305					
Dart	DS4	DS6	DS15	DS20	DS21	DS23	3168	E3406
Volvo B6	V201	E3241	E3246				
Lynx	E3341	E3342	E3343	E3346	E3347		
Scania coach	E4352	E4353					
DAF Ikarus	E4335	E4336	E4337	E4339			
Volvo Citybus	613	614	617	7615	7643		
Olympian	E5389	E5397	E5398	E5404	E5407	E5408	E5409

Cranleigh (Mansfield Park, Guildford Road) - CR - Guildford & West Surrey

Dart	DSL25	DSL26	DSL28	DSL30	DSL31	DSL33	DSL35	DSL36
	DSL591	DSL592						
Lance	LSL008							
DAF Cadet	3923	3924						

Dartford (Central Road) - DA - Kent Thameside

MetroRider	1850	1851	1852					
Dart	3112	3179	3218	3232	3261	3262	3263	3264
	3265	3266	3267	3268	3269	3270	3271	3272
	3276	3277	3278	3279	3280	3281	3282	3283
	3284	3285	3286	3287	3288	3291	3292	3293
	3294	3295	3296	3297	3298	3299	3301	3302
	3303							
DAF Cadet	3945	3946	3947	3948	3949	3950	3951	3952
	3953							
VDL Bus Cadet	3954	3955	3956	3957	3958			
DAF Gemini	6213	6214	6215	6216	6217	6218	6219	

Gillingham (Nelson Road) - GI - Medway Towns

Mercedes-Benz	1118	1119	1120	1121	1122	E2392		
Dart	1606	1607	1608	1609	1610	1611	1612	1613
	1614	1615	1616	1617	3178	3216	3219	3220
	3221	3223	3224	3225	3226	3227	3228	3229
	3230	3231	3232	3233	3234	3235	3236	3237
	3238	3239	3240	3241	3242	3243	3244	3245
	DS24	DSL39	DSL70	DSL71	DSL72	DSL73	DSL75	DSL76
	DSL77							
Volvo B6	3601	3602	3603	3604	3605			
Olympian	5770							
Volvo Citybus	7624	7625	7626	7627	7629	7630	7631	7632
	7633	7634	7635	7636				
Volvo B7TL	6401	6402	6403	6404	6405	6406	6407	6408
	6409	6410	6411	6412	6413	6414	6415	6416
	6417	6418	6419	6420	6421	6422	6423	6424
	6425	6426	6427	6428	6429	6430	6431	6432
	6433	6434	6435	6436	6437	6438	6439	6440
	6441	6442	6443	6444	6445	6446	6447	6448
	6449							

Grays (Europa Park, London Road) - GY - East Herts & Essex

Dart	E3388	E3389	E3390	E3400	E3401	E3402	E3403	E3405
	E3421	E3423	E3424	E3425	E3426	E3427	E3428	E3429
	E3431							
DAF Cadet	E4500	E4501	E4502	E4503	E4504	E4505	E4506	E4507
	E4508	E4509	E4510	E4511	E4512	E4513		
Olympian	E5388							

Guildford (Leas Road) - GU - Guildford & West Surrey

Dart	3197	3198	DS22	DSL27	DSL29	DSL47	DSL50	DSL51
	DSL53	DSL84	DSL86	DSL87	DSL88	DSL89	DSL90	DSL91
	DSL92	DSL93	DSL94	DSL95	DSL96	DSL97	DSL98	DSL99
	DSL100	DSL101	DSL102	DSL103	DSL104	DSL105	DSL106	DSL109
	DSL110							
DAF Cadet	3925	3926	3927	3928	3929	3930	3931	3932
	3933	3934	3935	3937	3938	3939	3940	3941
	3942	3943	3944					
Volvo B6	512							
Lance	LS21	LS23	LS24					
Dominator	DD13	DD14	DD15					
Volvo B7TL	6200							

Hawkhurst (Rye Road) - HK - Kent & Sussex

Outstation at Tenterden

Dart	3103	3104	3105	3106	3210	3211	3212	3213
	DS2	DS5						
Lynx	3065							
Olympian	5891	5892	5893	5894	5895	5897	5898	5899
	5900	5902	5903	5910	5911	5922	5923	5924
	5925							

Arriva Kent and Sussex operate London-liveried 6219, GK53AOG. This Wright Pulsar Gemini-bodied batch of DAF DB250s is allocated for the TfL route 492 to Bluewater. The photograph was taken at Dartford.
Richard Godfrey

Horsham (Station Road, Warnham) - HO - West Sussex

Dart	3170	3248	DS19	DSL32	DSL37	DSL68	DSL69	DSL74
	DSL80	DSL81	DSL82	DSL83	DSL85			
Olympian	901	907	908					

Maidstone (Armstrong Road) - ME - Kent & Sussex

Volvo B10M coach	2846							
DAF Première	2903	2904	2905	2906	2907	2908	2909	2910
	2911	2912						
Dart	DSL46	3172	3176	3177	3181	3192	3193	3194
	3195	3196	3202	3203	3205	3206	3207	3208
	3209	3215	3249	3307	3308	3702		
Volvo B6	513	516	3614					
VDL Bus Cadet	3959	3960						
Lynx	3046	3049	3052					
Lance	LS20							
VDL Bus Cmdr	3961	3962	3963	3964	3965	3966	3967	3968
	3969							
Olympian	5561	5563	5564	5901	5909	5912	5913	5914
	5915	5916	5917	5919	5920	5926	5927	5928
	5929	5930	5931	5932	5933	5934	5935	5936
	5937							

LS21, N221TPK is one of five low-floor examples of the Dennis Lance in the fleet. These carry East Lancs bodies with a special version of the 2000 body styling. LS21 is currently allocated to Guildford and was seen at the Park Barn terminus. *Richard Godfrey*

Northfleet (London Road) - NF - Kent Thameside

Mercedes-Benz	E2380	E2381					
MetroRider	1805	1806	1807	1808	1809	1810	1811	1812
	1813	1814					
Dart	3113	3132	3133	3134	3135	3143	3155	3156
	3158	3186	3187	3188	3189	3190	3191	3273
	3274	3275	3289					
Volvo B6	V203	V204					
Lynx	3051						
Scania	3250	3251	3252	3253	3254	3255	3256	3257
	3258	3259					
DAF Prestige	3911	3912	3913	3914	3915	3916	3921
Olympian	5557	5558	5559				
Volvo Citybus	7616	7706					

Sheerness (Bridge Road) - SR - Medway Towns

Dart	3175						
Volvo B6	3606						
Olympian	E5403	5562	5565	5765	5766	5767	5768	5769
	5887	5918					
Volvo Citybus	7642						

Sittingbourne (Crown Quay Lane) - SI - Medway Towns

Mercedes-Benz	1475	E2383	E2186	E2388	E2391		
Dart	3165	3166	3171	3174	3199	3201	DSL39	DSL45
	DSL54	DSL55					

Southend (Short Street) - SE - Southend

Mercedes-Benz	1751	1752	1753	1754	1755	1756	E2188	E2191
	E2192	E2193						
Dart	DS7	DS8	DS9	DS24	E3218	E3220	E3221	E3222
	E3223	E3224	E3225	E3226	E3379	E3381	E3382	E3383
	E3384	E3387	E3391	E3392	E3393	E3394	E3395	E3396
	E3397	E3404						
Dominator	DD16	E5273	E5274	E5275	E5276	E5278	E5286	E5287
	E5288							
Olympian	E5386	E5387	E5392	E5393	E5394	E5395	E5396	E5399
	E5415	E5416	E5417	E5418	E5419			
Trident	E5434	E5435	E5436	E5437	E5438	E5439	E5441	E5442
	E5443	E5445	E5446	E5447	E5451			

Tonbridge (Cannon Lane) - TO - New Enterprise Coaches

Volvo B6	3615	3619						
Tiger coach	2194							
Volvo B10M coach	2830	2831	2835	2851				
DAF coach	2894	2895	2896	2897	2898	2899	2900	2901
	2902							
Scania coach	2031	2051	2054					
Metrobus	M586	M1263	M1275	M1280				
Olympian	5905							

Tunbridge Wells (St John's Road) - TW - Kent & Sussex; Kent Thameside

Mercedes-Benz	1476	1477	1479	1480	E2187	E2378	E2379	
Volvo B6	3608	3609	3610	3611	3612	3613	3616	3617
Dart	1601	1602	1603	1604	1605	3184	3185	E3408
	E3409	E3410	E3411	E3412				
Lance	LS22							
DAF Prestige	3918	3919						
DAF Palatine	6204	6205	6206	6207	6208	6209	6210	6211
	6212							
Lynx	3041	3045						
Olympian	5896	5904	5906	5907	5908			

Unallocated and stored - u/w

Mercedes-Benz	E2115	E2134	E2384					
Dart	3217	3701	3703	3704	3705	3706	DS14	E3092
	E3349	E3350	E3370	E3373				
Volvo B6	3601	3602	3603	3604	3605	3607		
Lynx	3043	3044	3054					
DAF Cadet	E3407							
Metrobus	M615							
Volvo Citybus	7640	7641	7702	7708				
Olympian	5402	5405						

ARRIVA DANMARK

Arriva Danmark A/S; Arriva Scandinavia A/S
Herstedvang 7C, DK-2650 Albertslund, Danmark

101	NM88.326	Mercedes-Benz O407GN Duo bus	Mercedes-Benz	AB60D	1998	On loan from HT
155	MY91.485	DAB GS200 8.6m	DAB	NM18D	1992	On loan from HT
156	MY91.485	DAB GS200 8.6m	DAB	NM18D	1992	On loan from HT
160	MY91.438	DAB GS200 8.6m	DAB	NM18D	1992	On loan from HT
161	MY91.439	DAB GS200 8.6m	DAB	NM18D	1992	On loan from HT

401-404
Mercedes-Benz Sprinter 312   Mercedes-Benz   M8   1997   Handicap service

401	OX90.567	402	OZ97.632	403	OY95.589	404	OX91.313.873

406	NM88.046	Mercedes-Benz Sprinter 310	Mercedes-Benz	M8	1993	Handicap service
407	OX91.412	Mercedes-Benz Sprinter 310	Mercedes-Benz	M8	1992	Handicap service

408-411
Mercedes-Benz Sprinter 312   Mercedes-Benz   M8   1997   Handicap service

408	OX90.5607	409	OZ90.635	410	OU96.648	411	OU96.505

412	EB99.503	Mercedes-Benz 409	Mercedes-Benz	M8	1988	Handicap service
414	SM90.147	Mercedes-Benz Sprinter 312	Mercedes-Benz	M8	1998	Handicap service
415	RL94.003	Mercedes-Benz 310	Mercedes-Benz	M8	1991	Handicap service
416	SM90.263	Mercedes-Benz Sprinter 312	Mercedes-Benz	N8	1998	Handicap service
417	SM90.290	Mercedes-Benz Sprinter 312	Mercedes-Benz	N8	1998	Handicap service
418	NK91.881	Mercedes-Benz 410	Mercedes-Benz	M8	1993	Handicap service
420	PE94.546	Mercedes-Benz Sprinter 412	Mercedes-Benz	N8	1998	Handicap service
422	PE94.547	Mercedes-Benz Sprinter 412	Mercedes-Benz	N8	1998	Handicap service
423	EE98.983	Mercedes-Benz Vario 711	Mercedes-Benz	M8	1988	Handicap service
424	PE94.548	Mercedes-Benz Sprinter 412	Mercedes-Benz	N8	1998	Handicap service
426	NR90.952	Mercedes-Benz Sprinter 310	Mercedes-Benz	M8	1994	Handicap service
427	NY90.316	Mercedes-Benz Sprinter 310	Mercedes-Benz	M8	1995	Handicap service
428	NY90.313	Mercedes-Benz Sprinter 310	Mercedes-Benz	M8	1995	Handicap service
429	NY90.314	Mercedes-Benz Sprinter 310	Mercedes-Benz	M8	1995	Handicap service
434	RH97.631	Fiat Ducato 18.2.5	Fiat	M8	1996	Handicap service
435	OL96.516	Fiat Ducato 18.2.5	Fiat	M8	1996	Handicap service
436	OU96.508	Mercedes-Benz Sprinter 312	Mercedes-Benz	N8	1997	Handicap service
437	PE94.549	Mercedes-Benz Sprinter 312	Mercedes-Benz	N8	1998	Handicap service
440	NU91.449	Mercedes-Benz Sprinter 310	Mercedes-Benz	M8	1995	Handicap service
442	PE94.550	Mercedes-Benz Sprinter 312	Mercedes-Benz	N8	1998	Handicap service
447	HD99.516	Mercedes-Benz 609	Mercedes-Benz	M8	1987	Handicap service
448	DZ99.640	Mercedes-Benz 609	Mercedes-Benz	M8	1987	Handicap service

451-456
Mercedes-Benz Sprinter 412   Mercedes-Benz   N-   1998-99   Handicap service

451	SB92.849	453	SB92.850	455	PJ96.270	456	SM90.201
452	SM90.148	454	SB92.851				

464	LS97.271	Mercedes-Benz 609	Mercedes-Benz	M8	1989	Handicap service

1001-1013
Volvo B10LE   Säffle   AN62D   1998

1001	PC90.745	1005	PC95.842	1008	PC95.862	1011	PC95.873
1002	PC95.805	1006	PC95.843	1009	PC95.872	1012	PC95.885
1003	PC95.830	1007	PC95.849	1010	PC95.863	1013	PC95.892
1004	PC95.836						

1014-1027
Volvo B10BLE   Åbenrå   N43D   1998

1014	PJ88.334	1018	PJ88.338	1022	PJ88.342	1025	PJ88.345
1015	PJ88.335	1019	PJ88.339	1023	PJ88.343	1026	PJ88.346
1016	PJ88.336	1020	PJ88.340	1024	PJ88.344	1027	PJ88.347
1017	PJ88.337	1021	PJ88.341				

Arriva is one of the principal operators to provide transport in Copenhagen, the capital of Denmark. Buses carry a yellow livery and the operator's name is shown below the driver's window. LPG-powered DAB Citibus 1094, PE97.350 is seen leaving from the central bus terminal. *Bill Potter*

1028-1049 Volvo B10BLE Säffle N43D 1998

1028	PJ97.769	1034	PE94.601	1040	PE94.607	1045	PJ97.561
1029	PJ97.770	1035	PE94.591	1041	PE94.608	1046	PJ97.558
1030	PJ97.771	1036	PE94.592	1042	PE94.617	1047	PJ97.559
1031	PJ97.772	1037	PE94.602	1043	PE94.628	1048	PJ97.573
1032	PE94.590	1038	PE94.616	1044	PJ97.560	1049	PJ97.574
1033	PJ97.846	1039	PE94.603				

1051-1080 Mercedes-Benz O405N Mercedes-Benz N--D 1998

1051	PE96.623	1059	PE96.600	1067	PE96.550	1074	PE96.519
1052	PE96.481	1060	PE96.548	1068	PE96.517	1075	PE96.615
1053	PE96.614	1061	PE96.611	1069	PE96.518	1076	PE96.630
1054	PE96.641	1062	PE96.624	1070	PE96.584	1077	PE96.549
1055	PE96.510	1063	PE96.462	1071	PE96.483	1078	PE96.545
1056	PE96.520	1064	PE96.461	1072	PE96.482	1079	PE96.583
1057	PE96.599	1065	PE96.610	1073	PE96.509	1080	PE96.508
1058	PE96.516	1066	PE96.557				

1084-1147 DAB Citibus S15 LPG DAB N43D+27 1998

1084	PE97.340	1100	PE97.445	1116	PJ96.961	1132	PM95.408
1085	PE97.341	1101	PE97.446	1117	PJ96.962	1133	PM95.409
1086	PE97.342	1102	PJ96.813	1118	PJ96.963	1134	PM95.410
1087	PE97.343	1103	PJ96.814	1119	PJ96.964	1135	PM95.453
1088	PE97.344	1104	PJ96.815	1120	PL95.949	1136	PM95.454
1089	PE97.345	1105	PJ96.860	1121	PL95.977	1137	PM95.455
1090	PE97.346	1106	PJ96.861	1122	PL95.978	1138	PM95.490
1091	PE97.347	1107	PJ96.862	1123	PL95.979	1139	PM95.491
1092	PE97.348	1108	PJ96.904	1124	PL95.999	1140	PM95.507
1093	PE97.349	1109	PJ96.905	1125	PL96.000	1141	PM95.508
1094	PE97.350	1110	PJ96.906	1126	PL96.001	1142	PM95.509
1095	PE97.351	1111	PJ96.907	1127	PL96.059	1143	PP94.068
1096	PE97.352	1112	PJ96.922	1128	PL96.060	1144	PP94.069
1097	PE97.359	1113	PJ96.958	1129	PL96.061	1145	PP94.070
1098	PE97.424	1114	PJ96.959	1130	PM95.387	1146	PP94.071
1099	PE97.444	1115	PJ96.960	1131	PM95.388	1147	PP94.072

The 'S' services are a limited stop network across Copenhagen. Buses are identified for these services with a blue band on the cantrail. New buses have this as a blue block on the nearside front and off-side rear corners. Kokkedal depot's 1006, PC95.843 is a Volvo B10LE articulated bus with Saffle bodywork. *Bill Potter*

1148-1153   Volvo B10BLE   Åbenrå   AN43D+27 1994

| 1148 | PP94.661 | 1150 | PP94.662 | 1152 | PP94.664 | 1153 | PP94.659 |
| 1149 | PP94.663 | 1151 | PP94.660 | | | | |

1157-1171   Scania L113CLL   Berkhof   N43D   1998-99

1157	PP94.307	1161	PP94.355	1165	PR93.211	1169	PR93.373
1158	PP94.306	1162	PP94.356	1166	PR93.283	1170	PR93.374
1159	PP94.325	1163	PP94.280	1167	PR93.314	1171	PR93.328
1160	PP94.326	1164	PR93.210	1168	PR93.327		

1172-1181   DAB Citibus S15 LPG   DAB   N43D   1999

1172	PP94.305	1175	PZ89.716	1178	PZ89.855	1180	PZ89.893
1173	PZ90.195	1176	PZ89.723	1179	PZ89.856	1181	PZ89.894
1174	PZ89.	1177	PZ89.838				

1182-1186   Volvo B10BLE 12m   Åbenrå   NC39D   1999-2000

| 1182 | RE94.301 | 1184 | RE94.302 | 1185 | RE94.296 | 1186 | RE94.303 |
| 1183 | RE94.295 | | | | | | |

1340-1384   Volvo B10BLE 12m   Åbenrå   N36D   2000

1340	RM90.995	1352	RM91.007	1363	RM91.018	1374	RM91.084
1341	RM90.996	1353	RM91.008	1364	RM91.019	1375	RN90.321
1342	RM90.997	1354	RM91.009	1365	RM91.020	1376	RN90.322
1343	RM90.998	1355	RM91.010	1366	RM91.021	1377	RN90.323
1344	RM90.999	1356	RM91.011	1367	RM91.022	1378	RN90.379
1345	RM91.000	1357	RM91.012	1368	RM91.023	1379	RN90.380
1346	RM91.001	1358	RM91.013	1369	RM91.024	1380	RN90.381
1347	RM91.002	1359	RM91.014	1370	RM91.025	1381	RN90.382
1348	RM91.003	1360	RM91.015	1371	RM91.026	1382	RN90.413
1349	RM91.004	1361	RM91.016	1372	RM91.082	1383	RN90.414
1350	RM91.005	1362	RM91.017	1373	RM91.083	1384	RP91.062
1351	RM91.006						

1385-1403   Volvo B10BLE 13.7m   Åbenrå   NC41D   2000

1385	SN89.817	1390	RN95.489	1395	RN95.514	1400	RP88.736
1386	RN90.444	1391	RN95.490	1396	RN95.515	1401	RP88.737
1387	RN95.486	1392	RN95.511	1397	RP88.732	1402	RP88.738
1388	RN95.487	1393	RN95.512	1398	RP88.733	1403	RP88.734
1389	RN95.488	1394	RN95.513	1399	RP88.735		

1404-1435 — Volvo B10BLE 13.7m — Åbenrå — NC41D — 2001

1404	RX93.855	1412	RX93.811	1420	RX93.891	1428	RX93.860
1405	RX93.854	1413	RX93.857	1421	RX93.892	1429	RV96.460
1406	RX93.856	1414	RV92.762	1422	RX93.893	1430	RV96.461
1407	RX93.853	1415	RX93.812	1423	RX93.894	1431	RV96.462
1408	RX93.882	1416	RX93.858	1424	RX93.895	1432	RX93.885
1409	RX93.883	1417	RX93.884	1425	RV92.764	1433	RV96.463
1410	RV92.761	1418	RX93.859	1426	RV92.765	1434	RV96.464
1411	RV92.729	1419	RV92.763	1427	RV96.459	1435	RX96.754

1441-1454 — Volvo B7LT 12m — East Lancs Vyking — N(73)D — 2001

1441	RZ92.675	1445	RZ97.043	1449	RZ92.782	1452	SB95.711
1442	SB95.709	1446	RZ92.781	1450	RZ97.045	1453	SB95.712
1443	RZ92.799	1447	RZ97.044	1451	SB95.593	1454	SB95.594
1444	RZ92.676	1448	SB95.710				

1455-1473 — Volvo B10BLE 13.7m — Åbenrå — N41D — 2002

1455	SC90.610	1460	SC90.691	1465	SD88.214	1470	SD88.252
1456	SC90.611	1461	SD88.164	1466	SB93.616	1471	SD88.253
1457	SC90.651	1462	SD88.165	1467	SB93.617	1472	SD88.254
1458	SC90.652	1463	SD88.166	1468	SB93.618	1473	SD88.255
1459	SC90.677	1464	SD88.212	1469	SD88.251		

1700-1733 — Volvo B10BLE 12m — Åbenrå — AN38D — 1999

1700	PZ95.450	1709	PZ95.459	1718	PZ95.500	1726	PZ95.547
1701	PZ95.451	1710	PZ95.492	1719	PZ95.501	1727	PZ95.548
1702	PZ95.452	1711	PZ95.493	1720	PZ95.502	1728	PZ95.549
1703	PZ95.453	1712	PZ95.494	1721	PZ95.503	1729	PZ95.550
1704	PZ95.454	1713	PZ95.495	1722	PZ95.504	1730	PZ95.551
1705	PZ95.455	1714	PZ95.496	1723	PZ95.505	1731	PZ95.552
1706	PZ95.456	1715	PZ95.497	1724	PZ95.506	1732	PZ95.553
1707	PZ95.457	1716	PZ95.498	1725	PZ95.546	1733	PZ95.554
1708	PZ95.458	1717	PZ95.499				

1740	PZ95.592	Volvo B10BLE	Åbenrå	N68D	1999
1741	PZ95.593	Volvo B10BLE	Åbenrå	N68D	1999
1742	PZ95.594	Volvo B10BLE	Åbenrå	N68D	1999
1750	RU97.094	DAB	DAB	N14D	2001
1751	RU97.095	DAB	DAB	N14D	2002
1752	SR93.368	Volvo B10L	Åbenrå	N-	1996
1753	PP94.330	DAB	DAB	N14D	1998
1762	OK89.136	Volvo B10M	Åbenrå	B38D	1996
1765	PC95.879	Volvo B10M	Åbenrå	B38D	1998
1770	OV91.913	Volvo B10BLE	Åbenrå	N32D	1997
1771	OV91.900	Volvo B10BLE	Åbenrå	N32D	1997
1772	PP89.362	Volvo B10BLE	Åbenrå	N32D	1997
1773	PP89.440	Volvo B10BLE	Åbenrå	N32D	1997
1775	LZ88.558	Volvo B10M	Åbenrå	B38D	1990
1776	LZ88.559	Volvo B10M	Åbenrå	B38D	1990
1777	PB91.328	DAB Citybus S15 III	DAB	N34D	1997
1778	PL97.752	Volvo B10BLE	Åbenrå	N32D	1998
1779	RC89.415	Volvo B10BLE	Åbenrå	N32D	1998
1780	RC89.416	Volvo B10BLE	Åbenrå	N32D	1998
1781	RC89.417	Volvo B10BLE	Åbenrå	N32D	1998
1782	RH97.569	Volvo B10BLE	Åbenrå	N32D	1998

1783-1794 — Scania OmniLink CL94UB 12m — Scania — N42D — 2003

1783	SU96.129	1786	SU96.126	1789	SU96.123	1792	SU96.135
1784	SU96.128	1787	SU96.125	1790	SU96.122	1793	SU96.148
1785	SU96.127	1788	SU96.124	1791	SU96.136	1794	SU96.147

1795-1813 — Scania OmniLink CL94UB 13.7m — Scania — N-D — 2003

1795	SV97.011	1800	SX90.752	1805	SY89.362	1810	SY89.417
1796	SV97.012	1801	SX90.819	1806	SY89.361	1811	SY89.416
1797	SV97.013	1802	SX90.854	1807	SY89.360	1812	SY89.479
1798	SV97.044	1803	SX90.839	1808	SY89.393	1813	SY89.496
1799	SX90.788	1804	SX90.875	1809	SY89.392		

Recent arrivals for Arriva's Danish operation have been the integral Scania OmniLink. The first S-route for them was the 150S operated from Kokkedal with 1812, SY89.479, representing the batch. Further vehicles of this type are currently being supplied for general routes. *Nicolai Longhi*

1814-1819		Volvo B10BLE 12m		Åbenrå		N32D	1995-96
1814	NR88.857	**1814**	NY91.010	**1814**	NY91.033	**1814**	NY91.050
1815	NY91.009	**1814**	NY91.011				

1820	SR96.531	Volvo B10L	Åbenrå	N32D	1996
1821	SR96.545	Volvo B10L	Åbenrå	N32D	1996
1822	SR96.559	Volvo B10L	Åbenrå	N32D	1996
1823	ST94.135	MAN/DAB Citybus S15	DAB	N32D	1994
1824	ST94.140	MAN/DAB Citybus S15	DAB	N32D	1994
1825	ST93.232	Volvo B10L	Åbenrå	N32D	1996
1826	OM97.996	Volvo B10L	Åbenrå	N32D	1996

1827-1858		Scania OmniLink CL94UB 13.7m		Scania		N-D	2003-04
1827	SY93.825	**1835**	SY93.783	**1843**	TB88.449	**1851**	TB88.489
1828	SY93.784	**1836**	SZ91.745	**1844**	TB88.417	**1852**	TB88.477
1829	SY93.824	**1837**	SZ91.744	**1845**	TB88.418	**1853**	TB88.490
1830	SY93.774	**1838**	SZ91.749	**1846**	TB88.450	**1854**	TB88.491
1831	SY93.775	**1839**	SZ91.755	**1847**	TB88.444	**1855**	TB88.493
1832	SY93.776	**1840**	SZ91.756	**1848**	TB88.445	**1856**	TB88.492
1833	SY93.777	**1841**	SZ91.765	**1849**	TB88.483	**1857**	TB88.469
1834	SY93.778	**1842**	TB88.448	**1850**	TB88.484	**1858**	TB88.470

1859	OL88.346	Volvo B10L	Åbenrå	N32D	1996
1860	OV92.039	Volvo B10L	Åbenrå	N32D	1997
1861	RN88.117	Volvo B10L	Åbenrå	N32D	2000
1862	NV93.382	MAN/DAB Citybus S15	DAB	N32D	1994
1863	NV93.383	MAN/DAB Citybus S15	DAB	N32D	1994
1864	NY91.031	Volvo B10L	Åbenrå	N32D	1995
1865	NY91.032	Volvo B10L	Åbenrå	N32D	1995
1866	NY91.051	Volvo B10L	Åbenrå	N32D	1995
1892	NB93.821	Mercedes-Benz O405	Mercedes-Benz	B35D	1992

1912-1926 DAB RS200L 12m · DAB · N26D · 1993

1912 SN94.318	1916 NJ97.883	1919 NK88.003	1923 NK88.023
1914 NJ97.881	1917 NJ97.934	1922 NK88.013	1926 NK88.026
1915 NJ97.882	1918 NK88.002		

1927-1937 Volvo B10BLE 12m · Åbenrå · AN33D · 1994

1927 NU88.584	1930 NU88.591	1933 NU88.603	1936 NU88.642
1928 NU88.588	1931 NU88.600	1934 NU88.631	1937 NU88.651
1929 NU88.590	1932 NU88.599	1935 NU88.632	

1938-1942 Mercedes-Benz O405GN · Mercedes-Benz · AN57D · 1994

1938 NV90.317	1940 NV90.315	1941 NV90.314	1942 NV90.313

1946-1970 DAB GS200 · Silkeborg · NC34D · 1995

1946 OC93.611	1953 OC93.621	1959 OC93.650	1965 OD92.388
1947 OC93.618	1954 OC93.622	1960 OC93.651	1966 OD92.416
1948 OC93.592	1955 OC93.623	1961 OD92.384	1967 OD92.417
1949 OC93.612	1956 OC93.642	1962 OD92.385	1968 OD92.418
1950 OC93.613	1957 OC93.643	1963 OD92.386	1969 OD92.419
1951 OC93.619	1958 OC93.649	1964 OD92.387	1970 OD92.420
1952 OC93.620			

1971-1984 Mercedes-Benz O405GN · Mercedes-Benz · AN54D · 1995-96

1971 OK94.243	1975 OK94.294	1979 OK94.484	1982 OM89.895
1972 OK94.242	1976 OK94.342	1980 OM89.830	1983 OM89.939
1973 OK94.241	1977 OK94.384	1981 OM89.857	1984 OM89.941
1974 OK94.240	1978 OK94.385		

Fleet	Reg	Body	Operator	Type	Year
1985	OK91.590	DAB GS200	Silkeborg	BC34D	1996
1986	OK91.591	DAB GS200	Silkeborg	BC34D	1996
1987	OK91.592	DAB GS200	Silkeborg	BC34D	1996
1988	OP93.607	Mercedes-Benz O405N	Mercedes-Benz	N34D	1996

1989-1998 Volvo B10BLE · Åbenrå · N34D · 1997

1989 OV92.054	1992 OX94.338	1995 OX94.347	1997 OX94.366
1990 OX94.333	1993 OX94.339	1996 OX94.365	1998 OX94.372
1991 OX94.334	1994 OX94.346		

Fleet	Reg	Body	Operator	Type	Year
1999	PB91.329	DAB GS200	Silkeborg	BC37D	1997
2007	LV91.554	Volvo B10M	Åbenrå	B39D	1989
2012	NZ93.950	DAB	Silkeborg	B47F	1995
2013	MR93.333	DAB	Silkeborg	B47F	1991
2018	MB92.612	DAB	Silkeborg	B39D	1990
2019	NX92.970	DAB	Silkeborg	B39D	1994
2020	NX92.969	DAB	Silkeborg	B39D	1994
2023	NX93.044	DAB	Silkeborg	B47F	1990
2025	MV95.152	Setra	Setra	B44F	1992
2027	NK95.279	Setra	Setra	B45F	1993
2039	NS91.543	Volvo B10	Åbenrå	B39F	1994

2045-2057 Volvo B10B · Åbenrå · N29D · 1997

2045 OU92.250	2049 OU92.263	2052 OV91.884	2055 OV91.885
2046 OU92.249	2050 OU92.271	2053 OV91.887	2056 OV91.883
2047 OU92.248	2051 OU92.275	2054 OV91.886	2057 OV91.896
2048 OU92.255			

Fleet	Reg	Body	Operator	Type	Year
2059	PE91.021	Volvo B10BLE	Åbenrå	N44F	1998
2060	PP89.432	Volvo B10BLE	Åbenrå	N44F	?
2061	PP89.434	Volvo B10BLE	Åbenrå	N44F	1998
2062	RD91.902	Volvo B10BLE	Åbenrå	N44F	1999
2063	RD91.904	Volvo B10BLE	Åbenrå	N44F	1999
2064	RD91.919	Volvo B10BLE	Åbenrå	N44F	1999
2065	RN88.014	Volvo B10BLE	Åbenrå	N44F	?
2066	RV89.287	Mercedes-Benz Cito S	Mercedes-Benz	N29F	2002
2067	RV89.288	Mercedes-Benz Cito S	Mercedes-Benz	N29F	2002
2080	LH90.503	Volvo B10M	Åbenrå	B--D	1987
2095	LC91.642	Volvo B10M	Silkeborg	B--D	1989
2134	LP94.417	Volvo B10M	Åbenrå	B--D	1988
2136	LP94.443	Volvo B10M	Åbenrå	B--D	1988
2173	LX94.925	Volvo B10M	Åbenrå	B--D	1989
2193	LY93.236	Volvo B10BLE	Silkeborg	B--D	1989

While the yellow colours of Copenhagen may be familiar, in the rural areas the local transport authority colours are also used. Operating in the area around Ringsted number 2048, OU92.255, carries an orange and ivory scheme. This Volvo B10B has bodywork by Åbenrå. *Bill Potter*

2195	LY93.265	Volvo B10BLE	Silkeborg	B--D	1989
2212	MB92.838	Volvo B10BLE	Åbenrå	B--D	1990
2216	MC97.181	Volvo B10BLE	Åbenrå	B--D	1990

2229-2244   Volvo B10M   Silkeborg   B38D   1990

2229	MC92.659	2238	ME94.454	2241	ME94.483	2243	ME94.488
2230	MC92.667	2240	ME94.473	2242	ME94.484	2244	ME94.489

2249-2263   Volvo B10M   Åbenrå   B38D   1991

2249	MJ95.476	2252	ML88.128	2260	MN92.185	2262	MN92.281
2251	MJ95.618	2258	MN92.151	2261	MN92.186	2263	MN92.282

2264	MN92.322	Volvo B10M	Åbenrå	B--D	1991
2266	MR93.432	Volvo B10M	Silkeborg	B--D	1991
2268	MR93.469	Volvo B10M	Silkeborg	B--D	1991
2270	MR93.471	Volvo B10M	Silkeborg	B--D	1991
2285	MS91.111	Volvo B10M	Silkeborg	B--D	1991
2287	MS91.113	Volvo B10M	Silkeborg	B--D	1991
2291	MS97.752	Volvo B10M	Åbenrå	B--D	1991
2292	MS97.753	Volvo B10M	Åbenrå	B--D	1992
2293	MS97.754	Volvo B10M	Åbenrå	B--D	1992
2297	MS97.752	Volvo B10M	Åbenrå	B--D	1992

2303-2311   Volvo B10M   Åbenrå   B38D   1992

2303	NB97.060	2305	NB97.088	2310	OY95.455	2311	OE93.171
2304	NB97.087	2309	NB97.101				

2312-2325   Volvo B10M   Silkeborg   B38D   1992

2312	NB89.308	2317	NB89.355	2322	NB89.424	2324	NB97.433
2314	NB89.310	2318	NB89.356	2323	NB97.432	2325	NB97.476
2315	NB89.311						

2327	MZ89.352	DAF/DAB Citybus	Silkeborg		B--D	1992		
2328	NB97.583	DAF/DAB Citybus	Silkeborg		B--D	1992		
2344	NB97.681	Volvo B10M	Silkeborg		B--D	1992		
2345	NE89.728	Volvo B10M	Åbenrå		B--D	1993		

2348-2354 Volvo B10M Åbenrå B38D 1993

2348	NJ93.668	2350	RS89.441	2352	NJ93.810	2354	NJ93.800
2349	NJ93.700	2351	NJ93.727	2353	NJ93.818		

2358	NK96.706	Volvo B10M HLB	Åbenrå		BC35D	1993		
2359	NK96.749	Volvo B10M HLB	Åbenrå		BC35D	1993		
2360	NK96.750	Volvo B10M HLB	Åbenrå		BC35D	1993		

2365-2379 Volvo B10M Silkeborg B38D 1993

2365	NN89.572	2368	NN89.574	2370	NN89.576	2378	NK96.626
2366	NN89.542	2369	NN89.575	2377	NN89.627	2379	NK96.625
2367	NN89.573						

2389	NN91.877	Volvo B10BLE	Åbenrå		N44D	1994		
2390	NN91.909	Volvo B10BLE	Åbenrå		N44D	1994		

2393-2425 Volvo B10M Silkeborg B38D 1994

2393	NN97.536	2406	NX93.002	2417	NX93.067	2420	NX93.070
2394	NN97.537	2414	NX93.041	2418	NX93.068	2421	NX93.071
2395	NN97.538	2415	NX93.042	2419	NX93.069	2425	NX90.912
2405	NX93.001	2416	NX93.066				

2427	NX90.942	Volvo B10M HLB	Åbenrå		BC--D	1994		
2431	NX90.842	Volvo B10BLE	Åbenrå		N44D	1994		
2442	NZ93.543	Volvo B10M HLB	Åbenrå		BC--D	1995		
2443	OB94.328	Volvo B10M	Åbenrå		B44D	1995		
2456	OD92.566	Scania N113	Lahti		B39D	1995		

2457-2463 Volvo B10M Silkeborg B38D 1995

2457	OD92.635	2460	OD92.657	2462	OD92.659	2463	OD92.660
2459	OD92.656	2461	OD92.658				

2471	OD91.011	Volvo B10M HLB	Åbenrå		BC--D	1995		
2472	OD97.337	Volvo B10M HLB	Åbenrå		BC--D	1995		
2473	OD97.349	Volvo B10M HLB	Åbenrå		BC--D	1995		
2474	OE94.307	Volvo B6LE	Vest		BC--D	1995		
2475	OE94.308	Volvo B6LE	Vest		BC--D	1995		

2481-2485 Volvo B10M DAB/Silkeborg B38D 1996

2481	OJ92.349	2483	OS97.952	2484	OJ92.352	2485	OJ92.353
2482	OJ92.350						

2486	OL97.128	Volvo B10LA	Saffle S		N--D	1996		
2489	OL88.369	Volvo B10M HLB	Åbenrå		B--D	1996		
2490	OL96.926	Volvo B10M	Åbenrå		B--D	1996		
2491	OL96.921	Volvo B10M HLB	Åbenrå		B--D	1996		
2506	OM97.903	Volvo B10M HLB	Åbenrå		B--D	1996		
2509	OM97.854	Volvo B10M	Åbenrå		B--D	1996		
2510	OM97.918	Volvo B10M HLB	Åbenrå		B--D	1996		
2511	OM97.927	Volvo B10M HLB	Åbenrå		B--D	1996		
2512	OU94.973	Volvo B6LE	Vest		B--D	1997		
2515	OV91.912	Volvo B9M	DAB/Silkeborg		B--D	1997		
2516	OV91.931	Volvo B9M	DAB/Silkeborg		B--D	1997		
2521	OX91.625	Volvo B10M	DAB/Silkeborg		B--D	1997		
2526	OX91.679	Volvo B10M	DAB/Silkeborg		B--D	1997		
2527	OS89.334	DAF/DAB Citybus	DAB/Silkeborg		B--D	1997		
2528	OS89.335	DAF/DAB Citybus	DAB/Silkeborg		B--D	1997		
2531	OX94.453	Volvo B9M	DAB/Silkeborg		B--D	1997		
2534	OX94.494	Volvo B10M HLB	Åbenrå		B--D	1997		
2535	OY97.183	Volvo B10M HLB	Åbenrå		B--D	1997		

2536-2543 Scania N112CL Scania B--D 1997

2536	PB91.473	2538	PB91.475	2541	PB91.480	2543	PB91.482
2537	PB91.474	2539	PB91.476	2542	PB91.481		

2544	PB89.173	Volvo B10M HLB	Åbenrå		B--D	1997		
2545	PB89.180	Volvo B10M HLB	Åbenrå		B--D	1997		
2546	PB91.477	Scania N112CL	Scania		B--D	1997		

STS provide the transport services to the south east of Copenhagen and Arriva's 2534, OX94.494 is seen in that livery. The vehicle is a Swedish-built Volvo B10M with Åbenrå bodywork. Most buses have a front entrance and rear exit. *Bill Potter*

2547	PB91.478	Scania N112CL	Scania	B--D	1997
2548	PB89.069	Volvo B10M	Åbenrå	B--D	1997
2549	PB89.077	Volvo B10M	Åbenrå	B--D	1997

2550-2555 Volvo B10M HLB — Åbenrå — B--D — 1997

2550	PB89.084	**2552**	PB89.095	**2554**	PB89.102	**2555**	PB89.108
2551	PB89.085	**2553**	PB89.103				

2556-2569 Volvo B10M HLB — Vest — B--D — 1997-98

2556	OZ94.278	**2561**	PC90.717	**2564**	PC95.835	**2567**	PC89.073
2559	OZ94.283	**2562**	PC90.719	**2565**	PC89.056	**2568**	PC89.080
2560	PC90.718	**2563**	PC90.720	**2566**	PC89.064	**2569**	PC89.105

2572	PC89.157	Volvo B10M	Åbenrå	B--D	1998
2574	PC97.949	Scania N112CL	Scania	B--D	1998
2575	PE92.039	Volvo B10M HLB	Vest	B--D	1998
2576	PE92.042	Volvo B10M HLB	Vest	B--D	1998
2578	PP89.431	Volvo B10M	Åbenrå	B--D	1998

2581-2589 Volvo B10M — Vest — B--D — 1998

2581	PE92.002	**2585**	PP93.852	**2587**	PP93.854	**2589**	PR94.089
2582	PE92.001	**2586**	PP93.855	**2588**	PP93.852		

2590-2634 Volvo B10M HLB — Åbenrå — B--D — 1998-99

2590	PE94.629	**2596**	PP89.417	**2633**	PT95.382	**2634**	PT95.381
2595	PP89.414	**2619**	PT95.340				

2647	PX96.158	Volvo B10M HLB	Åbenrå	B--D	1999
2648	PX96.158	Volvo B10M HLB	Åbenrå	B--D	1999
2649	PX96.158	Volvo B10M HLB	Åbenrå	B--D	1999

The Cito was Mercedes-Benz integral midibus, but has recently been withdrawn from the product list. Arriva operate ten of the type in Denmark for which 2067, RV89.288, shown here in Frederiksberg bus station, and a further five with the Cremona operation in Italy. The model seated 29 as standard with many standing. *Bill Potter*

2652-2656

Volvo B10M | Vest | B--D | 1999

2652	RC91.287	2654	RC91.289	2655	RC91.290	2656	RC91.291
2653	RC91.288						

2658-2663

Volvo B10M | Åbenrå | B--D | 1999

2658	PX96.253	2660	PX96.265	2662	RC89.372	2663	RC89.383
2659	PX96.266	2661	PX96.271				

2664	RD94.746	DAF/DAB Citybus	DAB	B--D	1999
2665	RD94.747	DAF/DAB Citybus	DAB	B--D	1999
2666	RD90.971	Volvo B10M	Vest	B--D	1999
2667	RC89.395	Volvo B10M	Åbenrå	B--D	1999
2668	RC89.396	Volvo B10M	Åbenrå	B--D	1999
2669	RC89.397	Volvo B10M	Åbenrå	B--D	1999
2671	RD91.987	Volvo B10LA	Saffle S	N--D	1999

2672-2676

Volvo B10M | Åbenrå | B--D | 1999

2672	RD91.994	2674	PX96.241	2675	RE94.201	2676	RD91.993
2673	RD91.999						

2682	RH97.538	Volvo B10M	Åbenrå	B--D	2000
2683	RK95.314	Scania	DAB/Silkeborg	N--D	2000
2685	RL96.925	Scania	DAB/Silkeborg	N--D	2000
2701	RL92.435	Volvo B10LA	Saffle S	N--D	2000

2707-2718

Scania L113CLL | DAB/Silkeborg | N--D | 2000

2707	RM96.994	2712	RN96.024	2715	RN96.188	2717	RN95.954
2710	RM96.996	2713	RN96.048	2716	RN96.189	2718	RN95.953

2720	RN88.013	Volvo B10BLE	Åbenrå	N38D	2000
2723	RP91.142	Volvo B10BLE	Åbenrå	N38D	2000
2745	RN96.076	Scania	DAB/Silkeborg	N--D	2000
2746	RN96.123	Scania	DAB/Silkeborg	N--D	2000
2747	RN96.124	Scania	DAB/Silkeborg	N--D	2000
2749	RP91.084	Volvo B10M	Åbenrå	B--D	2000
2751	RT95.351	MAN 9m lavgulv		N--F	2001
2752	RT95.350	MAN 9m lavgulv		N--F	2001

Fynbus is the fleetname for the operations on the Island of Fyn, situated between the larger islands of Jutland and Zealand. Arriva operate from two depots both serving Odense, the major centre. Recent deliveries include a large batch of Scania's integral OmniLine and 2799, RV95.347, is shown in the town. *Bill Potter*

2753-2769   Volvo B10BLE   Åbenrå   N38D   2001

2753	RT95.277	2758	RT95.268	2762	RT95.272	2766	RT95.276
2754	RT95.261	2759	RT95.269	2763	RT95.273	2767	RT95.267
2755	RT95.262	2760	RT95.270	2764	RT95.274	2768	RT95.266
2756	RT95.263	2761	RT95.271	2765	RT95.275	2769	RT95.265
2757	RT95.264						

2770-2819   Scania OmniLine CL94UB 12m   Scania   N--D   2001   *2774 is an OmniLink

2770	RT96.882	2787	RV95.338	2798	RV95.384	2809	RV95.394
2774	RV95.418	2788	RV95.339	2799	RV95.347	2810	RV95.395
2777	RV95.328	2789	RV95.340	2800	RV95.385	2811	RV95.396
2778	RV95.329	2790	RV95.341	2801	RV95.386	2812	RV95.397
2779	RV95.330	2791	RV95.342	2802	RV95.387	2813	RV95.398
2780	RV95.331	2792	RV95.343	2803	RV95.388	2814	RV95.399
2781	RV95.332	2793	RV95.344	2804	RV95.389	2815	RV95.400
2782	RV95.333	2794	RV95.345	2805	RV95.390	2816	RV95.401
2783	RV95.334	2795	RV95.382	2806	RV95.391	2817	RV95.402
2784	RV95.335	2796	RV95.383	2807	RV95.392	2818	RV95.403
2785	RV95.336	2797	RV95.346	2808	RV95.393	2819	RV95.404
2786	RV95.337						

2820-2825   Scania 13.6m   Lahti   N--D   2001-02

2820	RV95.405	2822	RV95.407	2824	SJ94.192	2825	RX97.975
2821	RV95.406	2823	RV95.408				

2826	RX96.850	Volvo B10M 13.7m	Åbenrå	NC44D	2002
2827	SM97.944	Scania 13.6m	Lahti	N--D	2002
2830	RZ88.061	Scania Omniline	DAB	N--D	2002
2831	RY88.058	Scania 13.6m	Lahti	N--D	2002
2837	RX96.843	Volvo B10M 13.7m	Åbenrå	NC44D	2002

2840-2844   Scania OmniLine CL94UB 12m   Scania   N--D   2002   *2843 is an OmniLink

2840	RZ97.927	2842	SD91.475	2843	SJ93.967	2844	SH93.791
2841	RZ97.946						

2845	SM95.889	Volvo B12M	Vest	NC44D	2002

2846-2851 Scania OmniLine CL94UB 12m Scania N--D 2002

2846	SL96.650	2848	SL95.855	2850	SL95.857	2851	SL95.953
2847	SL95.830	2849	SL95.856				

2852-2865 Scania OmniLink CL94UB 12m Scania N--D 2003-03

2852	SM97.681	2856	SX97.339	2860	SX97.367	2863	SX97.369
2853	SX97.361	2857	SX97.364	2861	SX97.340	2864	SX97.303
2854	SX97.362	2858	SX97.365	2862	SX97.368	2865	SX97.338
2855	SX97.363	2859	SX97.366				

2866-2871 MAN 13.310 HOCL Jonckheere Modulo C--D 2004

2866	SY89.049	2868	SY89.051	2870	SY89.081	2871	SY89.082
2867	SY89.050	2869	SY89.052				

3009	LJ93.182	Volvo B10M	Åbenrå	B36D	1985
3010	LJ96.657	Volvo B10M	Åbenrå	B36D	1985
3022	NB89.392	DAB	Silkeborg	B14F	1992
3025	NV89.197	Volvo B10BLE	Säffle	B36D	1994
3026	NV89.198	Volvo B10BLE	Säffle	B36D	1994
3064	RH97.568	Volvo B10BLE	Åbenrå	N39D	2000
3065	RH97.577	Volvo B10BLE	Åbenrå	N39D	2000
4001	OV92.022	Volvo B10L	Carrus	N40D	1997
4006	OP90.477	MAN/DAB	Silkeborg	N35D	1996
4007	OP90.478	MAN/DAB	Silkeborg	N35D	1996
4008	OY91.823	DAF/DAB	Silkeborg	N--D	1997

4021-4030 Volvo B10BLE Vest N36D 2002

4021	SN90.043	4024	SN90.046	4027	SM97.699	4029	SM97.737
4022	SN90.044	4025	SN90.047	4028	SM97.714	4030	SM97.752
4023	SN90.045	4026	SM97.688				

4275	MJ95.580	Volvo B10M	Åbenrå	B--D	1991

4308-4320 MAN/DAB Silkeborg N35D 1995

4307	OE92.914	4311	OE92.917	4319	OE92.963	4320	OE92.964
4308	OE92.915	4315	OE92.939				

4331	RP89.787	Volvo B10L	Carrus	N40D	1996
4355	OS89.286	DAF/DAB	Silkeborg	N--D	1996
4356	OS89.287	MAN/DAB	Silkeborg	N35D	1996

4361-4367 Volvo B10L Carrus N40D 1997

4361	PB89.204	4363	PB89.218	4365	PB89.226	4367	PB89.507
4362	PB89.215	4364	PB89.223	4366	PB89.488		

4368	PP94.329	DAB	Silkeborg	N35D	1998
4369	PP94.330	DAB	Silkeborg	N35D	1998
4370	PP94.331	DAB	Silkeborg	N35D	1998
4371	PP94.332	DAB	Silkeborg	N35D	1998
4372	PX96.281	Volvo B7L	Åbenrå	N39D	1999

4375-4388 Volvo B10BLE Åbenrå N--D 2000

4375	RE94.369	4377	RE94.371	4386	RN88.149	4388	RN88.151
4376	RE94.370	4378	RE94.372	4387	RN88.150		

4389-4393 Scania OmniLink 13.7m N--D 2002

4389	RU97.030	4391	RU97.078	4392	RU97.079	4393	RU97.080
4390	RU97.031						

4394	SJ89.557	Volvo B10BLE 13.7m	Åbenrå	NC--D	2002

4395-4409 Volvo B10BLE Vest N--D 2002

4395	SJ88.780	4399	SJ88.784	4403	SJ88.788	4407	SJ88.792
4396	SJ88.781	4400	SJ88.785	4404	SJ88.789	4408	SJ88.793
4397	SJ88.782	4401	SJ88.786	4405	SJ88.790	4409	SJ88.794
4398	SJ88.783	4402	SJ88.787	4406	SJ88.791		

Fifteen Berkhof-bodied Scania L94UB buses from 1999 are operated on Copenhagen routes. Illustrating the type is 1171, PR93.328. *Bill Potter*

4410-4419		Mercedes-Benz Cito		Mercedes-Benz		N17F	2002	
4410	SD96.842	**4413**	SD96.845	**4416**	SD96.848		**4418**	SD96.850
4411	SD96.843	**4414**	SD96.846	**4417**	SD96.849		**4419**	SD96.851
4412	SD96.844	**4415**	SD96.847					

7029	MV95.794	Scania N113CLB		-		B34D	1992	
7056	NJ97.968	DAB		Silkeborg		B26D	1989	

7077-7082		MAN 13.310 HOCL		Jonckheere Modulo		C--D	2004	
7077	SX88.391	**7079**	SX88.393	**7081**	SX88.395		**7082**	SX88.396
7078	SX88.392	**7080**	SX88.394					

7088-7122		DAB		Silkeborg		B26D	1994-98	
7088	NR96.589	**7096**	NR96.619	**7107**	NS95.974		**7114**	NS96.034
7089	NR96.590	**7099**	NR96.621	**7108**	NS95.987		**7115**	NS96.035
7091	NR96.592	**7101**	NS95.940	**7109**	NS95.988		**7116**	NS96.052
7092	NR96.593	**7102**	NS95.941	**7110**	NS95.989		**7117**	NS96.053
7093	NR96.594	**7103**	NS95.942	**7111**	NS95.990		**7119**	NS96.074
7094	NR96.595	**7105**	NS95.944	**7113**	NS96.013		**7122**	NV93.256
7095	NR96.618	**7106**	NS95.973					

7143-7159		Volvo B10B		Åbenrå		B29D	1996	
7143	OL88.190	**7148**	OL88.238	**7152**	OL88.242		**7156**	OL88.261
7144	OL88.191	**7149**	OL88.239	**7153**	OL88.242		**7157**	OL88.262
7145	OL88.192	**7150**	OL88.240	**7154**	OL88.250		**7158**	OL88.279
7146	PC95.824	**7151**	OL88.241	**7155**	OL88.260		**7159**	OL88.280
7147	OL88.194							

7208	NR96.200	Volvo B10	Åbenrå	B39D	1994
7209	NN91.908	Volvo B10	Åbenrå	B39D	1994
7210	NX90.841	Volvo B10	Åbenrå	B39D	1994
7211	OB94.391	Volvo B10	Åbenrå	B39D	1995
7229	PX96.500	MAN ?	MAN	N26F	1999
7230	PX96.499	MAN ?	MAN	N26F	1999

8017	NJ89.122	DAF/DAB Citybus	Silkeborg	B47D	1993	
8050	NX93.077	DAF 12m	?	B47D	1994	
8067	LP94.376	Volvo B10M	Åbenrå	B36D	1988	
8076	MR93.187	DAF/DAB Citybus	Silkeborg	B47D	1991	
8094	ME91.072	Volvo B10M	Åbenrå	B36D	1990	

8095-8120 DAF/DAB Citybus Silkeborg B47D 1991-93

8095	ML93.941	**8098**	NM90.134	**8099**	NM90.133	**8120** ME94.417
8097	ML93.995					

8134	OD92.514	Scania/DAB	Silkeborg	B47D	1995	
8141	MZ89.176	DAF/DAB Citybus	Silkeborg	B47D	1992	
8153	NR96.632	DAF 10m	Silkeborg	B--D	1989	
8165	OS95.223	DAF/DAB Citybus	Silkeborg	B47D	1991	

8262-8281 DAF/DAB Citybus Silkeborg B47D 1992

8262	MK92.126	**8270**	SB92.891	**8280**	NB97.629	**8281** NB97.670
8265	ML93.784					

8288	NU93.379	MAN/DAB Citybus Mk2	Silkeborg	B35D	1994	
8308	OZ91.788	Scania/DAB	Silkeborg	N38D	1997	
8323	NY91.120	Volvo B10M	Åbenrå	B39D	1995	
8332	OD90.885	Scania N113CLB	Lahti	N--D	1995	
8342	NM90.545	Volvo B9M 10m	Åbenrå	B--D	1993	

8353-8379 Volvo B10M Åbenrå B36D 1988-95

8353	NY91.118	**8377**	NB97.121	**8378**	OD92.522	**8379** MC97.193
8354	NY91.119					

8380	OY91.949	Scania OmniCity	DAB Silkeborg	N--D	1997	

8381-8391 MAN/DAB 12m Lavgulv B--D 1994-95

8381	OS89.278	**8384**	NY93.044	**8387**	NX92.950	**8390** NS96.012
8382	NZ93.971	**8385**	NY93.045	**8388**	NX92.951	**8391** OM90.436
8383	NZ93.973	**8386**	NX92.949	**8389**	NX92.952	

8392	OP90.576	DAF/DAB Citybus Mk III	Silkeborg	N--D	1996	
8393	OP90.577	DAF/DAB Citybus Mk III	Silkeborg	N--D	1996	
8394	NS95.943	MAN/DAB 12m	Lavgulv	B--D	1994	
8395	PP94.263	MAN/DAB 12m	Lavgulv	B--D	1994	
8396	NR96.643	MAN/DAB 12m	Lavgulv	B--D	1994	
8397	NR96.620	MAN/DAB 12m	Lavgulv	B--D	1994	
8398	ML93.951	DAF/DAB Citybus	Silkeborg	B38D	1991	
8399	ML93.952	DAF/DAB Citybus	Silkeborg	B38D	1991	
8401	MC92.630	DAF 12m	Silkeborg	B--D	1990	
8403	NJ97.905	DAF/DAB Citybus	Silkeborg	B38D	1990	
8417	MS97.695	Volvo B10M	Åbenrå	B39D	1992	
8418	OD97.597	Volvo B10M	Vest	B--D	1996	
8419	RH95.798	Volvo B10M	Vest	B--D	2000	
9057	KV94.738	Volvo B10M	DAB Silkeborg	B39D	1986	
9060	KV94.741	Volvo B10M	DAB Silkeborg	B39D	1986	
9061	KV94.742	Volvo B10M	DAB Silkeborg	B39D	1986	
9978	OX93.195	Volvo B10M	Åbenrå	B39D	1984	
9982	JR89.438	Volvo B10M	Åbenrå	B39D	1984	
9985	JR89.456	Volvo B10M	Åbenrå	B39D	1984	

Vestbus operation

77	Nj89.094	DAF/DAB Citybus	Silkeborg	BC--D	1993	

77-94 Volvo B10M - C--D 1994-2000

78	NU88.541	**85**	NY92.871	**88**	OS89.960	**92** NX90.900
79	NU88.542	**86**	NY92.872	**89**	OS89.961	**93** RL92.430
84	NY92.870	**87**	NZ93.570	**91**	NX90.899	**94** RL92.431

97	NM90.252	DAF/DAB Citybus	Silkeborg	BC--D	1992	

99-105 Volvo B10M - C--D 2000-01

99	RS90.131	**101**	RT94.703	**103**	SB94.567	**105** SB94.593
100	RS90.289	**102**	SB94.592	**104**	SB94.594	

2084	LH90.616	Volvo B10M	-	C--D	1987	
2130	LP94.394	Volvo B10M	-	C--D	1988	

ARRIVA SVERIGE

Arriva Sverige, Helsingborg, Sweden

6101	HSO203	Scania L113CLB	Scania	B55D	1995
6102	HSL103	Scania L113CLB	Scania	B55D	1995
6103	PFT339	Scania L113CLB	Carrus	B52D	1994
6108	GDA037	Scania CN112ALB	Scania	AB68D	1987
6109	FZP197	Scania CN112ALB	Scania	AB68D	1987
6110	GCE247	Scania CN112ALB	Scania	AB68D	1987
6112	HLR063	Scania L113CLB	DAB	B55D	1995
6113	HTS063	Scania L113CLB	DAB	B55D	1995
6114	TFY796	Volvo B10B	Carrus Delta Star	B42D	1993
6117	GNX410	Scania CN113ALB	Scania	AB70D	1996
6118	GOE130	Scania CN113ALB	Scania	AB70D	1996
6119	GPR410	Scania CN113ALB	Scania	AB70D	1996

6125-6132 Scania L113TLL Carrus AB56D 1996

6125	AER681	**6127**	AER941	**6129**	AES661	**6131**	ASX692
6126	AEO541	**6128**	AEO661	**6130**	AES611	**6132**	ASX602

6143	DLE670	Volvo B10M-70	Vest	AB55D	1997
6144	DLE630	Volvo B10M-70	Vest	AB55D	1997
6145	DLD590	Volvo B10M-70	Vest	AB55D	1997

6146-6159 Scania L94UB 14.8m Lahti N38D 2002-03

6146	STU583	**6150**	TPM	**6154**		**6157**	
6147	TPM241	**6151**	TPM	**6155**		**6158**	
6148	TPM238	**6152**	TPM	**6156**		**6159**	
6149	TPM232	**6153**	TPM				

6160-6166 Scania L94UB 13.5m Vest N34D 2002-03

6160	TPL913	**6162**	TPL955	**6164**	TPL712	**6166**	TPM811
6161	TPL940	**6163**	TPL685	**6165**	TPM802		

6167-6171 Scania L94UB 13.5m Vest N34D 2003

6167	TSX610	**6169**	TSX601	**6170**	TSX559	**6171**	TSX583
6168	TSX562						

6172-6176 Scania L94UB 14.8m Vest N38D 2003

6172	TSX574	**6174**	TSX532	**6175**	TSX538	**6176**	TSX547
6173	TSX580						

6198	RGP523	Scania L94UB	Vest	N34D	2000
6199	RGP529	Scania L94UB	Vest	N34D	2000
6211	FYP402	Scania CK112	Kutter	AB54D	1987
6219	NOE995	Volvo B10M-55	Säffle	AB49D	1989
6220	NOC595	Volvo B10M-70	Säffle	AB49D	1989
6364	NOH925	Volvo B10M-70	Säffle	B49D	1989
6366	NRS705	Volvo B10M-70	Säffle	B49D	1989
6381	PJT229	Mercedes-Benz Sprinter 410D	Mercedes-Benz	B17F	1992
6388	TUS376	Volvo B10L	Åbenrå	N32D	1997
6389	TYJ706	Volvo B10L	Åbenrå	N32D	1997
6390	UAF976	Volvo B10L	Åbenrå	N32D	1997

6391-6398 Scania OmniLink CL94UB Scania N32D 2001

6391	SFW553	**6393**	SHA709	**6395**	SHB571	**6397**	SOB811
6392	SFW559	**6394**	SHA715	**6396**	SOB844	**6398**	SOB832

6399	TUS256	DAB GS200 8.6m	DAB	N18D	1996
6400	TWG436	DAB GS200 8.6m	DAB	N18D	1996

One of the first Scania Omnicity buses delivered to Arriva was a batch for the operation in Lund, a town 21km north of Malmo. Eight of these were CNG-powered and operate along-side a batch of CNG-powered Volvo B10Ls. Under the more stringent environmental regulations only the gas-powered buses operate at weekends leaving the diesel-powered Scanias on weekday duties only. Number 6452, JKA408, illustrates the attractive livery applied by the local transport authority. *Bill Potter.*

6403-6426   Volvo B10BLE   Carrus City L   N36D   1997

6403	DYE741	6421	DHD620	6423	DHE580	6425	DHE680
6411	DGZ660	6422	DHD690	6424	DHE670	6426	DHE960
6420	DHD590						

6451-6458   Scania Omnicity CN94UB CNG   Scania   N32D   1998-99

6451	JKF208	6453	JJZ208	6455	JKA158	6457	DSO512
6452	JKA408	6454	JKC218	6456	JJZ138	6458	DSO632

6459	DKO530	Scania CN113CLL	Scania Maxi	N35D	1997
6460	JTM555	Scania CN113CLL	Scania Maxi	N35D	1997

6461-6480   Scania Omnicity CL94UB   Scania   N32D   2001

6461	SEA778	6466	SFA697	6471	SFA682	6476	SFW565
6462	SEA769	6467	SFC013	6472	SFA679	6477	SFW595
6463	SEA841	6468	SFA691	6473	SFW571	6478	SFW538
6464	SEA847	6469	SFA796	6474	SFW580	6479	SHA700
6465	SFA700	6470	SFA685	6475	SFX187	6480	SHA736

6481	DFS589	Scania Omnicity CN94UB	Scania	N32D	1997

6501-6515   Volvo B10L   Carrus City L   N36D   1997

6501	DSD690	6505	DSE550	6509	DSF570	6513	DSG850
6502	DSD780	6506	DSE590	6510	DSF590	6514	DSG940
6503	DSD870	6507	DSE650	6511	DSG560	6515	DSH520
6504	DSD890	6508	DSE580	6512	DSG590		

6516-6538   Volvo B10BLE   Åbenrå   N30D   2001

6516	SHC256	6522	SHC274	6528	SHC727	6534	SHB772
6517	SHC259	6523	SHC277	6529	SHC736	6535	SHB781
6518	SHC252	6524	SHC280	6530	SHC739	6536	SHD922
6519	SHC265	6525	SHC283	6531	SHC748	6537	SHD925
6520	SHC288	6526	SHC708	6532	SHB760	6538	SHD931
6521	SHC271	6527	SHC718	6533	SHB763		

The buses on Arriva's share of the Malmo services were substantially replaced in 2001 with batches of Volvo B10BLE and B10LA. The other buses at Malmo being 6501-15. Showing bodywork by Volvo subsidiary Åbenrå is 6522, SHC274. *Bill Potter*

6539-6544		Volvo B10AL			Saffle			AN48D	2001
6539	SHH016	**6541**	SHH025	**6543**	SHH031		**6544**	SHH034	
6540	SHH019	**6542**	SHH028						

6551-6574		Volvo B10L			Carrus			N32D	1999
6551	DCH730	**6557**	DBT690	**6563**	DBX640	**6569**	DCC780		
6552	DBU790	**6558**	DCA750	**6564**	DCB560	**6570**	OOP953		
6553	DBS990	**6559**	DCA850	**6565**	DBU650	**6571**	EZZ628		
6554	DCA880	**6560**	DBU720	**6566**	DBU610	**6572**	HKK690		
6555	DCN930	**6561**	DBS960	**6567**	DCH510	**6573**	ELP614		
6556	DBW580	**6562**	DBZ910	**6568**	DCE600	**6574**	LDP685		

6575	CDR237	Volvo B10L			Säffle			N32D	1998

6701-6729		Scania Omnicity CN94UA 18m			Scania			AN44D	2001
6701	SCH208	**6709**	SDD967	**6716**	SDM457	**6723**	SFA859		
6702	SCH223	**6710**	SDD955	**6717**	SEA832	**6724**	SFA721		
6703	SCH199	**6711**	SDD952	**6718**	SEA820	**6725**	SFA706		
6704	SCH181	**6712**	SDE007	**6719**	SEA817	**6726**	SFW556		
6705	SCH184	**6713**	SDD958	**6720**	SEA784	**6727**	SFW568		
6706	SCH226	**6714**	SDD949	**6721**	SEA775	**6728**	SFW547		
6707	SCH220	**6715**	SDM460	**6722**	SEA766	**6729**	SFZ649		
6708	SDD964								

ARRIVA NEDERLAND

Arriva Nederlands BV, Trambaan 3, postbus 626, 8440 AP Heerenveen

122-132			Mercedes-Benz 0405			Mercedes-Benz		B38D	1989		
122	LK	VF-14-VX	125	SG	VG-24-BH	128	GR	VF-25-YS	131	GR	VF-27-YS
123	GR	VF-11-VX	126	LK	VF-50-XJ	129	GR	VF-39-ZX	132	GR	VG-19-BH
124	LK	VF-52-XJ	127	LK	VF-26-YF	130	GR	VF-37-ZX			

133-138			Mercedes-Benz 0405G			Mercedes-Benz		AB49D	1990		
133	GR	VJ-58-LT	135	GR	VJ-71-ZV	137	GR	VN-59-GX	138	GR	VN-19-HG
134	GR	VJ-77-TK	136	GR	VJ-75-TK						

139	GR	VN-72-JX	Mercedes-Benz 0405		Mercedes-Benz		C38F	1991
140	GR	VN-63-GX	Mercedes-Benz 0405		Mercedes-Benz		BC37F+33	1991
141	GR	VN-15-HG	Mercedes-Benz 0405		Mercedes-Benz		BC37F+33	1991

142-157			Mercedes-Benz 0405G			Mercedes-Benz		AB49D	1992-93		
142	GR	VR-27-LR	146	GR	VR-85-JS	150	GR	VR-39-DF	154	GR	VV-72-XH
143	GR	VR-12-JT	147	GR	VR-98-JS	151	GR	VR-58-FJ	155	GR	VV-64-XH
144	GR	VR-09-XS	148	GR	VR-06-XS	152	GR	VR-10-LR	156	GR	VV-99-XB
145	GR	VR-13-XS	149	GR	VR-09-LR	153	GR	VV-69-XH	157	GR	VV-65-XH

158-165			Mercedes-Benz 0530G			Mercedes-Benz Citaro		AB50F	1999-2002 Seating varies		
158	GR	BH-VJ-15	160	GR	BH-XX-29	162	GR	BN-HN-57	164	GR	BN-HN-60
159	GR	BH-XX-31	161	GR	BH-XX-30	163	GR	BN-HN-59	165	GR	BN-HN-61

185	GR	VR-17-LK	Bova FHD 12.290	Bova Futura		C50F	1992
186	WT	VV-85-KK	DAF SB3000	Smit Orion Grandluxe		C50F	1993
187	GR	VV-80-PL	Mercedes-Benz 0350	Smit		C49F	1993

189-199			Mercedes-Benz 0350			Mercedes-Benz Tourismo		C51F	1995-2002		
189	GR	BB-ZP-54	192	GR	BG-NP-90	195	HV	BL-VH-80	198	SN	BJ-BG-36
190	GR	BD-RX-88	193	GR	BL-VH-95	196	WT	BH-FH-71	199	GR	BL-BG-74
191	GR	BF-LH-16	194	GR	BL-VH-96	197	WT	BH-HG-65			

201-206			DAF DE02LB SB220			Berkhof 2000NL		N36D	1995	LPG bus	
201	GR	BD-FZ-03	203	GR	BD-FZ-01	205	GR	BD-FZ-08	206	GR	BD-FZ-09
202	GR	BD-FZ-10	204	GR	BD-FZ-05						

451	GR	VV-78-GZ	Bova FHD 12.290	Bova Futura		C47F	1993
452	DR	VV-89-GZ	Bova FHD 12.290	Bova Futura		C47F	1993
453	HV	BB-LT-71	Iveco 380.12.35HD	Berkhof E3000HD		C50F	1994
454	LS	BB-LT-69	Iveco 380.12.35HD	Berkhof E3000HD		C50F	1994
456	SN	BD-BZ-70	Iveco 380.12.35HD	Berkhof E3000HD		C50F	1995

521-540			Mercedes-Benz 0530			Mercedes-Benz Citaro		N35D	2002-03		
521	GR	BN-JD-07	526	GR	BN-JD-02	531	GR	BN-JB-96	536	GR	BN-TS-65
522	GR	BN-JD-06	527	GR	BN-JD-01	532	GR	BN-JB-95	537	GR	BN-TS-66
523	GR	BN-JD-05	528	GR	BN-JB-99	533	GR	BN-JB-93	538	GR	BN-TS-67
524	GR	BN-JD-04	529	GR	BN-JB-98	534	GR	BN-TS-61	539	GR	BN-TS-62
525	GR	BN-JD-03	530	GR	BN-JB-97	535	GR	BN-TS-64	540	GR	BN-TS-68

1080-1086			Volvo B10M-55			Berkhof 2000NL		B45D+34	1995		
1080	LS	BD-BG-94	1082	LS	BD-BG-92	1084	DR	BD-BG-29	1086	LS	BD-BG-96
1081	LS	BD-BG-33	1083	LS	BD-BG-26	1085	LS	BD-BG-98			

1087-1096			Iveco EuroRider 391.12.29A			Berkhof 2000NL		B44D+34	1996		
1087	LS	BD-NN-44	1090	DM	BD-NN-46	1092	DM	BD-NN-48	1095	SN	BD-NN-52
1088	DM	BD-NN-21	1091	DM	BD-NN-47	1094	SN	BD-NN-50	1096	SN	BD-NN-42
1089	DM	BD-NN-51									

Pictured as it emerges from the paint-shop in March 2004 having received Arriva colours, DAF SB220 205, BD-FZ-08, illustrates the Berkhof 2000NL body styling. *Harry Laming*

1117-1126   Mercedes-Benz O408   Mercedes-Benz   B49D+31   1995

1117	SV	BD-FS-86	**1120**	SK	BD-FX-84	**1123**	WT	BD-FT-09	**1125**	AP	BD-FT-05
1118	SK	BD-FS-87	**1121**	SK	BD-FV-88	**1124**	WT	BD-FT-06	**1126**	UZ	BD-FT-03
1119	SV	BD-FS-88	**1122**	VD	BD-TV-38						

1138-1147   Iveco EuroRider B89   Den Oudsten   N45D   1995

1138	DM	BD-JB-29	**1141**	LS	BD-HV-14	**1144**	LS	BD-JP-95	**1146**	MG	BD-JP-94
1139	DM	BD-HV-12	**1142**	LS	BD-JB-28	**1145**	LS	BD-JP-96	**1147**	MG	BD-HV-26
1140	LS	BD-HV-13	**1143**	LS	BD-HV-24						

1152-1162   Den Oudsten B91   Den Oudsten Alliance   BC47D+30 1996

1152	VD	BD-BS-19	**1155**	WT	BD-BS-18	**1158**	ZP	BD-BS-12	**1161**	AP	BD-BS-09
1153	SK	BD-BS-16	**1156**	UZ	BD-BS-11	**1159**	AP	BD-BS-21	**1162**	SU	BD-RX-80
1154	WT	BD-BS-15	**1157**	ZP	BD-BS-13	**1160**	AP	BD-BS-20			

1254-1257   Den Oudsten B96   Den Oudsten Alliance   N31D+62 1996

1254	AS	BD-ZJ-61	**1255**	EM	BD-ZJ-52	**1256**	EM	BD-ZJ-51	**1257**	AS	BD-ZJ-66

1258-1267   Mercedes-Benz O408   Mercedes-Benz   B49D+30 1996

1258	VD	BD-ZB-16	**1261**	DM	BD-ZF-13	**1264**	SK	BD-ZF-10	**1266**	DM	BD-ZF-16
1259	VD	BD-ZF-18	**1262**	DM	BD-ZF-05	**1265**	VD	BD-ZF-14	**1267**	DM	BD-ZF-15
1260	ZK	BD-ZF-03	**1263**	UZ	BD-ZF-08						

1268-1276   Den Oudsten B95   Den Oudsten Alliance   N45D+33 1997

1268	AP	BD-TS-78	**1271**	WT	BD-TS-66	**1273**	SK	BD-TS-70	**1275**	SN	BD-TS-72
1269	AP	BD-TS-63	**1272**	ZK	BD-TS-69	**1274**	VD	BD-TS-71	**1276**	SN	BD-TS-67
1270	AP	BD-TS-64									

1279-1288   Iveco EuroRider   Berkhof 2000NL   N44D   1997

1279	MG	BF-GJ-28	**1282**	DM	BF-GJ-34	**1285**	SN	BF-GJ-29	**1287**	SN	BF-GJ-86
1280	MG	BF-GJ-38	**1283**	SN	BF-GJ-31	**1286**	SN	BF-GJ-26	**1288**	SN	BF-GJ-13
1281	DM	BF-GJ-36	**1284**	DM	BF-GJ-30						

Arriva Nederland 4041, BZ-05-ZV, is one of the oldest route buses still in service. It is seen at Zwartsluis and is a DAF MB230 with Den Oudsten B88 bodywork. *Harry Laming*

2194-2203
Den Oudsten B95   Den Oudsten Alliance   B45D+33   1997

2194	SN	BF-LG-44	2197	SN	BF-LG-87	2199	SN	BF-LJ-29	2202	SN	BF-LG-42
2195	ZW	BF-LG-43	2198	SN	BF-LG-83	2200	SN	BF-LG-40	2203	SN	BF-LH-20
2196	SN	BF-LG-89									

2217-2221
Den Oudsten B95   Den Oudsten Alliance   B45D+32   1997

2217	DG	BF-XV-78	2219	EM	BF-XV-23	2220	EM	BF-XV-22	2221	DR	BF-XV-21
2218	ML	BF-XV-24									

3601	GR	BP-96-TT	DAF MB200 DKDL600	Den Oudsten		B44D	1986
3625	DR	BR-36-JN	DAF MB200 DKDL600	Den Oudsten		B44D	1986
3631	AP	BV-46-VK	DAF MB200 DKDL600	Den Oudsten		B44D	1986

3816-3832
DAF MB200 DKDL600   Den Oudsten   B44D   1987

3816	WT	BV-85-VR	3826	AP	BV-71-XX	3829	VD	BV-28-YS	3832	AP	BY-44-ND
3825	PP	BV-72-XX	3828	LS	BV-27-YS						

3886-3936
DAF MB200 DKDL600   Den Oudsten   B44D   1987-88

3886	LS	BY-82-LJ	3890	ZK	BY-75-TK	3893	ZK	BY-68-VV	3936	HV	BY-52-XB
3889	ZK	BY-45-ND	3892	LK	BY-96-TK	3894	WT	BY-53-XB			

4014-4076
DAF MB230 LC615600   Den Oudsten B88   B45D+31   1988

4014	VD	BZ-71-SV	4020	VD	BZ-47-SP	4041	DV	BZ-05-ZV	4048	ZK	VB-26-DY
4015	EM	BZ-74-SV	4023	EM	BZ-50-SP	4042	HO	BZ-06-ZV	4049	ZK	VB-25-DY
4016	LK	BZ-73-SV	4024	WT	BZ-44-SP	4043	EM	BZ-07-ZV	4065	VD	VB-98-KJ
4017	AP	BZ-72-SV	4025	SK	BZ-94-VJ	4044	HV	BZ-98-ZT	4075	SU	VB-65-KJ
4018	LK	BZ-46-SP	4039	EM	BZ-03-ZV	4045	EM	VB-71-BN	4076	WT	VB-64-KJ
4019	LK	BZ-45-SP	4040	DV	BZ-04-ZV	4047	LK	VB-73-BN			

4116-4155 DAF MB230 LC615 Den Oudsten B88 B45D+32 1989

4116	EM	VF-37-JG	4126	WT	VF-19-GN	4143	SN	VF-08-GH	4150	DV	VF-02-GH
4117	EM	VF-11-HY	4127	VD	VF-79-GN	4144	ED	VF-12-GH	4151	DV	VF-27-GK
4118	LK	VF-06-HY	4128	VD	VF-30-HG	4146	AS	VF-99-GG	4152	AP	VF-94-GG
4119	LK	VF-71-HX	4129	WT	VF-28-HG	4147	DV	VF-95-GG	4153	EM	VF-87-GG
4122	LK	VF-20-HY	4130	ZK	VF-25-HG	4148	ML	VF-92-GG	4154	DV	VF-32-PP
4123	LK	VF-18-HY	4131	WT	VF-26-HG	4149	ML	VF-86-GG	4155	HO	VF-91-NP
4125	UZ	VF-23-GN	4142	ZW	VF-16-GH						

4233	ZW	VH-91-JX	DAF MB230 LC61564	Den Oudsten B88	B45D	1990
4234	ZW	VH-01-JY	DAF MB230 LC61564	Den Oudsten B88	B45D	1990

4239-4267 DAF MB230 LC61564 Den Oudsten B88 B45D+32 1990

4239	ML	VH-69-HF	4247	EM	VH-93-HF	4254	AP	VH-65-KO	4261	SK	VH-91-KB
4240	ML	VH-72-HF	4248	AP	VH-94-HF	4255	SK	VH-14-KP	4262	LK	VH-26-KD
4241	EM	VH-31-HG	4249	EM	VH-92-KD	4256	WT	VH-81-KB	4263	SK	VH-34-KD
4242	w	VH-35-HG	4250	DV	VH-89-KB	4257	WT	VH-95-KB	4264	SK	VH-37-KD
4243	DV	VH-42-HG	4251	EM	VH-94-KD	4258	WT	VH-04-KD	4265	SK	VH-44-NR
4244	EM	VH-44-HG	4252	AP	VH-66-KD	4259	SK	VH-43-KD	4266	WT	VH-41-NR
4245	HO	VH-88-HF	4253	AM	VH-79-KB	4260	SK	VH-47-KD	4267	WT	VH-42-NR

4299	LS	VS-31-RB	Mercedes-Benz 0408	Mercedes-Benz/Zabo	BC49D	1992

4301-4328 DAF MB230 LC615 Den Oudsten B88 B45D+32 1990

4301	LK	VH-32-NK	4304	SK	VH-35-NX	4308	AP	VH-25-SV	4327	ZW	VH-93-VX
4302	VD	VH-33-NK	4306	VD	VH-27-TF	4309	SK	VH-23-SV	4328	ED	VH-82-XG
4303	WT	VH-04-NX	4307	VD	VH-26-SV	4310	ZK	VH-35-SV			

4437-4447 Mercedes-Benz 0408 Mercedes-Benz/Zabo BC49D 1991

4437	SN	VK-65-TS	4441	LK	VK-19-ZZ	4444	LK	VK-62-LD	4446	VD	VK-11-SB
4439	VD	VK-01-VN	4442	AP	VK-21-ZZ	4445	WT	VK-13-SB	4447	LK	VK-57-PG
4440	GR	VK-12-YN	4443	SN	VK-60-PB						

4448-4472 Mercedes-Benz 0408 Mercedes-Benz/Zabo BC49D 1991

4448	AS	VL-97-GG	4455	LK	VL-29-SY	4461	DR	VN-61-DL	4467	LK	VN-68-BB
4449	AS	VL-99-GG	4456	LK	VN-71-BB	4462	SN	VL-01-GH	4469	OO	VL-25-SY
4450	HE	VL-35-JB	4457	SN	VN-01-BS	4463	DU	VL-98-GG	4470	DR	VL-19-VH
4451	LK	VL-40-LN	4458	LK	VN-09-DF	4464	DR	VL-45-GG	4471	TG	VN-69-GF
4452	OO	VL-49-LS	4459	LK	VN-77-DL	4465	WT	VL-62-PB	4472	VD	VN-63-GF
4453	AM	VL-30-TV	4460	OO	VN-75-DL	4466	LS	VL-03-SZ			
4454	LK	VN-85-NN									

4473-4489 Mercedes-Benz 0408 Mercedes-Benz/Zabo BC49D+31 1991

4473	SN	VL-81-NZ	4478	SN	VN-03-BS	4482	LK	VN-62-DL	4486	DM	VL-02-SZ
4474	SN	VL-36-JB	4479	SN	VN-61-DF	4483	SN	VL-59-PB	4487	DM	VL-21-VH
4475	SN	VL-14-SB	4480	SN	VN-07-DF	4484	DM	VL-87-PG	4488	DM	VN-74-BB
4476	SN	VL-37-LN	4481	SN	VN-80-FF	4485	DM	VL-86-PG	4489	DM	VN-64-DL
4477	SN	VL-33-VV									

4577-4602 DAF MB230 LC615 Den Oudsten B88 B45D+32 1990-91

4577	ZW	VL-49-SY	4584	AP	VL-51-PG	4591	ZW	VL-90-PB	4597	ML	VL-04-SB
4578	ZW	VL-52-SY	4585	AP	VL-07-PB	4592	UZ	VL-85-PB	4598	DV	VL-01-SB
4579	DU	VL-47-SY	4586	AP	VL-93-PK	4593	UZ	VL-79-PB	4599	DV	VL-98-RZ
4580	SK	VH-59-PG	4587	AP	VL-66-PB	4594	UZ	VL-83-PB	4600	EM	VL-96-RZ
4581	VD	VL-62-PG	4588	VD	VL-74-PB	4595	ZW	VL-92-PB	4601	AS	VL-38-TL
4582	AP	VL-54-PG	4590	SK	VH-98-PK	4596	DV	VL-05-SB	4602	EM	VL-20-SB
4583	AP	VL-52-PG									

4603-4632 DAF MB230 LO615 Den Oudsten Alliance B89 BC45D+31 1992

4603	HO	VR-03-GJ	4611	ZW	VR-22-GN	4618	DR	VP-72-XJ	4625	SK	VP-78-XX
4604	HO	VR-58-HH	4612	ZW	VR-27-GN	4619	ED	VP-48-XJ	4626	SK	VP-60-XJ
4605	ML	VR-11-GJ	4613	DV	VR-30-GN	4620	DR	VP-53-XJ	4628	VD	VP-41-XJ
4606	AS	VR-09-GJ	4614	DV	VR-28-GN	4621	EM	VP-12-XN	4629	WT	VP-14-YP
4607	EM	VR-06-GJ	4615	DR	VP-80-XJ	4622	DR	VP-56-XJ	4630	HE	VP-05-YP
4608	EM	VR-18-GN	4616	w	VP-44-XJ	4623	HE	VP-59-XK	4631	SN	VP-78-YN
4609	ZW	VR-24-GN	4617	DR	VP-77-XJ	4624	AP	VP-43-XK	4632	ED	VP-61-YN
4610	ZW	VR-21-GN									

The Mercedes-Benz O408 type with Mercedes-Benz/Zabo bodywork are predominantly used on inter-urban work for which several carry Q-liner markings. Pictured in Groningen bus station is recently-repainted 4455, VL-29-SY. *Harry Laming*

4677-4684

			Mercedes-Benz O408			Mercedes-Benz/Zabo		B49D	1992		
4677	SK	VR-60-VG	4679	UZ	VS-01-DB	4681	VD	VS-94-BZ	4683	ZK	VS-87-BZ
4678	SU	VR-61-VG	4680	ZK	VS-96-BZ	4682	VD	VS-90-BZ	4684	VD	VS-85-BZ

4700	DR	VR-23-GJ	DAF MB230 LO615			Den Oudsten Alliance B89		B45D	1992		
4701	SN	VR-25-GJ	DAF MB230 LO615			Den Oudsten Alliance B89		B45D	1992		
4735	DM	VS-75-LN	Mercedes-Benz O408			Mercedes-Benz/Zabo		B49D	1992		
4736	LS	VS-84-LN	Mercedes-Benz O408			Mercedes-Benz/Zabo		B49D	1992		

4738-4652

			Volvo B10M-61			Berkhof 2000NL		B45D	1993		
4738	DR	VV-14-XD	4742	DR	VV-23-XD	4747	MG	VV-29-XD	4750	MG	VX-09-DL
4739	DR	VV-17-XD	4743	DR	VV-24-XD	4748	MG	VX-66-DY	4751	TG	VX-18-DL
4740	DR	VV-20-XD	4744	LS	VV-25-XD	4749	MG	VX-36-DL	4752	LS	VX-58-DK
4741	DR	VV-22-XD	4746	LS	VV-27-XD						

4753-4757

			Mercedes-Benz O408			Mercedes-Benz/Zabo		B49D+31	1993		
4753	AM	VX-27-GJ	4755	SN	VX-17-GJ	4756	LS	VX-15-GJ	4757	SN	VX-23-GJ
4754	HE	VX-35-GJ									

4771-4777

			Mercedes-Benz O408			Mercedes-Benz		B49D+31	1993		
4771	ZK	BB-DL-39	4773	SK	BB-DL-76	4775	VD	BB-DL-35	4777	SK	BB-DL-37
4772	VD	BB-DL-31	4774	AP	BB-DL-33	4776	SK	BB-DL-86			

4833-4848

			DAF SB220 LC575			Den Oudsten B89 Alliance		BC47D	1992		
4833	HO	BB-LB-10	4837	DV	BB-LB-60	4841	EM	BB-JZ-95	4846	DV	VX-07-LK
4834	w	BB-LB-11	4838	ZW	BB-JV-77	4842	EM	BB-JV-80	4847	EM	BB-LB-14
4835	DG	BB-JX-59	4839	ED	BB-NL-24	4843	EM	BB-JV-89	4848	HO	BB-LB-61
4836	ED	BB-JZ-94	4840	ZW	BB-NL-23	4845	EM	BB-LB-13			

5531-5576

			DAF SB3000			Den Oudsten B95 Intercity		BC45D	1993-94		
5531	AS	VV-23-JP	5536	EM	VV-25-JP	5569	DV	BB-HJ-76	5573	DV	BB-HJ-87
5532	ZW	VV-14-JP	5537	ML	VV-19-JP	5570	EM	BB-HJ-73	5574	DV	BB-HJ-82
5533	AS	VV-16-JP	5538	AS	VV-11-JP	5571	AS	BB-HJ-90	5575	HO	BB-HJ-80
5534	ED	VV-07-JV	5567	ED	BB-HJ-86	5572	HO	BB-HJ-88	5576	ML	BB-HJ-69
5535	ZW	VV-35-JV	5568	EM	BB-HJ-78						

Mercedes-Benz O550 Integro number 5820, BH-TS-01, lost its Aggloliner colours for Arriva Qliner scheme during 2003. It is seen in Groningen bus station. *Harry Laming*

5577-5586

			Den Oudsten B91 DM580			Den Oudsten Alliance		B47D+32 1993		
5577	SK	BB-GS-55	5580	SU	BB-GS-03	5583	SK	BB-GR-98	5585	UZ	BB-GT-03
5578	ZK	BB-GS-54	5581	SK	BB-GS-01	5584	WT	BB-GR-97	5586	AP	BB-GS-23
5579	ZK	BB-GS-02	5582	ZK	BB-BR-99						

5700-5704

			DAF SBR3015 WS580 15m		Berkhof Excellence 500NL		BC45D	1994-95		
5700	EM	BB-PP-08	5702	HE	BB-PD-64	5703	EM	BB-PD-63	5704	EM	BB-PD-62
5701	HE	BB-PP-11									

5742-5746

			DAF SBR3015 WS580 15m		Berkhof Excellence 500NL		BC44D+35 1995			
5742	LK	BD-HG-61	5744	VD	BD-HG-64	5745	VD	BD-HG-69	5746	VD	BD-HH-22
5743	LK	BD-HG-59									

5747	EM	BB-HH-19	DAF SBR3015	Den Oudsten Interliner 500NL	BC44D	1995
5748	HE	BB-HG-38	DAF SBR3015	Den Oudsten Interliner 500NL	BC44D	1995
5783	DM	BF-XR-66	DAF DR33WS15	Berkhof Radial	BC58D	1997
5784	HE	BF-XR-65	DAF DR33WS15	Berkhof Radial	BC58D	1997
5785	EM	BF-XR-63	DAF DR33WS15	Berkhof Radial	BC58D	1997
5800	AS	46-DL-RX	Mercedes-Benz Vito 208D	Mercedes-Benz	M8	1999
5802	HO	03-DN-BL	Mercedes-Benz Vito 208D	Mercedes-Benz	M8	1999
5803	DV	42-DL-XT	Mercedes-Benz Vito 208D	Mercedes-Benz	M8	1999

5810-5821

			Mercedes-Benz O550ÜL		Mercedes-Benz Integro L		NC50D	2000		
5810	LK	BH-TD-29	5813	AP	BH-TN-93	5816	LK	BH-TN-90	5819	LK	BH-TR-99
5811	LK	BH-TN-95	5814	LK	BH-TN-92	5817	LK	BH-TR-97	5820	LK	BH-TS-01
5812	AP	BH-TN-94	5815	LK	BH-TN-91	5818	LK	BH-TR-98	5821	LK	BH-TS-02

5822-5834

			DAF SB220 LF		Berkhof Excellence 2000		N36D+4	2000		
5822	SG	BJ-DF-10	5826	TG	BJ-DF-16	5829	TG	BJ-DF-21	5832	SG	BJ-DF-25
5823	AM	BJ-DF-12	5827	TG	BJ-DF-18	5830	SG	BJ-DF-23	5833	SG	BJ-DF-27
5824	AM	BJ-DF-14	5828	TG	BJ-DF-19	5831	SG	BJ-DF-24	5834	EM	BJ-DR-02
5825	AM	BJ-DF-15									

Almost 200 DAF SB200s with Wrightbus Commander bodies are now operating with Arriva Nederland. As shown by 5965, BN-DS-90, the front door is narrower than on the British examples. The bus is seen at Zwartsluis bus station about to return to its home depot in Zwolle. *Harry Laming*

5835-5845

DAF SB220 GS · Berkhof Excellence 2000 · N42D+39 · 2000

5835	EM	BJ-DP-99	5838	DV	BJ-DP-93	5841	ZW	BJ-DP-90	5844	ZW	BJ-DP-86
5836	HO	BJ-DP-96	5839	DV	BJ-DP-92	5842	ZW	BJ-DP-89	5845	ED	BJ-DP-83
5837	ML	BJ-DP-95	5840	DV	BJ-DP-91	5843	ZW	BJ-DP-88			

5846	DR	96-JS-XX	Mercedes-Benz Vito 208D	Mercedes-Benz	M8	2002
5847	DR	97-JS-XX	Mercedes-Benz Vito 208D	Mercedes-Benz	M8	2002
5848	OO	98-JS-XX	Mercedes-Benz Vito 208D	Mercedes-Benz	M8	2002
5849	HE	99-JS-XX	Mercedes-Benz Vito 208D	Mercedes-Benz	M8	2002

5850-5899

Dennis Dart SLF · Alexander ALX200 · N39D+30 · 2000-01

5850	DG	BL-JD-45	5863	AS	BJ-ZF-51	5875	DR	BJ-ZT-87	5887	OO	BL-BJ-82
5851	EM	BJ-VB-33	5864	AS	BJ-ZF-50	5876	DR	BJ-ZT-90	5888	OO	BL-BJ-83
5852	DR	BJ-XN-84	5865	AS	BJ-ZF-46	5877	DR	BJ-ZT-89	5889	OO	BL-BJ-78
5853	EM	BJ-XN-81	5866	DG	BJ-ZT-77	5878	DR	BJ-ZT-91	5890	HE	BL-BJ-79
5854	EM	BJ-XN-82	5867	AS	BJ-ZJ-38	5879	DR	BJ-ZT-86	5891	HE	BL-BS-19
5855	EM	BJ-XN-78	5868	HO	BJ-ZJ-39	5880	DR	BJ-ZT-94	5892	DR	BL-BS-20
5856	EM	BJ-XN-80	5869	HO	BJ-ZJ-40	5881	DR	BJ-ZT-93	5893	LS	BL-BS-21
5857	EM	BJ-XN-77	5870	HO	BJ-ZJ-41	5882	DR	BJ-ZT-92	5894	HE	BL-BS-22
5858	EM	BJ-XN-83	5871	HO	BJ-ZJ-42	5883	DR	BL-DX-66	5895	HE	BL-BV-38
5859	ML	BL-BS-18	5872	HO	BJ-ZJ-43	5884	DR	BL-BJ-77	5896	HE	BL-BV-37
5860	ML	BJ-ZF-49	5873	DR	BJ-ZJ-44	5885	OO	BJ-ZT-76	5898	HE	BL-GN-77
5861	EM	BJ-ZF-48	5874	DR	BJ-ZJ-45	5886	OO	BL-BJ-80	5899	ML	BJ-TB-91
5862	ML	BJ-ZF-47									

5900-5919

Volvo B10BLE · Carrus · N40D · 1997 · Arriva Sverige, 2002

5900	LK	BL-SH-07	5906	LK	BN-BS-01	5912	LK	BL-TX-80	5916	LK	BN-HT-39
5902	ZK	BL-VJ-93	5907	LK	BN-FJ-84	5913	LK	BL-ZP-63	5917	LK	BN-FR-71
5903	ZK	BN-FH-34	5909	LK	BN-DG-29	5914	LK	BL-TN-74	5918	LK	BN-HV-20
5904	LK	BL-VZ-99	5910	LK	BL-SP-71	5915	LK	BL-VF-77	5919	LK	BL-SH-08
5905	LK	BL-XR-75	5911	LK	BN-FN-94						

The 2004 Arriva Bus Handbook

Recent arrivals are low floor minibuses for the *Servicebus* operation. These are Mercedes-Benz Vito 208s and from the 2003 delivery, pictured in Assen is Mercedes-Benz 411, 6110, BN-HP-85. *Harry Laming*

5920-5927 — DAF DE12CSSB120 — Wright Cadet — N24D — 2002

5920	LS	BL-TG-43	5922	LS	BL-TG-49	5924	LS	BL-TG-47	5926	LS	BL-TG-48
5921	LS	BL-TG-50	5923	LS	BL-TG-46	5925	LS	BL-TG-45	5927	LS	BL-TG-44

5928-5999 — DAF SB200 — Wrightbus Commander — N37D — 2002

5928	LS	BL-XH-68	5931	LS	BL-XH-67	5934	LS	BL-XH-70	5937	LS	BL-XH-80
5929	LS	BL-XH-73	5932	LS	BL-XH-71	5935	LS	BL-XH-77	5938	LS	BL-XH-76
5930	LS	BL-XH-66	5933	LS	BL-XH-74	5936	LS	BL-XH-78	5939	LS	BL-XH-79

5940	SK	TD-GD-80	Fiat Ducato	Fiat	M8	1998

5941-5999 — DAF DE12CSSB200 — Wrightbus Commander — N42D — 2002 — Seating varies

5941	WT	BL-BP-84	5956	OO	BL-DS-81	5971	DR	BN-HD-75	5986	ED	BN-HS-82
5942	WT	BL-BP-85	5957	OO	BL-DS-82	5972	DR	BN-HD-76	5987	SK	BN-HS-66
5943	WT	BL-BP-86	5958	DR	BN-DS-83	5973	DR	BN-HD-78	5988	AP	BN-HS-67
5944	WT	BL-BP-87	5959	DR	BN-DS-84	5974	DR	BN-HD-79	5989	TI	BN-HS-68
5945	WT	BL-BP-89	5960	DR	BN-DS-85	5975	DR	BN-HD-81	5990	TI	BN-HS-69
5946	WT	BL-BP-90	5961	DR	BN-DS-86	5976	OO	BN-HD-87	5991	TI	BN-HS-83
5947	WT	BL-BP-91	5962	DR	BN-DS-87	5977	OO	BN-HD-73	5992	TI	BN-HS-76
5948	WT	BL-BP-92	5963	ZW	BN-DS-88	5978	OO	BN-HD-77	5993	TI	BN-HS-77
5949	WT	BL-BP-94	5964	ZW	BN-DS-89	5979	OO	BN-HD-88	5994	TI	BN-HS-78
5950	AP	BL-BP-96	5965	ZW	BN-DS-90	5980	HE	BN-HD-89	5995	TI	BN-HS-80
5951	AP	BL-BP-97	5966	ZW	BN-DS-91	5981	HE	BN-HD-90	5996	TI	BN-HS-81
5952	AP	BL-BP-82	5967	ZW	BN-DS-93	5982	DV	BN-HS-70	5997	TI	BN-HS-73
5953	HE	BL-DS-78	5968	ZW	BN-DS-95	5983	DV	BN-HS-71	5998	TI	BN-HS-74
5954	OO	BL-DS-79	5969	ZW	BN-DS-96	5984	DV	BN-HS-72	5999	TI	BN-HS-75
5955	OO	BL-DS-80	5970	ZW	BN-DS-97	5985	ED	BN-HS-79			

6012	GR	VL-59-LF	Van Hool A508	Van Hool	B24D+32	1992
6014	GR	VP-81-KX	Van Hool A508	Van Hool	B24D+32	1992
6015	GR	VP-79-KX	Van Hool A508	Van Hool	B24D+32	1992

6100-6109   DAF DE12CSSB200   Berkhof Ambassador   N43D   2002

6100	SN	BN-HX-03	6103	SN	BN-JB-07	6106	SN	BN-HH-82	6108	SN	BN-JT-79
6101	SN	BN-HX-04	6104	SN	BN-JB-08	6107	SN	BN-HH-85	6109	SN	BN-JT-80
6102	SN	BN-HX-06	6105	SN	BN-JB-09					

6110	AS	BN-HP-85	Mercedes-Benz Sprinter 411 CDi	Mercedes-Benz	M8	2002

6111-6122   Mercedes-Benz Vito 208   Mercedes-Benz   M8   2003

6111	SN	35-LD-NK	6114	TI	08-LF-XH	6117	TI	07-LF-XH	6120	PP	27-LK-BF
6112	SN	36-LD-NK	6115	TI	05-LF-XH	6118	PP	09-LF-XH	6121	PP	28-LK-BF
6113	DM	34-LD-NK	6116	TI	06-LF-XH	6119	PP	26-LK-BF	6122	PP	29-LK-BF

6131-6158   Mercedes-Benz O550   Mercedes-Benz Integro   NC43D   2003

6131	HE	BN-NF-13	6138	LS	BN-NF-24	6145	PP	BN-NG-16	6152	MK	BN-NF-98
6132	DR	BN-NF-15	6139	LS	BN-NF-25	6146	MK	BN-NG-13	6153	PP	BN-NG-40
6133	DR	BN-NF-17	6140	SN	BN-NF-06	6147	PP	BN-NG-08	6154	PP	BN-NX-74
6134	DR	BN-NF-20	6141	PP	BN-NG-39	6148	MK	BN-NG-04	6155	GO	BN-NX-78
6135	DR	BN-NF-21	6142	PP	BN-NG-38	6149	PP	BN-NG-02	6156	GO	BN-NX-76
6136	DR	BN-NF-22	6143	PP	BN-NG-34	6150	PP	BN-NG-01	6157	SN	BN-NX-77
6137	DR	BN-NF-23	6144	GO	BN-NG-19	6151	MK	BN-NF-99	6158	LS	BN-NX-73

6171-6189   DAF DE12CSSB200   Berkhof Ambassador   NC43D   2003

6171	DM	BN-VX-54	6176	DM	BN-VX-59	6181	LS	BN-VX-64	6186	LS	BN-VX-69
6172	DM	BN-VX-55	6177	DM	BN-VX-60	6182	LS	BN-VX-65	6187	MG	BN-VX-70
6173	DM	BN-VX-56	6178	DM	BN-VX-61	6183	LS	BN-VX-66	6188	MG	BN-VX-71
6174	DM	BN-VX-57	6179	DM	BN-VX-62	6184	LS	BN-VX-67	6189	MG	BN-VX-72
6175	DM	BN-VX-58	6180	LS	BN-VX-63	6185	LS	BN-VX-68			

6200-6301   DAF DE12CSSB200   Wrightbus Commander   N42D   2003

6200	TI	BN-PN-24	6226	PP	BN-RP-10	6252	MK	BN-SG-15	6277	PP	BN-TB-25
6201	MK	BN-PN-27	6227	PP	BN-RP-11	6253	MK	BN-SG-17	6278	PP	BN-TB-26
6202	MK	BN-PN-30	6228	PP	BN-RP-12	6254	MK	BN-TB-43	6279	PP	BN-TB-27
6203	MK	BN-PN-32	6229	PP	BN-RP-13	6255	PP	BN-TB-45	6280	MK	BN-TB-28
6204	MK	BN-PN-33	6230	PP	BN-RP-15	6256	PP	BN-TB-47	6281	PP	BN-TB-29
6205	GO	BN-PN-38	6231	MK	BN-RP-17	6257	PP	BN-TB-49	6282	PP	BN-TB-30
6206	GO	BN-PN-39	6232	MK	BN-RP-18	6258	PP	BN-TB-51	6283	PP	BN-TB-31
6207	GO	BN-PN-35	6233	MK	BN-RP-20	6259	PP	BN-TB-53	6284	PP	BN-TB-32
6208	GO	BN-PN-41	6234	MK	BN-RP-21	6260	PP	BN-TB-56	6285	PP	BN-TB-33
6209	GO	BN-PN-42	6235	MK	BN-RP-23	6261	PP	BN-TR-58	6286	PP	BN-TB-35
6210	GO	BN-RD-38	6236	GO	BN-RP-26	6262	PP	BN-TR-59	6287	PP	BN-TB-37
6211	PP	BN-RD-39	6237	PP	BN-RP-28	6263	PP	BN-TR-61	6288	PP	BN-TB-38
6212	PP	BN-RD-40	6238	GO	BN-RP-30	6264	PP	BN-TR-62	6289	PP	BN-TB-41
6213	PP	BN-RD-41	6239	GO	BN-RP-32	6265	PP	BN-TR-63	6290	SK	BN-TR-69
6214	PP	BN-RD-47	6240	PP	BN-SF-92	6266	PP	BN-TR-64	6291	SK	BN-TR-70
6215	PP	BN-RD-48	6241	PP	BN-SF-94	6267	PP	BN-TR-66	6292	VD	BN-TR-71
6216	PP	BN-RD-49	6242	PP	BN-SF-96	6268	PP	BN-TR-67	6293	VD	BN-TR-76
6217	PP	BN-RD-50	6243	PP	BN-SF-98	6269	SK	BN-TR-68	6294	VD	BN-TR-77
6218	PP	BN-RD-51	6244	PP	BN-SF-99	6270	PP	BN-SG-19	6295	VD	BN-TR-78
6219	PP	BN-RD-52	6245	PP	BN-SG-01	6271	PP	BN-SG-24	6296	AS	BN-TR-79
6220	PP	BN-RN-83	6246	PP	BN-SG-03	6272	PP	BN-SG-25	6297	AS	BN-TR-81
6221	PP	BN-RN-87	6247	MK	BN-SG-04	6273	PP	BN-SG-26	6298	AS	BN-TR-83
6222	PP	BN-RN-84	6248	MK	BN-SG-06	6274	PP	BN-SG-27	6299	AS	BN-TR-84
6223	PP	BN-RN-85	6249	MK	BN-SG-08	6275	PP	BN-SG-28	6300	AS	BN-TR-85
6224	PP	BN-RN-86	6250	MK	BN-SG-11	6276	MK	BN-TB-24	6301	AS	BN-TR-86
6225	PP	BN-RP-08	6251	MK	BN-SG-13						

6315	TG	VF-43-PP	Volvo B10M 10m	Hainje	B29D+42	1989
6317	LS	VF-70-PP	Volvo B10M 10m	Hainje	B29D+42	1989
6340	LS	VJ-58-TD	Volvo B10M 10m	Berkhof	B29D+43	1990
6341	LS	VJ-32-TB	Volvo B10M 10m	Berkhof	B29D+43	1990
6381	SN	BD-VV-35	Iveco Daily 45.10	Iveco	M17	1996
6382	GR	BD-VV-36	Iveco Daily 45.10	Iveco	M17	1996
6387	HE	BF-XL-12	MAN 11.220 HOCL	Berkhof 2000NLE	B25D	1997
6388	UZ	BF-XL-09	MAN 11.220 HOCL	Berkhof 2000NLE	B25D	1997
6721	FA	BT-92-NP	DAF MB 230 10m	Den Oudsten Alliance	B26F	1987
7119	LK	VT-55-FG	DAF SBG220 LB506	Den Oudsten Alliance	AB61D+63	1992
7120	AP	VT-54-LD	DAF SBG220 LB506	Den Oudsten Alliance	AB61D+63	1992
7284	DM	RG-XN-42	Iveco 35.10	Iveco	M8	1997
7285	TI	RG-XN-44	Iveco 35.10	Iveco	M8	1997
7287	ML	RG-FG-89	Mercedes-Benz Sprinter 208D	Mercedes-Benz	M8	1996
7288	AS	RG-FG-86	Mercedes-Benz Sprinter 208D	Mercedes-Benz	M8	1996

7291	AP	RZ-XG-70	Mercedes-Benz Sprinter 208D	Mercedes-Benz	M8	1997
7301	AP	SN-FZ-80	Mercedes-Benz Sprinter 208D	Mercedes-Benz	M8	1997
7302	AS	SX-GZ-04	Mercedes-Benz Sprinter 208D	Mercedes-Benz	M8	1997
7303	ML	SX-PG-91	Mercedes-Benz Sprinter 208D	Mercedes-Benz	M8	1997
7304	DV	SX-GZ-02	Mercedes-Benz Sprinter 208D	Mercedes-Benz	M8	1997
7305	DR	SP-NG-36	Iveco 35.10	Iveco	M8	1997
7306	EM	SP-NG-38	Iveco 35.10	Iveco	M8	1997
7316	AS	TS-VV-22	Mercedes-Benz Sprinter 208D	Mercedes-Benz	M8	1998

7620-7651
DAF MBG200 DKFL530 — Den Oudsten — AB68D+55 1987-88

7620	ZK	BX-78-PT	7625	LS	BX-36-SL	7645	LK	BZ-40-KT	7649	AP	BZ-79-LJ
7621	SK	BX-77-PT	7628	LK	BX-72-YZ	7647	LK	BZ-32-KT	7650	AP	BZ-75-LJ
7622	ZK	BX-80-PT	7644	LK	BZ-24-KF	7648	VD	BZ-48-LD	7651	GR	BZ-76-LJ
7623	ZK	BX-03-RG									

7657-7661
Volvo B10MG-60 — Hainje-Duvedec — AB65D+54 1989

7657	AS	VF-41-DL	7659	LK	VF-36-HG	7660	AS	VF-39-HG	7661	EM	VF-81-HB
7658	AS	VF-76-HB									

7668-7672
Volvo B10MG-55 — Berkhof — AB65D+59 1990

7668	AS	VJ-36-KH	7670	AS	VJ-98-KV	7671	LK	VJ-16-PJ	7672	LK	VJ-13-PJ
7669	DR	VJ-18-LD									

7752-7759
Volvo B10MG-55 III — Berkhof — AB65D+59 1991

7752	AS	VL-88-PB	7754	DV	VL-33-SB	7756	EM	VL-48-TH	7758	ZW	VL-31-LN
7753	ZW	VL-21-SB	7755	DV	VL-97-SY	7757	EM	VL-98-SY	7759	ZW	VL-17-LN

Depots and Codes:

AM	Ameland	GR	Groningen	SG	Schiermonnikoog
AP	Appingedam	HE	Heerenveen	SK	Stadskanaal
AS	Assen	HV	Heerenveen	SN	Sneek
DG	Dieverbrug	LK	Groningen Srreek/Leek	SV	Surhuisterveen
DM	Dokkum	LS	Leeuwarden Stad	TG	Terschelling
DR	Drachten	MG	Minnertsga	UZ	Uithuizen
DV	Dedernsvaart	ML	Meppel	VD	Veendam
ED	Emmeloord	OO	Oosterworlde	WT	Winschoten
EN	Emmen	PP	Papendrecht	ZW	Zwartsluis

This Noordned DAF SB200 with Berkhof Ambassador bodywork is 6102 BN-HX-06, in the Arriva Nederland fleet. It is seen in Sneek. *Harry Laming*

ARRIVA PORTUGAL

Arriva Portugal, Edificio Guimarães, Rua Eduardo de Almeida, No 162, 2°Sala-C,
4810-440 Guimarães, Portugal

20	RT-83-65	Volvo B58-55	Irmãos Mota (1991)	BC53D	1971	Hotelcar, Lisboa, 1990
23	TM-67-93	AEC Reliance 10U3ZL	UTIC (Porto)	BC55D	1980	
48	OS-22-02	AEC Reliance 6U3ZL	UTIC (Porto)	B32D	1972	
52	MS-65-03	AEC Reliance 6U3ZL	UTIC (Porto)	BC59D	1972	
54	NN-94-78	AEC Reliance 6U3ZL	UTIC (Porto)	B34D	1975	
55	ON-25-62	AEC Reliance 6U3ZL	UTIC (Porto)	BC73D	1973	
62	NP-74-16	AEC Reliance 10U2L	UTIC (Lisboa)	C53D	1979	
64	NP-74-18	AEC Reliance 10U2L	UTIC (Lisboa)	C51D	1979	
65	EU-58-65	UTIC-AEC U2077	UTIC (Lisboa)	C51D	1980	
68	GR-84-44	UTIC-AEC U2077	UTIC (Lisboa)	C55D	1980	
69	IV-72-34	Scania BR116S	Irmãos Mota	BC47D	1981	
70	BZ-09-52	Scania BR116S	Irmãos Mota	C47D	1981	
71	BZ-09-50	Scania BR116S	Irmãos Mota	C49D	1981	
72	DO-02-26	Scania BR116S	Irmãos Mota	C55D	1982	
73	EB-09-81	Scania BR116S	Irmãos Mota	C55D	1982	
74	ND-16-05	Scania BR116S	Irmãos Mota	C49D	1983	Barraqueiro, Malaveira, 1999
75	CJ-48-40	Scania K112S	Alfredo Caetano	C51D	1984	Belos Transportes, Setúbal, 1999
78	NT-91-12	UTIC Leyland MTL11R	UTIC (Porto)	C54D	1983	
79	OT-51-12	Volvo B10M-60	Irmãos Mota	C49D	1983	
80	OT-51-13	Volvo B10M-60	Irmãos Mota	C49D	1983	
81	TN-95-90	Scania K112S	Irmãos Mota	C49D	1984	
82	TN-95-91	Scania K112S	Irmãos Mota	C49D	1984	
84	JS-97-52	Scania K112S	Irmãos Mota	C49D	1986	
85	JS-97-53	Scania K112S	Irmãos Mota	C49D	1986	
86	FQ-88-17	Scania K112S	Irmãos Mota	C49D	1987	
87	FQ-88-18	Scania K112S	Irmãos Mota	C49D	1987	
92	NR-36-07	AEC Reliance 6U3ZL	UTIC (Porto)	BC59D	1972	
94	DU-95-69	Scania BR116S	Irmãos Mota	C55D	1981	
95	DU-99-92	Scania BR86S	Irmãos Mota	BC51D	1981	
96	IM-02-26	Scania BR116S	Irmãos Mota	C55D	1981	
98	ND-16-04	Scania BR116S	Irmãos Mota	C49D	1983	

Several of the buses operating with Arriva Portugal have been mid-life buses purchased from Germany. An example of this is Mercedes-Benz O305 number 123, 23-36-CL which was pictured at Famalicão bus station in October 2003. Harry Laming

Pictured at Parada depot, number 98, ND-16-04 is a Scania BR116S with Irmãos Mota bodywork. This is now one of the older buses, though displays the corporate colours very well. *Harry Laming*

100	PA-65-24	Scania K112-60	Irmãos Mota	C53D	1989	
101	RF-74-82	Scania K113CLB	Irmãos Mota	C49D	1989	
102	RF-74-81	Scania K113CLB	Irmãos Mota	C49D	1989	

116-122		MAN SL200		MAN	B39D	1977	Hamburg, 1992
116	56-18-AU	118	56-20-AU	121	56-16-AU	122	56-17-AU
117	56-19-AU	119	56-14-AU				

123-129		Mercedes-Benz O305		Mercedes-Benz	B44D	1981	Germany 1993-94
123	23-36-CL	125	23-38-CL	127	23-40-CL	129	52-91-EC
124	23-37-CL	126	23-39-CL	128	52-90-EC		

| 130 | 99-70-EH | Mercedes-Benz O303 | Mercedes-Benz | BC55D | 1986 | Germany, 1994 |

131-143		Mercedes-Benz O305		Mercedes-Benz	B44D*	1979-84	Germany 1994-95
					*131 is BC44D; 137-40 are B37D; 141/2 are B41D		
131	99-74-EI	134	39-63-EJ	140	61-64-FU	142	98-37-FV
132	99-75-EI	137	79-05-FT	141	98-36-FV	143	21-02-FX
133	99-76-EI	139	12-22-FU				

145	GP-80-07	UTIC-AEC U2075	UTIC (Lisboa)	B40D	1977	VIMECA, Queiuz de Baixo, 1996
147	16-81-HT	Mercedes-Benz 0303	Mercedes-Benz	C51D	1984	Germany, 1997
148	13-06-HJ	Mercedes-Benz 0303	Mercedes-Benz	C51D	1988	Germany, 1996
150	08-86-DC	MAN SL200	MAN	B41D	1981	VIMECA, Queiuz de Baixo, 1997
152	63-36-CC	MAN SL200	MAN	B44D	1981	VIMECA, Queiuz de Baixo, 1997
154	55-39-KF	Mercedes-Benz O305	Mercedes-Benz	B44D	1983	Germany, 1997
155	64-00-JL	Mercedes-Benz O305	Mercedes-Benz	B44D	1982	Germany, 1998
156	56-56-JO	Mercedes-Benz O305	Mercedes-Benz	B37D	1983	Germany, 1998
157	95-75-MJ	Mercedes-Benz 0303	Mercedes-Benz	B44D	1986	Germany, 1998
158	95-76-MJ	Mercedes-Benz O305	Mercedes-Benz	B44D	1986	Germany, 1998
159	46-36-ML	Mercedes-Benz O405	Mercedes-Benz	B44D	1986	Germany, 1998
160	46-37-ML	Mercedes-Benz 0303	Mercedes-Benz	BC53D	1991	Germany, 1998
161	79-18-ML	Mercedes-Benz O305	Mercedes-Benz	B37D	1986	Germany, 1998
162	79-19-ML	Mercedes-Benz O305	Mercedes-Benz	B38D	1986	Germany, 1998

Acquired in 2002, coach 592, UA-48-68, is a Scania K113 with UTIC (Lisboa) bodywork. Originally received for the Metro replacement service, this type of coach is now found on the principal routes in the area.
Marco António Lindo

163-179		Mercedes-Benz O405		Mercedes-Benz		B44D+32*	1987-91	Germany, 2003
								*Seating varies

163	98-34-VU	168	25-06-VU	172	45-10-VX	176	98-35-VU
164	25-10-VU	169	45-08-VX	173	98-36-VU	177	98-37-VU
165	25-08-VU	170	25-11-VU	174	45-09-VX	178	98-33-VU
166	25-09-VU	171	98-32-VU	175	25-12-VU	179	25-13-VU
167	25-07-VU						

196	OO-21-50	AEC Reliance U2076 (Volvo)	UTIC (Porto) (1988)	BC43D	1978	A V Minho, 1992
197	TM-30-63	AEC Reliance U2076 (Volvo)	UTIC (Porto)	B35D	1979	
206	IG-86-75	UTIC-AEC U2001	J D Martins (1985)	C47D	1963	
207	II-27-28	UTIC-AEC U2001	UTIC (Porto) (1981)	C47D	1964	
209	NN-56-30	UTIC-AEC U2047	UTIC (Lisboa)	BC73D	1974	
212	GI-41-27	UTIC-AEC U2001	J D Martins (1985)	C47D	1966	
218	ST-91-65	Volvo B58-60R	Irmãos Mota (1989)	BC53D	1976	
222	OR-84-90	Volvo B58-60R	J D Martins	BC73D	1977	
223	NN-99-29	Volvo B58-60R	Irmãos Mota (1988)	BC55D	1975	SOTUBE, 1982
240	RT-72-92	AEC Reliance U2021	J D Martins	C51D	1971	
243	RT-81-80	Volvo B58-55	Irmãos Mota	BC49D	1971	Machado Fernandes, 1983
246	OS-23-59	UTIC-AEC U2047	UTIC (Lisboa)	BC59D	1972	
248	NR-39-48	UTIC-AEC U2047	UTIC (Lisboa)	BC59D	1972	
251	AO-12-13	UTIC-AEC U2055	UTIC (Lisboa)	B39D	1973	RBI, Castelo Branco, 1996
252	OS-60-31	UTIC-AEC U2047	UTIC (Lisboa)	BC59D	1972	
253	NR-76-54	UTIC-AEC U2055	UTIC (Lisboa)	BC73D	1973	
254	NR-76-55	UTIC-AEC U2055	UTIC (Lisboa)	BC73D	1973	
255	AO-12-20	UTIC-AEC U2047	UTIC (Lisboa)	BC73D	1973	Covas & Filhos, 2001
259	PM-47-25	UTIC-AEC U2055	UTIC (Lisboa)	BC59D	1974	
261	72-54-HT	Mercedes-Benz O303/15R	Mercedes-Benz	C49D	1987	
263	PO-47-04	Magirus Deutz 260B120A	Salvador Caetano	C49D	1977	
264	PO-70-16	Volvo B58-60R	J D Martins	BC73D	1977	
265	SR-56-38	Volvo B58-60R	J D Martins	BC73D	1977	
267	PS-35-43	Volvo B58-60R	Irmãos Mota	BC53D	1977	
269	76-65-NM	Mercedes-Benz O303/15R	Mercedes-Benz	C49D	1987	
270	76-66-NM	Mercedes-Benz O303/15R	Mercedes-Benz	C49DT	1984	

Eight articulated Volvo B10M buses were acquired in 2002. These have CAMO bodies and 304, RP-95-43, is illustrated. New in 1987, these buses are employed on school transport work and, following the withdrawal of the Scanias are the only remaining articulated buses in the fleet. *Marco António Lindo*

271	SR-74-98	Volvo B58-60P	Irmãos Mota (1998)	C53D	1978
273	PO-96-69	Magirus Deutz 260C120E	Salvador Caetano	C53D	1977
275	OM-98-37	Volvo B10M-60	Alfredo Caetano	C49D	1982	Ag Viagens Sta Filomena, 1996
278	OO-39-95	Volvo B58-60R	J D Martins	BC59D	1979
279	OO-39-88	Volvo B58-60P	Irmãos Mota (1993)	BC53D	1979
284	HS-58-14	UTIC-AEC U2077	UTIC (Lisboa)	C49D	1979
286	TS-22-34	UTIC-AEC U2077	UTIC (Lisboa)	C49D	1980
291	RS-17-88	Volvo B10M-60	Ramp	C49D	1983	Ag Viagens Sta Filomena,
292	OR-78-64	Volvo B58-60R	Salvador Caetano	C53F	1976	Ag Viagens Sta Filomena,
293	TM-75-73	AEC Reliance 10U3ZL	UTIC (Lisboa)	BC53D	1980
294	TM-75-74	AEC Reliance 10U3ZL	UTIC (Lisboa)	C55D	1980
295	OO-99-57	Volvo B58-60P	J D Martins	B36D	1979
296	TS-24-63	Volvo B58-60P	Irmãos Mota	C49D	1980
298	SP-51-23	Volvo B10M-60	Irmãos Mota	C49D	1981	Ag Viagens Sta Filomena,
299	RS-59-61	Pegaso 5036	Salvador Caetano	C47D	1983
300	RS-59-62	Pegaso 5036	Salvador Caetano	C47D	1983

301-308		Volvo B10M-55G	CAMO	AB49D	1987	Acquired, 2002
301	QN-06-15	**303**	RP-69-35	**305**	QN-54-94	**307**	QT-33-69
302	QN-06-19	**304**	RP-95-43	**306**	QN-83-83	**308**	QQ-79-80

350	QS-93-85	Volvo B10R	Irmãos Mota	B36D	1990	TUG, Guimaraes, 2003
351	RQ-11-70	Volvo B10R	CAMO	B36D	1991	TUG, Guimaraes, 2003
352	SQ-29-93	Volvo B10R	Irmãos Mota	B36D	1992	TUG, Guimaraes, 2003
376	70-16-TI	Volvo B10M-60	DAB	BC51D	1988	Arriva Danmark, 2002
377	85-57-TL	Volvo B10M-60	Åbenrå	BC51D	1989	Arriva Danmark, 2002

378-390		Volvo B10M-60	DAB	BC51D	1989-90	Arriva Denmark, 2001-03
378	81-15-TH	**381**	89-21-SR	**386**	97-07-TD	**389**	85-58-TL
379	70-18-TI	**383**	97-09-TD	**387**	81-16-TH	**390**	35-65-UP
380	70-17-TI	**384**	97-08-TD	**388**	81-17-TH		

391	89-73-UP	Volvo B10R	Åbenrå	BC49D	1987	Arriva Danmark, 2003

392-400 Volvo B10M-60 Åbenrå BC51D* 1987-91 Arriva Denmark, 2003 *seating varies

392	59-25-UP	395	35-61-UP	397	35-59-UP	399	89-62-UP
393	35-64-UP	396	35-63-UP	398	35-62-UP	400	97-43-UZ
394	35-60-UP						

401-420 Mercedes-Benz OH1634L/63 Irmãos Mota C51D 1994

401	23-30-EH	406	90-45-EI	411	79-16-EJ	416	42-79-EL
402	49-07-EH	407	90-46-EI	412	79-37-EJ	417	42-80-EL
403	49-08-EH	408	90-47-EI	413	79-38-EJ	418	42-81-EL
404	49-09-EH	409	90-48-EI	414	79-39-EJ	419	42-82-EL
405	90-35-EI	410	79-15-EJ	415	42-78-EL	420	42-88-EL

421	VI-16-66	Mercedes-Benz O303/63	Irmãos Mota	C51D	1990
501	75-37-DJ	Scania K113CLB	Irmãos Mota	C51D	1994
502	66-89-FI	Scania K113CLB	Irmãos Mota	C51D	1995
503	61-34-ND	Scania K124IB4x2	Irmãos Mota	C51D	1999
504	70-12-NT	Scania K124IB4x2	Irmãos Mota	C55D	1999

521-527 Scania K114IB4x2 Caetano Bus C59D 2002

521	10-70-TT	523	10-68-TT	525	10-66-TT	527	10-64-TT
522	10-69-TT	524	10-67-TT	526	10-65-TT		

581	JJ-81-37	Scania K112S	UTIC (Lisboa) (1990)	C49D	1984	EVA Transportes, Faro, 2002
582	JA-86-73	Scania K112S	UTIC (Lisboa) (1990)	C49D	1985	EVA Transportes, Faro, 2002
589	RD-57-84	Scania K113CLB	UTIC (Lisboa)	C49D	1988	
590	RG-68-73	Scania K113CLB	UTIC (Lisboa)	C51D	1989	
591	UA-48-65	Scania K113CLB	UTIC (Lisboa)	C49D	1989	Cruz e Neves, Ilhavo, 2002
592	UA-48-68	Scania K113CLB	UTIC (Lisboa)	C49D	1989	Cruz e Neves, Ilhavo, 2002
593	VC-38-22	Scania K113CLB	UTIC (Lisboa)	C49D	1990	EVA Transportes, Faro, 2002
594	VC-38-25	Scania K113CLB	UTIC (Lisboa)	C49D	1990	EVA Transportes, Faro, 2002
601	68-35-SD	Scania L94IB4x2	CAMO	B47D	2001	
602	68-34-SD	Scania L94IB4x2	CAMO	B47D	2001	
603	62-12-SG	Scania L94IB4x2	CAMO	B47D	2001	
604	62-06-SG	Scania L94IB4x2	CAMO	B47D	2001	
651	32-05-GU	Scania K113CLL AA	Irmãos Mota	B47D	1996	
652	32-06-GU	Scania K113CLL AA	Irmãos Mota	B47D	1996	
701	QX-01-42	Scania K113CLB	Irmãos Mota	C(63)DT	1991	
702	QX-01-43	Scania K113CLB	Irmãos Mota	C(63)DT	1991	
703	29-69-FB	Scania K113CLB	Irmãos Mota	C(61)DT	1995	
704	29-70-FB	Scania K113CLB	Irmãos Mota	C(61)DT	1995	
705	06-01-IG	Scania K113CLB	Irmãos Mota	C(59)DT	1997	
706	42-09-NH	Scania K124IB4x2	Irmãos Mota	C(59)DT	1999	

Arriva Portugal's 267, PS-35-43, is a Volvo B58 with Irmãos Mota bodywork. It is seen turning at the bus station in Famalicão in October 2003.
Harry Laming

ARRIVA NOROESTE

Arriva (Iasa-Finisterre), Poligono de Sabon, Parcela 31-32, 15142 Arteixo, La Coruña, España

0177	C-2375-Z	Setra S215HU	Setra	BC55D	1984
0178	C-5716-AC	Pegaso 5031-L4	Unicar	C55D	1986
0179	C-5717-AC	Pegaso 5031-L4	Unicar	C55D	1986
0180	C-8337-AC	Pegaso 5031-L4	Unicar	C55D	1986
0204	C-1248-AF	Volvo B10M-60	Irizar	C55D	1986
0205	C-1249-AF	Volvo B10M-60	Irizar	C55D	1986
0206	C-1813-AF	Mercedes-Benz O303	Irizar	C55D	1986
0207	C-1814-AF	Mercedes-Benz O303	Irizar	C55D	1986
0208	C-1918-AF	Pegaso 5036-S1	Castrosua	C55D	1986
0209	C-1919-AF	Pegaso 5036-S1	Castrosua	C55D	1986
0212	C-7688-AF	Pegaso 5036-S1	Castrosua	C55D	1987
0213	C-7689-AF	Pegaso 5036-S1	Castrosua	C55D	1987
0214	C-2324-A	Setra S215HU	Setra	BC55D	1989
0215	C-2325-A	Setra S215HU	Setra	BC55D	1989
0216	C-2326-A	Setra S215HU	Setra	BC55D	1989
0217	C-2327-A	Setra S215HU	Setra	BC55D	1989
0218	C-2328-A	Setra S215HU	Setra	BC55D	1989
0219	C-2329-A	Setra S215HU	Setra	BC55D	1989
0221	C-8224-AT	Setra S215HD	Setra	C55D	1990
0222	C-8225-AT	Setra S215HD	Setra	C55D	1990
0223	C-8226-AT	Setra S215HU	Setra	BC55D	1990
0224	C-8227-AT	Setra S215HD	Setra	C55D	1990
0225	C-8228-AT	Setra S215HU	Setra	BC55D	1990
0226	C-8229-AT	Setra S215HD	Setra	C55D	1990
0227	LU-9759-I	Mercedes-Benz O303	Hispano Carrocera	C55D	1987
0229	LU-5545-J	Mercedes-Benz O303 15	Irizar	C56F	1988
0231	C-6734-A	Setra S215HU	Setra	BC55D	1991
0232	C-6735-A	Setra S215HU	Setra	BC55D	1991
0233	C-6736-A	Setra S215HU	Setra	BC55D	1991
0234	C-6737-A	Setra S215HU	Setra	BC55D	1991
0235	LU-5547-J	Mercedes-Benz O303 15	Castrosua	C55D	1988
0236	LU-5546-J	Mercedes-Benz O303 15	Castrosua	C55D	1988
0243	C-1910-AY	DAF SB3000DKX	Castrosua	C55D	1991
0245	C-1912-AY	DAF SB3000DKX	Castrosua	C55D	1991
0246	C-1913-AY	DAF SB3000DKX	Castrosua	C55D	1991
0248	C-0746-AZ	Mercedes-Benz O303 15	Irizar	C55D	1992
0249	C-0747-AZ	Mercedes-Benz O303 15	Irizar	C55D	1992
0250	C-2011-BB	Mercedes-Benz O303 15	Irizar	C55D	1992
0251	C-2012-BB	Mercedes-Benz O303 15	Irizar	C55D	1992
0254	LU-9758-I	Mercedes-Benz O303	Hispano Carrocera	C55D	1987
0255	C-7264-BB	Pegaso 5226	Castrosua	C55D	1992
0256	C-7265-BB	Pegaso 5226	Castrosua	C55D	1992
0257	C-7266-BB	Pegaso 5226	Castrosua	C55D	1992
0258	C-7267-BB	Pegaso 5226	Castrosua	C55D	1992
0264	C-9126-BD	Pegaso 5226	Castrosua	C55D	1993
0265	C-9127-BD	Pegaso 5226	Castrosua	C55D	1993
0266	C-9128-BD	Pegaso 5226	Castrosua	C55D	1993
0267	C-9129-BD	Pegaso 5226	Castrosua	C55D	1993
0268	LU-5964-O	Setra S215HD	Setra	C55D	1993
0269	LU-5965-O	Setra S215HD	Setra	C55D	1993
0270	C-9130-BD	Volvo B12	Irizar	C55D	1993
0271	C-9131-BD	Volvo B12	Irizar	C55D	1993
0279	M-4106-GK	Mercedes-Benz O303	Obradors	C54D	1985
0280	M-4916-GK	Mercedes-Benz O303	Obradors	C54D	1985
0281	M-4917-GK	Mercedes-Benz O303	Obradors	C54D	1985
0282	M-3844-GL	Mercedes-Benz O303	Obradors	C54D	1985
0283	M-3845-GL	Mercedes-Benz O303	Obradors	C54D	1985
0284	M-8982-JK	Mercedes-Benz	Ayats	C50D	1989
0285	O-8206-AH	Scania K113TLA	Irizar Dragon	C(75)D	1986
0286	C-1998-BH	Scania K113TLA	Irizar Dragon	C(81)D	1994
0291	C-2166-AB	Setra S215HU	Setra	C55D	1985
0292	C-8424-AC	Setra S215HU	Setra	C55D	1986
0293	C-8425-AC	Setra S215HU	Setra	C55D	1986
0294	C-0245-AH	Setra S215HU	Setra	C55D	1987
0295	C-5051-AK	Setra S215HU	Setra	C55D	1988

0296	C-7818-AM	Setra S215HU	Setra	C55D	1989
0297	C-7289-AW	Setra S215HU	Setra	C55D	1991
0298	C-9928-AX	Setra S215HD	Setra	C55D	1991
0299	C-0041-BD	Setra S215HD	Setra	C55D	1993
0300	C-4724-BJ	Mercedes-Benz O404 RH	Irizar	C55D	1994
0301	C-4725-BJ	Mercedes-Benz O404 RH	Irizar	C55D	1994
0302	S-7337-P	Scania K112TL	Ayats	BC75D	1988
0303	LU-4913-O	Pegaso 5226	Castrosua	C56D	1993
0304	C-2809-BK	Pegaso 5226	Hispano Carrocera	C55D	1994
0305	C-2808-BK	Pegaso 5226	Hispano Carrocera	C55D	1994
0306	C-9809-BK	Pegaso CC959E18	Unvi	C36D	1995
0307	C-9810-BK	Pegaso CC959E18	Unvi	C36D	1995
0308	C-3741-BL	Mercedes-Benz O1117	Ferqui	C36C	1995
0309	C-3742-BL	Mercedes-Benz O1117	Ferqui	C36C	1995
0310	S-7109-V	Scania K113	Ayats	BC75D	1990
0314	C-6100-BN	Mercedes-Benz O1117	Ferqui	C36C	1996
0315	C-6101-BN	Mercedes-Benz O1117	Ferqui	C36C	1996
0316	C-6424-BN	Mercedes-Benz O1117	Ferqui	C36C	1996
0317	C-6425-BN	Mercedes-Benz O1117	Ferqui	C36C	1996
0320	C-2523-BT	Mercedes-Benz O1829	Irizar	C55D	1997
0321	C-2524-BT	Mercedes-Benz O1829	Irizar	C55D	1997
0322	C-5538-BT	Setra Seida 412MH	Setra	C55D	1997
0323	C-5539-BT	Setra Seida 412MH	Setra	C55D	1997
0324	C-5748-BT	Setra Seida 412MH	Setra	C55D	1997
0325	C-5749-BT	Setra Seida 412MH	Setra	C55D	1997
0326	C-0297-BU	MAN 10.220 FOCL	Ferqui	C38C	1997
0327	C-0358-BV	MAN 10.220 FOCL	Ferqui	C38C	1997
0328	C-0359-BV	MAN 10.220 FOCL	Ferqui	C38C	1997
0329	C-0360-BV	MAN 10.220 FOCL	Ferqui	C38C	1997
0330	C-3683-BX	MAN 13.220 HOCL	Ugarte	C43D	1998
0331	C-3684-BX	MAN 13.220 HOCL	Ugarte	C43D	1998
0332	C-3685-BX	MAN 13.220 HOCL	Ugarte	C43D	1998
0333	C-3686-BX	MAN 13.220 HOCL	Ugarte	C43D	1998
0334	C-7698-BY	MAN 13.220 HOCL	Ugarte	C43D	1998
0335	C-7699-BY	MAN 13.220 HOCL	Ugarte	C43D	1998
0336	C-7700-BY	MAN 13.220 HOCL	Ugarte	C43D	1998
0337	C-7701-BY	MAN 13.220 HOCL	Ugarte	C43D	1998
0338	C-0336-CB	Scania K94IB	OVI	C47D	1999
0339	C-0337-CB	Scania K94IB	OVI	C47D	1999
0340	C-0338-CB	Scania K94IB	OVI	C47D	1999
0341	C-0339-CB	Scania K94IB	OVI	C47D	1999
0400	C-8493-BZ	Iveco Mago 59.12	Indcar	C27D	1999
0401	C-8494-BZ	Iveco Mago 59.12	Indcar	C27D	1999
0402	C-8495-BZ	Iveco Mago 59.12	Indcar	C27D	1999
0403	C-8496-BZ	Iveco Mago 59.12	Indcar	C27D	1999
0424	C-1285-AB	Setra S215HD	Setra	C55D	1985
0425	C-6884-AC	Setra S215HD	Setra	C56D	1986
0426	C-6885-AC	Setra S215HD	Setra	C56D	1986
0428	C-2204-AD	Pegaso 5031-S1	Unicar	C56D	1986
0429	C-2205-AD	Pegaso 5031-S1	Unicar	C56D	1986
0430	C-7120-AF	Setra S215HU	Setra	BC56D	1987
0431	C-7121-AF	Setra S215HU	Setra	BC56D	1987
0432	C-7122-AF	Setra S215HU	Setra	BC56D	1987
0433	C-0878-AH	Pegaso 5036-S1	Unicar	C56D	1987
0434	C-0228-A	Volvo B10M	Irizar	C56D	1987
0435	C-0229-A	Volvo B10M	Irizar	C56D	1987
0436	C-1675-AJ	DAF SB3000DKK	Obradors	C54D	1988
0437	BI-1336-AU	MAN-Caetano	Caetano	C56D	1988
0439	C-5189-AJ	MAN-Caetano	Caetano	C56D	1988
0440	C-5190-AJ	MAN-Caetano	Caetano	C56D	1988
0441	C-5385-AJ	MAN-Caetano	Caetano	C56D	1988
0442	C-6357-AJ	MAN-Caetano	Caetano	C56D	1988
0443	C-6474-AJ	MAN-Caetano	Caetano	C56D	1988
0444	C-4538-BX	MAN-Caetano	Caetano	C56D	1988
0445	M-9035-IZ	Mercedes-Benz O303 15	Irizar	C56D	1988
0446	M-9036-IZ	Mercedes-Benz O303 15	Irizar	C54D	1988
0447	C-8875-BU	Setra S215HU	Setra	C56D	1988
0448	C-8743-BU	MAN 10.180 HOCL	Hispano Carrocera	C37D	1989
0449	C-1365-BZ	DAF SB3000DKV	Castrosua	C56D	1989
0450	O-1919-AU	MAN 16.360	Obradors	C55D	1989
0451	C-8874-BU	Setra S215HU	Setra	C56D	1989
0452	C-8352-AP	Setra S215HU	Setra	C56D	1989
0453	C-8986-AP	Setra S215HU	Setra	C56D	1989

0454	C-9637-AP	Volvo B10M-60	Hispano Carrocera	C56D	1989
0455	C-9638-AP	Volvo B10M-60	Hispano Carrocera	C56D	1989
0456	C-6114-AS	Volvo B10M-60	Hispano Carrocera	C56D	1990
0457	C-4673-AU	DAF SB3000DKX	Sunsundegui	C56D	1990
0458	C-5106-AU	DAF SB3000DKV	Castrosua	C56D	1990
0459	C-5107-AU	DAF SB3000DKV	Castrosua	C56D	1990
0460	C-5108-AU	DAF SB3000DKV	Castrosua	C56D	1990
0462	C-5110-AU	DAF SB3000DKV	Castrosua	C56D	1990
0463	C-9926-CB	DAF FA 1000	Noge	C25D	1991
0464	C-9239-BX	MAN 16.360 HOCL	Irizar	C64D	1991
0465	C-9360-BU	MAN 16.360 HOCL	Irizar	C56D	1991
0466	C-2037-AX	Pegaso 5226	Beulas	C56D	1991
0467	C-5546-AX	DAF SB3000DKX	Sunsundegui	C56D	1991
0468	C-0913-BC	DAF SB3000DKV	Castrosua	C56D	1992
0469	C-0914-BC	DAF SB3000DKV	Castrosua	C56D	1992
0470	C-0915-BC	DAF SB3000DKV	Castrosua	C56D	1992
0471	C-0916-BC	DAF SB3000DKV	Castrosua	C56D	1992
0472	C-1524-BC	Pegaso 5226	Castrosua	C56D	1992
0473	C-9452-BF	Pegaso 5226	Castrosua	C56D	1993
0474	C-9544-BF	Pegaso 5226	Castrosua	C56D	1993
0475	C-0017-BG	DAF SB3000DKX	Castrosua	C56D	1993
0476	C-3745-BX	Pegaso CC959E18	Indicar	C35D	1994
0477	C-7700-BJ	Mercedes-Benz OH 1627L	Castrosua	C56D	1994
0478	C-1177-BM	MAN 18310	Irizar	C56D	1995
0479	C-4402-BM	MAN 18310 HOCL	Castrosua	C56D	1995
0480	C-3568-BP	MAN 18310	Irizar	C57D	1996
0481	C-9560-BP	MAN 18310 HOCL	Castrosua	C56D	1996
0482	C-9561-BP	MAN 18.310 HOCL	Castrosua	C56D	1996
0483	C-9562-BP	MAN 18310 HOCL	Castrosua	C56D	1996
0484	C-2371-BV	MAN 18.350	Irizar	C56D	1997
0486	C-5304-BX	MAN 18.350	Irizar	C57D	1999
0487	C-5305-BX	MAN 18.350	Irizar	C57D	1999
0488	C-1013-CD	MAN 18.310 HOCL	Irizar	C56D	1999
0489	C-1014-CD	MAN 18.310 HOCL	Irizar	C56D	1999
0490	C-1015-CD	MAN 18.310 HOCL	Irizar	C56D	1999
0491	C-5395-CF	Volvo B12	Irizar Century	C50D	1999
0492	C-5396-CF	Volvo B12	Irizar Century	C50D	1999
0493	C-5397-CF	Volvo B12	Irizar Century	C50D	1999
0494	C-5398-CF	Volvo B12	Irizar Century	C50D	1999
0495	C-5399-CF	Volvo B12	Irizar Century	C50D	1999
0496	C-5400-CF	Volvo B12	Irizar Century	C50D	1999
0497	C-5401-CF	Volvo B12	Irizar Century	C50D	1999
0498	C-5402-CF	Volvo B12	Irizar Century	C50D	1999
0499	C-8930-CF	Volvo B12	Irizar Century	C50D	1999
0500	C-8928-CF	Volvo B12	Irizar Century	C50D	1999
0501	C-8929-CF	Volvo B12	Irizar Century	C50D	1999
0502	C-9814-CF	Volvo B12	Irizar Century	C50D	1999
0503	C-9815-CF	Volvo B12	Irizar Century	C50F	1999
0504	C-9816-CF	Volvo B12	Irizar Century	C50F	1999
0505	C-9817-CF	Volvo B12	Irizar Century	C50F	1999
0506	C-0637-CG	Volvo B10M	Irizar InterCentury	C54F	1999
0507	C-0638-CG	Volvo B12	Irizar Century	C50F	1999
0508	C-0639-CG	Volvo B10M	Irizar InterCentury	C54F	1999
0509	C-0640-CG	Volvo B10M	Irizar InterCentury	C54F	1999
0510	C-0641-CG	Volvo B10M	Irizar InterCentury	C54F	1999
0511	C-0642-CG	Volvo B10M	Irizar InterCentury	C54F	1999
0512	C-0643-CG	Volvo B10M	Irizar InterCentury	C54F	1999
0513	C-0644-CG	Volvo B10M	Irizar InterCentury	C54F	1999
0514	C-0645-CG	Volvo B10M	Irizar InterCentury	C54F	1999
0515	C-0646-CG	Volvo B10M	Irizar InterCentury	C54F	1999
0516	C-0647-CG	Volvo B10M	Irizar InterCentury	C54F	1999
0517	C-0648-CG	Volvo B12	Irizar Century	C50F	1999
0518	C-0649-CG	Volvo B12	Irizar Century	C50F	1999
0519	C-0650-CG	Volvo B10M	Irizar InterCentury	C54F	1999
0520	C-0651-CG	Volvo B10M	Irizar InterCentury	C54F	1999
0521	C-0625-CG	Volvo B10M	Irizar InterCentury	C54F	1999
0522	C-0653-CG	Volvo B10M	Irizar InterCentury	C54F	1999
0523	C-0654-CG	Volvo B10M	Irizar InterCentury	C54F	1999
0524	C-0655-CG	Volvo B12	Irizar Century	C50F	1999
0525	C-0656-CG	Volvo B10M	Irizar InterCentury	C54F	1999
0526	C-0657-CG	Volvo B10M	Irizar InterCentury	C54F	1999
0527	C-0658-CG	Volvo B10M	Irizar InterCentury	C54F	1999
0528	C-0659-CG	Volvo B10M	Irizar InterCentury	C54F	1999

Traditional DAR livery is carried on Palma's 66, IB-2138-DT, a MAN 22.360 with Camelsa Yumbo bodywork. It is seen in Palma bus station. *Colin Martin*

0529	C-0660-CG	Volvo B10M	Irizar InterCentury	C54F	1999
0530	C-0661-CG	Volvo B10M	Irizar InterCentury	C54F	1999
0531	4277-BSW	Volvo B12	Irizar Century	C55F	1995
0532	4278-BSW	Volvo B12	Irizar Century	C55F	1996
0533	4276-BSW	Volvo B12	Sunsundegui	C56F	1996
0534	3838-BWJ	Volvo B12	Irizar Century	C55F	1995
0535	3839-BWJ	Volvo B12	Irizar Century	C55F	1996
0536	4016-BWJ	Volvo B12	Irizar Century	C55F	1997
0537	0471-BZN	Scania 420	Irizar Century	C71F	2002
0538	0547-BZN	Scania 420	Irizar Century	C71F	2002
0539	0343-BZN	Scania K114	Irizar Century	C59F	2002
0540	0517-BZN	Scania K114	Irizar Century	C59F	2002
0541	7452-BZN	Scania K114	Irizar Century	C59F	2002
0542	0324-BZN	Scania K114	Irizar Century	C59F	2002
0543	9571-BZN	Scania K114	Irizar Century	C59F	2002
0544	0359-BZN	Scania K114	Irizar Century	C59F	2002
0545	0402-BZN	Scania K114	Irizar Century	C59F	2002

Autocares Mallorca

Camino Vell Mal Pas, Alcudia

Autocares Pujol

1	PM-1070-AB	Pegaso 5036	Beulas Super	C59D	1984
2	PM-0345-AN	Mercedes-Benz OH1628	Obradors Sagaro 3.50	C55D	1987
3	PM-0743-BN	MAN 11.190 HOCL	Beulas Midi Star	C35D	1992
5	PM-2126-AV	Pegaso 5231	Beulas Stergo	C55D	1988

One of the four Autocares Pujol buses, 5, PM2126AV is a Pegaso 5231 with Beulas Stergo bodywork. it is seen in Inca bus station for on the service to Palma. *Colin Martin*

Palma de Mallorca

19	PM-2033-W	Setra S215H	Setra	C59D	1982
20	PM-1337-AB	Pegaso 5036	Camelsa Yhetero	C59D	1984
23	PM-2261-AF	Pegaso 6100S	Camelsa Yhetero	C55D	1984
25	PM-0091-AJ	Mercedes-Benz 180	Mercedes	M10	1986
32	PM-4524-AH	Setra S215HD	Setra	C55D	1986
33	PM-6726-BD	Pegaso 5231	Hispano Phoenix	C55D	1990
34	PM-9943-BD	Pegaso 5231	Hispano Phoenix	C55D	1990
35	PM-4846-BZ	Iveco 391E	Castrosua	B39D	1995
36	PM-4851-BZ	Iveco 391E	Castrosua	B39D	1995
37	PM-0457-CB	Iveco 391E	Ugarte CX-Elite	C55D	1995
38	PM-1248-CB	Iveco 391E	Ugarte CX-Elite	C55D	1995
39	PM-0304-CH	Iveco 391E	Castrosua	B39D	1996
40	PM-0305-CH	Iveco 391E	Castrosua	B39D	1995
41	PM-4402-CG	Ford Transit	Ford	C14D	1996
42	PM-1249-CM	Iveco 80E18	Indcar Mago	C30F	1997
43	PM-9734-CM	Iveco 391E	Irizar Century	BC55D	1997
44	PM-9735-CM	Iveco 391E	Irizar Century	BC55D	1997
45	PM-3530-CN	Iveco 391E	Castrosua	B39D	1997
46	PM-3531-CN	Iveco 391E	Castrosua	B39D	1997
47	IB-8194-CV	Iveco 391E	Irizar Century	C55D	1998
48	IB-7901-CW	Iveco 391E	Unvi Cidade II	B26D	1998
51	IB-2184-CZ	Mercedes-Benz 0405	Mercedes-Benz	B55D	1998
53	IB-3540-DG	Iveco 391E	Ayats Atlas	C55D	1999
54	IB-0143-BM	Ford Transit	Ford	C14D	1992
55	IB-5156-DG	Iveco Daily 35-10	Iveco	C13D	1999
56	IB-5157-DG	Iveco Daily 35-10	Iveco	C13D	1999
57	IB-5158-DG	Iveco Daily 35-10	Iveco	C13D	1999
58	IB-3046-DN	Iveco 391E	Noge Touring	C27D	2000
60	IB-9413-DN	Iveco 391E	Unvi Cidade II	B44D	2000
61	IB-9414-DN	Iveco 391E	Unvi Cidade II	B44D	2000
62	IB-4796-DP	Iveco 391E	Ugarte Nobus	C36D	2000
63	IB-4737-CY	MAN 1190 HOCL	Arabus	C35D	1998
64	IB-5685-CY	Iveco 391E	Irizar InterCentury	BC53D	1998
65	IB-5686-CY	Iveco 391E	Irizar InterCentury	BC53D	1998

66	8867BWL	68	8784BWL	69	7280CHJ	70	7321CHJ
67	8678BWL						

71-76 Iveco EuroRider 397E Unvi Cidade II B44D 2003

71	2543CHR	73	2671CHR	75	6244CJD	76	6293CJD
72	2630CHR	74	2717CHR				

Bus Nort Balear, Palma

19 Gremi Fusters, Poligono Son Castello, Palma

44	IB-4854-AT	Scania K112	Irizar 360	C55D	1984
45	IB-8182-AT	Scania K112	Irizar 360	C55D	1984
46	IB-0596-BC	Ford Transit	Ford	M14	1989
49	IB-6800-CG	MAN 8150 FOCL	Alvilla	C26D	1996
53	IB-2534-AU	MAN 16.290 HOCL	Unicar 3000 GLS	C55D	1988
54	IB-2535-AS	Setra S215H	Setra	C55D	1988
57	IB-2038-AT	MAN 16.290 HOCL	Caetano Algarve	C55D	1988
58	IB-2655-AY	MAN 22.360 HOCL N	Camelsa Yumbo	C(79)D	1989
59	IB-2124-DB	MAN 24.420 HOCL N	Obradors ST400	C(75)D	1995
60	IB-8635-BJ	Pegaso 5226	Beulas Stergo	C55D	1991
61	IB-1675-BM	Pegaso 5226	Camelsa	C55D	1991
62	IB-0120-DF	Iveco EuroRider 391E 12-29	OVI Radial	B44D	1999
63	IB-4614-BC	MAN 22.330 HOCL N	Camelsa Yumbo	BC(80)D	1990
65	M-1994-KT	Scania K93CLB	Burillo	B52D	1990
66	IB-2138-DT	MAN 22.360 HOCL N	Camelsa Yumbo	B80D	1989
71	IB-0365-BM	Pegaso 5226	Noge Xaloc II	C55D	1992
72	SE-8048-AY	MAN 16.290 HOCL N	Andecar Sahara	C55D	1989
73	M-3689-OC	Pegaso 5226	Ugarte 3000N	C55D	1993
74	IB-6814-AV	Scania K112	Castrosua Master 35	C55D	1988
75	IB-7717-CL	Ford Transit	Ford	M14	1997
76	IB-9451-DD	MAN 18.310 HOCL	Sunsundegui Stylo	B55D	1999
78	IB-7573-CN	Iveco EuroRider 391E	Ugarte CX-Elite	C55D	1997
81	9830BWT	Iveco EuroRider 391E	Irizar InterCentury	C55D	2002
82	LU-1200-H	Mercedes-Benz	Irizar 360	C52D	1984
83	LU-1212-H	Mercedes-Benz	Irizar 360	C52D	1984
84	C-7724-AM	Mercedes-Benz O303	Castrosua Master 35	C54D	1990
85	C-7726-AM	Mercedes-Benz O303	Castrosua Master 35	C54D	1990
86	3283CHJ	Iveco EuroRider 397E	Irizar InterCentury	C55D	1996
87	3129CHG	Iveco EuroRider 397E	Irizar InterCentury	C55D	1996
88	3061CHG	Iveco EuroRider 397E	Irizar InterCentury	C55D	1996
89	3290CHG	Iveco EuroRider 397E	Irizar InterCentury	C55D	1996

Auto Mallorca 70, 7321CHJ, is one of the recent delivery of Iveco EuroRiders with Irizar Inter-Century bodywork. The tour bus illustrates the TIB colour scheme as it rests in Alandia.
Colin Martin

ARRIVA ITALY

SAB Autoservizi srl, Piazza Marconi 4, 24122 Bergamo

26-38		Iveco 370.97.24		Portesi		Regional bus	1985-89
26	BG744315	30	BG776473	33	BG872091	36	BG922940
27	BG758737	31	BG776492	34	BG876301	37	BG930888
28	BG758736	32	BG819302	35	BG922939	38	BG940393
29	BG776402						

39	BGA52588	Iveco 370.97.S24	Portesi	Regional bus	1991
40	BGA50162	Iveco 370.97.S24	Portesi	Regional bus	1991
41	BG794807	Iveco 315.8.17	Orlandi	Regional bus	1986
42	BGA50161	Iveco 370.97.S24	Portesi	Regional bus	1991
43	BGA48631	Iveco 370.97.S24	Portesi	Regional bus	1991
44	BGA50160	Iveco 370.97.S24	Portesi	Regional bus	1991
45	BGA34200	Iveco 370.97.S24	Portesi	Regional bus	1990
49	BG740961	Iveco 315.8.17	Garbarini	Regional bus	1984
50	BG777875	Iveco 315.8.17	Orlandi	Regional bus	1985

51-75		Mercedes-Benz O303/10R		Bianchi		Regional bus	1981-87
51	BG626692	61	BGA17224	68	BG710038	72	BG825373
52	BG626694	62	BGA17234	69	BG711242	73	BG825372
55	BG627151	63	BGA17226	70	BG711243	74	BG828183
59	BGA17233	64	BGA17232	71	BGD17574	75	BA759JL
60	BGA17227	65	BGA17230				

76	AW749PY	Mercedes-Benz O303/9R	Mercedes	Regional bus	1990
77	BA635JC	Mercedes-Benz O303/9R	Mercedes	Coach	1991
79	AW288TM	Mercedes-Benz O303/10R	Mercedes	Coach	1987
80	BGD12750	Mercedes-Benz O303/10R	Mercedes	Coach	1994

The Italian operations are based in the north east of the country with headquarters at Bergamo where SAB is also located. City buses carry a livery of burnt yellow while country, or rural, buses are in blue. In Lombardy, the region of Italy served by Arriva, the central stripe is green. Operators compete for routes and select their own buses. The SAB depot houses more than the 400 buses allocated and Setra 145, BGB01837, shows the rural livery scheme. *Bill Potter*

The SAB fleet is dominated by products from Mercedes-Benz and Fiat/Iveco/Irisbus. From the 2000 delivery, Iveco 393 number 340, BG297PC, moves from the depot into the adjacent bus station. Bodywork is Irisbus-Orlandi MyWay. *Bill Potter*

81-84 — Mercedes-Benz O303/10R — Bianchi — Regional bus — 1987-90

81	BG918869	**82**	AW092TN	**83**	BG918870	**84**	BGA40904

Iveco 380.10.29 EuroClass — Orlandi — Regional bus

85	AH913KM	Iveco 380.10.29 EuroClass	Orlandi	Regional bus	1996
86	AH911KM	Iveco 380.10.29 EuroClass	Orlandi	Regional bus	1996
87	AH915KM	Iveco 380.10.29 EuroClass	Orlandi	Regional bus	1996
88	AH128JK	Iveco 370.97.24	Portesi	Regional bus	1987

89-93 — Iveco 370.10.24 — Iveco — Regional bus — 1986

89	BG787336	**91**	BG787337	**92**	BGB64702	**93**	BGB59004
90	BG787335						

94-97 — Iveco 370.10.24 — Portesi — Regional bus — 1985

94	BG762750	**95**	BG762751	**96**	BG762752	**97**	BG771140

98	BG766040	Iveco 370.10.24	Iveco	Regional bus	1985
99	BG773987	Iveco 370.10.24	Bianchi	Regional bus	1985
100	BG865704	Iveco 370.10S.24	Portesi	Regional bus	1987
101	BG878119	Iveco 370.10S.24	Bianchi	Regional bus	1987
102	BG888744	Iveco 370.10S.24	Bianchi	Regional bus	1988
103	BG890276	Iveco 370.10S.24	Bianchi	Regional bus	1988

104-107 — Iveco 370.10S.24 — Iveco — Regional bus — 1987-89

104	BG875640	**105**	BG877365	**106**	BG893072	**107**	BG952197

108-113 — Iveco 370.10S.24 — Portesi — Regional bus — 1989

108	BG952200	**110**	BG952198	**112**	BG960676	**113**	BG960675
109	BG952199	**111**	BG953420				

114	AD666TP	Iveco 370.10S.24	Desimon	Regional bus	1990

115-120 — Iveco 380.10.29 EuroClass — Orlandi — Regional bus — 1995

115	AH401KF	**117**	AH876KF	**119**	AH877KF	**120**	AH875KF
116	AH878KF	**118**	AH402KF				

121-135 — Man SG 280 — Portesi — City bus — 1985-88

121	BG884606	**123**	BG744316	**125**	BGB34394	**135**	BG923925
122	BG814714	**124**	BGB34395				

138	BGA65439	Setra SG 221 UL	Kassbohrer		Regional bus	1991	
139	BGA74947	Setra SG 221 UL	Kassbohrer		Regional bus	1991	
140	BGB18812	Setra SG 221 UL	Kassbohrer		Regional bus	1992	

142-145   Setra S 215 UL   Kassbohrer   Regional bus   1991-92

142	BGB51904	143	BGB51903	144	BGB01838	145	BGB01837

155	BG860952	Mercedes-Benz O303/10R	Bianchi		Regional bus	17/07/1987
156	BG861737	Mercedes-Benz O303/10R	Bianchi		Regional bus	23/07/1987
157	BG861736	Mercedes-Benz O303/10R	Bianchi		Regional bus	23/07/1987
159	BS458WY	Cacciamali TCI 970 Sigma 2	Cacciamali		Regional bus	10/05/2001
160	BS460WY	Cacciamali TCI 970 Sigma 2	Cacciamali		Regional bus	10/05/2001
161	BG886418	Iveco 315.8.17	Iveco		Regional bus	10/06/1988
162	BG886413	Iveco 315.8.17	Iveco		Regional bus	10/06/1988
163	AH669KM	Iveco 315.8.17	Iveco		Regional bus	08/08/1985
164	AN015PP	Iveco 315.8.18	Orlandi		Regional bus	17/12/1996
165	AN014PP	Iveco 315.8.18	Orlandi		Regional bus	17/12/1996
166	AN013PP	Iveco 315.8.18	Orlandi		Regional bus	17/12/1996
167	AW525RA	Iveco 315.8.17	Iveco		Regional bus	02/01/1986

168-186   Cacciamali TCI 970 Sigma 2   Cacciamali   Regional bus   2001-03

168	BS456WY	172	BS790WZ	176	BS777WT	181	BV382VR
169	BS459WY	173	BS791WZ	177	BV355VS	185	BX177BE
170	BS457WY	174	BS895WZ	178	BV356VS	186	CE896TB
171	BS560WT	175	BS896WZ	179	BV357VS		

221	AW523TL	Setra S 215 HD	Kassbohrer		Coach	1982

222-227   Mercedes-Benz O303/15R   Bianchi   Regional bus   1983-85

222	BG942534	224	BG707215	226	BG754859	227	BG754860
223	BG707214	225	BG754858				

228-232   Mercedes-Benz O303/15R   Bianchi   Regional-Coach   1985

228	BG746477	230	BG752672	231	BG775999	232	BG757432
229	BG752671						

236-252   Mercedes-Benz O303/15R   Bianchi   Regional bus   1979-82

236	BG543326	240	BG545354	251	BH892WL	252	BK086GH

253-259   Mercedes-Benz O303/15R   Bianchi   Regional-Coach   1983-84

253	BG694239	255	BG700422	257	BA215JD	259	BG741064
254	BG695918	256	BG705571	258	BG728280		

261-264   Iveco 370.12.S30   Bianchi   Regional bus   1991

261	BGA48629	262	BGA52589	263	BGA48630	264	BGA52590

304-309   Mercedes-Benz O303/15R   Bianchi   Regional bus   1985-91

304	BG781439	306	BG921921	308	BGA55605	309	BGA55606
305	BG781440	307	BGA52587				

310	BGB54150	Setra S 215 HRI	Kassbohrer		Regional bus	29/10/1992
311	BGB54151	Setra S 215 HRI	Kassbohrer		Regional bus	29/10/1992

321-329   Iveco 380.12.35 EuroClass   Orlandi   Regional bus   1995-96

321	AH880KF	324	AH882KF	326	AH912KM	328	AH914KM
322	AH403KF	325	AH400KF	327	AH910KM	329	AH909KM
323	AH881KF						

332-349   Iveco 393.12.35 My Way   Irisbus-Orlandi   Regional bus   2000

332	BG305PC	336	BG301PC	340	BG297PC	344	BG293PC
333	BG304PC	337	BG300PC	341	BG296PC	345	BG292PC
334	BG303PC	338	BG299PC	342	BG295PC	346	BG291PC
335	BG302PC	339	BG298PC	343	BG294PC		

348	AW278TP	Mercedes-Benz O404	Mercedes		Regional bus	1998
349	AW279TP	Mercedes-Benz O404	Mercedes		Regional bus	1998

350-364   Mercedes-Benz O408   Mercedes   Regional bus   1997

350	AT083SN	353	AT084SN	356	AT080SN	358	AT088SN
351	AT086SN	354	AT087SN	357	AT079SN	364	AT085SN
352	AT081SN	355	AT082SN				

SAB operate the Mercedes-Benz Citaro in both articulated 18m and rigid 12m examples. Seen between trips, 394, BN681RW, represents the rigid 12-metre type. *Bill Potter*

365-387 — Mercedes-Benz O405 NU — Mercedes — Regional bus — 1998

365	AW205TM	371	AW386TM	377	AW383TM	383	AW396TM
366	AW220TM	372	AW387TM	378	AW395TM	384	AW392TM
367	AW203TM	373	AW388TM	379	AW384TM	385	AW394TM
368	AW206TM	374	AW382TM	380	AW391TM	386	BE193NY
369	AW204TM	375	AW389TM	381	AW393TM	387	BE194NY
370	AW219TM	376	AW390TM	382	AW397TM		

388-399 — Mercedes-Benz Citaro O530 NU — Evobus — Regional bus — 2001

388	BN683RW	391	BN689RW	394	BN681RW	397	BN690RW
389	BN688RW	392	BP287ZA	395	BN687RW	398	BP288ZA
390	BN677RW	393	BN693RW	396	BN694RW	399	BN685RW

400-403 — Setra S 300 NC — Kassbohrer — City bus — 1991-92

400	AT158SM	401	AT159SM	402	AT889SM	403	AT989SM

404	AN974PP	Menarini M 221.1	Menarini	City bus	14/01/1997

405-418 — Mercedes-Benz Citaro O530 NU — Evobus — Regional bus — 2000-01

405	BN678RW	409	BS475XA	413	BP292ZA	416	BN686RW
406	BP289ZA	410	BP291ZA	414	BN682RW	417	BM871EW
407	BN684RW	411	BN692RW	415	BN679RW	418	BN680RW
408	BP290ZA	412	BN691RW				

419-422 — Mercedes-Benz O407 — Mercedes — Regional bus — 1992

419	BZ825WZ	420	BZ826WZ	421	BZ827WZ	422	BZ828WZ

430-447 — Iveco 393.12.35 My Way — Iveco — Regional bus — 2000

430	BM961EV	435	BM262EW	440	BM259EW	444	BM874EW
431	BM962EV	436	BM263EW	441	BM257EW	445	BM875EW
432	BM963EV	437	BM260EW	442	BM872EW	446	BM876EW
433	BM964EV	438	BM264EW	443	BM873EW	447	BM877EW
434	BM261EW	439	BM258EW				

448-452   Iveco 393.12.35 My Way   Irisbus-Orlandi   Regional bus   2000-03

| 448 | BM569EY | | | | | |
| 449 | BM571EY | | 450 | BM570EY | 451 | BM568EY | 452 | CE897TB |

448	BM569EY
449	BM571EY
450	BM570EY
451	BM568EY
452	CE897TB

| 453 | CH278PD | Setra S 300 NC | Kassbohrer | City bus | 1992 |
| 454 | CH633NZ | Setra S 300 NC | Kassbohrer | City bus | 1992 |

462-478   Mercedes-Benz O303/15R   Bianchi   Coach   1985-86

462	BG770681	465	BG776713	470	BG782510	474	BG806386
463	BG769199	466	BG777451	472	BG796681	475	BG807955
464	BG776712	467	AH342KN	473	BA800JC	478	BG818432

481-487   Mercedes-Benz O303/15R   Bianchi   Regional-Coach   1986-88

| 481 | AH406KF | 484 | BG498PC | 486 | BG499PC | 487 | BG497PC |
| 482 | AH405KF | | | | | | |

488	BG907343	Mercedes-Benz O303/15R	Bianchi	Coach	1988
489	BG912768	Mercedes-Benz O303/15R	Bianchi	Coach	1988
490	BGA06869	Iveco 370.12.S30	Bianchi	Coach	1990
491	BGA09074	Iveco 370.12.S30	Bianchi	Coach	1990
492	BGA65274	Iveco 370.12.S30	Bianchi	Coach	1991
493	CB768MJ	Iveco 370.12.S30	Orlandi	Regional bus	1992
494	BGB29553	Iveco 370.12.S30	Orlandi	Coach	1992
495	BGB29554	Iveco 370.12.S30	Orlandi	Coach	1992
496	BGB31233	Iveco 370.12.S30	Orlandi	Coach	1992
497	AH404KF	Mercedes-Benz O303/15RHD	Mercedes	Coach	1992
498	AT356TE	Mercedes-Benz O350 Tourismo	Mercedes	Coach	1997
499	AT537TE	Mercedes-Benz O350 Tourismo	Mercedes	Coach	1997

501-511   Mercedes-Benz O404   Mercedes   Coach   1992-93

501	AW352RV	504	AW786PZ	507	AW888PZ	510	BE213NY
502	AW785PZ	505	AW145PZ	508	AW488RA	511	BF264NR
503	AW144PZ	506	AW146PZ	509	BE246NZ		

512	CD086FF	Mercedes-Benz O350 Tourismo	Mercedes	Coach	13/09/2002
513	CD743FE	Mercedes-Benz O350 Tourismo	Mercedes	Coach	05/09/2002
978	BX755BF	Iveco Daily F45.12	Iveco	Regional bus	27/11/2001
979	BS105XA	Iveco EuroPolis 9.15	Iveco	City bus	08/03/2001
980	BS224XA	Iveco EuroPolis 9.15	Iveco	City bus	13/03/2001
984	CE543TA	Fiat Ducato L2.8JTD	Fiat	Coach	28/01/2003
985	BX274BG	Iveco 65.C15 THESI	Cacciamali	Regional bus	11/12/2001
986	BY309EF	Iveco 65.C15 THESI	Cacciamali	Regional bus	10/01/2002
987	BX275BG	Iveco 65.C15 THESI	Cacciamali	Regional bus	11/12/2001
988	BY308EF	Iveco 65.C15 THESI	Cacciamali	Regional bus	10/01/2002
989	AW386TL	Mercedes-Benz O402	Mercedes	City bus	13/01/1987
990	AT431TG	Mercedes-Benz O402	Mercedes	City bus	01/11/1986
991	AT949TT	Iveco Dayli F45.12	Iveco	Regional bus	15/09/1997
992	AT948TT	Iveco Dayli F45.12	Iveco	Regional bus	15/09/1997
993	AT947TT	Iveco Dayli F45.12	Iveco	Regional bus	15/09/1997
994	AT950TT	Iveco Dayli F45.12	Iveco	Regional bus	15/09/1997
995	BE248NZ	Iveco Dayli F45.12	Iveco	Regional bus	02/08/1999
996	BE249NZ	Iveco Dayli F45.12	Iveco	Regional bus	02/08/1999
999	AW385TM	Fiat Ducato	Fiat	Regional bus	06/06/1996
001	BG853433	Iveco 370.97.24	Portesi	Regional bus	15/12/1987
004	BG963500	Iveco 370.97.S24	Portesi	Regional bus	21/06/1989
011	BGB28561	Iveco 370.12.S30	Orlandi	Regional bus	14/05/1992
013	BGB28562	Iveco 370.12.S30	Orlandi	Regional bus	14/05/1992
026	BG834773	Mercedes-Benz O303/15R	Menarini	Regional bus	04/02/1987
027	BG834774	Mercedes-Benz O303/15R	Menarini	Regional bus	04/02/1987
041	BG756834	Menarini 110 M	Menarini	Regional bus	18/04/1985
042	BG756835	Menarini 110 M	Menarini	Regional bus	18/04/1985
043	BG774002	Mercedes-Benz O303/10R	Menarini	Regional bus	19/09/1985
045	BG774004	Mercedes-Benz O303/10R	Menarini	Regional bus	19/09/1985
046	BG803871	Menarini 110 M	Menarini	Regional bus	16/05/1986
047	BG803869	Menarini 110 M	Menarini	Regional bus	16/05/1986
049	AH745KN	Menarini 110 M	Menarini	Regional bus	07/12/1985
051	BG883403	Iveco 370.97.S24	Portesi	Regional bus	22/01/1988
053	BG874860	Iveco 370.12.L25	Portesi	Regional bus	13/11/1987
054	BG853434	Iveco 370.12.L25	Portesi	Regional bus	28/05/1987
055	BG874861	Iveco 370.12.L25	Portesi	Regional bus	13/11/1987
056	BG874862	Iveco 370.12.L25	Portesi	Regional bus	13/11/1987
057	BG853435	Iveco 370.12.L25	Portesi	Regional bus	28/06/1987

Articulated buses feature in both the city and rural operations. Six of the ten Volvo B7LAs with Snodato bodywork carry city livery with the remaining four in blue. Waiting its next duty at the central depot is 1202, CH281PD. The fleet also contains coaches for operation on non-tendered work and these are liveried in bright colours on a dark grey background. *Bill Potter*

1058	BG963501	Iveco 370.97.S24	Portesi	Regional bus	21/06/1989
1059	BG860165	Iveco 370.97.24	Portesi	Regional bus	14/07/1987
1060	BG853436	Iveco 370.12.L25	Portesi	Regional bus	28/05/1987
1061	AT219SM	Iveco 370.12.L25	Portesi	Regional bus	26/07/1989
1062	BG969683	Iveco 370.12.L25	Portesi	Regional bus	26/07/1989
1063	BG970248	Iveco 370.12.L25	Portesi	Regional bus	28/07/1989
1064	BG970249	Iveco 370.12.L25	Portesi	Regional bus	28/07/1989
1067	BGA57919	Iveco 370.10S.24	Iveco	Regional bus	25/02/1991
1069	BGB11432	Setra SG 221 UL	Kassbohrer	Regional bus	12/02/1992

1081-1086

1081-1086		Mercedes-Benz O530GNU	Mercedes-Benz Citaro	Regional bus	2001		
1081	BS585XB	1083	BS844XB	1085	BS988WY	1086	BS101WY
1082	BS455WY	1084	BS578WY				

1087	BB553TB	BredaMenarini M 321	BredaMenarini	City bus	22/02/1999
1100	AH605KF	Mercedes-Benz O303/15R	Bianchi	Regional bus	15/03/1983
1101	AH606KF	Mercedes-Benz O303/15R	Bianchi	Regional bus	20/03/1983
1102	BG627123	Mercedes-Benz O303/15R	Menarini	Regional bus	10/11/1981
1106	BG692729	Mercedes-Benz O303/15R	Menarini	Regional bus	28/06/1983
1110	BG871072	Iveco 370.12.L25	Iveco	Regional bus	16/10/1987
1111	BG922858	Mercedes-Benz O303/10R	Bianchi	Regional bus	19/10/1988
1112	BG940225	Mercedes-Benz O303/10R	Menarini	Regional bus	03/02/1989
1113	BGA68889	Volvo B 10 M	Portesi	Regional bus	24/04/1991
1114	BGA68890	Volvo B 10 M	Portesi	Regional bus	24/04/1991

1201-1210

1201-1210		Volvo B7LA	Snodato	City/Regional bus	2000-01		
1201	CH280PD	1204	CH483PD	1207	CH096NZ	1209	CH635NZ
1202	CH281PD	1205	CH563PD	1208	CH140NZ	1210	CH636NZ
1203	CH484PD	1206	CH139NZ				

4005	BE570BF	Iveco 370.10.25	Iveco	Regional bus	1982

SAL

SAL srl, Via della Pergola 2, 23900 Lecco

1	AG416TK	Mercedes-Benz0303/15R	Mercedes	Coach	1987
2	AN848EV	MAN 11.190 HOCL	MACCHI	City bus	1996
5	AN942EW	MAN 11.190 HOCL	MACCHI	City bus	1997
13	COD59447	MAN 11.190 HOCL	MACCHI	City bus	1994
15	AN438EW	Setra S 300 NC	Setra	City bus	1992
16	AN439EW	Setra S 300 NC	Setra	City bus	1997
17	AN440EW	Setra S 300 NC	Setra	City bus	1993
18	AN441EW	Setra S 300 NC	Setra	City bus	1993
19	C0838445	Menarini M 201/2 LS	Menarini	City bus	1985
20	CO838444	Menarini M 201/2 LS	Menarini	City bus	1985
25	CO833367	Menarini M 201/2 LS	Menarini	City bus	1985
26	AG533TR	BredaMenarini M 3001.12L	Bredamenarinbus	City bus	1996
27	AG534TR	BredaMenarini M 3001.12L	Bredamenarinbus	City bus	1996
29	AN731EW	BredaMenarini M 221	Bredamenarinbus	City bus	1997
31	AN442EW	Setra S 300 NC	Setra	City bus	1992
32	C0B03782	Setra S 210 H	Setra	City bus	1990
33	COD39220	Iveco 370.97.24	Portesi	Regional bus	1985
34	AN988EW	Setra S 300 NC	Setra	Regional bus	1991
35	COB83012	BredaMenarini M120/1	Bredamenarinbus	City bus	1992
36	COA95307	Iveco 370.97.24	Portesi	Regional bus	1990
40	BB257KC	Inbus I 240	Desimon	Regional bus	1984
43	COA01929	Iveco 370.97.24	Portesi	Regional bus	1989
44	CO846144	Iveco 370.97.24	Portesi	Regional bus	1986
48	COA95306	Mercedes-Benz0303/15R	Bianchi	Regional bus	1990
49	CO704745	Mercedes-Benz0303/15R	Bianchi	Regional bus	1982
50	CO704744	Mercedes-Benz0303/15R	Bianchi	Regional bus	1982
51	CO716748	Mercedes-Benz0303/15R	Bianchi	Regional bus	1982

SAL operates from a base at Lecco on the shores of Lake Como with services extending into the surrounding area. The fleet contains six Setra S300 buses of which 31, AN442EW is seen at the depot. *Bill Potter*

The central terminal in Lecco is, as with much of continental Europe, outside the rail station. Six Iveco EuroPolis vehicle featured in the 2001 vehicle programme, of which the first four were 9m examples. Here the longer 10.5metre 138, BP539ZY, is seen waiting time. *Bill Potter*

52	CO825029	Mercedes-Benz O303/15R	Bianchi	Regional bus	1985
53	CO846143	Mercedes-Benz O303/15R	Padane	Regional bus	1986
54	CO951309	Mercedes-Benz O303/15R	Bianchi	Regional bus	1988
55	CO956066	Mercedes-Benz O303/15R	Bianchi	Regional bus	1988
56	COA05267	Mercedes-Benz O303/15R	Bianchi	Regional bus	1989
57	COD59602	Setra S 212 H	Setra	Regional bus	1994
58	COD61582	Iveco 370.12.L25	Iveco	Regional bus	1990
59	COD61581	Iveco 370.12.L25	Iveco	Regional bus	1990
60	BGB60678	Iveco 370.10.24	Desimon	Regional bus	1990
62	AE270JA	Iveco 370.12.35	Iveco	Regional bus	1989
63	AN080EZ	Mercedes-Benz O303/15R	Bianchi	Regional bus	1987
64	AP574VZ	Mercedes-Benz O303/15R	Bianchi	Regional bus	1986
65	AN939EY	Mercedes-Benz O303/15R	Bianchi	Coach	1986
71	MI08874S	Mercedes-Benz O303/15R	Padane	Coach	1983
72	MI46254Z	Mercedes-Benz O303/15R	Bianchi	Coach	1986
73	MI46255Z	Mercedes-Benz O303/15R	Bianchi	Regional bus	1986
74	MI7G7326	Mercedes-Benz O303/15R	Bianchi	Regional bus	1988
75	MI1N3923	Mercedes-Benz O303/15R	Padane	Regional bus	1989
77	MIOU7810	Iveco 580.12.24	Iveco	Regional bus	1991
96	AN570EV	MAN SR 280 F	Bianchi	Regional bus	1986
98	AN943EW	Mercedes-Benz O303/10R	Menarini	City bus	1987
105	BB764KB	Mercedes-Benz O303/9R	Mercedes	Regional bus	1986
106	BB199KC	Mercedes-Benz O303/14R	Mercedes	Regional bus	1999
107	BC670FV	MAN A05 NM152	MAN	Regional bus	1994
108	BD947VR	MAN A05 NM152	MAN	Regional bus	1994
109	BE328MY	Iveco Dayli F45.12	Iveco	City bus	1999
110	BF504TD	Mercedes-Benz O303/15R	Bianchi	City bus	1981
111	BF506TD	Mercedes-Benz O303/15R	Bianchi	Regional bus	1979
112	BF505TD	Mercedes-Benz O303/15R	Bianchi	Regional bus	1980
114	BF634TD	Mercedes-Benz O408	Mercedes	Regional bus	1997
115	BF635TD	Mercedes-Benz O408	Mercedes	Regional bus	1997
116	BF636TD	Mercedes-Benz O408	Mercedes	Regional bus	1997
117	BF637TD	Mercedes-Benz O408	Mercedes	Regional bus	1997
118	BF638TD	Mercedes-Benz O408	Mercedes	Regional bus	1997

119	BF830TD	Iveco Dayli F45.12	Iveco	Regional bus	1998
120	BF829TD	Iveco Dayli F45.12	Iveco	Regional bus	2000
121	BF828TD	Iveco Dayli F45.12	Iveco	School bus	2000
122	BY901MN	Iveco 393.12.35 My Way	Iveco	School bus	2000
123	BK965MA	Mercedes-Benz O404	Mercedes	School bus	1993
124	BJ017NR	Iveco 393.12.35 My Way	Iveco	Regional bus	2000
125	BJ015NR	Iveco 393.12.35 My Way	Iveco	Coach	2000
126	BJ018NH	Iveco 393.12.35 My Way	Iveco	Regional bus	2000
127	BJ016NR	Iveco 393.12.35 My Way	Iveco	Regional bus	2000
128	BJ014NR	Iveco 393.12.35 My Way	Iveco	Regional bus	2000
129	BJ012NR	Iveco 393.12.35 My Way	Iveco	Regional bus	2000
130	BJ013NR	Iveco 393.12.35 My Way	Iveco	Regional bus	2000
131	BP600PP	DeSimon Starline 55.12	Desimon	Regional bus	2001
132	BP722PP	DeSimon Starline 55.12	Desimon	Regional bus	2001
133	BP262PR	Iveco EuroPolis 9.15	Iveco	City bus	2001
134	BP261PR	Iveco EuroPolis 9.15	Iveco	Regional bus	2001
135	BP260PR	Iveco EuroPolis 9.15	Iveco	City bus	2001
136	BP259PR	Iveco EuroPolis 9.15	Iveco	City bus	2001
137	BP694ZY	Iveco EuroPolis 10.50	Iveco	City bus	2001
138	BP539ZY	Iveco EuroPolis 10.50	Iveco	Regional bus	2001
139	BP696ZY	Mercedes-Benz Citaro O530 NU	Mercedes	Regional bus	2001
140	BP695ZY	Mercedes-Benz Citaro O530 NU	Mercedes	Regional bus	2001
141	BP540ZY	Mercedes-Benz Citaro O530 NU	Mercedes	City bus	2001
142	BP541ZY	Mercedes-Benz Citaro O530 NU	Mercedes	City bus	2001
143	BP538ZY	Mercedes-Benz Citaro O530 NU	Mercedes	City bus	2001
144	BV031SY	Inbus 181	De Simon	City bus	1992
145	BV004 SZ	Inbus 181	De Simon	Regional bus	1987
146	BV937SX	Iveco Dayli F45.12	Iveco	City bus	2001
147	BZ 262 SZ	Mercedes-Benz O350 TURISMO	Mercedes	City bus	2002
148	CD147SA	DeSimon Starline 55.12	Desimon	School bus	2002
149	BZ646TB	Cacciamali TCI 970 Sigma 2	Cacciamali	Coach	2002

With Lecco station building and mountains behind, number 133, BP262PR illustrates the nearside of the 9metre Iveco EuroPolis. *Bill Potter*

SIA

Società Italiana Autoservizi Spa, Via Cassala 3/a, 25126 Brescia

8	BS770254	Inbus G.T. 330		Padane	Regional bus	1982
9	BS784466	Inbus G.T. 330		Padane	Regional bus	1982
16	BS985450	Iveco 370.12.35		Orlandi	Coach	1987
18	AZ 513NG	Iveco 370.12.35		Orlandi	Coach	1987
19	BSA23490	Iveco 370.12.35		Orlandi	Coach	1987

20-25		Iveco 370.12.30		Dallavia	Coach	1987-88
20	BSA21499	**22**	BSA41550	**24**	BSA83566	**25**	BSA83567
21	BSA41552	**23**	BSA41551				

26	BSB64403	BredaMenarini 5001.12SL	Bredabus	Regional bus	1990
28	BSD42532	Iveco 370.12.S30	Dallavia	Coach	1991
29	BSB69700	Iveco 370.12.30	Bianchi	Regional bus	1990
32	BSE05236	Iveco 370.12.S30	Orlandi	Coach	1992
33	BSE05235	Iveco 370.12.S30	Orlandi	Coach	1992
34	BSE72407	Iveco 315.8.18	Orlandi	Coach	1993
35	BSF08559	Iveco 370.12.S30	Dallavia	Coach	1994
36	AF 080XT	Iveco 370.12.SE35	Dallavia	Coach	1996
37	AF 330XW	Iveco 370.12.SE35	Dallavia	Coach	1996
38	AZ 085MC	Iveco 380.12.38 EuroClass HD	Orlandi	Coach	1998
39	AZ 423MC	Mercedes-Benz O404/15R HD	Mercedes-Benz	Coach	1998
40	AZ 431MC	Mercedes-Benz O404/15R HD	Mercedes-Benz	Coach	1998
41	BE 792ZJ	Iveco 380.12.38 EuroClass HD	Orlandi	Coach	1999
42	BT062GC	Iveco 391.12.35 EuroRider	Orlandi	Coach	2001
43	BSB41099	Mercedes-Benz O303/15R	Bianchi	Regional bus	1989
44	BSB73813	Mercedes-Benz O303/15R	Bianchi	Regional bus	1990
45	CD209BW	Mercedes-Benz O350	Mercedes-Benz Tourismo	Coach	2002
46	CD124BW	Mercedes-Benz O350	Mercedes-Benz Tourismo	Coach	2002
47	CD125BW	Mercedes-Benz O350	Mercedes-Benz Tourismo	Coach	2002

50-56		Inbus I 330		Inbus	Regional bus	1984-86
50	BS873474	**52**	BS873472	**54**	AA 418GD	**56**	BS937360
51	BS873471	**53**	BS873473	**55**	BS937361		

63-66		Iveco 370.12.S30		Iveco	Regional bus	1987-89
63	BSA28909	**64**	BSA70782	**65**	BSA70783	**66**	BSB29140

74-79		BredaMenarini M 5001.12SL		Bredabus	Regional bus	1990-95
74	BSD15607	**76**	BSD24107	**78**	BSD24110	**79**	AF 386XJ
75	BSD24109	**77**	BSD24108				

84-87		Iveco 370.12.SE35 12m		Orlandi	Regional bus	1998
84	AZ 264MD	**85**	AZ 888MC	**86**	AZ 783MD	**87**	AZ 784MD

91-94		BredaMenarini M 3001.12L		Bredabus	City bus	1989
91	BSB55791	**92**	BSB55781	**93**	BSB55771	**94**	BSB55779
95	BSB90063	BredaMenarini M 2001.10L	Bredabus	City bus	18/05/1990	

102-115		Inbus AID 280 FT 17.5m		Inbus	Regional bus	1985
102	BS897393	**105**	BS897395	**111**	BS899160	**114**	BS899157
103	BS897394	**106**	BS897396	**112**	BS899159	**115**	BS899156
104	BS899162	**110**	BS899161	**113**	BS899158		

116	BSE19611	Inbus AID 280 FT	Inbus	Regional bus	1992
117	BSE62370	MAN SG 292	Inbus	Regional bus	1993
118	AF 079XT	Inbus AID 280 FT	Inbus	Regional bus	1985
119	AF 078XT	Inbus AID 280 FT	Inbus	Regional bus	1985
121	AP 164NW	Inbus AID 280 FT	Inbus	Regional bus	1991

122-126		Mercedes-Benz O530 GNU 18m	Mercedes-Benz Citaro	Regional bus	2001
122	BV 951 DY	**124**	BV 579 DW	**125**	BV 580 DW	**126**	BV 585 DW
123	BV 581 DW						

SIA operate from offices in Brescia, a town they share with another Arriva operator SAIA. Generally, the operation of SIA are to the north with depots in Sarezzo and other urban centers. SIA operate a few coaches, including 37, AF 330XW, an Iveco 370 with DallaviaCoach body. It is seen at the company offices. *Bill Potter*

149-162

Iveco 315.8.17 7.5m   Iveco   Regional bus   1983-87

149	AZ 177NG	153	BS917310	157	BS951858	160	BSA32181
150	BS814619	154	BS925626	158	BSA28908	161	BSB29110
151	BS814618	155	BS925628	159	BSA28907	162	BSB29130
152	BS912625	156	BS944758				

163-167

Iveco 315.8.18 7.6m   Orlandi   Regional bus   1993

163	BSE62369	165	BSE62367	166	BSE62366	167	BSE62365
164	BSE62368						

168-172

Iveco 315.8.S18 7.6m   Orlandi   Regional bus   1996-98

168	AF870XR	170	AF869XR	171	AZ350NF	172	AZ351NF
169	AF868XR						

250-290

Mercedes-Benz O408   Mercedes-Benz   Regional bus   1996-97

250	AF436XX	261	AF440XX	272	AP634NW	282	AP636NW
251	AF701XX	262	AF441XX	273	AP481NW	283	AP632NW
252	AF437XX	263	AF787XX	274	AP490NW	284	AP635NW
253	AF710XX	265	AF705XX	275	AP683NW	285	AP489NW
254	AF708XX	266	AF709XX	276	AP491NW	286	AP488NW
256	AF707XX	267	AP487NW	277	AP492NW	287	AP486NW
257	AF702XX	268	AP482NW	278	AP493NW	288	AP631NW
258	AF703XX	269	AP495NW	279	AP494NW	289	AP633NW
259	AF704XX	270	AP485NW	280	AP483NW	290	AP682NW
260	AF439XX	271	AP496NW	281	AP484NW		

291-295

Mercedes-Benz O405 NU   Mercedes-Benz   Regional bus   1998

291	BH071WK	293	BH073WK	294	BH074WK	295	BH075WK
292	BH072WK						

Newly into service is a batch of Mercedes-Benz Conecto air-conditioned rural buses. Brought out for the camera is 359, CL984AY. The depot is about 500 metres from the company's covered bus station and comprises several large garages in addition to an extensive maintenance area. *Bill Potter*

296-322
Mercedes-Benz O530 NU   Mercedes-Benz Citaro   Regional bus   2001

296	BT242GD	303	BT108GD	310	BT 763 GD	317	BV 403 DV
297	BT100GD	304	BT109GD	311	BT 107 GD	318	BV 582 DW
298	BT101GD	305	BT110GD	312	BT 244 GD	319	BV 402 DV
299	BT102GD	306	BT112GD	313	BT 764 GD	320	BV 583 DW
300	BT103GD	307	BT111GD	314	BT 761 GD	321	BV 401 DV
301	BT104GD	308	BT106GD	315	BT 243 GD	322	BV 584 DW
302	BT105GD	309	BV 404 DV	316	BT 762 GD		

339-345
Iveco 370.12.25   Iveco   Regional bus   1982

339	BS794050	340	BS794051	341	BS794052	345	BS796084

350-362
Mercedes-Benz O345   Mercedes-Benz Conecto   Regional bus   2003-04

350	CL043AY	354	CL982AY	357	CL190AY	360	CL979AY
351	CL042AY	355	CL983AY	358	CL191AY	361	CL985AY
352	CL980AY	356	CL981AY	359	CL984AY	362	CL099AY
353	CL189AY						

401-414
Iveco 370.10.25   Iveco   Regional bus   1981-85

401	BSA82710	405	BS854525	409	BS878689	412	BS917312
402	BSA86942	406	BS854522	410	BS912624	413	BS917313
403	AF 156WG	407	BS854520	411	BS917311	414	BS925627
404	BS854521	408	BS854524					

415	BS912626	Iveco 370.10.24	Dallavia	Regional bus	14/08/1985
416	BS912627	Iveco 370.10.24	Dallavia	Regional bus	14/08/1985
417	BS937362	Iveco 370.10.24	Dallavia	Regional bus	04/03/1986
418	BS981593	Iveco 370.97.24	Portesi	Regional bus	21/01/1987
419	BSA18358	Iveco 370.97.24	Portesi	Regional bus	10/09/1987
420	BSA32610	Iveco 370.97.S24	Portesi	Regional bus	18/12/1987

Dating from the mid 1980s 103, BS897394, is an Inbus AID 280. Around twenty of the type are still in service and display the angular styling from the period. *Bill Potter*

421-426   Iveco 370.10.S24   Iveco   Regional bus   23/06/1989

421	BSA32612	**423**	BSA64151	**425**	BSB29120	**426**	BSB29080
422	BSA32611	**424**	BSA65280				

427-431   Iveco 370.97.S24   Portesi   Regional bus   1990-91

427	BSD12666	**429**	BSD33608	**430**	BSD33604	**431**	BSD24106
428	BSD33607						

432	BSD39302	Iveco 370.10.S24	Iveco	Regional bus	15/03/1991
433	BSE53607	Iveco 370.97.24	Portesi	Regional bus	09/07/1987
434	BSE53610	Iveco 370.97.24	Portesi	Regional bus	22/07/1987
435	BSE53609	Iveco 370.97.24	Portesi	Regional bus	07/08/1987
436	BSE53606	Iveco 370.10.24	Iveco	Regional bus	17/01/1986
437	BSE53605	Iveco 370.10.24	Iveco	Regional bus	17/01/1986
438	AD 459WC	Iveco 370.97.S24	Portesi	Regional bus	31/03/1995
439	AD 458WC	Iveco 370.97.S24	Portesi	Regional bus	31/03/1995
501	BS925664	Iveco 370.12.L25	Portesi	Regional bus	05/12/1985
502	BSB36607	Mercedes-Benz O303/15R	Padane	Regional bus	01/08/1989
503	MI4S3982	Volvo B 10 M	Portesi	Regional bus	14/11/1995
504	BSE88082	Iveco 370.12.L25	Portesi	Regional bus	01/01/1993
505	BSE97138	Iveco 370.12.L25	Portesi	Regional bus	01/01/1993
506	AF649XH	Iveco 370.12.SE35	Orlandi	Regional bus	01/01/1994
507	AD126VP	Iveco 370.12.SE35	Orlandi	Regional bus	17/01/1995
508	AF784XJ	Iveco 370.12.SE35	Orlandi	Regional bus	06/12/1995
509	AP382NT	Mercedes-Benz O408	Mercedes-Benz	Regional bus	11/06/1997
510	AZ605ND	Mercedes-Benz O408	Mercedes-Benz	Regional bus	26/05/1998
511	AZ736NF	Mercedes-Benz O405 N2	Mercedes-Benz	City bus	25/08/1998
512	BE684ZJ	Iveco 391.12.29 EuroRider	Orlandi	Regional bus	27/07/1999
513	BR642FF	Iveco 391.12.29 EuroRider	Orlandi	Regional bus	05/12/2000
514	BR112FG	Iveco 391.12.29 EuroRider	Orlandi	Regional bus	15/12/2000
576	BSA00383	Inbus S 210	Inbus	City bus	11/05/1987
577	BSA00384	Inbus S 210	Inbus	City bus	11/05/1987
638	BSB93697	Iveco 370.12.25	Iveco	Regional bus	22/12/1982

Mercedes-Benz O405 number 825, AZ 117NF, is seen departing the SIA bus terminal in central Brescia for Caino a distance of some 10km to the north east. *Bill Potter*

639	BSB93708	Iveco 370.12.25	Iveco	Regional bus	24/12/1982		
642	BSD39306	Iveco 370.12.L25	Iveco	Regional bus	15/03/1991		
643	BSD39402	Iveco 370.12.L25	Iveco	Regional bus	15/03/1991		
644	BSD39303	Iveco 370.12.L25	Iveco	Regional bus	15/03/1991		
645	BSD39308	Iveco 370.12.L25	Iveco	Regional bus	15/03/1991		

646-658		Iveco 370.12.SE35		Iveco		Regional bus	1995
646	AF 402XJ	650	AF 405XJ	653	AF 395XJ	656	AF 392XJ
647	AF 404XJ	651	AF 396XJ	654	AF 393XJ	657	AF 401XJ
648	AF 417XL	652	AF 406XJ	655	AF 403XJ	658	AF 391XJ
649	AF 394XJ						

659-690		Iveco 393.12.35 My Way		Iveco		Regional bus	2000
659	BM 314 FV	676	BM 417 FV	681	BM 689 FV	686	BM 692 FV
666	BM 685 FV	677	BM 418 FV	682	BM 690 FV	687	BM 555 FF
667	BM 321 FV	678	BM 687 FV	683	BM 420 FV	688	BM 554 FF
668	BM 686 FV	679	BM 419 FV	684	BM 691 FV	689	BM 553 FF
674	BM 416 FV	680	BM 688 FV	685	BM 326 FV	690	BM 552 FF
675	BM 325 FV						

802-810		Setra S300 NC		Setra		City bus	1992-94
802	AP 002NZ	805	AP 005NZ	807	AP 007NZ	809	AP 009NZ
803	AP 003NZ	806	AP 006NZ	808	AP 008NZ	810	AP 010NZ
804	AP 004NZ						

811-831		Mercedes-Benz O405 N2		Mercedes-Benz		City bus	1998-99
811	AZ 933NE	817	AZ 112NF	822	AZ 935NE	827	AZ 119NF
812	AZ 932NE	818	AZ 114NF	823	AZ 934NE	828	AZ 937NE
813	AZ 108NF	819	AZ 115NF	824	AZ 938NE	829	AZ 107NF
814	AZ 110NF	820	AZ 936NE	825	AZ 117NF	830	BE 794ZJ
815	AZ 109NF	821	AZ 116NF	826	AZ 118NF	831	BE 793ZJ
816	AZ 113NF						

SAIA

SAIA Trasporti, Via Foro Boario 4/b, 25124 Brecia.

Additonal depots are located at Palazzolo sull'Oglio, Orzinuovi, Fiesse, Pralboino and Desenzano del Garda.

1	BSB72612	Menarini M101/1 12m	Menarini	Coach	1990
3	BS E64899	Iveco 370S 12.30	Domino	Coach	1996
9	AZ 528 NF	Renault FRI GTX	Renault	Coach	1993
11	AF 737 XL	Scania	Ikarus	Coach	1996
12	BS 792546	Iveco 370.12.25	Iveco	Regional bus	1982
13	AF 946 XR	Iveco 370E.12.35.	DallaVia Palladio	Coach	1996
14	BS 793292	Iveco 370.12.25	Iveco	Regional bus	1982
15	AP 032 NY	Iveco 370E.12.35.	Iveco	Coach	1997
17	AN 528 JX	Iveco 380 12.38.	Irisbus-Orlandi	Coach	1997
19	AP 139 NW	Renault Iliade GTX	Renault	Coach	1997
21	AP 209 NZ	Renault Iliade GTX	Renault	Coach	1998
23	AP 289 NZ	Iveco 380 12.38.	Irisbus-Orlandi	Coach	1998
25	BR 459 ZT	Renault Iliade GTX	Renault	Coach	2001
26	BS 794053	Iveco 370.12.25	Iveco	Regional bus	1982
27	BS A42593	Iveco 49	Cacciamali	Coach	1988
28	BS 794048	Iveco.370.12.25	Iveco	Regional bus	1982
29	BS D23781	Iveco 70	Cacciamali	Coach	1990
30	BS B97299	Iveco 370.12.25	Iveco	Regional bus	1982
31	BS B97340	Irisbus 389E.12.43	Iveco	Coach	2003
32	BS B97296	Iveco.370.12.25	Iveco	Regional bus	1982
34	AZ 845 MC	Iveco.370.12.25	Inbus	Regional bus	1982
40	BS 902692	Iveco 370.12.30	Iveco	Regional bus	1984
42	BS 873470	Iveco 370,12,35	Iveco	Regional bus	1984
44	VR 674897	Iveco 370.12.25	Portesi	Regional bus	1984
46	BS 914719	Iveco 370.12.30	Padane	Regional bus	1985
48	AF 429 XP	Iveco.370.12.L.25	Iveco	Regional bus	1985
50	BS 920315	Iveco.370.12.L.25	Iveco	Regional bus	1985
52	BS 920316	Iveco.370.12.L.25	Iveco	Regional bus	1985
54	BS 897398	Inbus AID 280.FT	Inbus	Regional bus	1985
56	BS 897392	Inbus AID 280.FT	Inbus	Regional bus	1985
58	BS 887824	Iveco.370.12.35	Iveco	Regional bus	1983
60	BS 897397	Inbus AID 280.FT	Inbus	Regional bus	1985
62	BS 897399	Inbus AID 280.FT	Inbus	Regional bus	1985
64	BS 943084	Iveco 370.12.30.	Iveco	Regional bus	1986
66	AZ 733 ND	Mercedes-Benz 0.402	Mercedes-Benz	Regional bus	1986
68	AZ 734 ND	Mercedes-Benz 0.402	Mercedes-Benz	Regional bus	1986
70	BS 932802	Iveco 370.12.25L	Portesi	Regional bus	1986
72	BS 974553	Iveco 370.12.L.25	Iveco	Regional bus	1986
74	AF 872 XN	Iveco.370.12.L.25	Iveco	Regional bus	1986
76	VR 732641	Iveco 370.12.L25	Iveco	Regional bus	1986
78	BV 263 DZ	Menarini 370.12.30.	Breda Menarini	Regional bus	1987
80	BS A31136	Menarini 370.12.30.	Breda Menarini	Regional bus	1987
82	BS A20189	Iveco 370.12.30	Portesi	Regional bus	1987
84	BG 301 NT	Inbus I.210	Inbus	Regional bus	1987
86	BS A11037	Iveco.370.12.L..25	Iveco	Regional bus	1987
88	BS A18977	Iveco 671.12.24	Iveco	Regional bus	1987
90	BS A18978	Iveco 671.12.24	Iveco	Regional bus	1987
92	BS A28911	Imbus I.330.30	Inbus	Regional bus	1987
96	VR 798892	Iveco 370.12.30S	Iveco	Regional bus	1987
98	BS A28910	Inbus I.330.30	Inbus	Regional bus	1987
100	BS A77137	Renault FRI R50	Renault	Regional bus	1988
102	BS A80969	Setra 215 UL	Setra	Regional bus	1988
104	AN 220 JY	Iveco 370 12 35	Orlandi	Regional bus	1988
106	BS A88951	Iveco.370 12.L.25	Iveco	Regional bus	1988
108	BS A88952	Iveco.370 12.L.25	Iveco	Regional bus	1988
110	BS B31560	Iveco 315.8.17	Iveco	Regional bus	1989
112	BS B46884	Mercedes-Benz 0303	Padane	Regional bus	1989
114	BS B03701	Mercedes-Benz 0303	Bianchi	Regional bus	1989
116	BS B40368	Inbus I.330.30	Inbus	Regional bus	1989
118	BS B94283	Bredabus 5001.12sl	Breda Menarini	Regional bus	1990
120	BS B40369	Inbus I.330.30	Inbus	Regional bus	1989
122	VR 864004	Iveco 370.12.30S	Iveco	Regional bus	1989

The SAIA bus station in Brescia is located outside the rail station, raised up over a service area. The station is fan-shaped with buses parked nose-in. Pictured on depoarture is 228, BM 323FV, a Irisbus 393.12.35 with Irisbus-Orlandi My Way bodywork. On this example the Iveco lettering is still shown. *Bill Potter*

124	BS D23647	Inbus AID 280 FT	Inbus	Regional bus	1990
126	BS D05104	Iveco 370.12.L.25	Iveco	Regional bus	1990
128	AP 354 NZ	Mercedes-Benz 0405 N	Mercedes-Benz	Regional bus	1991
130	MI 7T2510	Mercedes-Benz 0303	Bianchi	Regional bus	1991
132	AF 503 XX	Iveco 370 12.30.	Orlandi	Regional bus	1991
134	BS D65556	Iveco 370.12.L.25	Iveco	Regional bus	1991
136	VR 955482	Inbus I 330	Inbus	Regional bus	1991
138	AP 163 NW	Inbus AID. 280.FT	Inbus	Regional bus	1991
140	BS D98773	Setra 215 UL	Setra	Regional bus	1992
142	BS D99326	Volvo B10M-60	Barbi	Regional bus	1992
144	BS D99327	Volvo B10M-60	Barbi	Regional bus	1992
146	BH 433WC	Iveco GTS	Irisbus-Orlandi Domino	Regional bus	1992
148	AP 001NZ	Setra S330 NC	Setra	Regional bus	1992
150	AP 425NW	MAN NG272	MAN	Regional bus	1993
152	BC 217VM	Iveco GTS	Irisbus-Orlandi Domino	Regional bus	1993
154	BF 021VJ	MAN NG272	MAN	Regional bus	1993
156	AF 284XK	Volvo B10B SL12	Barbi	Regional bus	1995

158-178		Mercedes-Benz 0408	Mercedes-Benz	Regional bus	1996-97

158	AF 957XX	**164**	AF 706XX	**170**	AP 033NX	**176**	AP 036NX
160	AF 958XX	**166**	AF 438XX	**172**	AP 034NX	**178**	AP 037NX
162	AF 959XX	**168**	AP 032NX	**174**	AP 035NX		

180	AZ 944NF	Mercedes-Benz 0405 NU	Mercedes-Benz	Regional bus	1998
182	AZ 710NF	Mercedes-Benz 0405 NU	Mercedes-Benz	Regional bus	1998
184	AZ 927NF	Mercedes-Benz 0405 NU	Mercedes-Benz	Regional bus	1998
186	BS B93695	Iveco 370.12.25	Iveco	Regional bus	1982
188	BS B93698	Iveco 370.12.25	Iveco	Regional bus	1982
190	AY 420CV	De Simon UL Scania	Desimon	Regional bus	1998
192	BA 087SM	Iveco 391E 12.35/M	Padane	Regional bus	1999
194	BE 218DN	Mauri 18EP30-1	Mauri	Regional bus	1999
196	BN 300SX	Mercedes-Benz Integro 0550	Mercedes-Benz	Regional bus	2000
198	BN 518SX	Mercedes-Benz Integro 0550	Mercedes-Benz	Regional bus	2000
200	BN 695SX	Mercedes-Benz Integro 0550	Mercedes-Benz	Regional bus	2000

SAIA operate just eight articulated buses, two MAN and six Inbus AID 280.FTs including 54, BS 897398, seen here at the Brescia depot. Note the exceedingly small registration plate, common on vehicles from the mid 1980s. *Bill Potter*

202	BN 694SX	Ayats Bravo I	Ayats	Regional bus	2000
204	BR 094FE	Ayats Bravo I	Ayats	Regional bus	2000
206	BR 096FE	Mercedes-Benz Integro O550	Mercedes-Benz	Regional bus	2000
208	BR 095FE	Mercedes-Benz Integro O550	Mercedes-Benz	Regional bus	2000

210-236

Irisbus 393.12.35 My Way — Irisbus-Orlandi — Regional bus — 2000

210	BR 928FE	218	BM 324FV	226	BM 320FV	232	BM 315FV
212	BR 964FE	220	BM 316FV	228	BM 323FV	234	BM 415FV
214	BR 772FE	222	BM 317FV	230	BM 313FV	236	BM 318FV
216	BM 322FV	224	BM 319FV				

| 238 | BP 180BG | MAN NL263 F | Autodromo | Regional bus | 2000 |
| 240 | BP 177BG | MAN NL263 F | Autodromo | Regional bus | 2000 |

242-254

Mercedes-Benz Citaro O530 NU — Mercedes-Benz — Regional bus — 2001

| 242 | BT 351GC | 246 | BT 348GC | 250 | BT 537GC | 254 | BT 204GD |
| 244 | BT 350GC | 248 | BT 349GC | 252 | BT 538GC | | |

256	BT203GD	Ayats Bravo I	Ayats	Regional bus	2000
258	BT941GD	Mercedes-Benz Citaro O530 NU	Mercedes-Benz	Regional bus	2001
260	BT940GD	Mercedes-Benz Citaro O530 NU	Mercedes-Benz	Regional bus	2001
262	BV410DV	Mercedes-Benz Citaro O530 NU	Mercedes-Benz	Regional bus	2001
264	AF359XE	Volvo B10M-60	Barbi	Regional bus	1985
266	BV873DZ	Irisbus Agora Moovy	Irisbus	Regional bus	2001
268	BV874DZ	Irisbus Agora Moovy	Irisbus	Regional bus	2001
270	BZ174XN	Setra S215 UL	Setra	Regional bus	1991
272	BZ169XN	MAN SU 313	MAN	Regional bus	2002
274	BZ170XN	MAN SU 313	MAN	Regional bus	2002
276	CF122JN	Irisbus 399E My Way	Irisbus Orlandi	Regional bus	2003
278	CJ391BX	Iveco 380 12.35.	Orlandi	Regional bus	1995
280	CJ309BY	MAN SG292 18m	MAN	Regional bus	1993

282-300

Mercedes-Benz Conecto O345 — Mercedes-Benz — Regional bus — 2001

282	CL542AX	288	CL544AX	294	CL052AY	298	CM023EW
284	CL543AX	290	CL220AX	296	CL5624Y	300	CL561AY
286	CL541AX	292	CL560AY				

KM

KM spa, Via Postumia 102, 26100 Cremona

No	Reg	Type	Body	Notes	Year
3	CR389359	Iveco 280 RA7	Cacciamali	School bus	1988
4	BG451PH	Iveco 45.10	Iveco	School bus	1995
5	BH060WY	Iveco CC80E18M/86	Cacciamali	School bus	2000
6	BV937GP	Iveco Scuolabus Turbo Daily	Cacciamali	School bus	1989
58	CR384191	Inbus U210/FT	Breda	City bus	1987
59	CR384192	Inbus U210/FT	Breda	City bus	1987
61	CR384194	Inbus U210/FT	Breda	City bus	1987
62	CR384195	Inbus U210/FT	Breda	City bus	1987
63	CR389020	Menarini 201/2 LU	Menarini	City bus	1987
64	CR390912	Menarini M 201/2NU	Menarini	City bus	1988
66	CR410068	Inbus U210/FTN	Breda	City bus	1989
67	CR410069	Inbus U210/FTN	Breda	City bus	1989
68	CR410070	Inbus U210/FTN	Breda	City bus	1989
70	CR413848	Menarini M 201/2NU	Menarini	City bus	1989
71	CR413849	Menarini M 201/2NU	Menarini	City bus	1989
72	CR454939	Menarini M 220/NU	Menarini	City bus	1991
73	CR454940	Menarini M 220/NU	Menarini	City bus	1991
74	AL597GD	CAM Bussotto NL202 FU	Carrozzeria Autiromo	City bus	1996
75	AP257XK	Breda Menarini M 230/1E2	Bredamenarinbus	City bus	1998
76	AP258XK	Breda Menarini M 230/1E2	Bredamenarinbus	City bus	1998

78-82

Kronos 10KV23-U — Mauri — City bus — 2001

78	BV620GK	**80**	BV621GK	**81**	BV826GK	**82**	BV827GK
79	BV680GK						

83-86

Mercedes-Benz CITO — Mercedes-Benz — City bus — 2002

83	BV916GS	**84**	BV014GT	**85**	BV917GS	**86**	BV936GP

87	-	Iveco 491.12.27 - Cityclass	Iveco	City bus	On order

Cremona is located to the south east of Milan. Until recently there was a trolleybus system which became part of the Arriva operation and although it has been withdrawn the overhead wires remain. Seen with overall advertising, 72, CR454939, is a Menarini M 220. *Bill Potter*

Representing the Regional bus members of the KM Fleet, 135, BS A11034, is seen departing from the rail station terminus. This Iveco 370 features a Portesi body. *Bill Potter*

100	BS 814084	Iveco 370.12.25	Iveco	Regional bus	1983
101	BS 814083	Iveco 370.12.25	Iveco	Regional bus	1983
103	BS D05103	Iveco 370.12.25L	Iveco	Regional bus	1990
104	BS918590	Iveco 370.12.25L	Iveco	Regional bus	1985
105	AF778 XJ	Cam Busotto 2LS-SR	Carrozzeria Autiromo	City bus	1995
106	BS870148	Iveco 370.12.25	Portesi	Regional bus	1984
107	CR463164	Inbus S 210	Breada	City bus	1987
108	AW765 EJ	Breda Menarini M 230/01 MS	Bredamenarinbus	City bus	1998
109	BE301DN	Mercedes-Benz O405NU	Mercedes-Benz	Regional bus	1999
110	AZ465 NF	Mercedes-Benz O405NU	Mercedes-Benz	Regional bus	1998
111	BM984FW	Mercedes-Benz O405NU	Mercedes-Benz	Regional bus	2000
112	BS918588	Iveco 370.12.25L	Iveco	Regional bus	1985
113	AF164 XD	Iveco 370.12.35	Dalla Via	Regional bus	1995
114	AZ469 NF	Mercedes-Benz O405NU	Mercedes-Benz	Regional bus	1998
115	AN900 JY	Iveco 370.12.25L	Dalla Via	Regional bus	1986
116	BS834021	Iveco 370.12.25	Portesi	Regional bus	1983
117	BS918589	Iveco 370.12.25L	Portesi	Regional bus	1985
118	BSA11038	Iveco 370.12.25L	Iveco	Regional bus	1987
119	BS902579	Iveco 370.12.25L	Iveco	Regional bus	1985
120	BS840857	Inbus I/330	Iveco	Regional bus	1994
121	BSA73986	Iveco 370.12.25L	Portesi	Regional bus	1988
122	BS920314	Iveco 370.12.25L	Iveco	Regional bus	1985
123	BSA11035	Iveco 370.12.25L	Portesi	Regional bus	1987
124	BS920313	Iveco 370.12.25L	Iveco	Regional bus	1985
125	BSA84583	Iveco 370.12.25L	Portesi	Regional bus	1988
126	BSA84584	Iveco 370.12.25L	Portesi	Regional bus	1988
127	BS967705	Iveco 370.12.25L	Portesi	Regional bus	1986
128	BSB69662	Iveco 370.12.25L	Iveco	Regional bus	1990
129	BSD05102	Iveco 370.12.25L	Iveco	Regional bus	1990
130	BH343WC	Iveco 391E.12.29 Eurorider	Iveco	Regional bus	1998
131	BH342WC	Iveco 391E.12.29 Eurorider	Iveco	Regional bus	1998
132	AZ 468NF	Mercedes-Benz O405 NU	Iveco	Regional bus	1998
133	BS 799902	Inbus S/210	Iveco	City bus	1983
134	BS 902580	Iveco 370.12.25	Iveco	Regional bus	1985
35	BS A11034	Iveco 370.12.25L	Portesi	Regional bus	1987

An interesting bus with KM is number 105, AF778 XJ. Joining the fleet in 1995 it is a Cam Busotto 2LS-SR with Carrozzeria Autiromo body. A further bus from the manufacturer came the following year. It is seen on a cross town service, number 4, though the scrolling destination, like ticker-tape, prevents the whole name being shown at any one time. *Bill Potter*

136	BS A84582		Iveco 370.12.25L		Portesi	Regional bus		1988
137-142			Mauri Ayats2 piani		Mauri	Regional bus		2001
137	BM 281DX	**139**	BM 283DX	**141**	BR 776FE		**142**	BR 905FE
138	BM 282DX	**140**	BR 775FE					
143	AF 163 XD		Iveco 370.12.35		Dalla Via	Regional bus		1995
144	BM 280DX		Iveco 393E.12.35 My Way		Iveco	Regional bus		2001
145	BM 285DX		Iveco 393E.12.35 My Way		Iveco	Regional bus		2001
146	BM 290DX		Iveco 393E.12.35 My Way		Iveco	Regional bus		2001
147	AF 747 XF		Iveco 370.12.35		Dalla Via	Regional bus		1995
148-155			Iveco 393E.12.35 My Way		Iveco	Regional bus		2001
148	BM 291DX	**150**	BM 284DX	**152**	BM 288DX		**154**	BM 292DX
149	BM 286DX	**151**	BM 287DX	**153**	BM 289DX		**155**	CD523YR
157	AZ 470 NF		Mercedes-Benz O405NU		Mercedes-Benz	Regional bus		1998
159	AZ 467 NF		Mercedes-Benz O405NU		Mercedes-Benz	Regional bus		1998
160	BS 693LE		Iveco 491.12.27 - Cityclass		Iveco	City bus		2001
161	BS 694LE		Iveco 491.12.27 - Cityclass		Iveco	City bus		2001
162	BS 695LE		Iveco 491.12.27 - Cityclass		Iveco	City bus		2001
189	BS D09800		Iveco 370.12.30S		Portesi	Regional bus		1990
195	AZ 466 NF		Mercedes-Benz O405NU		Mercedes-Benz	Regional bus		1998
401	CR 508523		Iveco 370E.12.35 - Palladio		Dalla Via	Coach		1994
402	AL 285 GG		Iveco 370E.12.35 - Palladio		Dalla Via	Coach		1996
403	AW 021 EM		Iveco 370E.12.35 - Domino		Iveco-Orlandi	Coach		1997
404	AW 491 EL		Iveco 370E.12.35 - Palladio		Dalla Via	Coach		1997
405	AP 785 XF		Iveco 370E.12.35 - Domino		Iveco-Orlandi	Coach		1998
406	AP 596 XG		Iveco 370E.12.35 - Palladio		Dalla Via	Coach		1998
407	BG 322PH		Mercedes-Benz O404 V8		Dalla Via	Coach		2000
408	BG 323PH		Mercedes-Benz O404 V8		Dalla Via	Coach		2000
409	BV103GM		Iveco GT 65C15		Cacciamali	Coach		2002

Trieste Trasporti

Trieste Trasporti Spa, Stazione Centrale di Plazza Della Liberta 8, Trieste

511-514 Europolis TCC760 Cacciamali City bus 1999-2000

511	BG 401 BS	512	BG 402 BS	513	BH 096 XY	514	BH 095 XY

521-528 Breda Menarini 231 MU/3P Bredamenarinbus City bus 1999-2000

521	BG 845 BS	523	BH 624 XX	525	BH 623 XX	527	BM 161 RA
522	BG 846 BS	524	BH 622 XX	526	BM 139 RA	528	BM 160 RA

531	AN 099 ER	Europolis TCC 635 L	Cacciamali	City bus	1997
541	AN 159 EP	Breda Menarini M230/1E	Bredamenarinbus	City bus	1997
542	AN 120 ES	Breda Menarini M230/1E	Bredamenarinbus	City bus	1997
543	AT 320 FD	Breda Menarini M230/1E	Bredamenarinbus	City bus	1998
544	AX 127 ZT	Breda Menarini M230/1E	Bredamenarinbus	City bus	1998

551-562 Breda Menarini 240 NU Bredamenarinbus City bus 1999

551	BD 691 AF	554	BD 694 AF	557	BD 829 AF	560	BD 828 AF
552	BD 692 AF	555	BD 695 AF	558	BD 826 AF	561	BD 893 AF
553	BD 693 AF	556	BD 696 AF	559	BD 827 AF	562	BD 894 AF

571-587 Europolis TCN105 Cacciamali City bus 1999

571	BF 203 AR	576	BF 207 AR	580	BF 208 AR	584	BF 267 AR
572	BF 204 AR	577	BF 362 AR	581	BF 265 AR	585	BF 210 AR
573	BF 205 AR	578	BF 363 AR	582	BF 209 AR	586	BF 268 AR
574	BF 424 AR	579	BF 364 AR	583	BF 266 AR	587	BF 211 AR
575	BF 206 AR						

591	CB 258 YE	Europolis 924	Cacciamali	City bus	2002
592	CB 350 YE	Europolis 924	Cacciamali	City bus	2002
593	CB 351 YE	Europolis 924	Cacciamali	City bus	2002
601	BM 667 RA	Setra S315 HD	Setra	Coach	1999
603	BM 762 RA	Mercedes-Benz O404	Mercedes-Benz	Coach	1999
604	BM 761 RA	Iveco 370E.12.35H Palladio	Iveco	Coach	2000
605	BV 038 ZB	Neoplan N516SHD Starliner	Neoplan	Coach	2000
606	BV 678 ZC	Domino 2001 HDH	Orlandi	Coach	2002
611	AK 653 RA	Breda Menarini M220 LU 4P	Bredamenarinbus	City bus	1996
612	AN 263 EN	Breda Menarini M220 LU 4P	Bredamenarinbus	City bus	1996
615	BM 666 RA	Iveco 380.12.38 HD-T	Iveco	Coach	1996
616	BM 668 RA	Iveco 380.12.38 HD-T	Iveco	Coach	1998
641	BM 868 RA	Iveco CC80E18M 86	Cacciamali	School bus	1999
642	BV 039 ZB	Iveco CC80E18M/86	Cacciamali	School bus	1999
643	BV 074 ZB	Iveco CC80E18M/86	Cacciamali	School bus	1999
644	BV 088 ZB	Iveco 100E18 E2 48	Cacciamali	School bus	1999
645	BV 073 ZB	Iveco 100E18 E2 48	Cacciamali	School bus	1999
646	BV 072 ZB	Iveco CC80E18M/86	Cacciamali	School bus	2000
647	BM 605 RA	Iveco 100E18 E2 48	Cacciamali	School bus	2000
648	CB 051 YE	Iveco 100E21N	Cacciamali	School bus	2002

712-767 Iveco Turbocity-U Desimon UN 70.02 City bus 1990-92

712	TS 349482	726	TS 350863	740	TS 352777	754	TS 361087
713	TS 349483	727	TS 350864	741	TS 353124	755	TS 377316
714	TS 349484	728	TS 350865	742	TS 353475	756	BD 503 AF
715	AN 522 ER	729	TS 350866	743	TS 353476	757	TS 377318
716	TS 350480	730	TS 350867	744	TS 353477	758	TS 377319
717	TS 349866	731	TS 350868	745	TS 353478	759	TS 377320
718	TS 349867	732	TS 350869	746	TS 353479	760	TS 377321
719	TS 349868	733	TS 350870	747	TS 353480	761	TS 377322
720	TS 349869	734	TS 351355	748	TS 353481	762	TS 377323
721	TS 349870	735	TS 351713	749	TS 353482	763	TS 377324
722	TS 350476	736	TS 351712	750	TS 353483	764	TS 377325
723	TS 350479	737	AK 663 RA	751	TS 361084	765	TS 377769
724	TS 350477	738	TS 352386	752	TS 361085	766	TS 377771
725	TS 350478	739	TS 352387	753	TS 361086	767	TS 377770

771-775

Van Hool AG300RA01 — Desimon — City bus — 1999

771	BD 795 AF	773	BF 005 AR	774	BF 007 AR	775	BF 006 AR
772	BF 008 AR						

781-790

Breda Menarini M321/1 — Bredamenarinbus — City bus — 1999

781	BD 895 AF	784	BD 898 AF	787	BD 900 AF	789	BD 902 AF
782	BD 896 AF	785	BD 796 AF	788	BD 901 AF	790	BD 903 AF
783	BD 897 AF	786	BD 899 AF				

801-833

Irisbus 491.12.29 CityClass — Irisbus — City bus — 2001

801	BM 827 RA	810	BM 595 RA	818	BM 681 RA	826	BM 599 RA
802	BM 399 RA	811	BM 518 RA	819	BM 597 RA	827	BM 601 RA
803	BM 398 RA	812	BM 455 RA	820	BM 519 RA	828	BM 520 RA
804	BM 397 RA	813	BM 596 RA	821	BM 453 RA	829	BM 678 RA
805	BM 396 RA	814	BM 454 RA	822	BM 456 RA	830	BM 602 RA
806	BM 521 RA	815	BM 395 RA	823	BM 517 RA	831	BM 603 RA
807	BM 680 RA	816	BM 452 RA	824	BM 677 RA	832	BM 604 RA
808	BM 457 RA	817	BM 522 RA	825	BM 598 RA	833	BM 679 RA
809	BM 594 RA						

861-892

Iveco 490.E10.22 — Iveco — City bus — 1996-97

861	AK 005 RD	869	AN 418 EN	876	AN 425 EN	886	AN 335 ES
862	AN 016 EN	870	AN 419 EN	877	AN 869 EN	887	AN 336 ES
863	AK 006 RD	871	AN 420 EN	881	AN 330 ES	888	AN 337 ES
864	AN 773 EN	872	AN 421 EN	882	BV 602 ZC	889	AN 338 ES
865	AN 020 EN	873	AN 422 EN	883	AN 332 ES	890	AN 339 ES
866	AN 018 EN	874	AN 423 EN	884	AN 333 ES	891	AN 340 ES
867	AN 021 EN	875	AN 424 EN	885	AN 334 ES	892	AN 341 ES
868	AN 019 EN						

1001-1005

ALE 7,7/3P E3 — Autiromo — City bus — 2001-03

1001	BV 785 ZB	1003	BV 787 ZB	1004	BV 786 ZB	1005	CB 450 YE
1002	BV 788 ZB						

1011-1020

Breda Menarini M231/E3 — Bredamenarinbus — City bus — 2001

1011	BV 501 ZB	1014	BV 562 ZB	1017	BV 561 ZB	1019	BV 656 ZB
1012	BV 502 ZB	1015	BV 503 ZB	1018	BV 637 ZB	1020	BV 655 ZB
1013	BV 635 ZB	1016	BV 636 ZB				

1031-1049

Breda Menarini M240/E3 NU — Bredamenarinbus — City bus — 2001

1031	BV 504 ZB	1036	BV 507 ZB	1041	BV 567 ZB	1046	BV 559 ZB
1032	BV 505 ZB	1037	BV 508 ZB	1042	BV 512 ZB	1047	BV 560 ZB
1033	BV 506 ZB	1038	BV 509 ZB	1043	BV 513 ZB	1048	BV 570 ZB
1034	BV 565 ZB	1039	BV 510 ZB	1044	BV 568 ZB	1049	BV 571 ZB
1035	BV 566 ZB	1040	BV 511 ZB	1045	BV 569 ZB		

1050-1080

Breda Menarini M240/E3 NU — Bredamenarinbus — City bus — 2002-03

1050	CB 352 YE	1058	CB 410 YE	1066	CB 413 YE	1074	CB 127 YE
1051	CB 180 YE	1059	CB 411 YE	1067	CB 414 YE	1075	CB 152 YE
1052	CB 181 YE	1060	CB 259 YE	1068	CB 415 YE	1076	CB 128 YE
1053	CB 409 YE	1061	CB 260 YE	1069	CB 416 YE	1077	CB 129 YE
1054	CB 182 YE	1062	CB 261 YE	1070	CB 417 YE	1078	CB 151 YE
1055	CB 183 YE	1063	CB 262 YE	1071	CB 418 YE	1079	CB 150 YE
1056	CB 195 YE	1064	CB 263 YE	1072	CB 125 YE	1080	CB 149 YE
1057	CB 196 YE	1065	CB 412 YE	1073	CB 126 YE		

1101-1110

Breda Menarini M240/E3 LU 3P — Bredamenarinbus — City bus — 2002

1101	CB 264 YE	1104	CB 238 YE	1107	CB 240 YE	1109	CB 241 YE
1102	CB 197 YE	1105	CB 239 YE	1108	CB 198 YE	1110	CB 266 YE
1103	CB 237 YE	1106	CB 265 YE				

1151-1170

Breda Menarini M240/E3 LU 18m — Bredamenarinbus — City bus — 2002-03

1151	CB 419 YE	1156	CB 355 YE	1161	CB 358 YE	1166	CB 425 YE
1152	CB 420 YE	1157	CB 430 YE	1162	CB 422 YE	1167	CB 426 YE
1153	CB 267 YE	1158	CB 421 YE	1163	CB 423 YE	1168	CB 427 YE
1154	CB 353 YE	1159	CB 356 YE	1164	CB 424 YE	1169	CB 359 YE
1155	CB 354 YE	1160	CB 357 YE	1165	CB 429 YE	1170	CB 428 YE

1201	CB 835 YE	Scania OmniCity CN94UB	Scania	City bus	2003

RT

RT buses are based in Imperia, in the Region of Liguria.

RT3202 IM158620	Iveco A55 F 10	Iveco	Regional bus	1979
RT3211 BK398WN	Iveco A45 E 12	Iveco	Regional bus	2002
RT4150 IM155885	Iveco 315.8.13	Iveco	Regional bus	1979
RT4151 IM156272	Iveco 315.8.13	Iveco	Regional bus	1979
RT4153 IM158617	Iveco 315.8.13	Iveco	Regional bus	1979
RT4154 IM158618	Iveco 315.8.13	Iveco	Regional bus	1979
RT4156 IM168348	Iveco 315.8.13	Iveco	Regional bus	1980
RT4157 IM178086	Iveco 315.8.13	Iveco	Regional bus	1981
RT4159 IM178087	Iveco 315.8.13	Iveco	Regional bus	1981
RT4164 BG308BX	Iveco 315.8.18	Iveco	Regional bus	1999
RT4168 BH026VV	Iveco 315.8.18	Iveco	Regional bus	1999
RT4300 IM217583	Iveco 316.8.13	Viberti	Regional bus	1991
RT4305 IM274912	Iveco 316.8.13	Viberti	Regional bus	1991
RT4306 IM274942	Iveco 316.8.13	Viberti	Regional bus	1991
RT4308 IM2768001	Iveco 316.8.13	Viberti	Regional bus	1991
RT4309 IM276802	Iveco 316.8.13	Viberti	Regional bus	1991
RT5074 AG103DY	MAN 11.220 HOCL	DeSimon	Regional bus	1996
RT5077 AG237DY	MAN 11.220 HOCL	DeSimon	Regional bus	1996
RT5079 AG238DY	MAN 11.220 HOCL	DeSimon	Regional bus	1996
RT5081 AG834DY	MAN 11.220 HOCL	DeSimon	Regional bus	1996
RT5082 AG835DY	MAN 11.220 HOCL	DeSimon	Regional bus	1996
RT5083 AG833DY	MAN 11.220 HOCL	DeSimon	Regional bus	1996
RT5085 BD041RN	MAN 11.220 HOCL	DeSimon	Regional bus	1999
RT5087 BK830WM	MAN 11.220 HOCL	DeSimon	Regional bus	2000
RT5350 IM201418	Inbus S150	Sicca	Regional bus	1986
RTL001 BZ417CB	Iveco A50 C 15	Iveco	Regional bus	2002
RTL002 BZ980CB	Mercedes-Benz0303/10R	Bianchi	Regional bus	1981

Arriva London's operation includes the private hire and coach operation Leaside Travel. One of the buses is a AEC Regent from the mid 1960s, numbered RV1, GJG750D. The bus was new to East Kent when that company was still owned by British Electric Traction. It is seen on wedding duty outside the Mansion House in London.
Richard Godfrey

Index to UK vehicles

3CLT	London	A574NWX	Yorkshire	B129WUL	London	B605UUM	The Shires
49XBF	Midlands	A575NWX	Yorkshire	B130WUL	London	B606UUM	Yorkshire
70CLT	London	A577NWX	Yorkshire	B134GAU	Midlands	B607UUM	Yorkshire
124CLT	London	A579NWX	Yorkshire	B135GAU	Midlands	B608UUM	Yorkshire
124YTW	North West & W	A580NWX	Yorkshire	B136GAU	Midlands	B609UUM	Yorkshire
185CLT	London	A581NWX	Yorkshire	B136WUL	London	B824AAT	OLST
205CLT	London	A582NWX	Yorkshire	B137GAU	Midlands	B825AAT	OLST
217CLT	London	A583NWX	Yorkshire	B138GAU	Midlands	B861XYR	The Shires
324CLT	London	A584NWX	Yorkshire	B139GAU	Midlands	B962WRN	North West & W
361CLT	London	A585NWX	Yorkshire	B140GAU	Midlands	B963WRN	North West & W
398CLT	London	A586NWX	Yorkshire	B140WUL	London	B964WRN	North West & W
453CLT	London	A588NWX	Yorkshire	B141GAU	Midlands	B965WRN	North West & W
464CLT	London	A589NWX	Yorkshire	B142GAU	Midlands	B967WRN	North West & W
480CLT	London	A590NWX	Yorkshire	B143GAU	Midlands	BAZ7384	Southern Counties
530MUY	London	A667XDA	OLST	B148TRN	North West & W	BCW824V	North West & W
593CLT	London	A700THV	London	B149TRN	North West & W	BF52NZM	Midlands
614WEH	Midlands	A855UYM	The Shires	B151TRN	North West & W	BF52NZN	Midlands
640CLT	London	A856UYM	The Shires	B152WUL	OLST	BF52NZO	Midlands
662NKR	Midlands	A895SUL	OLST	B154TRN	North West & W	BF52NZP	Midlands
725DYE	London	A903SUL	London	B170WUL	London	BF52NZR	Midlands
734DYE	London	A927SUL	OLST	B179WUL	London	BF52NZS	Midlands
776DYE	London	A930SUL	North East	B187BLG	Midlands	BF52NZT	Midlands
801DYE	London	A959SYF	North East	B190BLG	Midlands	BF52NZU	Midlands
803HOM	Midlands	A973SYF	North East	B194BLG	North West & W	BF52NZV	Midlands
815DYE	The Shires	A984SYF	London	B197DTU	North West & W	BF52NZW	Midlands
822DYE	London	ADZ4731	The Shires	B198DTU	North West & W	BF52NZX	Midlands
A11GTA	Southern Counties	ALD872B	London	B214WUL	London	BF52NZY	Midlands
A112KFX	OLST	ALD941B	London	B222VHW	OLST	BF52NZZ	Midlands
A113KFX	OLST	ALD968B	London	B224VHW	OLST	BF52OAA	Midlands
A114KFX	OLST	ALD975B	London	B225VHW	OLST	BF52OAB	Midlands
A129DTO	Midlands	ALD978B	London	B227WUL	OLST	BF52OAC	Midlands
A130DTO	Midlands	ALM50B	London	B231WUL	London	BF52OAD	Midlands
A131DTO	Midlands	ALM60B	London	B239WUL	OLST	BF52OAE	Midlands
A132DTO	Midlands	B75WUL	London	B240LRA	OLST	BF52OAG	Midlands
A132SMA	Midlands	B84WUL	London	B248WUL	London	BKE847T	The Shires
A133DTO	Midlands	B86WUL	North East	B251NVN	North West & W	BU02URX	Midlands
A134SMA	Midlands	B89WUL	North East	B253WUL	London	BU02URY	Midlands
A139MRN	North West & W	B90WUL	North East	B254WUL	London	BU02URZ	Midlands
A141MRN	North West & W	B91WUL	North East	B263WUL	Southern Counties	BU02USB	Midlands
A147OFR	North West & W	B92WUL	London	B265WUL	OLST	BU02USC	Midlands
A152UDM	North West & W	B94WUL	London	B274LPH	Midlands	BU03HPV	Midlands
A241GHN	North East	B95WUL	London	B275LPH	Midlands	BU03HPX	Midlands
A242GHN	North East	B96WUL	London	B275WUL	Southern Counties	BU03HPY	Midlands
A244GHN	North East	B97WUL	London	B277KPF	North East	BU03HPZ	Midlands
A250SVW	The Shires	B98WUL	London	B280WUL	Southern Counties	BU03HRA	Midlands
A501EJF	Midlands	B100WUL	London	B300WUL	London	BU03HRC	Midlands
A502EJF	Midlands	B101WUL	London	B303WUL	London	BU03HRD	Midlands
A503EJF	Midlands	B103WUL	London	B513LFP	North West & W	BU03HRE	Midlands
A504EJF	Midlands	B104WUL	London	B514LFP	Midlands	BU03HRF	Midlands
A508EJF	Midlands	B105WUL	London	B591SWX	Yorkshire	BU03HRG	Midlands
A509EJF	Midlands	B112WUL	North East	B594SWX	Yorkshire	BU03HRJ	Midlands
A512EJF	Midlands	B115ORU	OLST	B596SWX	Yorkshire	BU03HRK	Midlands
A565NWX	Yorkshire	B116WUL	North East	B597SWX	Yorkshire	BU03HRL	Midlands
A566NWX	Yorkshire	B121ORU	OLST	B599SWX	Yorkshire	BU51KWJ	Midlands
A567NWX	North East	B121WUL	London	B600UUM	Yorkshire	BU51KWK	Midlands
A569NWX	Yorkshire	B123WUL	London	B601UUM	Yorkshire	BU51KWL	Midlands
A570NWX	Yorkshire	B124WUL	London	B603UUM	Yorkshire	BU51KWM	Midlands
A571NWX	Yorkshire	B126WUL	London	B604UUM	Yorkshire	BU51KWN	Midlands

Reg	Region	Reg	Region	Reg	Region	Reg	Region
BU53AWP	Midlands	C56CHM	London	CUV280C	London	D166FYM	The Shires
BU53AWR	Midlands	C58CHM	London	CUV287C	London	D167FYM	The Shires
BX04MWW	London	C59CHM	The Shires	CUV292C	London	D168FYM	The Shires
BX04MWY	London	C65CHM	London	CUV294C	London	D169FYM	The Shires
BX04MWZ	London	C66CHM	London	CUV301C	London	D170FYM	Midlands
BX04MXA	London	C102CHM	London	CUV304C	London	D171FYM	Midlands
BX04MXB	London	C118FKH	OLST	CUV307C	London	D172FYM	Southern Counties
BX04MXC	London	C133CFB	OLST	CUV315C	London	D174FYM	North East
BX04MXD	London	C141SPB	Midlands	CUV322C	London	D178FYM	North East
BX04MXE	London	C144NRR	Midlands	CUV323C	London	D179FYM	London
BX04MXG	London	C145NRR	Midlands	CUV324C	London	D181FYM	The Shires
BX04MXH	London	C146NRR	Midlands	CUV325C	London	D185FYM	London
BX04MXJ	London	C147NRR	Midlands	CUV326C	London	D186FYM	London
BX04MXK	London	C148NRR	Midlands	CUV328C	London	D187FYM	The Shires
BX04MXL	London	C212GTU	North West & W	CUV329C	London	D188FYM	London
BX04MXM	London	C260UAJ	North East	CUV330C	London	D189FYM	North East
BX04MXN	London	C261UAJ	North East	CUV333C	London	D190FYM	Midlands
BX04MXP	London	C262UAJ	North East	CUV334C	London	D191FYM	London
BX04MXR	London	C263XEF	North East	CUV340C	London	D192FYM	London
BX04MXS	London	C264XEF	North East	CUV341C	London	D194FYM	London
BX04MXT	London	C268XEF	North East	CUV343C	London	D196FYM	London
BX04MXU	London	C310BUV	OLST	CUV344C	London	D196WJC	The Shires
BX04MXV	London	C312BUV	London	CUV346C	London	D197FYM	London
BX04MXW	London	C313BUV	London	CUV347C	London	D198FYM	London
BX04MXY	London	C314BUV	London	CUV350C	London	D201FYM	London
BX04MXZ	London	C318BUV	London	CUV351C	London	D203FYM	The Shires
BX04MYA	London	C319BUV	London	CUV354C	London	D211FYM	The Shires
BX04MYB	London	C320BUV	London	CUV355C	London	D214FYM	London
BX04MYC	London	C322BUV	London	CUV356C	London	D216FYM	North East
BX04MYD	London	C324BUV	London	CUV359C	London	D218FYM	London
BX04MYF	London	C324LDT	North West & W	CWR514Y	Scotland	D223FYM	London
BX04MYY	London	C326BUV	London	CWR517Y	Yorkshire	D224FYM	The Shires
BX04NDD	London	C327BUV	London	CWR518Y	Scotland	D226FYM	London
BX04NDG	London	C332BUV	London	CWR519Y	Scotland	D228FYM	London
BX04NDV	London	C354BUV	North East	CWR521Y	Yorkshire	D230FYM	London
BYX121V	OLST	C367BUV	London	CWR524Y	Yorkshire	D231FYM	The Shires
BYX123V	OLST	C398BUV	London	CX04AXW	North West & W	D232FYM	London
BYX143V	OLST	C399BVU	London	CX04AXY	North West & W	D234FYM	Southern Counties
BYX185V	OLST	C401BUV	OLST	CX04AXZ	North West & W	D237FYM	London
BYX210V	North East	C402BUV	London	CX04AYA	North West & W	D240FYM	The Shires
BYX245V	OLST	C404BUV	Scotland	CX04AYB	North West & W	D242FYM	The Shires
BYX251V	OLST	C405BUV	London	CX04AYC	North West & W	D246FYM	London
BYX296V	OLST	C406BUV	London	CX04EHV	North West & W	D251FYM	London
BYX304V	OLST	C610ANW	Yorkshire	CX04EHW	North West & W	D257FYM	London
BYX310V	OLST	C611ANW	Yorkshire	CX04EHY	North West & W	D258FYM	London
BYX314V	OLST	C612ANW	Yorkshire	CX04EHZ	Midlands	D443UHC	North West & W
C21CHM	London	C805BYY	London	D108NDW	North West & W	D553YNO	OLST
C22CHM	London	C906GUD	OLST	D135FYM	London	D634BBV	North West & W
C24CHM	London	C907GUD	OLST	D143FYM	London	DE520KV	Southern Counties
C25CHM	London	C920FMP	Yorkshire	D146FYM	The Shires	DE520KW	Southern Counties
C31CHM	The Shires	CUB66Y	North East	D147FYM	London	DE520KX	Southern Counties
C32CHM	Southern Counties	CUB68Y	North East	D150FYM	London	DE520KZ	Southern Counties
C35CHM	London	CUV122C	London	D155FYM	North East	DE520LM	Southern Counties
C36CHM	The Shires	CUV179C	London	D155HML	North West & W	DE520LN	Southern Counties
C37CHM	London	CUV185C	London	D157FYM	North East	DOC26V	North West & W
C38CHM	The Shires	CUV217C	London	D157HML	North West & W	DOC37V	North West & W
C41HHJ	Southern Counties	CUV261C	London	D159FYM	London	E23ECH	Midlands
C45CHM	London	CUV264C	London	D160FYM	North East	E25ECH	Midlands
C46CHM	London	CUV265C	London	D161FYM	London	E26ECH	Scotland
C49CHM	London	CUV266C	London	D162FYM	London	E52UNE	North West & W
C50CHM	London	CUV267C	London	D164FYM	London	E72KBF	Midlands
C52VJU	OLST	CUV277C	London	D165FYM	North East	E149BTO	Midlands

Reg	Region	Reg	Region	Reg	Region	Reg	Region
E150BTO	Midlands	F106TML	North West & W	F578SMG	Southern Counties	G35HKY	North West & W
E151BTO	Midlands	F107TML	North West & W	F579SMG	Southern Counties	G36HKY	Midlands
E152BTO	Midlands	F108TML	North West & W	F580SMG	Southern Counties	G37HKY	Midlands
E153BTO	Midlands	F109TML	North West & W	F621HGO	Southern Counties	G38YHJ	Midlands
E1580MD	Midlands	F110TML	North West & W	F634LMJ	The Shires	G40YHJ	Midlands
E1590MD	Midlands	F111TML	Midlands	F636LMJ	The Shires	G41VME	North West & W
E1600MD	Midlands	F112TML	North West & W	F637LMJ	The Shires	G45VME	Southern Counties
E1610MD	Midlands	F114TML	Midlands	F639LMJ	The Shires	G49CVC	North West & W
E205TUB	Yorkshire	F117XTX	North West & W	F640LMJ	The Shires	G1080UG	Midlands
E224WBG	North West & W	F151KGS	The Shires	F641LMJ	The Shires	G1100UG	Midlands
E225CFC	The Shires	F152KGS	The Shires	F642LMJ	The Shires	G122RGT	North West & W
E226CFC	The Shires	F153DET	Midlands	F643LMJ	The Shires	G123RGT	North West & W
E227WBG	North West & W	F153KGS	The Shires	F644LMJ	The Shires	G125RGT	North West & W
E228CFC	The Shires	F154DET	Midlands	F701ECC	North East	G129YEV	The Shires
E229CFC	The Shires	F155DET	Midlands	F747XCS	The Shires	G130YEV	The Shires
E265WUB	North West & W	F157DET	Midlands	F792DWT	North East	G131YWC	The Shires
E268WUB	North West & W	F158DET	Midlands	F892BKK	Southern Counties	G132YWC	The Shires
E3230MG	The Shires	F188HKK	North East	F893BKK	Southern Counties	G140GOL	Yorkshire
E49WEM	North West & W	F189HKK	North East	F894BKK	Southern Counties	G141GOL	Midlands
E564BNK	The Shires	F245MTW	Southern Counties	F895BKK	Southern Counties	G149CHP	North West & W
E565BNK	The Shires	F246MTW	Southern Counties	F896DKK	Southern Counties	G154TYT	Scotland
E641VFY	North West & W	F251YTJ	North West & W	F897DKK	Southern Counties	G209HCP	North East
E642VFY	North West & W	F252YTJ	North West & W	F898DKK	Southern Counties	G210HCP	North East
E767JAR	OLST	F253YTJ	North West & W	F899DKK	Southern Counties	G212HCP	North East
E768JAR	OLST	F254YTJ	North West & W	F899GUM	Southern Counties	G214HCP	North East
E769JAR	OLST	F255YTJ	North West & W	F900DKK	Southern Counties	G218LGK	Midlands
E770JAR	OLST	F256YTJ	North West & W	F901GUM	Southern Counties	G230VWL	The Shires
E771JAR	OLST	F257YTJ	North West & W	F991UME	North West & W	G231VWL	The Shires
E772JAR	OLST	F258GWJ	Midlands	FD02UKB	Midlands	G232VWL	The Shires
E773JAR	OLST	F258YTJ	North West & W	FD02UKC	Midlands	G234VWL	The Shires
E885KYW	Southern Counties	F259YTJ	North West & W	FD02UKE	Midlands	G235VWL	The Shires
E887KYW	Southern Counties	F260YTJ	North West & W	FD02UKG	Midlands	G251SRG	North East
E888KYW	Southern Counties	F261YTJ	North West & W	FD02UKJ	Midlands	G252SRG	North East
E890KYW	Southern Counties	F262YTJ	North West & W	FD02UKK	Midlands	G253SRG	North East
E891AKN	Southern Counties	F263YTJ	North West & W	FD02UKL	Midlands	G254SRG	North East
E964JAR	OLST	F264YTJ	North West & W	FD02UKN	Midlands	G255UVK	North East
E965JAR	OLST	F266YTJ	North West & W	FD02UKO	Midlands	G256UVK	North East
E965PME	Southern Counties	F267YTJ	North West & W	FD02UKP	Midlands	G257UVK	North East
E966JAR	OLST	F268YTJ	North West & W	FD02UKR	Midlands	G258UVK	North East
E966PME	Southern Counties	F269YTJ	North West & W	FD02UKS	Midlands	G283UMJ	The Shires
EGF220B	London	F270YTJ	North West & W	FD02UKT	Midlands	G286UMJ	The Shires
EWW541Y	Yorkshire	F280AWW	North West & W	FD02UKU	Midlands	G287UMJ	The Shires
EWW542Y	Yorkshire	F281AWW	Midlands	FD52GGO	Midlands	G288UMJ	The Shires
EWW544Y	The Shires	F284AWW	Midlands	FD52GGP	Midlands	G290UMJ	The Shires
EWX528Y	Yorkshire	F301AWW	North West & W	FD52GGU	Midlands	G291UMJ	The Shires
EWX530Y	Yorkshire	F402PUR	The Shires	FD52GGV	Midlands	G292UMJ	The Shires
F27JRC	Midlands	F404PUR	The Shires	FE51WSU	Midlands	G293UMJ	The Shires
F28JRC	Midlands	F406DUG	Midlands	FE51WSV	Midlands	G294UMJ	The Shires
F33ENF	Midlands	F406DUG	Midlands	FE51YWH	Midlands	G301DPA	Midlands
F34ENF	Midlands	F425UVW	The Shires	FE51YWJ	Midlands	G302DPA	Midlands
F36ENF	Midlands	F455BKF	North West & W	FE51YWK	Midlands	G303DPA	Midlands
F39ENF	Midlands	F457BKF	North West & W	FE51YWL	Midlands	G304DPA	Midlands
F40ENF	Midlands	F459BKF	North West & W	FE51YWM	Midlands	G305DPA	Midlands
F45ENF	Southern Counties	F467UVW	The Shires	FIL3451	Midlands	G306DPA	Midlands
F46ENF	Southern Counties	F506OYW	The Shires	FJ04PFX	Midlands	G307DPA	Midlands
F47ENF	Southern Counties	F571SMG	Southern Counties	FK52MML	Midlands	G308DPA	Midlands
F48ENF	Southern Counties	F572SMG	Southern Counties	FKM866V	The Shires	G309DPA	Midlands
F51ENF	Midlands	F573SMG	Southern Counties	FL52MML	Midlands	G310DPA	Midlands
F61PRE	North West & W	F574SMG	Southern Counties	FN04AFJ	Midlands	G319NNW	North West & W
F96PRE	North West & W	F575SMG	Southern Counties	FN52XBG	Midlands	G322NNW	Yorkshire
F97PRE	North West & W	F576SMG	Southern Counties	G21HHG	North East	G324NUM	Midlands
F104TML	North West & W	F577SMG	Southern Counties	G34HKY	Midlands	G324NWW	North West & W

Reg	Region	Reg	Region	Reg	Region	Reg	Region
G327NUM	North West & W	G539VBB	London	G648CHF	Southern Counties	GK52YUX	Southern Counties
G329NUM	North West & W	G540VBB	London	G648UPP	The Shires	GK52YUY	Southern Counties
G330NUM	Yorkshire	G541VBB	London	G649UPP	The Shires	GK52YVA	Southern Counties
G331NUM	Yorkshire	G542VBB	London	G650EKA	North West & W	GK52YVB	Southern Counties
G332NUM	Yorkshire	G543VBB	London	G650UPP	The Shires	GK52YVC	Southern Counties
G381EKA	Midlands	G544VDB	London	G651EKA	North West & W	GK52YVD	Southern Counties
G382EKA	Midlands	G545VBB	London	G651UPP	The Shires	GK52YVF	Southern Counties
G383EKA	Midlands	G546VBB	London	G652EKA	North West & W	GK52YVF	Southern Counties
G384EKA	Midlands	G547VBB	London	G652UPP	The Shires	GK52YVG	Southern Counties
G385EKA	Midlands	G548VBB	London	G653EKA	North West & W	GK52YVJ	Southern Counties
G386EKA	Midlands	G549VBB	London	G653UPP	The Shires	GK52YVL	Southern Counties
G387EKA	Midlands	G550VBB	London	G654UPP	The Shires	GK53AOA	Southern Counties
G388EKA	Midlands	G551VBB	London	G655UPP	The Shires	GK53AOB	Southern Counties
G38HKY	Midlands	G552SGT	The Shires	G656UPP	The Shires	GK53AOC	Southern Counties
G501SFT	Midlands	G552VBB	London	G657UPP	The Shires	GK53AOD	Southern Counties
G502SFT	Midlands	G553VBB	London	G659DTJ	Southern Counties	GK53AOE	Southern Counties
G503SFT	Midlands	G554SGT	The Shires	G660DTJ	Yorkshire	GK53AOF	Southern Counties
G504SFT	Midlands	G554VBB	London	G661DTJ	North West & W	GK53AOG	Southern Counties
G505SFT	Midlands	G555VBB	London	G663FKA	Southern Counties	GK53AOH	Southern Counties
G506SFT	North West & W	G556VBB	London	G664FKA	Southern Counties	GK53AOJ	Southern Counties
G507SFT	Midlands	G560SGT	The Shires	G665FKA	Southern Counties	GK53AOL	Southern Counties
G508EAJ	North East	G570SGT	The Shires	G70PKR	Southern Counties	GK53AON	Southern Counties
G508SFT	North West & W	G612BPH	Yorkshire	G711LKW	Midlands	GK53AOO	Southern Counties
G509EAJ	North East	G613BPH	Southern Counties	G714LKW	Midlands	GK53AOP	Southern Counties
G509SFT	North West & W	G614BPH	Southern Counties	G754UYT	North West & W	GK53AOR	Southern Counties
G510EAJ	North East	G615BPH	Southern Counties	G755UYT	North West & W	GK53AOT	Southern Counties
G510SFT	Midlands	G616BPH	Southern Counties	G756UYT	North East	GK53AOU	Southern Counties
G511EAJ	Scotland	G617BPH	Southern Counties	G757UYT	North East	GK53AOV	Southern Counties
G511SFT	Midlands	G618BPH	Yorkshire	G758UYT	North West & W	GK53AOW	Southern Counties
G512EAJ	North East	G619BPH	Yorkshire	G759UYT	North West & W	GK53AOX	Southern Counties
G512SFT	North West & W	G620BPH	Yorkshire	G760UYT	North East	GK53AOY	Southern Counties
G513SFT	North West & W	G621YMG	The Shires	G761UYT	North East	GK53AOZ	Southern Counties
G514VBB	London	G622BPH	Yorkshire	G762UYT	North East	GKA449L	North West & W
G515VBB	London	G624BPH	Southern Counties	G801BPG	Southern Counties	GN04UCW	Southern Counties
G516VBB	London	G625BPH	Southern Counties	G801THA	North West & W	GN04UCX	Southern Counties
G517VBB	London	G626BPH	Southern Counties	G802THA	North West & W	GN04UCY	Southern Counties
G518VBB	London	G626EKA	Southern Counties	G901SKP	Southern Counties	GN04UCZ	Southern Counties
G519VBB	London	G627BPH	Southern Counties	G902SKP	Southern Counties	GN04UDB	Southern Counties
G520VBB	London	G628EKA	Southern Counties	G903SKP	Southern Counties	GN04UDD	Southern Counties
G521VBB	London	G629BPH	Southern Counties	G904SKP	Southern Counties	GN04UDE	Southern Counties
G521WJF	North West & W	G630BPH	Southern Counties	G905SKP	Southern Counties	GN04UDG	Southern Counties
G522VBB	London	G631BPH	Southern Counties	G906TYR	London	GN04UDH	Southern Counties
G522WJF	North West & W	G632BPH	Southern Counties	G908TYR	London	GN04UDJ	Southern Counties
G523VBB	London	G633BPH	Southern Counties	G916LHA	North West & W	GN04UDK	Southern Counties
G523WJF	North West & W	G634BPH	Southern Counties	G917LHA	North West & W	GN04UDL	Southern Counties
G524VBB	London	G635BPH	Southern Counties	G918LHA	North West & W	GN04UDM	Southern Counties
G524WJF	North West & W	G636BPH	Southern Counties	G919LHA	North West & W	GN04UDP	Southern Counties
G525VBB	London	G637BPH	Yorkshire	G97VMM	The Shires	GN04UDS	Southern Counties
G525WJF	North West & W	G638BPH	Yorkshire	GEY389Y	North West & W	GN04UDT	Southern Counties
G526VBB	London	G639BPH	Yorkshire	GIL6949	Midlands	GN04UDU	Southern Counties
G527VBB	London	G640BPH	Southern Counties	GJG750D	London	GN04UDV	Southern Counties
G528VBB	London	G641BPH	Southern Counties	GK51SYY	Southern Counties	GN04UDW	Southern Counties
G529VBB	London	G641CHF	Southern Counties	GK51SYZ	Southern Counties	GN04UDX	Southern Counties
G530VBB	London	G642BPH	Southern Counties	GK51SZC	Southern Counties	GN04UDY	Southern Counties
G531VBB	London	G642CHF	Yorkshire	GK51SZD	Southern Counties	GN04UDZ	Southern Counties
G532VBB	London	G643BPH	Southern Counties	GK51SZE	Southern Counties	GN04UEA	Southern Counties
G533VBB	London	G645UPP	The Shires	GK51SZF	Southern Counties	GN04UEB	Southern Counties
G534VBB	London	G646BPH	Midlands	GK51SZG	Southern Counties	GN04UEC	Southern Counties
G535VBB	London	G646UPP	The Shires	GK51SZJ	Southern Counties	GN04UED	Southern Counties
G536VBB	London	G647BPH	Midlands	GK51SZL	Southern Counties	GN04UEE	Southern Counties
G537VBB	London	G647EKA	North West & W	GK51SZN	Southern Counties	GN04UEF	Southern Counties
G538VBB	London	G647UPP	The Shires	GK52YUW	Southern Counties	GN04UEG	Southern Counties

Reg	Location	Reg	Location	Reg	Location	Reg	Location
GNO4UEH	Southern Counties	GYE533W	OLST	H253PAJ	North East	H655GPF	Midlands
GNO4UEJ	Southern Counties	GYE537W	London	H254GEV	The Shires	H656GPF	Midlands
GNO4UEK	Southern Counties	GYE537W	London	H254PAJ	North West & W	H658GPF	Midlands
GNO4UEL	Southern Counties	GYE539W	OLST	H255GEV	The Shires	H659GPF	Midlands
GNO4UEM	Southern Counties	GYE553W	OLST	H256GEV	Southern Counties	H660GPF	North West & W
GNO4UEP	Southern Counties	GYE555W	OLST	H256YLG	Southern Counties	H661GPF	North West & W
GNO4UER	Southern Counties	GYE558W	OLST	H257GEV	Southern Counties	H662GPF	North West & W
GNO4UES	Southern Counties	GYE569W	London	H262GEV	Southern Counties	H663GPF	Midlands
GNO4UET	Southern Counties	GYE575W	London	H263GEV	Southern Counties	H664GPF	Midlands
GNO4UEU	Southern Counties	GYE586W	Southern Counties	H264GEV	Southern Counties	H665GPF	North West & W
GNO4UEV	Southern Counties	GYE591W	London	H265GEV	Southern Counties	H667GPF	North West & W
GNO4UEW	Southern Counties	GYE603W	OLST	H266CFT	North East	H668GPF	Scotland
GNO4UEX	Southern Counties	H28MJN	North West & W	H267CFT	North East	H669GPF	Midlands
GNO4UEY	Southern Counties	H31PAJ	North East	H278LEF	North West & W	H670GPF	Scotland
GNO4UEZ	Southern Counties	H32PAJ	North East	H279LEF	North West & W	H671GPF	Midlands
GNO4UFA	Southern Counties	H34PAJ	North West & W	H335TYG	Yorkshire	H672GPF	Midlands
GNO4UFB	Southern Counties	H47MJN	Southern Counties	H336TYG	Yorkshire	H674GPF	Midlands
GNO4UFC	Southern Counties	H48MJN	Southern Counties	H337TYG	Yorkshire	H675GPF	Scotland
GNO4UFD	Southern Counties	H49MJN	Southern Counties	H338TYG	Yorkshire	H676GPF	Scotland
GNO4UFE	Southern Counties	H73DVM	Midlands	H338UWT	Yorkshire	H677GPF	Scotland
GNO4UFG	Southern Counties	H74DVM	Midlands	H339UWT	Yorkshire	H679GPF	North West & W
GNO4UFH	Southern Counties	H76DVM	Midlands	H341UWT	Yorkshire	H680GPF	Midlands
GNO4UFJ	Southern Counties	H78DVM	North West & W	H342UWT	Yorkshire	H681GPF	Scotland
GNO4UFK	Southern Counties	H79DVM	North West & W	H343UWT	Yorkshire	H682GPF	Midlands
GNO4UFL	Southern Counties	H81DVM	Midlands	H343UWX	Yorkshire	H684GPF	·Midlands
GNO4UFM	Southern Counties	H82DVM	Midlands	H344UWX	Yorkshire	H733HWK	North West & W
GNO4UFP	Southern Counties	H83DVM	Midlands	H345UWX	Yorkshire	H755WWW	Yorkshire
GNO4UFR	Southern Counties	H84DVM	Midlands	H346UWX	Yorkshire	H756WWW	Yorkshire
GNO4UFS	Southern Counties	H85DVM	North West & W	H347UWX	Yorkshire	H757WWW	Yorkshire
GNO4UFT	Southern Counties	H86DVM	North West & W	H350PNO	The Shires	H765EKJ	Southern Counties
GNO4UFU	Southern Counties	H87DVM	North West & W	H355WWX	Yorkshire	H766EKJ	Southern Counties
GNO4UFV	Southern Counties	H91MOB	Midlands	H356WWX	Yorkshire	H767EKJ	Southern Counties
GNO4UFW	Southern Counties	H101GEV	North West & W	H357WWX	Yorkshire	H768EKJ	Southern Counties
GNO4UFX	Southern Counties	H102GEV	North West & W	H358WWY	Yorkshire	H769EKJ	Southern Counties
GNO4UFY	Southern Counties	H103GEV	North West & W	H359WWY	Yorkshire	H770EKJ	Southern Counties
GNO4UFZ	Southern Counties	H104GEV	North West & W	H367XGC	The Shires	H803AHA	North West & W
GNO4UGA	Southern Counties	H105GEV	North West & W	H368XGC	The Shires	H803RWJ	Midlands
GNO4UGB	Southern Counties	H106GEV	North West & W	H369XGC	The Shires	H804AHA	North West & W
GNO4UGC	Southern Counties	H106RWT	Yorkshire	H370XGC	The Shires	H804RWJ	Midlands
GNO4UGD	Southern Counties	H107GEV	North West & W	H393WWY	Yorkshire	H805AHA	North West & W
GNO4UGE	Southern Counties	H108GEV	North West & W	H407ERO	The Shires	H805RWJ	Midlands
GNO4UGF	Southern Counties	H108RWT	Yorkshire	H408ERO	The Shires	H806AHA	North West & W
GNO4UGG	Southern Counties	H109GEV	North West & W	H408YMA	North West & W	H814EKJ	Southern Counties
GSU347	Scotland	H110GEV	North West & W	H409ERO	The Shires	H815EKJ	Southern Counties
GTO301V	Midlands	H112GEV	North West & W	H410ERO	The Shires	H816EKJ	Southern Counties
GYE346W	OLST	H113GEV	North West & W	H459UGO	Midlands	H845AHS	The Shires
GYE351W	OLST	H114GEV	North West & W	H460WWY	Yorkshire	H846AHS	Southern Counties
GYE353W	OLST	H115GEV	North West & W	H470UGO	Midlands	H851NOC	North West & W
GYE365W	North West & W	H130LPU	North West & W	H501GHA	Midlands	H878LOX	Yorkshire
GYE389W	OLST	H192JNF	North West & W	H512YCX	Yorkshire	H881BGN	The Shires
GYE396W	North East	H196GRO	The Shires	H567MPD	The Shires	H912XYT	North East
GYE399W	OLST	H197GRO	The Shires	H575DVM	Midlands	H913XYT	Scotland
GYE456W	North West & W ·	H199AOD	The Shires	H577DVM	Midlands	H914XYT	Midlands
GYE469W	London	H199GRO	The Shires	H580DVM	Midlands	H915XYT	Scotland
GYE495W	OLST	H202GRO	The Shires	H588DVM	North West & W	H916XYT	Scotland
GYE500W	OLST	H203GRO	The Shires	H616UWR	The Shires	H917XYT	North East
GYE507W	Scotland	H242MUK	Scotland	H649GPF	Midlands	H918XYT	Midlands
GYE509W	OLST	H244MUK	Scotland	H650GPF	Midlands	H919XYT	Midlands
GYE510W	Scotland	H245MUK	The Shires	H651GPF	Midlands	H920XYT	Scotland
GYE515W	North East	H251GEV	Southern Counties	H652GPF	Midlands	H921XYT	Scotland
GYE525W	OLST	H252GEV	Southern Counties	H653GPF	Midlands	H922LOX	The Shires
GYE530W	OLST	H253GEV	Southern Counties	H654GPF	Midlands	H922XYT	North East

H923LOX	Southern Counties	J347BSH	OLST	J929CYL	North East	JJD569D	London
H923XYT	North East	J348BSH	OLST	J930CYL	North East	JJD571D	London
H925LOX	The Shires	J349BSH	OLST	J931CYL	North East	JJD572D	London
H925XYT	North East	J350BSH	London	JDZ2353	The Shires	JJD573D	London
H926LOX	The Shires	J351BSH	London	JHK495N	The Shires	JJD574D	London
HIL2148	Scotland	J352BSH	London	JIL5367	Midlands	JJD577D	London
HIL3652	Midlands	J353BSH	London	JJD366D	London	JJD582D	London
HIL7595	The Shires	J354BSH	London	JJD370D	London	JJD586D	London
IIL7269	OLST	J362YWX	Yorkshire	JJD372D	London	JJD588D	London
J3SLT	North West & W	J363YWX	Yorkshire	JJD373D	London	JJD589D	London
J6SLT	North West & W	J364YWX	Yorkshire	JJD375D	London	JJD591D	London
J7SLT	North West & W	J365YWX	Yorkshire	JJD380D	London	JJD595D	London
J8SLT	North West & W	J366YWX	Yorkshire	JJD382D	London	JJD597D	London
J9SLT	North West & W	J367YWX	Yorkshire	JJD383D	London	JJD598D	London
J25UNY	Southern Counties	J368YWX	Yorkshire	JJD386D	London	JTL804V	North West & W
J26UNY	The Shires	J369YWX	Yorkshire	JJD387D	London	K27EWC	North West & W
J27UNY	Southern Counties	J370YWX	Yorkshire	JJD391D	London	K36XNE	Southern Counties
J31SFA	Midlands	J371AWT	Yorkshire	JJD394D	London	K37XNE	Southern Counties
J32SFA	Midlands	J371YWX	Yorkshire	JJD401D	London	K38YVM	Southern Counties
J34SRF	Midlands	J372AWT	Yorkshire	JJD406D	London	K101OHF	North West & W
J36GCX	Southern Counties	J373AWT	Yorkshire	JJD407D	London	K102OHF	North West & W
J154NKN	Southern Counties	J374AWT	Yorkshire	JJD408D	London	K103OHF	North West & W
J220HGY	Yorkshire	J375AWT	Yorkshire	JJD409D	London	K104OHF	North West & W
J221HGY	Yorkshire	J376AWT	Yorkshire	JJD416D	London	K105OHF	North West & W
J23GCX	Yorkshire	J377AWT	Yorkshire	JJD418D	London	K106OHF	North West & W
J307WHJ	Southern Counties	J379BWU	Yorkshire	JJD434D	London	K107OHF	North West & W
J310WHJ	Southern Counties	J380BWU	Yorkshire	JJD452D	London	K108OHF	North West & W
J311WHJ	North West & W	J381BWU	Yorkshire	JJD457D	London	K124TCP	Southern Counties
J312WHJ	North West & W	J382BWU	Yorkshire	JJD468D	London	K130TCP	North West & W
J313WHJ	North West & W	J402XVX	The Shires	JJD477D	London	K131TCP	North West & W
J314XVX	North West & W	J403XVX	The Shires	JJD483D	London	K132TCP	North West & W
J315BSH	London	J404XVX	The Shires	JJD491D	London	K133TCP	North West & W
J315XVX	North West & W	J413NCP	North East	JJD492D	London	K140RYS	North East
J316BSH	London	J414NCP	North East	JJD494D	London	K211UHA	Midlands
J316XVX	Southern Counties	J433BSH	OLST	JJD503D	London	K212UHA	Midlands
J317BSH	London	J463MKL	Southern Counties	JJD504D	London	K213UHA	Midlands
J317XVX	Southern Counties	J465MKL	Southern Counties	JJD505D	London	K214UHA	Midlands
J318BSH	London	J465UFS	The Shires	JJD510D	London	K215UHA	Midlands
J319BSH	London	J466OKP	Southern Counties	JJD512D	London	K216UHA	Midlands
J320BSH	OLST	J467OKP	Yorkshire	JJD514D	London	K217UHA	Midlands
J321BSH	OLST	J468OKP	Southern Counties	JJD518D	London	K218UHA	Midlands
J322BSH	London	J469OKP	Southern Counties	JJD521D	London	K219UHA	Midlands
J323BSH	London	J470SKO	Southern Counties	JJD523D	London	K318CVX	The Shires
J324BSH	London	J471SKO	Southern Counties	JJD524D	London	K319CVX	The Shires
J327VAW	Midlands	J556GTP	North West & W	JJD525D	London	K320CVX	Southern Counties
J328BSH	London	J56GCX	Southern Counties	JJD526D	London	K321CVX	The Shires
J328VAW	North West & W	J620UHN	North East	JJD527D	London	K322CVX	The Shires
J331BSH	London	J64BJN	The Shires	JJD528D	London	K323CVX	Southern Counties
J332BSH	London	J651UHN	North East	JJD531D	London	K390RLR	The Shires
J334BSH	London	J652UHN	North East	JJD533D	London	K401HWW	Yorkshire
J335BSH	OLST	J653UHN	North East	JJD534D	London	K402HWW	Yorkshire
J336BSH	OLST	J654UHN	North West & W	JJD536D	London	K403HWW	Yorkshire
J337BSH	London	J655UHN	North West & W	JJD538D	London	K404HWW	Yorkshire
J338BSH	OLST	J656UHN	North East	JJD544D	London	K405FHJ	The Shires
J339BSH	London	J657UHN	North East	JJD545D	London	K405HWX	Yorkshire
J340BSH	London	J658UHN	North East	JJD546D	London	K406FHJ	The Shires
J341BSH	OLST	J65BJN	The Shires	JJD548D	London	K407FHJ	The Shires
J342BSH	OLST	J701NHA	North West & W	JJD549D	London	K408BHN	North East
J343BSH	OLST	J802KHD	Yorkshire	JJD552D	London	K408FHJ	The Shires
J344BSH	OLST	J866UPY	North East	JJD562D	London	K409BHN	North East
J345BSH	OLST	J926CYL	Southern Counties	JJD563D	London	K409FHJ	The Shires
J346BSH	London	J927CYL	Southern Counties	JJD567D	London	K410BHN	North East

Reg	Region	Reg	Region	Reg	Region	Reg	Region
K410FHJ	The Shires	K908SKR	Southern Counties	KL52CXF	The Shires	L35PNN	Midlands
K411BHN	North East	K909SKR	Southern Counties	KL52CXG	The Shires	L36PNN	Midlands
K411FHJ	The Shires	K910SKR	Southern Counties	KL52CXH	The Shires	L37PNN	Midlands
K412BHN	North East	K911OEM	North West & W	KL52CXJ	The Shires	L38PNN	Midlands
K412FHJ	The Shires	K946OEM	North West & W	KL52CXK	The Shires	L43MEH	The Shires
K413BHN	North East	K946SGG	Scotland	KL52CXM	The Shires	L94HRF	Midlands
K413FHJ	The Shires	K947SGG	Scotland	KL52CXN	The Shires	L95HRF	Midlands
K414BHN	North East	K955PBG	North West & W	KL52CXO	The Shires	L100SBS	North East
K414FHJ	The Shires	KC51NFO	Southern Counties	KL52CXP	The Shires	L102MEH	North East
K415BHN	North East	KC51PUX	Southern Counties	KL52CXR	The Shires	L112YVK	Southern Counties
K416BHN	North East	KE03OUK	The Shires	KL52CXS	The Shires	L113YVK	Southern Counties
K417BHN	North East	KE03OUL	The Shires	KS51KOE	The Shires	L114YVK	Yorkshire
K447XPA	The Shires	KE03OUM	The Shires	KS51KOH	The Shires	L115YVK	North West & W
K448XPA	The Shires	KE03OUN	The Shires	KS51KPG	The Shires	L116YVK	North West & W
K504BHN	North East	KE03OUP	The Shires	KYO609X	OLST	L117YVK	London
K505BHN	North East	KE03OUS	The Shires	KYO610X	Scotland	L117YVK	North West & W
K506BHN	North East	KE03OUU	The Shires	KYO615X	Southern Counties	L118YVK	The Shires
K507BHN	North East	KE04CZF	The Shires	KYO617X	London	L119YVK	The Shires
K508BHN	North East	KE04CZG	The Shires	KYV646X	North East	L120YVK	North West & W
K509BHN	North East	KE04CZH	The Shires	KYV646X	OLST	L121YVK	North West & W
K510BHN	North East	KE51PSZ	The Shires	KYV652X	London	L122YVK	North West & W
K510RJX	North West & W	KE51PTO	The Shires	KYV659X	OLST	L123YVK	North West & W
K511BHN	North East	KE51PTU	The Shires	KYV663X	North West & W	L124YVK	The Shires
K512BHN	North East	KE51PTX	The Shires	KYV664X	Scotland	L125YVK	North West & W
K513BHN	North East	KE51PTY	Southern Counties	KYV665X	London	L126YVK	North West & W
K514BHN	North East	KE51PTZ	Southern Counties	KYV671X	North East	L127YVK	Yorkshire
K515BHN	North East	KE51PUA	Southern Counties	KYV672X	OLST	L128YVK	Yorkshire
K516BHN	North East	KE51PUF	Southern Counties	KYV682X	OLST	L129YVK	Yorkshire
K517BHN	North East	KE51PUH	Southern Counties	KYV689X	North West & W	L130YVK	Yorkshire
K518BHN	North East	KE51PUJ	Southern Counties	KYV699X	London	L131YVK	Yorkshire
K538ORH	Scotland	KE51PUK	Southern Counties	KYV707X	OLST	L132YVK	Southern Counties
K539ORH	Scotland	KE51PUO	Southern Counties	KYV710X	OLST	L133HVS	The Shires
K540ORH	Scotland	KE51PUU	Southern Counties	KYV715X	London	L133YVK	Southern Counties
K541ORH	Scotland	KE51PUV	Southern Counties	KYV718X	London	L134YVK	Southern Counties
K542ORH	Midlands	KE51PUY	Southern Counties	KYV721X	London	L135YVK	Southern Counties
K543ORH	Midlands	KE51PVA	Southern Counties	KYV724X	OLST	L136YVK	Yorkshire
K544ORH	Midlands	KE51PVF	The Shires	KYV729X	OLST	L137YVK	Yorkshire
K545ORH	Midlands	KE51PVK	The Shires	KYV732X	London	L138YVK	Southern Counties
K547ORH	Midlands	KE51PVZ	The Shires	KYV733X	London	L139YVK	Midlands
K548ORH	Midlands	KE53NEU	The Shires	KYV734X	Scotland	L140YVK	Yorkshire
K549ORH	Midlands	KE53NFA	The Shires	KYV746X	OLST	L141YVK	Yorkshire
K550ORH	Midlands	KE53NFC	The Shires	KYV747X	London	L142YVK	Midlands
K551ORH	Midlands	KGH858A	London	KYV748X	OLST	L143YVK	Southern Counties
K552ORH	Midlands	KGH975A	London	KYV751X	Scotland	L144YVK	Midlands
K601HWR	Yorkshire	KGJ118A	London	KYV752X	London	L145YVK	Southern Counties
K668PLH	The Shires	KGJ142A	London	KYV754X	London	L146YVK	Yorkshire
K726HUG	North East	KL52CWJ	The Shires	KYV762X	London	L148WAG	North West & W
K73SRG	North West & W	KL52CWK	The Shires	KYV765X	London	L148YVK	Southern Counties
K74SRG	North West & W	KL52CWN	The Shires	KYV770X	London	L149WAG	North West & W
K75SRG	North West & W	KL52CWO	The Shires	KYV772X	London	L149YVK	Yorkshire
K760JVX	The Shires	KL52CWP	The Shires	KYV773X	The Shires	L150SBG	North West & W
K761JVX	The Shires	KL52CWR	The Shires	KYV777X	London	L150WAG	North West & W
K762JVX	The Shires	KL52CWT	The Shires	KYV778X	London	L150YVK	Southern Counties
K801HWW	Yorkshire	KL52CWU	The Shires	KYV787X	London	L151SBG	North West & W
K802HWW	Yorkshire	KL52CWV	The Shires	KYV798X	London	L151WAG	London
K803HWW	Yorkshire	KL52CWW	The Shires	KYV798X	London	L151YVK	North West & W
K804HWW	Yorkshire	KL52CWZ	The Shires	KYV799X	OLST	L152SBG	North West & W
K805HWX	Yorkshire	KL52CXA	The Shires	L1SLT	North West & W	L152WAG	London
K817NKH	North West & W	KL52CXB	The Shires	L2SLT	North West & W	L152YVK	Yorkshire
K877UDB	North West & W	KL52CXC	The Shires	L11SLT	North West & W	L153UKB	North West & W
K906SKR	Southern Counties	KL52CXD	The Shires	L25LSX	Scotland	L153WAG	London
K907SKR	Southern Counties	KL52CXE	The Shires	L34PNN	Midlands	L153YVK	Southern Counties

Reg	Region	Reg	Region	Reg	Region	Reg	Region
L154UKB	North West & W	L234TKA	North West & W	L424CPB	The Shires	L530FHN	North East
L154WAG	London	L235TKA	North West & W	L437CPJ	Southern Counties	L531FHN	North East
L154YVK	Southern Counties	L236TKA	North West & W	L460NMJ	The Shires	L532EHD	North East
L155UKB	North West & W	L237TKA	North West & W	L500BUS	The Shires	L532FHN	North East
L155WAG	London	L238TKA	North West & W	L500DKT	Southern Counties	L533EHD	North East
L155YVK	Southern Counties	L239TKA	North West & W	L501TKA	North West & W	L533FHN	North East
L156UKB	North West & W	L240TKA	North West & W	L502DNX	Midlands	L534FHN	North East
L156WAG	London	L241TKA	North West & W	L502CPJ	Southern Counties	L535FHN	North East
L156YVK	Southern Counties	L242TKA	North West & W	L502TKA	North West & W	L536FHN	North East
L157WAG	London	L243TKA	North West & W	L503BNX	Midlands	L537FHN	North East
L157YVK	Yorkshire	L244TKA	North West & W	L503HKM	Southern Counties	L539FHN	North East
L158BFT	Southern Counties	L247WAG	North West & W	L503TKA	North West & W	L540FHN	North East
L158WAG	London	L271FVN	North East	L504BNX	Midlands	L541FHN	North East
L159BFT	Yorkshire	L272FVN	North East	L504TKA	North West & W	L542FHN	North East
L159GYL	North East	L273FVN	North East	L505CPJ	Southern Counties	L543FHN	North East
L160GYL	North East	L274FVN	North East	L505CPJ	Southern Counties	L544GHN	North East
L161GYL	North East	L275FVN	North East	L505TKA	North West & W	L545GHN	North East
L200BUS	The Shires	L300BUS	The Shires	L506BNX	Midlands	L546GHN	North East
L201TKA	North West & W	L300SBS	Midlands	L506CPJ	Southern Counties	L547GHN	North East
L201YCU	Southern Counties	L301NFA	Midlands	L506TKA	North West & W	L548GHN	North East
L202TKA	North West & W	L301TEM	North West & W	L507BNX	Midlands	L549GHN	North East
L202YCU	Southern Counties	L302NFA	Midlands	L507TKA	North West & W	L550GHN	North East
L203TKA	North West & W	L302TEM	North West & W	L508BNX	Midlands	L551GHN	North East
L203YCU	Southern Counties	L303NFA	Midlands	L508CPJ	Southern Counties	L557YCU	Southern Counties
L204TKA	North West & W	L303TEM	North West & W	L508TKA	North West & W	L558YCU	Southern Counties
L204YCU	Southern Counties	L304NFA	Midlands	L509BNX	Midlands	L559YCU	Southern Counties
L205TKA	North West & W	L305HPP	The Shires	L509CPJ	Southern Counties	L561YCU	Southern Counties
L205YCU	Southern Counties	L305NFA	Midlands	L509TKA	North West & W	L562YCU	Southern Counties
L206TKA	North West & W	L306HPP	The Shires	L510BNX	Midlands	L563YCU	Southern Counties
L206YCU	Southern Counties	L307HPP	The Shires	L510CPJ	Southern Counties	L564YCU	Southern Counties
L207YCU	Southern Counties	L308HPP	The Shires	L510TKA	North West & W	L565YCU	Southern Counties
L207YCU	Southern Counties	L309HPP	The Shires	L511BNX	Midlands	L588JSG	North West & W
L208TKA	North West & W	L310HPP	The Shires	L511CPJ	Southern Counties	L600BUS	Southern Counties
L209TKA	North West & W	L311HPP	The Shires	L511TKA	North West & W	L601EKM	Southern Counties
L210TKA	North West & W	L312HPP	The Shires	L512BNX	Midlands	L602EKM	Southern Counties
L210YCU	Southern Counties	L313HPP	The Shires	L512CPJ	Southern Counties	L603EKM	Southern Counties
L211SBG	North West & W	L314HPP	The Shires	L512TKA	North West & W	L604EKM	Southern Counties
L211TKA	North West & W	L315HPP	The Shires	L513BNX	Midlands	L604FHN	North East
L211YCU	Southern Counties	L316HPP	The Shires	L513CPJ	Southern Counties	L605BNX	Midlands
L212TKA	North West & W	L400BUS	The Shires	L513TKA	North West & W	L605EKM	Southern Counties
L212YCU	Southern Counties	L402TKB	North West & W	L514BNX	Midlands	L606EKM	Southern Counties
L213TKA	North West & W	L403TKB	North West & W	L514CPJ	Southern Counties	L607EKM	Southern Counties
L214TKA	North West & W	L404TKB	North West & W	L515BNX	Midlands	L608EKM	Southern Counties
L215TKA	North West & W	L405TKB	North West & W	L515CPJ	Southern Counties	L609EKM	Southern Counties
L216TKA	North West & W	L406NUA	Yorkshire	L516BNX	Midlands	L610EKM	Southern Counties
L217TKA	North West & W	L406TKB	North West & W	L516CPJ	Southern Counties	L618BNX	North West & W
L218TKA	North West & W	L407NUA	Yorkshire	L517BNX	Midlands	L620BNX	Midlands
L219TKA	North West & W	L407TKB	North West & W	L519BNX	Midlands	L700BUS	North East
L220TKA	North West & W	L408NUA	Yorkshire	L519FHN	North East	L766DPE	Midlands
L221TKA	North West & W	L408TKB	North West & W	L520FHN	North East	L773RWW	Midlands
L222TKA	North West & W	L409NUA	Yorkshire	L521BNX	Midlands	L800BUS	Southern Counties
L223TKA	North West & W	L409TKB	North West & W	L521FHN	North East	L806NNW	Yorkshire
L224TKA	North West & W	L410TKB	North West & W	L522BNX	Midlands	L807NNW	Yorkshire
L225TKA	North West & W	L411UFY	North West & W	L522FHN	North East	L808NNW	Yorkshire
L226TKA	North West & W	L412UFY	North West & W	L523BNX	Midlands	L809NNW	Yorkshire
L227TKA	North West & W	L413TKB	North West & W	L523FHN	North East	L810NNW	Yorkshire
L228TKA	North West & W	L415NHJ	The Shires	L524FHN	North East	L811NNW	Yorkshire
L229TKA	North West & W	L418FHN	North East	L525FHN	North East	L812NNW	Yorkshire
L230TKA	North West & W	L419FHN	North East	L526FHN	North East	L813NNW	Yorkshire
L231TKA	North West & W	L420FHN	North East	L527FHN	North East	L814NNW	Yorkshire
L232TKA	North West & W	L421FHN	North East	L528FHN	North East	L815NNW	Yorkshire
L233TKA	North West & W	L422FHN	North East	L529FHN	North East	L816NWY	Yorkshire

L817NWY	Yorkshire	LF02POH	London	LF52UPT	London	LG03MDE	London
L818NWY	Yorkshire	LF02PRZ	London	LF52UPV	London	LG03MDF	London
L819NWY	Yorkshire	LF02PSO	London	LF52UPW	London	LG03MDK	London
L820NWY	Yorkshire	LF02PSU	London	LF52UPX	London	LG03MDN	London
L821NWY	Yorkshire	LF02PSX	London	LF52UPY	London	LG03MDU	London
L822NWY	Yorkshire	LF02PSY	London	LF52UPZ	London	LG03MEV	London
L823NWY	Yorkshire	LF02PSZ	London	LF52URA	London	LG03MFA	London
L824NWY	Yorkshire	LF02PTO	London	LF52URB	London	LG03MFE	London
L825NWY	Yorkshire	LF02PTU	London	LF52URC	London	LG03MFF	London
L826NYG	Yorkshire	LF02PTX	London	LF52URD	London	LG03MFK	London
L827NYG	Yorkshire	LF02PTY	London	LF52URE	London	LG03MLL	London
L828NYG	Yorkshire	LF02PTZ	London	LF52URG	London	LG03MLN	London
L829NYG	Yorkshire	LF02PVA	Southern Counties	LF52URH	London	LG03MLV	London
L830NYG	Yorkshire	LF02PVE	London	LF52URJ	London	LG03MMU	London
L855WRG	North East	LF02PVJ	London	LF52URK	London	LG03MMV	London
L922LJO	The Shires	LF02PVK	London	LF52URL	London	LG03MMX	London
L923LJO	The Shires	LF02PVL	London	LF52URM	London	LG03MOA	London
L934GYL	North West & W	LF02PVN	London	LF52URN	London	LG03MOF	London
L935GYL	North West & W	LF02PVO	London	LF52URO	London	LG03MOV	London
L936GYL	North West & W	LF52UNV	London	LF52URP	London	LG03MPE	London
L937GYL	North West & W	LF52UNW	London	LF52URR	London	LG03MPF	London
L938GYL	North West & W	LF52UNX	London	LF52URS	London	LG03MPU	London
L939GYL	North West & W	LF52UNY	London	LF52URT	London	LG03MPV	London
L940GYL	North West & W	LF52UNZ	London	LF52URU	London	LG03MPX	London
L941GYL	North West & W	LF52UOA	London	LF52URV	London	LG03MPY	London
L970VGE	Scotland	LF52UOB	London	LF52URW	London	LG03MPZ	London
LAZ5785	Scotland	LF52UOC	London	LF52URX	London	LG03MRU	London
LDS279A	London	LF52UOD	London	LF52URY	London	LG03MRV	London
LDS402A	London	LF52UOE	London	LF52URZ	London	LG03MRX	London
LF02PKA	London	LF52UOG	London	LF52USB	London	LG03MRY	London
LF02PKC	London	LF52UOH	London	LF52USC	London	LG03MSU	London
LF02PKD	London	LF52UOJ	London	LF52USD	London	LG03MSV	London
LF02PKE	London	LF52UOK	London	LF52USE	London	LG03MSX	London
LF02PKJ	London	LF52UOL	London	LF52USG	London	LG52DAA	London
LF02PKO	London	LF52UOM	London	LF52USH	London	LG52DAO	London
LF02PKU	London	LF52UON	London	LF52USJ	London	LG52DAU	London
LF02PKV	London	LF52UOO	London	LF52USL	London	LG52DBO	London
LF02PKX	London	LF52UOP	London	LF52USM	London	LG52DBU	London
LF02PKY	London	LF52UOR	London	LF52USN	London	LG52DBV	London
LF02PKZ	London	LF52UOS	London	LF52USO	London	LG52DBY	London
LF02PLJ	London	LF52UOT	London	LF52USS	London	LG52DBZ	London
LF02PLN	London	LF52UOU	London	LF52UST	London	LG52DCE	London
LF02PLO	London	LF52UOV	London	LF52USU	London	LG52DCF	London
LF02PLU	London	LF52UOW	London	LF52USV	London	LG52DCO	London
LF02PLV	London	LF52UOX	London	LF52USW	London	LG52DCU	London
LF02PLX	London	LF52UOY	London	LF52USX	London	LG52DCV	London
LF02PLZ	London	LF52UPA	London	LF52USY	London	LG52DCX	London
LF02PMO	London	LF52UPB	London	LF52USZ	London	LG52DCY	London
LF02PMV	London	LF52UPC	London	LF52UTA	London	LG52DCZ	London
LF02PMX	London	LF52UPD	London	LF52UTB	London	LG52DDA	London
LF02PMY	London	LF52UPE	London	LF52UTC	London	LG52DDE	London
LF02PNE	London	LF52UPG	London	LF52UTE	London	LG52DDF	London
LF02PNJ	London	LF52UPH	London	LF52UTG	London	LG52DDJ	London
LF02PNK	London	LF52UPJ	London	LF52UTH	London	LG52DDK	London
LF02PNL	London	LF52UPK	London	LF52UTJ	London	LG52DDL	London
LF02PNN	London	LF52UPL	London	LF52UTL	London	LJ03MDV	London
LF02PNO	London	LF52UPM	London	LF52UTM	London	LJ03MDX	London
LF02PNU	London	LF52UPN	London	LG03MBF	London	LJ03MDY	London
LF02PNV	London	LF52UPO	London	LG03MBU	London	LJ03MDZ	London
LF02PNX	London	LF52UPP	London	LG03MBV	London	LJ03MEU	London
LF02PNY	London	LF52UPR	London	LG03MBX	London	LJ03MFN	London
LF02POA	London	LF52UPS	London	LG03MBY	London	LJ03MFP	London

LJ03MFU	London	LJ03MUA	London	LJ03MYX	London	LJ04YWV	London
LJ03MFV	London	LJ03MUB	London	LJ03MYY	London	LJ04YWW	London
LJ03MFX	London	LJ03MUW	London	LJ03MYZ	London	LJ04YWX	London
LJ03MFY	London	LJ03MUY	London	LJ03MZD	London	LJ04YWY	London
LJ03MFZ	London	LJ03MVC	London	LJ03MZE	London	LJ04YWZ	London
LJ03MGE	London	LJ03MVD	London	LJ03MZF	London	LJ04YXA	London
LJ03MGU	London	LJ03MVE	London	LJ03MZG	London	LJ04YXB	London
LJ03MGV	London	LJ03MVF	London	LJ03MZL	London	LJ51DAA	London
LJ03MGX	London	LJ03MVG	London	LJ04LDA	London	LJ51DAO	London
LJ03MGY	London	LJ03MVT	London	LJ04LDC	London	LJ51DAU	London
LJ03MGZ	London	LJ03MVU	London	LJ04LDD	London	LJ51DBO	London
LJ03MHA	London	LJ03MVV	London	LJ04LDE	London	LJ51DBU	London
LJ03MHE	London	LJ03MVW	London	LJ04LDF	London	LJ51DBV	London
LJ03MHF	London	LJ03MVX	London	LJ04LDK	London	LJ51DBX	London
LJ03MHK	London	LJ03MVY	London	LJ04LDL	London	LJ51DBY	London
LJ03MHL	London	LJ03MVZ	London	LJ04LDN	London	LJ51DBZ	London
LJ03MHM	London	LJ03MWA	London	LJ04LDU	London	LJ51DCE	London
LJ03MHN	London	LJ03MWC	London	LJ04LDV	London	LJ51DCF	London
LJ03MHU	London	LJ03MWD	London	LJ04LDX	London	LJ51DCO	London
LJ03MHV	London	LJ03MWE	London	LJ04LDY	London	LJ51DCU	London
LJ03MHX	London	LJ03MWF	London	LJ04LDZ	London	LJ51DCV	London
LJ03MHY	London	LJ03MWG	London	LJ04LEF	London	LJ51DCX	London
LJ03MHZ	London	LJ03MWK	London	LJ04LEU	London	LJ51DCY	London
LJ03MJE	London	LJ03MWL	London	LJ04LFA	London	LJ51DCZ	London
LJ03MJF	London	LJ03MWM	London	LJ04LFB	London	LJ51DDA	London
LJ03MJK	London	LJ03MWN	London	LJ04LFD	London	LJ51DDE	London
LJ03MJU	London	LJ03MWP	London	LJ04LFE	London	LJ51DDF	London
LJ03MJV	London	LJ03MWU	London	LJ04LFF	London	LJ51DDK	London
LJ03MJX	London	LJ03MWV	London	LJ04LFG	London	LJ51DDL	London
LJ03MJY	London	LJ03MWX	London	LJ04LFH	London	LJ51DDN	London
LJ03MKA	London	LJ03MXH	London	LJ04LFK	London	LJ51DDO	London
LJ03MKC	London	LJ03MXK	London	LJ04LFL	London	LJ51DDU	London
LJ03MKD	London	LJ03MXL	London	LJ04LFM	London	LJ51DDV	London
LJ03MKE	London	LJ03MXM	London	LJ04LFN	London	LJ51DDX	London
LJ03MKF	London	LJ03MXN	London	LJ04LFP	London	LJ51DDY	London
LJ03MKG	London	LJ03MXP	London	LJ04LFR	London	LJ51DDZ	London
LJ03MKK	London	LJ03MXR	London	LJ04LFS	London	LJ51DEU	London
LJ03MKL	London	LJ03MXS	London	LJ04LFT	London	LJ51DFA	London
LJ03MKM	London	LJ03MXT	London	LJ04LFU	London	LJ51DFC	London
LJ03MKN	London	LJ03MXU	London	LJ04LFV	London	LJ51DFD	London
LJ03MKU	London	LJ03MXV	London	LJ04LFW	London	LJ51DFE	London
LJ03MKV	London	LJ03MXW	London	LJ04LFX	London	LJ51DFF	London
LJ03MKX	London	LJ03MXX	London	LJ04LFY	London	LJ51DFG	London
LJ03MKZ	London	LJ03MXY	London	LJ04LFZ	London	LJ51DFK	London
LJ03MLE	London	LJ03MXZ	London	LJ04LGA	London	LJ51DFL	London
LJ03MLF	London	LJ03MYA	London	LJ04LGC	London	LJ51DFN	London
LJ03MLK	London	LJ03MYB	London	LJ04LGD	London	LJ51DFO	London
LJ03MLX	London	LJ03MYC	London	LJ04LGE	London	LJ51DFP	London
LJ03MLY	London	LJ03MYD	London	LJ04LGF	London	LJ51DFU	London
LJ03MLZ	London	LJ03MYF	London	LJ04LGG	London	LJ51DFV	London
LJ03MMA	London	LJ03MYG	London	LJ04LGK	London	LJ51DFX	London
LJ03MME	London	LJ03MYH	London	LJ04LGL	London	LJ51DFY	London
LJ03MMF	London	LJ03MYK	London	LJ04LGN	London	LJ51DFZ	London
LJ03MMK	London	LJ03MYL	London	LJ04LGU	London	LJ51DGE	London
LJ03MSY	London	LJ03MYM	London	LJ04LGV	London	LJ51DGF	London
LJ03MTE	London	LJ03MYN	London	LJ04LGW	London	LJ51DGO	London
LJ03MTF	London	LJ03MYP	London	LJ04LGX	London	LJ51DGU	London
LJ03MTK	London	LJ03MYR	London	LJ04LGY	London	LJ51DGV	London
LJ03MTU	London	LJ03MYS	London	LJ04YWE	London	LJ51DGX	London
LJ03MTV	London	LJ03MYT	London	LJ04YWS	London	LJ51DGY	London
LJ03MTY	London	LJ03MYU	London	LJ04YWT	London	LJ51DGZ	London
LJ03MTZ	London	LJ03MYV	London	LJ04YWU	London	LJ51DHA	London

LJ51DHC	London	LJ53BBK	London	LJ53NGZ	London	M118RMS	Scotland
LJ51DHD	London	LJ53BBN	London	LJ53NHA	London	M119RMS	Scotland
LJ51DHE	London	LJ53BBO	London	LJ53NHB	London	M120RMS	Scotland
LJ51DHF	London	LJ53BBU	London	LJ53NHC	London	M121RMS	Scotland
LJ51DHG	London	LJ53BBV	London	LJ53NHD	London	M127YCM	North West & W
LJ51DHK	London	LJ53BBX	London	LJ53NHE	London	M129YCM	North West & W
LJ51DHL	London	LJ53BBZ	London	LJ53NHF	London	M156LNC	North West & W
LJ51DHN	London	LJ53BCF	London	LJ53NHG	London	M157LNC	North West & W
LJ51DHO	London	LJ53BCK	London	LJ53NHH	London	M157WKA	North West & W
LJ51DHP	London	LJ53BCO	London	LJ53NHK	London	M158WKA	North West & W
LJ51DHV	London	LJ53BCU	London	LJ53NHL	London	M159GRY	Midlands
LJ51DHX	London	LJ53BCV	London	LJ53NHM	London	M159WKA	North West & W
LJ51DHY	London	LJ53BCX	London	LJ53NHN	London	M160GRY	Midlands
LJ51DHZ	London	LJ53BCY	London	LJ53NHO	London	M160SKR	North West & W
LJ51DJD	London	LJ53BCZ	London	LJ53NHP	London	M160WKA	North West & W
LJ51DJE	London	LJ53BDE	London	LJ53NHT	London	M161GRY	Midlands
LJ51DJF	London	LJ53BDF	London	LJ53NHU	London	M161SKR	North West & W
LJ51DJK	London	LJ53BDO	London	LJ53NHV	London	M161WKA	North West & W
LJ51DJO	London	LJ53BDU	London	LJ53NHX	London	M162GRY	Midlands
LJ51DJU	London	LJ53BDV	London	LJ53NHY	London	M162SKR	North West & W
LJ51DJV	London	LJ53BDX	London	LJ53NHZ	London	M162WKA	North West & W
LJ51DJX	London	LJ53BDY	London	LJ53NJE	London	M163GRY	Midlands
LJ51DJY	London	LJ53BDZ	London	LJ53NJF	London	M163SKR	North West & W
LJ51DJZ	London	LJ53BEO	London	LJ53NJK	London	M163WKA	North West & W
LJ51DKA	London	LJ53BEU	London	LJ53NJN	London	M164WKA	North West & W
LJ51DKD	London	LJ53BEY	London	M2SLT	North West & W	M165GRY	Midlands
LJ51DKE	London	LJ53BFA	London	M5SLT	North West & W	M165WKA	North West & W
LJ51DKF	London	LJ53BFE	London	M20MPS	Midlands	M166GRY	Midlands
LJ51DKK	London	LJ53BFF	London	M30GGY	North West & W	M166WKA	North West & W
LJ51DKL	London	LJ53BFK	London	M30MPS	Midlands	M167WKA	North West & W
LJ51DKN	London	LJ53BFL	London	M38WUR	The Shires	M168GRY	Midlands
LJ51DKO	London	LJ53BFM	London	M43WUR	The Shires	M168WKA	North West & W
LJ51DKU	London	LJ53BFN	London	M45WUR	The Shires	M169GRY	Midlands
LJ51DKV	London	LJ53BFO	London	M46WUR	The Shires	M169WKA	North West & W
LJ51DKX	London	LJ53BFP	London	M47WUR	The Shires	M170GRY	Midlands
LJ51DKY	London	LJ53BFU	London	M51AWW	Southern Counties	M170WKA	North West & W
LJ51DLD	London	LJ53BFV	London	M52AWW	Southern Counties	M171GRY	Midlands
LJ51DLF	London	LJ53BFX	London	M53AWW	Southern Counties	M171YKA	North West & W
LJ51DLK	London	LJ53BFY	London	M54AWW	Southern Counties	M172GRY	Midlands
LJ51DLN	London	LJ53BGE	London	M65FDS	Scotland	M172YKA	North West & W
LJ51DLU	London	LJ53BGF	London	M67FDS	Scotland	M173GRY	Midlands
LJ51DLV	London	LJ53BGK	London	M95EGE	Scotland	M173YKA	North West & W
LJ51DLX	London	LJ53BGO	London	M100CBB	Southern Counties	M174GRY	Midlands
LJ51DLY	London	LJ53BGU	London	M102RMS	North West & W	M174YKA	North West & W
LJ51DLZ	London	LJ53NFE	London	M103RMS	North West & W	M175GRY	Midlands
LJ51DRA	London	LJ53NFF	London	M104RMS	Scotland	M175YKA	North West & W
LJ51ORC	London	LJ53NFG	London	M105RMS	North West & W	M176GRY	Midlands
LJ51ORF	London	LJ53NFT	London	M106RMS	Scotland	M176YKA	North West & W
LJ51ORG	London	LJ53NFU	London	M107RMS	Scotland	M177GRY	Midlands
LJ51ORH	London	LJ53NFV	London	M108RMS	Scotland	M177YKA	North West & W
LJ51ORK	London	LJ53NFX	London	M109RMS	Scotland	M178GRY	Midlands
LJ51ORL	London	LJ53NFY	London	M109XKC	North West & W	M178LYP	North East
LJ51OSK	London	LJ53NFZ	London	M110RMS	Scotland	M178YKA	North West & W
LJ51OSX	London	LJ53NGE	London	M110XKC	North West & W	M179LYP	North East
LJ51OSY	London	LJ53NGF	London	M112RMS	Scotland	M179YKA	North West & W
LJ51OSZ	London	LJ53NGG	London	M112XKC	North West & W	M180LYP	North East
LJ53BAA	London	LJ53NGN	London	M113RMS	Scotland	M180YKA	North West & W
LJ53BAO	London	LJ53NGO	London	M113XKC	North West & W	M181YKA	North West & W
LJ53BAU	London	LJ53NGU	London	M114RMS	Scotland	M182YKA	North West & W
LJ53BAV	London	LJ53NGV	London	M115RMS	Scotland	M183YKA	North West & W
LJ53BBE	London	LJ53NGX	London	M116RMS	Scotland	M184YKA	North West & W
LJ53BBF	London	LJ53NGY	London	M117RMS	Scotland	M185YKA	North West & W

M186YKA	North West & W	M301YBG	North West & W	M451HPF	Southern Counties	M557WTJ	North West & W
M187YKA	North West & W	M302SAJ	North East	M452HPG	North East	M558WTJ	North West & W
M188YKA	North West & W	M302YBG	North West & W	M453HPG	North East	M559WTJ	North West & W
M189YKA	North West & W	M303SAJ	North East	M501AJC	North East	M561WTJ	North West & W
M190YKA	North West & W	M303YBG	North West & W	M501PKJ	Southern Counties	M562WTJ	North West & W
M191YKA	North West & W	M304SAJ	North East	M502AJC	North East	M563WTJ	North West & W
M192YKA	North West & W	M305SAJ	North East	M502RKO	Southern Counties	M564YEM	North West & W
M193YKA	North West & W	M322AKB	North West & W	M503AJC	North East	M565YEM	North West & W
M194YKA	North West & W	M370FTY	North East	M503VJO	The Shires	M566YEM	North West & W
M195YKA	North West & W	M370KVR	North West & W	M504AJC	North East	M567YEM	North West & W
M196YKA	North West & W	M371FTY	North East	M504VJO	The Shires	M568YEM	North West & W
M197YKA	North West & W	M371KVR	North West & W	M514WHF	North West & W	M569YEM	North West & W
M198YKA	North West & W	M372FTY	North East	M515WHF	North West & W	M570YEM	North West & W
M199YKA	North West & W	M372KVR	North West & W	M516WHF	North West & W	M571YEM	North West & W
M200CBB	Southern Counties	M373FTY	North East	M517KPA	North West & W	M572YEM	North West & W
M201YKA	North West & W	M374FTY	North East	M517WHF	North West & W	M573YEM	North West & W
M202YKA	North West & W	M375FTY	North East	M518KPA	North West & W	M574YEM	North West & W
M203YKA	North West & W	M376FTY	North East	M518WHF	North West & W	M575YEM	North West & W
M204YKA	North West & W	M377FTY	North East	M519KPA	North West & W	M611PKP	Southern Counties
M205YKA	North West & W	M401EFD	Midlands	M519WHF	North West & W	M612PKP	Southern Counties
M206YKA	North West & W	M402EFD	Midlands	M520KPA	Southern Counties	M613PKP	Southern Counties
M207YKA	North West & W	M403EFD	Midlands	M520WHF	North West & W	M614PKP	Southern Counties
M208YKA	North West & W	M404EFD	Midlands	M521MPF	North West & W	M615PKP	Southern Counties
M209YKA	North West & W	M410UNW	Yorkshire	M521WHF	North West & W	M616PKP	Southern Counties
M20GGY	North West & W	M411UNW	Yorkshire	M522MPF	North West & W	M617PKP	Southern Counties
M210YKA	North West & W	M412UNW	Yorkshire	M522WHF	North West & W	M619PKP	Southern Counties
M211YKD	North West & W	M413UNW	Yorkshire	M523MPF	North West & W	M685HPF	North East
M212YKD	North West & W	M414UNW	Yorkshire	M523WHF	North West & W	M686HPF	North East
M213YKD	North West & W	M415UNW	Yorkshire	M524MPF	North West & W	M687HPF	North East
M214YKD	North West & W	M416UNW	Yorkshire	M524WHF	North West & W	M688HPF	North East
M215YKD	North West & W	M417UNW	Yorkshire	M525MPM	Southern Counties	M689HPF	North East
M216YKD	North West & W	M418UNW	Yorkshire	M525WHF	North West & W	M690HPF	North East
M217AKB	North West & W	M419UNW	Yorkshire	M526MPM	Southern Counties	M691HPF	North East
M218AKB	North West & W	M420UNW	Yorkshire	M526WHF	North West & W	M692HPF	North East
M218YKC	North West & W	M421UNW	Yorkshire	M527WHF	North West & W	M693HPF	North East
M219AKB	North West & W	M422GUS	Scotland	M528WHF	North West & W	M694HPF	London
M219YKC	North West & W	M422UNW	Yorkshire	M529WHF	North West & W	M695HPF	London
M220AKB	North West & W	M423GUS	Scotland	M530WHF	North West & W	M696HPF	London
M221AKB	North West & W	M423UNW	Yorkshire	M531WHF	North West & W	M697HPF	London
M223AKB	North West & W	M424UNW	Yorkshire	M532WHF	North West & W	M698HPF	London
M224AKB	North West & W	M425BLU	The Shires	M533WHF	North West & W	M699HPF	London
M225AKB	North West & W	M425UNW	Yorkshire	M534WHF	North West & W	M700HPF	London
M226AKB	North West & W	M426BLU	The Shires	M535WHF	North West & W	M701HPF	London
M227AKB	North West & W	M426UNW	Yorkshire	M536WHF	North West & W	M702HPF	London
M228AKB	North West & W	M427UNW	Yorkshire	M537WHF	North West & W	M703HPF	London
M229AKB	North West & W	M428UNW	Yorkshire	M538WHF	North West & W	M704HPF	London
M230AKB	North West & W	M429UNW	Yorkshire	M540WHF	North West & W	M7110MJ	The Shires
M231AKB	North West & W	M430UNW	Yorkshire	M541WHF	North West & W	M7120MJ	The Shires
M232AKB	North West & W	M431UNW	Yorkshire	M542WHF	North West & W	M7130MJ	The Shires
M247SPP	Scotland	M432UNW	Yorkshire	M543WHF	North West & W	M7140MJ	The Shires
M247WWR	Yorkshire	M433UNW	Yorkshire	M544WTJ	North West & W	M7150MJ	The Shires
M248SPP	Scotland	M440HPF	North East	M545WTJ	North West & W	M7160MJ	The Shires
M249SPP	Scotland	M441HPF	North East	M546WTJ	North West & W	M7170MJ	The Shires
M250SPP	Scotland	M442HPF	North East	M547WTJ	North West & W	M7180MJ	The Shires
M251SPP	Scotland	M443HPF	North East	M548WTJ	North West & W	M7190MJ	The Shires
M266VPU	The Shires	M444HPF	North East	M549WTJ	North West & W	M7200MJ	The Shires
M267VPU	The Shires	M445HPF	North East	M550WTJ	North West & W	M7210MJ	The Shires
M268VPU	The Shires	M446HPF	North East	M551WTJ	North West & W	M7220MJ	The Shires
M269VPU	Southern Counties	M447HPF	North East	M552WTJ	North West & W	M7230MJ	The Shires
M277FNS	Scotland	M448HPF	North East	M553WTJ	North West & W	M7240MJ	The Shires
M278FNS	Scotland	M449HPF	North East	M554WTJ	North West & W	M7250MJ	The Shires
M301SAJ	North East	M450HPF	Southern Counties	M556WTJ	North West & W	M7260MJ	The Shires

Reg	Region	Reg	Region	Reg	Region	Reg	Region
M726UTW	The Shires	M913MKM	Southern Counties	N108DWM	North West & W	N187EMJ	The Shires
M727OMJ	The Shires	M914MKM	Southern Counties	N108EVS	The Shires	N188EMJ	The Shires
M728OMJ	The Shires	M915MKM	Southern Counties	N109DWM	North West & W	N189EMJ	The Shires
M729OMJ	The Shires	M916MKM	Southern Counties	N109EVS	The Shires	N190EMJ	The Shires
M730OMJ	The Shires	M917MKM	Southern Counties	N110DWM	North West & W	N191EMJ	The Shires
M734AOO	North East	M918MKM	Southern Counties	N113DWM	North West & W	N192EMJ	The Shires
M746WWR	Yorkshire	M919MKM	Southern Counties	N114DWM	North West & W	N192RVK	North East
M748WWR	Yorkshire	M920MKM	Southern Counties	N115DWM	North West & W	N193EMJ	The Shires
M749WWR	Yorkshire	M921PKN	North West & W	N116DWM	North West & W	N194EMJ	The Shires
M750WWR	Yorkshire	M922PKN	Southern Counties	N117DWM	North West & W	N195EMJ	The Shires
M751WWR	Scotland	M923PKN	Southern Counties	N118DWM	North West & W	N196EMJ	The Shires
M752WWR	North East	M924PKN	Southern Counties	N119DWM	North West & W	N201NHS	Scotland
M753WWR	Scotland	M925PKN	Southern Counties	N120DWM	North West & W	N202NHS	Scotland
M761JPA	North West & W	M927EYS	North West & W	N121DWM	North West & W	N203NHS	Scotland
M762JPA	North West & W	M928EYS	North West & W	N122DWM	North West & W	N204NHS	Scotland
M763JPA	North West & W	M929EYS	North West & W	N123DWM	North West & W	N205NHS	Scotland
M764JPA	Southern Counties	M930EYS	North West & W	N124DWM	North West & W	N206NHS	Scotland
M792EUS	Scotland	M931EYS	North West & W	N125DWM	North West & W	N207NHS	Scotland
M793EUS	Scotland	M932EYS	North West & W	N126DWM	North West & W	N208NHS	Scotland
M794EUS	Scotland	M933EYS	North West & W	N127DWM	North West & W	N210TPK	North West & W
M802MOJ	Midlands	M934EYS	North West & W	N128DWM	North West & W	N211DWM	North West & W
M803MOJ	Midlands	M935EYS	North West & W	N129DWM	North West & W	N211TPK	North West & W
M804MOJ	Midlands	M936EYS	North West & W	N130DWM	North West & W	N212TPK	North West & W
M805MOJ	Midlands	M942LYR	The Shires	N131DWM	North West & W	N213TPK	North West & W
M811RCP	Yorkshire	M943LYR	The Shires	N132DWM	North West & W	N214TPK	North West & W
M812RCP	Yorkshire	M945LYR	North West & W	N133DWM	North West & W	N215TPK	North West & W
M813RCP	Yorkshire	M946LYR	The Shires	N134DWM	North West & W	N216TPK	North West & W
M814RCP	Yorkshire	M947LYR	The Shires	N160VVO	Midlands	N217TPK	North West & W
M815RCP	Yorkshire	M948LYR	The Shires	N161VVO	Midlands	N218TPK	North West & W
M816RCP	Yorkshire	M949LYR	The Shires	N162VVO	Midlands	N219TPK	North West & W
M817RCP	Yorkshire	M950LYR	North West & W	N163VVO	Midlands	N220TPK	Southern Counties
M818RCP	Yorkshire	M951LYR	The Shires	N164VVO	Midlands	N221TPK	Southern Counties
M819RCP	Yorkshire	MIL2350	The Shires	N165XVO	Midlands	N223TPK	Southern Counties
M831SDA	Midlands	MUH281X	The Shires	N166PUT	Midlands	N224TPK	Southern Counties
M832SDA	Midlands	N24FWU	North West & W	N166XVO	Midlands	N225TPK	Southern Counties
M833SDA	Midlands	N25FWU	North West & W	N167PUT	Midlands	N226TPK	Southern Counties
M834SDA	Midlands	N26KYS	Scotland	N168PUT	Midlands	N227TPK	Southern Counties
M835SDA	Midlands	N27KYS	Scotland	N168WNF	Midlands	N228MUS	Scotland
M841DDS	Southern Counties	N28KGS	The Shires	N169PUT	Midlands	N228TPK	Southern Counties
M841RCP	North West & W	N29KGS	The Shires	N169WNF	Midlands	N229TPK	Southern Counties
M842DDS	The Shires	N31KGS	The Shires	N170PUT	Midlands	N230TPK	Southern Counties
M842RCP	North West & W	N32KGS	The Shires	N170WNF	Midlands	N231TPK	Southern Counties
M843DDS	The Shires	N35JPP	The Shires	N170WNF	Midlands	N232TPK	Southern Counties
M843RCP	North West & W	N36JPP	The Shires	N171PUT	Midlands	N233CKA	North West & W
M844DDS	The Shires	N37JPP	The Shires	N172PUT	Midlands	N233TPK	Southern Counties
M846DDS	Southern Counties	N38JPP	The Shires	N172WNF	Yorkshire	N234CKA	North West & W
M847RCP	North West & W	N39JPP	The Shires	N173PUT	Midlands	N234TPK	Southern Counties
M849RCP	North West & W	N41JPP	The Shires	N174PUT	Midlands	N235CKA	North West & W
M863KCU	North East	N42JPP	The Shires	N175DWM	The Shires	N235TPK	Southern Counties
M866KCU	North East	N43JPP	The Shires	N175PUT	Midlands	N236CKA	North West & W
M867KCU	North East	N45JPP	The Shires	N176DWM	The Shires	N236TPK	Southern Counties
M869KCU	North East	N46JPP	The Shires	N176PUT	Midlands	N237CKA	North West & W
M870KCU	North East	N81PUS	Scotland	N177DWM	The Shires	N237VPH	Southern Counties
M871LBB	North East	N82PUS	Scotland	N177PUT	Midlands	N238CKA	North West & W
M872LBB	North East	N101YVU	North West & W	N178DWM	North West & W	N238VPH	Midlands
M873LBB	North East	N103YVU	North West & W	N178PUT	Midlands	N239CKA	North West & W
M874LBB	North East	N104YVU	North West & W	N179DWM	North West & W	N239VPH	Southern Counties
M875LBB	North East	N105YVU	North West & W	N179PUT	Midlands	N240CKA	North West & W
M876LBB	North East	N106DWM	North West & W	N181OYH	North East	N240VPH	Midlands
M878DDS	Scotland	N106EVS	The Shires	N182OYH	North East	N241CKA	North West & W
M911MKM	Southern Counties	N107DWM	North West & W	N183OYH	North East	N241VPH	Midlands
M912MKM	Southern Counties	N107EVS	The Shires	N186EMJ	The Shires	N242CKA	North West & W

N242VPH	Midlands	N285CKB	North West & W	N385OTY	North East	N524XVN	North East
N243CKA	North West & W	N285NCN	North East	N386JGS	The Shires	N525XVN	North East
N243VPH	Midlands	N286CKB	North West & W	N386OTY	North East	N527SPA	North West & W
N244CKA	North West & W	N286NCN	North East	N387JGS	The Shires	N528SPA	North West & W
N244VPH	Midlands	N287CKB	North West & W	N387OTY	North East	N529SPA	North West & W
N245CKA	North West & W	N287NCN	North East	N388OTY	North East	N530SPA	North West & W
N245VPH	Southern Counties	N288CKB	North West & W	N389OTY	North East	N531DWM	North West & W
N246CKA	North West & W	N288NCN	North East	N390OTY	North East	N532DWM	North West & W
N246VPH	Southern Counties	N289CKB	North West & W	N391OTY	North East	N539TPF	Southern Counties
N247CKA	North West & W	N289NCN	North East	N392OTY	North East	N540TPF	Southern Counties
N247VPH	Southern Counties	N290CKB	North West & W	N393OTY	North East	N541TPF	Southern Counties
N248CKA	North West & W	N290NCN	North East	N414NRG	The Shires	N542TPK	Southern Counties
N248GBM	The Shires	N291CKB	North West & W	N415NRG	The Shires	N543TPK	Southern Counties
N248VPH	Midlands	N292CKB	North West & W	N415NRG	The Shires	N544TPK	Southern Counties
N249CKA	North West & W	N293CKB	North West & W	N429XRC	Midlands	N551LUA	London
N249VPH	Midlands	N294CKB	North West & W	N430XRC	Midlands	N576CKA	North West & W
N250BKK	Southern Counties	N295CKB	North West & W	N431XRC	Midlands	N577CKA	North West & W
N250CKA	North West & W	N296CKB	North West & W	N432XRC	Midlands	N578CKA	North West & W
N251BKK	Southern Counties	N297CKB	North West & W	N433XRC	Midlands	N579CKA	North West & W
N251CKA	North West & W	N298CKB	North West & W	N439GHG	Scotland	N580CKA	North West & W
N252BKK	Southern Counties	N299CKB	North West & W	N440GHG	Scotland	N581CKA	North West & W
N252CKA	North West & W	N301CKB	North West & W	N463EHA	Midlands	N582CKA	North West & W
N253BKK	Southern Counties	N301ENX	Midlands	N464EHA	Midlands	N583CKA	North West & W
N253CKA	North West & W	N302CKB	North West & W	N465EHA	Midlands	N584CKA	North West & W
N254BKK	Southern Counties	N302ENX	Midlands	N466EHA	Midlands	N585CKA	North West & W
N254CKA	North West & W	N303CLV	North West & W	N467EHA	Midlands	N586CKA	North West & W
N254PGD	Scotland	N303ENX	Midlands	N468EHA	Midlands	N587CKA	North West & W
N255BKK	Southern Counties	N304CLV	North West & W	N468SPA	North West & W	N588CKA	North West & W
N255CKA	North West & W	N304ENX	Midlands	N469EHA	Midlands	N589CKA	North West & W
N256BKK	Southern Counties	N305CLV	North West & W	N470EHA	Midlands	N590CKA	North West & W
N256CKA	North West & W	N305ENX	Midlands	N470SPA	North West & W	N591CKA	North West & W
N256PGD	Scotland	N306CLV	North West & W	N471EHA	Midlands	N592CKA	North West & W
N257BKK	Southern Counties	N307CLV	North West & W	N472EHA	Midlands	N593CKA	North West & W
N257CKA	North West & W	N308CLV	North West & W	N472XRC	Midlands	N594CKA	North West & W
N257PGD	Scotland	N322TPK	Southern Counties	N473MUS	Scotland	N595CKA	North West & W
N258BKK	Southern Counties	N356OBC	Midlands	N473XRC	Midlands	N596CKA	North West & W
N258CKA	North West & W	N357OBC	Midlands	N474MUS	Scotland	N597CKA	North West & W
N258PGD	Scotland	N358OBC	Midlands	N474XRC	Midlands	N598CKA	North West & W
N259BKK	Southern Counties	N366JGS	The Shires	N475XRC	Midlands	N599CKA	North West & W
N259CKA	North West & W	N367JGS	The Shires	N476XRC	Midlands	N601CKA	North West & W
N260CKA	North West & W	N368JGS	The Shires	N477XRC	Midlands	N601DWY	North West & W
N261CKA	North West & W	N369JGS	The Shires	N478XRC	Midlands	N602DWY	North West & W
N262CKA	North West & W	N370JGS	The Shires	N479XRC	Midlands	N603CKA	North West & W
N263CKA	North West & W	N371JGS	The Shires	N480XRC	Midlands	N603DWY	North West & W
N264CKA	North West & W	N372JGS	The Shires	N481XRC	Midlands	N604CKA	North West & W
N271CKB	North West & W	N373JGS	The Shires	N511XVN	North East	N604DWY	North West & W
N272CKB	North West & W	N374JGS	The Shires	N512XVN	North East	N605CKA	North West & W
N273CKB	North West & W	N375JGS	The Shires	N513XVN	North East	N605DWY	North West & W
N274CKB	North West & W	N376JGS	The Shires	N514XVN	North East	N606CKA	North West & W
N275CKB	North West & W	N377JGS	The Shires	N515XVN	North East	N606DWY	North West & W
N276CKB	North West & W	N378JGS	The Shires	N516XVN	North East	N607CKA	North West & W
N277CKB	North West & W	N379JGS	The Shires	N517XVN	North East	N607DWY	North West & W
N278CKB	North West & W	N380JGS	The Shires	N518XVN	North East	N608CKA	North West & W
N279CKB	North West & W	N381JGS	The Shires	N519XVN	North East	N608DWY	North West & W
N281CKB	North West & W	N381OTY	North East	N520XVN	North East	N609CKA	North West & W
N281NCN	North East	N382JGS	The Shires	N521MJO	The Shires	N609DWY	North West & W
N282CKB	North West & W	N382OTY	North East	N521XVN	North East	N610CKA	North West & W
N282NCN	North East	N383JGS	The Shires	N522MJO	The Shires	N610DWY	North West & W
N283CKB	North West & W	N383OTY	North East	N522XVN	North East	N611CKA	North West & W
N283NCN	North East	N384JGS	The Shires	N523MJO	The Shires	N611DWY	North West & W
N284CKB	North West & W	N384OTY	North East	N523XVN	North East	N612CKA	North West & W
N284NCN	North East	N385JGS	The Shires	N524MJO	The Shires	N612DWY	North West & W

Reg	Region	Reg	Region	Reg	Region	Reg	Region
N613CKA	North West & W	N707TPK	North West & W	N808PDS	Scotland	NML648E	London
N613DWY	North West & W	N708EUR	The Shires	N808TPK	Yorkshire	NML653E	London
N614CKA	North West & W	N708GUM	Scotland	N808XHN	North East	NML655E	London
N615CKA	North West & W	N708TPK	North West & W	N809TPK	Yorkshire	NSG636A	London
N616CKA	North West & W	N709EUR	The Shires	N809XHN	North East	OJD840Y	OLST
N617CKA	North West & W	N709GUM	Scotland	N810TPK	Yorkshire	OJD858Y	North East
N618CKA	North West & W	N709TPK	North West & W	N810XHN	North East	OJD863Y	OLST
N619CKA	North West & W	N710EUR	The Shires	N852YKE	Southern Counties	OLV551M	North West & W
N620CKA	North West & W	N710GUM	Scotland	N877RTN	North East	OYM453A	London
N621CKA	North West & W	N711EUR	The Shires	N878RTN	North East	P3SLT	North West & W
N621FJO	The Shires	N711GUM	Scotland	N879RTN	North East	P41MVU	North West & W
N621KUA	Yorkshire	N712EUR	The Shires	N880RTN	North East	P42MVU	North West & W
N622CKA	North West & W	N712GUM	Scotland	N881RTN	North East	P43MVU	North West & W
N622FJO	The Shires	N713EUR	The Shires	N882RTN	North East	P45MVU	North West & W
N622KUA	Yorkshire	N713TPK	Southern Counties	N883RTN	North East	P46MVU	North West & W
N623CKA	North West & W	N714EUR	The Shires	N884RTN	North East	P49MVU	North West & W
N623FJO	The Shires	N714TPK	Southern Counties	N885RTN	North East	P51HOJ	North West & W
N623KUA	Yorkshire	N715EUR	The Shires	N886RTN	North East	P52HOJ	North West & W
N624FJO	The Shires	N715TPK	Southern Counties	N887RTN	North East	P52MVU	North West & W
N671GUM	North West & W	N716EUR	The Shires	N889RTN	North East	P53HOJ	North West & W
N672GUM	Scotland	N716TPK	North West & W	N890RTN	North East	P53MVU	North West & W
N673GUM	Midlands	N718DJC	North West & W	N891RTN	North East	P54HOJ	North West & W
N674GUM	Midlands	N719DJC	North West & W	N907ETM	The Shires	P56HOJ	North West & W
N675GUM	Scotland	N750LUS	Scotland	N908ETM	The Shires	P56MVU	North West & W
N676GUM	North West & W	N752LUS	Scotland	N909ETM	The Shires	P56XTN	North East
N677GUM	Scotland	N753LUS	Scotland	N911ETM	The Shires	P57HOJ	North West & W
N678GUM	North West & W	N754LUS	Scotland	N912ETM	The Shires	P57XTN	North East
N679GUM	Midlands	N754LWW	Yorkshire	N913ETM	The Shires	P58HOJ	North West & W
N680GUM	Midlands	N755LWW	Yorkshire	N914ETM	Southern Counties	P58MVU	North West & W
N681GUM	Scotland	N756LWW	Yorkshire	N916ETM	The Shires	P58XTN	North East
N682GUM	North West & W	N757LWW	Yorkshire	N918ETM	The Shires	P59HOJ	North West & W
N683GUM	Scotland	N780EUA	The Shires	N919ETM	Southern Counties	P59XTN	North East
N684GUM	Scotland	N781EUA	North West & W	N935ETU	The Shires	P61HOJ	North West & W
N685GUM	Scotland	N782EUA	North West & W	N936ETU	The Shires	P61MVU	North West & W
N686GUM	Scotland	N783EUA	North West & W	N941MGG	Scotland	P61XTN	North East
N687GUM	Scotland	N784EUA	North West & W	N942MGG	Scotland	P100LOW	The Shires
N688GUM	Scotland	N801BKN	North East	N991KUS	Scotland	P130RWR	North East
N689GUM	Midlands	N801PDS	Scotland	N993CCC	North West & W	P135GND	North West & W
N690GUM	Midlands	N801TPK	Yorkshire	N994CCC	North West & W	P136GND	North West & W
N691GUM	Scotland	N802BKN	North East	N995CCC	North West & W	P137GND	North West & W
N693EUR	The Shires	N802PDS	Scotland	NEY819	North West & W	P137MTU	The Shires
N694EUR	The Shires	N802TPK	Yorkshire	NK53HHX	North East	P138GND	North West & W
N695EUR	The Shires	N803BKN	Scotland	NK53HHY	North East	P139GND	North West & W
N696EUR	The Shires	N803PDS	Scotland	NK53HHZ	North East	P140GND	North West & W
N697EUR	The Shires	N803TPK	Yorkshire	NK53HJA	North East	P167BTV	Midlands
N698EUR	The Shires	N804BKN	Scotland	NK53VKA	North East	P168BTV	Midlands
N701EUR	The Shires	N804PDS	Scotland	NL52XZV	North East	P169BTV	Midlands
N701GUM	London	N804TPK	Yorkshire	NL52XZW	North East	P170VUA	Yorkshire
N702EUR	The Shires	N805BKN	Southern Counties	NL52XZX	North East	P171VUA	Yorkshire
N702GUM	London	N805PDS	Scotland	NL52XZY	North East	P172VUA	Yorkshire
N703EUR	The Shires	N805TPK	Yorkshire	NML608E	London	P173VUA	Yorkshire
N703GUM	London	N806BKN	Southern Counties	NML611E	London	P174VUA	Yorkshire
N704EUR	The Shires	N806EHA	Midlands	NML617E	London	P175SRO	The Shires
N704GUM	North West & W	N806TPK	Yorkshire	NML619E	London	P175VUA	Yorkshire
N705EUR	The Shires	N806XHN	North East	NML625E	London	P176LKL	Southern Counties
N705GUM	London	N807BKN	Southern Counties	NML627E	London	P176SRO	The Shires
N705TPK	North West & W	N807EHA	Midlands	NML628E	London	P176VUA	Yorkshire
N706EUR	The Shires	N807PDS	Scotland	NML632E	London	P177LKL	Southern Counties
N706GUM	London	N807TPK	Yorkshire	NML635E	London	P177SRO	The Shires
N706TPK	North West & W	N807XHN	North East	NML636E	London	P177VUA	Yorkshire
N707EUR	The Shires	N808BKN	Southern Counties	NML638E	London	P178FNF	North West & W
N707GUM	North West & W	N808EHA	Midlands	NML643E	London	P178LKL	Southern Counties

212

Reg	Region	Reg	Region	Reg	Region	Reg	Region
P178SRO	The Shires	P198LKJ	Southern Counties	P242MKN	Southern Counties	P294FPK	Southern Counties
P178VUA	Yorkshire	P198VUA	Yorkshire	P243MKN	Southern Counties	P295FPK	Southern Counties
P179FNF	North West & W	P199LKJ	Southern Counties	P244MKN	Southern Counties	P296FPK	Southern Counties
P179LKL	Southern Counties	P199VUA	Yorkshire	P244NBA	North West & W	P296OOA	Midlands
P179SRO	The Shires	P201HRY	Midlands	P245MKN	Southern Counties	P301HEM	North West & W
P179VUA	Yorkshire	P201LKJ	Southern Counties	P246MKN	Southern Counties	P302HEM	North West & W
P180FNF	North West & W	P201RWR	Midlands	P247MKN	Southern Counties	P303HEM	North West & W
P180GND	North West & W	P202HRY	Midlands	P250APM	Southern Counties	P305HEM	North West & W
P180LKL	North West & W	P202LKJ	Southern Counties	P250NBA	North West & W	P306FEA	Midlands
P180SRO	The Shires	P203HRY	Midlands	P251APM	Southern Counties	P306HEM	North West & W
P180VUA	Yorkshire	P203LKJ	Southern Counties	P253APM	Southern Counties	P307FEA	Midlands
P181FNF	North West & W	P204HRY	Midlands	P254APM	Southern Counties	P307HEM	North West & W
P181GND	North West & W	P204LKJ	Southern Counties	P255APM	Southern Counties	P308FEA	Midlands
P181LKL	Southern Counties	P205HRY	Midlands	P255HOJ	North West & W	P308HEM	North West & W
P181SRO	The Shires	P205LKJ	Southern Counties	P256FPK	The Shires	P309FEA	Midlands
P181VUA	Yorkshire	P205RWR	Midlands	P257FPK	Southern Counties	P309HEM	North West & W
P182FNF	North West & W	P206HRY	Midlands	P258FPK	Southern Counties	P310FEA	Midlands
P182GND	North West & W	P206LKJ	Southern Counties	P259FPK	Southern Counties	P310HEM	North West & W
P182LKL	North West & W	P207LKJ	Southern Counties	P259FPK	Southern Counties	P311FEA	Midlands
P182SRO	The Shires	P208LKJ	Southern Counties	P260HOJ	North West & W	P311HEM	North West & W
P182VUA	Yorkshire	P209LKJ	Southern Counties	P260NBA	North West & W	P312FEA	Midlands
P183FNF	North West & W	P210LKJ	Southern Counties	P261FPK	Southern Counties	P313FEA	Midlands
P183GND	North West & W	P211LKJ	Southern Counties	P262FPK	Southern Counties	P314FEA	Midlands
P183LKL	North West & W	P212LKJ	Southern Counties	P263FPK	Southern Counties	P315FAW	Midlands
P183SRO	The Shires	P213LKJ	Southern Counties	P264FPK	Southern Counties	P315FEA	Midlands
P183VUA	Yorkshire	P214LKJ	North West & W	P265FPK	Southern Counties	P316FAW	Midlands
P184GND	North West & W	P215LKJ	Southern Counties	P266FPK	Southern Counties	P316FEA	Midlands
P184LKL	Southern Counties	P216LKJ	Southern Counties	P267FPK	Southern Counties	P317FEA	Midlands
P184SRO	The Shires	P217MKL	Southern Counties	P268FPK	Southern Counties	P318FEA	Midlands
P184VUA	Yorkshire	P217SGB	Scotland	P269FPK	Southern Counties	P319HOJ	Midlands
P185LKL	Southern Counties	P218MKL	Southern Counties	P270FPK	Southern Counties	P320HOJ	Midlands
P185SRO	The Shires	P218SGB	Scotland	P271FPK	Southern Counties	P321HOJ	Midlands
P185VUA	Yorkshire	P219MKL	Southern Counties	P271VRG	North East	P322HOJ	Midlands
P186LKJ	Southern Counties	P219SGB	Scotland	P272FPK	Southern Counties	P323HOJ	Midlands
P186SRO	The Shires	P220MKL	Southern Counties	P272VRG	North East	P324HOJ	Midlands
P186VUA	Yorkshire	P220SGB	Scotland	P273FPK	Southern Counties	P324HVX	Southern Counties
P187LKJ	Southern Counties	P221MKL	Southern Counties	P273VRG	North East	P325HOJ	Midlands
P187SRO	The Shires	P221SGB	Scotland	P274FPK	Southern Counties	P325HVX	Southern Counties
P187VUA	Yorkshire	P223MKL	Southern Counties	P274VRG	North East	P326HOJ	Midlands
P188LKJ	Southern Counties	P223SGB	Scotland	P275FPK	Southern Counties	P326HVX	Southern Counties
P188SRO	The Shires	P224MKL	Southern Counties	P275VRG	North East	P327HOJ	Midlands
P188VUA	Yorkshire	P224SGB	Scotland	P276FPK	Southern Counties	P327HVX	Southern Counties
P189LKJ	Southern Counties	P225MKL	Southern Counties	P276VRG	North East	P328HVX	Southern Counties
P189SRO	The Shires	P225SGB	Scotland	P277FPK	Southern Counties	P329HVX	Southern Counties
P189VUA	Yorkshire	P226MKL	Southern Counties	P277VRG	North East	P330HVX	Southern Counties
P190LKJ	Southern Counties	P226SGB	Scotland	P278FPK	Southern Counties	P331HVX	Southern Counties
P190SRO	The Shires	P227MKL	Southern Counties	P278VRG	North East	P332HVX	Southern Counties
P190VUA	Yorkshire	P227SGB	Scotland	P279FPK	Southern Counties	P334HVX	The Shires
P191LKJ	Southern Counties	P228MKL	Southern Counties	P279VRG	North East	P380FPK	Southern Counties
P191VUA	Yorkshire	P229MKL	Southern Counties	P281FPK	Southern Counties	P394FEA	North West & W
P192LKJ	Southern Counties	P230MKL	Southern Counties	P282FPK	Southern Counties	P395FEA	North West & W
P192VUA	Yorkshire	P231MKL	Southern Counties	P283FPK	Southern Counties	P396FEA	North West & W
P193LKJ	Southern Counties	P232MKL	Southern Counties	P284FPK	Southern Counties	P397FEA	North West & W
P193VUA	Yorkshire	P233MKN	Southern Counties	P285FPK	Southern Counties	P398FEA	North West & W
P194LKJ	Southern Counties	P234MKN	Southern Counties	P286FPK	Southern Counties	P399FEA	North West & W
P194VUA	Yorkshire	P235MKN	Southern Counties	P287FPK	Southern Counties	P401FEA	North West & W
P195LKJ	Southern Counties	P236MKN	Southern Counties	P288FPK	Southern Counties	P402MLD	The Shires
P195VUA	Yorkshire	P237MKN	Southern Counties	P289FPK	Southern Counties	P403MLD	The Shires
P196LKJ	Southern Counties	P238MKN	Southern Counties	P290FPK	Southern Counties	P404MLD	The Shires
P196VUA	Yorkshire	P239MKN	Southern Counties	P291FPK	Southern Counties	P405MLD	The Shires
P197LKJ	Southern Counties	P240MKN	Southern Counties	P292FPK	Southern Counties	P410CCU	North East
P197VUA	Yorkshire	P241MKN	Southern Counties	P293FPK	Southern Counties	P411CCU	North East

P412CCU	North East	P540MBU	North West & W	P671OPP	The Shires	P836RWU	Midlands
P413CCU	North East	P541MBU	North West & W	P671PNM	The Shires	P837KES	Scotland
P414CCU	North East	P542MBU	North West & W	P672OPP	The Shires	P837RWU	Midlands
P415CCU	North East	P543MBU	North West & W	P673OPP	The Shires	P838KES	Scotland
P416CCU	North East	P544MBU	North West & W	P674OPP	The Shires	P838RWU	North West & W
P417CCU	North East	P545MBU	North West & W	P688KCC	North West & W	P839KES	Scotland
P418CCU	North East	P601CAY	Midlands	P697UFR	The Shires	P839RWU	Midlands
P419CCU	North East	P602CAY	Midlands	P698PRJ	Southern Counties	P840KES	Scotland
P419HVX	North West & W	P603CAY	Midlands	P753RWU	London	P840PWW	Midlands
P420CCU	North East	P604CAY	Midlands	P754RWU	London	P841PWW	Midlands
P420HVX	North West & W	P605CAY	Midlands	P801RWU	Scotland	P842PWW	Midlands
P421HVX	Southern Counties	P606CAY	Midlands	P802RWU	Scotland	P843PWW	Midlands
P422HVX	North West & W	P606FHN	North East	P803RWU	Scotland	P844PWW	Midlands
P423HVX	Southern Counties	P607CAY	Midlands	P804RWU	Scotland	P845PWW	Midlands
P424HVX	Southern Counties	P607FHN	North East	P805RWU	Scotland	P846PWW	Midlands
P425HVX	Southern Counties	P608CAY	Midlands	P806DBS	Scotland	P847PWW	Midlands
P426HVX	Southern Counties	P608FHN	North East	P807DBS	Scotland	P848PWW	Midlands
P427HVX	Southern Counties	P608JJU	Midlands	P808DBS	Scotland	P849PWW	Midlands
P428HVX	Southern Counties	P609CAY	Midlands	P809DBS	Scotland	P850PWW	Midlands
P429HVX	Southern Counties	P609FHN	North East	P810DBS	Scotland	P851PWW	Midlands
P430HVX	North West & W	P610CAY	Midlands	P811DBS	Scotland	P852PWW	Midlands
P431HVX	Southern Counties	P610FHN	North East	P812DBS	Scotland	P853PWW	Midlands
P438HKN	Midlands	P611CAY	Midlands	P813DBS	Scotland	P854PWW	Midlands
P472APJ	North East	P611FHN	North East	P814DBS	Scotland	P855PWW	Midlands
P473APJ	North West & W	P612CAY	Midlands	P814VTY	North East	P893XCU	North East
P474APJ	Southern Counties	P612FHN	North East	P815DBS	Scotland	P894XCU	North East
P475DPE	Southern Counties	P613CAY	Midlands	P816GMS	Scotland	P895XCU	Scotland
P476DPE	Southern Counties	P613FHN	North East	P817GMS	Scotland	P896XCU	Scotland
P477DPE	Southern Counties	P614FHN	North East	P818GMS	Scotland	P902DRG	North East
P478DPE	Southern Counties	P615FHN	North East	P819GMS	Scotland	P903DRG	North East
P479DPE	Southern Counties	P616FHN	North East	P820GMS	Scotland	P904DRG	North East
P480DPE	Southern Counties	P617FHN	North East	P821GMS	Scotland	P905JNL	North East
P481DPE	Southern Counties	P618FHN	North East	P822GMS	Scotland	P906JNL	North East
P482CAL	Midlands	P619FHN	North East	P822RWU	Scotland	P913PWW	Scotland
P482DPE	Southern Counties	P620FHN	North East	P823GMS	Scotland	P914PWW	Scotland
P483CAL	Midlands	P621FHN	North East	P823RWU	North West & W	P915PWW	Scotland
P484CAL	Midlands	P622FHN	North East	P824GMS	Scotland	P916PWW	London
P485CAL	Midlands	P623FHN	North East	P824RWU	Midlands	P917PWW	London
P486CAL	Midlands	P624FHN	North East	P825KES	Scotland	P918PWW	London
P487CAL	Midlands	P625FHN	North East	P825RWU	North West & W	P926MKL	Southern Counties
P488CAL	Midlands	P627FHN	North East	P826KES	Scotland	P927MKL	Southern Counties
P490CAL	Midlands	P628FHN	North East	P826RWU	North West & W	P928MKL	Southern Counties
P491CAL	Midlands	P629FHN	North East	P827KES	Scotland	P929MKL	Southern Counties
P491TGA	Scotland	P630FHN	North East	P827RWU	North West & W	P930MKL	Southern Counties
P492CAL	Midlands	P631FHN	North East	P828KES	Scotland	P930YSB	Scotland
P492TGA	Scotland	P632FHN	North East	P828RWU	North West & W	P931MKL	Southern Counties
P524UGA	North West & W	P633FHN	North East	P829KES	Scotland	P931YSB	Scotland
P525UGA	North West & W	P634FHN	North East	P829RWU	North West & W	P932MKL	Southern Counties
P525YJO	The Shires	P635FHN	North East	P830KES	Scotland	P932YSB	Scotland
P526UGA	Scotland	P636FHN	North East	P830RWU	North West & W	P933MKL	Southern Counties
P526YJO	The Shires	P637FHN	North East	P831KES	Scotland	P934MKL	Southern Counties
P527UGA	Scotland	P638FHN	North East	P831RWU	North West & W	P935MKL	Southern Counties
P527YJO	The Shires	P639FHN	North East	P832KES	Scotland	P936MKL	Southern Counties
P528UGA	Scotland	P640FHN	North East	P832RWU	North West & W	P936YSB	Scotland
P529UGA	Scotland	P641FHN	North East	P833HVX	The Shires	P937MKL	Southern Counties
P533MBU	North West & W	P642FHN	North East	P833KES	Scotland	P937YSB	Scotland
P534MBU	North West & W	P643FHN	North East	P833RWU	North West & W	P938MKL	North West & W
P535MBU	North West & W	P644FHN	North East	P834KES	Scotland	P939MKL	North West & W
P536MBU	North West & W	P645FHN	North East	P834RWU	North West & W	P940MKL	North West & W
P537MBU	North West & W	P658KEY	North West & W	P835KES	Scotland	P941MKL	North West & W
P538MBU	North West & W	P669PNM	The Shires	P835RWU	Midlands	P942MKL	North West & W
P539MBU	North West & W	P670PNM	The Shires	P836KES	Scotland	P943MKL	North West & W

P952RUL	Midlands	R110TKO	North West & W	R165UAL	Midlands	R206VPU	The Shires
P953RUL	North West & W	R112GNW	North West & W	R166UAL	Midlands	R207CKO	Southern Counties
P954RUL	Midlands	R112TKO	North West & W	R167UAL	Midlands	R207GMJ	The Shires
P955RUL	Midlands	R113GNW	North West & W	R168UAL	Midlands	R207VPU	The Shires
P956RUL	Midlands	R113TKO	North West & W	R169GNW	The Shires	R208CKO	Southern Counties
P957RUL	Midlands	R114TKO	North West & W	R169UAL	Midlands	R208GMJ	The Shires
P058RUL	Midlands	R115TKO	North West & W	R170GNW	The Shires	R208VPU	The Shires
P959RUL	North West & W	R116TKO	North West & W	R170UUT	Midlands	R209CKO	Southern Counties
P960RUL	North West & W	R117TKO	North West & W	R171VBM	The Shires	R209GMJ	The Shires
P961RUL	North West & W	R118TKO	Southern Counties	R172VBM	The Shires	R209VPU	The Shires
P962RUL	Scotland	R119TKO	Southern Counties	R173VBM	The Shires	R210CKO	Southern Counties
P963RUL	Scotland	R120TKO	Southern Counties	R174VBM	Southern Counties	R210GMJ	The Shires
P964RUL	Scotland	R121TKO	Southern Counties	R175VBM	The Shires	R211CKO	Southern Counties
P965RUL	Scotland	R122TKO	Southern Counties	R176VBM	The Shires	R211GMJ	The Shires
P966RUL	Scotland	R123TKO	North West & W	R177VBM	The Shires	R212CKO	Southern Counties
P967RUL	Scotland	R124TKO	North West & W	R178VBM	The Shires	R212GMJ	The Shires
P968RUL	Scotland	R127LNR	Midlands	R179VBM	The Shires	R213CKO	North West & W
PDZ6275	Southern Counties	R128LNR	Midlands	R180VBM	The Shires	R213GMJ	The Shires
PFY72J	North West & W	R129GNW	North West & W	R181DNM	The Shires	R214GMJ	The Shires
PIL9730	Yorkshire	R129LNR	Midlands	R182DNM	The Shires	R215GMJ	The Shires
PIL9731	Yorkshire	R130GNW	North West & W	R183DNM	The Shires	R233AEY	North West & W
PIL9732	Yorkshire	R130LNR	Midlands	R184DNM	The Shires	R234AEY	North West & W
PIL9733	Yorkshire	R131LNR	Midlands	R185DNM	The Shires	R235AEY	North West & W
PIL9734	Yorkshire	R132LNR	Midlands	R186DNM	Southern Counties	R236AEY	North West & W
PIL9735	Yorkshire	R133LNR	Midlands	R187DNM	Southern Counties	R237AEY	North West & W
PN52XBF	Midlands	R134LNR	Midlands	R188DNM	Southern Counties	R238AEY	North West & W
PN52XBH	Midlands	R135LNR	Midlands	R189DNM	The Shires	R239AEY	North West & W
PN52XRJ	Midlands	R136LNR	Midlands	R190DNM	The Shires	R251JNL	North East
PN52XRK	Midlands	R137LNR	Midlands	R191DNM	Southern Counties	R255WRJ	North West & W
PN52XRL	Midlands	R138LNR	Midlands	R191RBM	The Shires	R261EKO	Southern Counties
PN52XRM	Midlands	R139LNR	Midlands	R192DNM	Southern Counties	R262EKO	Southern Counties
PN52XRO	Midlands	R140LNR	Midlands	R192RBM	The Shires	R263EKO	Southern Counties
PN52XRP	Midlands	R141LNR	Midlands	R193DNM	Southern Counties	R264EKO	Southern Counties
PN52XRR	Midlands	R142LNR	Midlands	R193RBM	The Shires	R265EKO	Southern Counties
PN52XRS	Midlands	R143LNR	Midlands	R194DNM	The Shires	R266EKO	Southern Counties
PN52XRT	Midlands	R144LNR	Midlands	R194RBM	The Shires	R267EKO	Southern Counties
PN52XRU	Midlands	R145LNR	Midlands	R195DNM	The Shires	R268EKO	Southern Counties
PN52XRV	Midlands	R146LNR	Midlands	R195RBM	The Shires	R269EKO	Southern Counties
PN52XRW	Midlands	R147UAL	Midlands	R196DNM	The Shires	R270EKO	Southern Counties
PUK637R	North West & W	R148UAL	Midlands	R196RBM	The Shires	R271EKO	Southern Counties
PUK652R	North West & W	R149UAL	Midlands	R197DNM	The Shires	R272EKO	Southern Counties
R45VJF	Midlands	R150UAL	Midlands	R197RBM	The Shires	R291KRG	North East
R46VJF	Midlands	R151GNW	North West & W	R198DNM	The Shires	R292KRG	North East
R47XVM	North West & W	R151UAL	Midlands	R198RBM	The Shires	R293KRG	North East
R48XVM	North West & W	R152GNW	North West & W	R199RBM	The Shires	R294KRG	North East
R51XVM	North West & W	R152UAL	Midlands	R201CKO	North West & W	R295KRG	North East
R54XVM	North West & W	R153GNW	North West & W	R201RBM	The Shires	R296CMV	Southern Counties
R57XVM	North West & W	R153UAL	Midlands	R201VPU	The Shires	R297CMV	Southern Counties
R59XVM	North West & W	R154UAL	Midlands	R202CKO	North West & W	R298CMV	Southern Counties
R69GNW	Yorkshire	R155UAL	Midlands	R202RBM	The Shires	R299CMV	Southern Counties
R101GNW	London	R156UAL	Midlands	R202VPU	The Shires	R301CMV	Southern Counties
R101TKO	North West & W	R157GNW	Southern Counties	R203CKO	North West & W	R301PCW	North West & W
R102TKO	North West & W	R157UAL	Midlands	R203RBM	The Shires	R302CMV	North West & W
R103GNW	Yorkshire	R158UAL	Midlands	R203VPU	The Shires	R302CVU	North West & W
R103TKO	North West & W	R159UAL	Midlands	R204CKO	Southern Counties	R303CMV	Southern Counties
R104TKO	North West & W	R160UAL	Midlands	R204RBM	The Shires	R303CVU	North West & W
R105TKO	North West & W	R161UAL	Midlands	R204VPU	The Shires	R304CMV	Southern Counties
R107TKO	North West & W	R162GNW	London	R205CKO	Southern Counties	R304CVU	North West & W
R108TKO	North West & W	R162UAL	Midlands	R205RBM	The Shires	R305CMV	Southern Counties
R109TKO	North West & W	R163UAL	Midlands	R205VPU	The Shires	R305CVU	North West & W
R10WAL	Yorkshire	R164UAL	Midlands	R206CKO	Southern Counties	R307CMV	Southern Counties
R110GNW	North West & W	R165GNW	The Shires	R206GMJ	The Shires	R308CMV	Southern Counties

Reg	Region	Reg	Region	Reg	Region	Reg	Region
R308CVU	North West & W	R418COO	North West & W	R452SKX	The Shires	R624MNU	Midlands
R309CVU	North West & W	R418HVX	The Shires	R453KWT	Yorkshire	R625MNU	Midlands
R309WVR	North West & W	R418TJW	Midlands	R453SKX	The Shires	R626MNU	Midlands
R310CMV	Southern Counties	R419COO	North West & W	R454KWT	Yorkshire	R627MNU	Midlands
R310CVU	North West & W	R419TJW	Midlands	R454SKX	The Shires	R629MNU	Midlands
R310NGM	Southern Counties	R420COO	North West & W	R455KWT	Yorkshire	R630MNU	Midlands
R310WVR	North West & W	R420TJW	Midlands	R455SKX	Southern Counties	R631MNU	Midlands
R311CVU	North West & W	R421COO	London	R456KWT	Yorkshire	R632MNU	Midlands
R311NGM	Southern Counties	R421TJW	Midlands	R456SKX	Southern Counties	R633MNU	Midlands
R311WVR	North West & W	R422COO	London	R457KWT	Yorkshire	R634MNU	Midlands
R312CVU	North West & W	R422TJW	Midlands	R458KWT	Yorkshire	R636MNU	Midlands
R312NGM	Southern Counties	R423COO	London	R459KWT	Yorkshire	R637MNU	Midlands
R312WVR	North West & W	R423RPY	North East	R460KWT	Yorkshire	R638MNU	Midlands
R313CVU	North West & W	R423TJW	Midlands	R461KWT	Yorkshire	R639MNU	Midlands
R313NGM	Southern Counties	R424COO	London	R486UCC	North West & W	R640MNU	Midlands
R313WVR	North West & W	R424RPY	North East	R487UCC	North West & W	R641MNU	Midlands
R314WVR	North West & W	R424TJW	Midlands	R521UCC	North West & W	R642MNU	Midlands
R315WVR	North West & W	R425COO	London	R522UCC	North West & W	R643MNU	Midlands
R317WVR	North West & W	R425RPY	North East	R546ABA	North West & W	R685MHN	North West & W
R319WVR	North West & W	R425TJW	Midlands	R547ABA	North West & W	R701KCU	North East
R321WVR	North West & W	R426COO	London	R548ABA	North West & W	R701MHN	North East
R322WVR	North West & W	R426RPY	North East	R549ABA	North West & W	R702MHN	North East
R324WVR	North West & W	R426TJW	Midlands	R550ABA	North West & W	R703MHN	North East
R326WVR	North West & W	R427COO	London	R551ABA	North West & W	R704MHN	North East
R327WVR	North West & W	R427RPY	North East	R552ABA	North West & W	R705MHN	North East
R329TJW	Midlands	R427TJW	Midlands	R553ABA	North West & W	R706MHN	North East
R329WVR	North West & W	R428COO	London	R554ABA	North West & W	R707MHN	North East
R330TJW	Midlands	R428RPY	North East	R556ABA	North West & W	R708MHN	North East
R330WVR	North West & W	R428TJW	Midlands	R557ABA	North West & W	R709MHN	North East
R331TJW	Midlands	R429COO	London	R558ABA	North West & W	R710MHN	North East
R331WVR	North West & W	R429RPY	North East	R559ABA	North West & W	R711MHN	North East
R332TJW	Midlands	R429TJW	Midlands	R560ABA	North West & W	R712MHN	North East
R332WVR	North West & W	R430COO	London	R561ABA	North West & W	R713MHN	North East
R334TJW	Midlands	R430RPY	North East	R562ABA	North West & W	R714MHN	North East
R334WVR	North West & W	R431COO	London	R563ABA	North West & W	R715MHN	North East
R335TJW	Midlands	R431RPY	North East	R564ABA	North West & W	R716MHN	North East
R335WVR	North West & W	R432RPY	North East	R565ABA	North West & W	R717MHN	North East
R336TJW	Midlands	R433RPY	North East	R566ABA	North West & W	R718MHN	North East
R336WVR	North West & W	R434RPY	North East	R567ABA	North West & W	R719MHN	North East
R337TJW	Midlands	R435RPY	North East	R568ABA	North West & W	R720MHN	North East
R337WVR	North West & W	R436RPY	North East	R569ABA	North West & W	R721MHN	North East
R338TJW	Midlands	R437RPY	North East	R570ABA	North West & W	R722MHN	North East
R339TJW	Midlands	R438RPY	North East	R571ABA	North West & W	R723MHN	North East
R340TJW	Midlands	R439RPY	North East	R601MHN	North West & W	R724MHN	North East
R341KGG	North West & W	R440GWY	Yorkshire	R602MHN	North West & W	R725MHN	North East
R341TJW	Midlands	R440RPY	North East	R603MHN	North West & W	R758DUB	The Shires
R342TJW	Midlands	R441KWT	Yorkshire	R604MHN	North West & W	R759DUB	The Shires
R343TJW	Midlands	R442KWT	Yorkshire	R606FBU	North West & W	R760DUB	The Shires
R344KGG	North West & W	R443KWT	Yorkshire	R606MHN	North West & W	R761DUB	The Shires
R344TJW	Midlands	R445KWT	Yorkshire	R607MHN	North West & W	R762DUB	The Shires
R381JYS	Scotland	R446KWT	Yorkshire	R608MHN	North West & W	R763DUB	Southern Counties
R382JYS	Scotland	R447KWT	Yorkshire	R609MHN	North East	R764DUB	The Shires
R383JYS	Scotland	R447SKX	The Shires	R614MNU	Midlands	R765DUB	Midlands
R384JYS	Scotland	R448KWT	Yorkshire	R615MNU	Midlands	R766DUB	The Shires
R385JYS	Scotland	R448SKX	The Shires	R616MNU	Midlands	R767DUB	The Shires
R415TJW	Midlands	R449KWT	Yorkshire	R617MNU	Midlands	R768DUB	Midlands
R416COO	North West & W	R449SKX	The Shires	R618MNU	Midlands	R769DUB	Midlands
R416HVX	The Shires	R450KWT	Yorkshire	R619MNU	Midlands	R770DUB	Midlands
R416TJW	Midlands	R450SKX	The Shires	R620MNU	Midlands	R785DUB	Midlands
R417COO	North West & W	R451KWT	Yorkshire	R621MNU	Midlands	R787DUB	Midlands
R417HVX	The Shires	R451SKX	The Shires	R622MNU	Midlands	R788DUB	Midlands
R417TJW	Midlands	R452KWT	Yorkshire	R623MNU	Midlands	R789DUB	Midlands

Reg	Location	Reg	Location	Reg	Location	Reg	Location
R790DUB	Midlands	R942VPU	Southern Counties	S205JUA	London	S262JUA	London
R791DUB	Midlands	R943VPU	The Shires	S206JUA	London	S263JUA	London
R792DUB	North West & W	R944VPU	The Shires	S207DTO	Midlands	S264JUA	London
R793DUB	North West & W	R945VPU	The Shires	S207JUA	London	S265JUA	London
R794DUB	North West & W	R946VPU	The Shires	S208DTO	Midlands	S266JUA	London
R795DUB	North West & W	R947VPU	The Shires	S208JUA	London	S267JUA	London
R796DUB	North West & W	R948VPU	Southern Counties	S209JUA	London	S268JUA	London
R797DUB	North West & W	R949VPU	Southern Counties	S210JUA	London	S269JUA	London
R798DUB	North West & W	R950VPU	Southern Counties	S211JUA	London	S270JUA	London
R799DUB	North West & W	R951VPU	Southern Counties	S212JUA	London	S271JUA	London
R801YJC	North West & W	R952VPU	Southern Counties	S213JUA	London	S272JUA	London
R802YJC	North West & W	R953VPU	Southern Counties	S214JUA	London	S273JUA	London
R803YJC	North West & W	R954VPU	Southern Counties	S215JUA	London	S274JUA	London
R804YJC	North West & W	R962FYS	North West & W	S216JUA	London	S275JUA	London
R805YJC	North West & W	RDZ1701	North West & W	S216XPP	The Shires	S276JUA	London
R807YJC	North West & W	RDZ1702	North West & W	S217JUA	London	S277JUA	London
R808YJC	North West & W	RDZ1703	North West & W	S217XPP	The Shires	S278JUA	London
R809TKO	Southern Counties	RDZ1704	North West & W	S218JUA	London	S279JUA	London
R809YJC	North West & W	RDZ1705	North West & W	S219JUA	London	S280JUA	London
R810TKO	Southern Counties	RDZ1706	North West & W	S220JUA	London	S281JUA	London
R810YJC	North West & W	RDZ1707	North West & W	S221JUA	London	S282JUA	London
R811TKO	Southern Counties	RDZ1708	North West & W	S223JUA	London	S283JUA	London
R811YJC	North West & W	RDZ1709	North West & W	S224JUA	London	S284JUA	London
R812TKO	Southern Counties	RDZ1710	North West & W	S225JUA	London	S285JUA	London
R812YJC	North West & W	RDZ1711	North West & W	S226JUA	London	S286JUA	London
R813TKO	Southern Counties	RDZ1712	North West & W	S227JUA	London	S287JUA	London
R813YJC	North West & W	RDZ1713	North West & W	S228JUA	London	S288JUA	London
R814TKO	Southern Counties	RDZ1714	North West & W	S229JUA	London	S289JUA	London
R814YJC	North West & W	RDZ4279	Southern Counties	S230JUA	London	S290JUA	London
R815YJC	North West & W	S146KNK	The Shires	S231JUA	London	S291JUA	London
R816YJC	North West & W	S147KNK	The Shires	S232JUA	London	S292JUA	London
R817YJC	North West & W	S148KNK	The Shires	S233JUA	London	S301JUA	London
R818YJC	North West & W	S149KNK	The Shires	S234JUA	London	S302JUA	London
R819YJC	North West & W	S150KNK	The Shires	S235JUA	London	S303JUA	London
R821YJC	North West & W	S151KNK	The Shires	S236JUA	London	S304JUA	London
R823CNB	The Shires	S152KNK	The Shires	S237JUA	London	S305JUA	London
R903BKO	Southern Counties	S153KNK	The Shires	S238JUA	London	S306JUA	London
R904BKO	Southern Counties	S154KNK	The Shires	S239JUA	London	S307JUA	London
R905BKO	Southern Counties	S156KNK	The Shires	S240JUA	London	S308JUA	London
R906BKO	Southern Counties	S157KNK	The Shires	S241JUA	London	S309JUA	London
R907BKO	Southern Counties	S158KNK	The Shires	S242JUA	London	S310JUA	London
R907JNL	North East	S159KNK	The Shires	S243JUA	London	S311JUA	London
R908BKO	Southern Counties	S160KNK	The Shires	S244JUA	London	S312JUA	London
R908JNL	North East	S161KNK	The Shires	S245JUA	London	S313JUA	London
R909BKO	Southern Counties	S169JUA	London	S246JUA	London	S314JUA	London
R909JNL	North East	S170JUA	London	S247JUA	London	S315JUA	London
R910BKO	Southern Counties	S171JUA	London	S248UVR	North West & W	S316JUA	London
R910JNL	North East	S172JUA	London	S249JUA	London	S317JUA	London
R912JNL	North East	S173JUA	London	S249UVR	North West & W	S318JUA	London
R913JNL	North East	S174JUA	London	S250JUA	London	S322JUA	London
R914JNL	North East	S175JUA	London	S251JUA	London	S341KHN	North East
R915JNL	North East	S176JUA	London	S252JUA	London	S342KHN	North East
R916JNL	North East	S177JUA	London	S253JUA	London	S343KHN	North East
R917JNL	North East	S178JUA	London	S254JUA	London	S344KHN	North East
R918JNL	North East	S179JUA	London	S255JUA	London	S345KHN	North East
R919JNL	North East	S180JUA	London	S256JUA	London	S345YOG	Midlands
R920JNL	North East	S181JUA	London	S257JUA	London	S346KHN	North East
R921JNL	North East	S182JUA	London	S258JUA	London	S346YOG	Midlands
R922JNL	North East	S183JUA	London	S259JUA	London	S347KHN	North East
R923JNL	North East	S202JUA	London	S260JUA	London	S347YOG	Midlands
R940VPU	The Shires	S203JUA	London	S261JUA	London	S348KHN	North East
R941VPU	The Shires	S204JUA	London			S348YOG	Midlands

S349KHN	North East	S616KHN	North East	S848RJC	North West & W	SMK756F	London
S349YOG	Midlands	S617KHN	North East	S860OGB	Scotland	SMK759F	London
S350KHN	North East	S618KHN	North East	S861OGB	Scotland	SN03DZY	North West & W
S350PGA	North West & W	S619KHN	North East	S862OGB	Scotland	SN03DZZ	North West & W
S350YOG	Midlands	S620KHN	North East	S863OGB	Scotland	SN03LDV	Midlands
S351KHN	North East	S621KHN	North East	S864OGB	Scotland	SN03LDX	Midlands
S351PGA	North West & W	S622KHN	North East	S865OGB	Scotland	SN03LGC	Midlands
S351YOG	Midlands	S623KHN	North East	S866OGB	Scotland	SN03LGD	Midlands
S352KHN	North East	S624KHN	North East	S867OGB	Scotland	SN03LGE	Midlands
S352PGA	North West & W	S625KHN	North East	S868OGB	Scotland	SN03LGF	Midlands
S352YOG	Midlands	S626KHN	North East	S872SNB	North West & W	SN53ESG	Midlands
S353KHN	North East	S627KHN	North East	S873SNB	North West & W	SN53ESO	Midlands
S353PGA	North West & W	S628KHN	North East	S874SNB	North West & W	SNV933W	The Shires
S353YOG	Midlands	S629KHN	North East	S875SNB	North West & W	SVS617	London
S354KHN	North East	S630KHN	North East	S876SNB	North West & W	SVS618	London
S354PGA	North West & W	S631KHN	North East	S877SNB	North West & W	T47WUT	Midlands
S355KHN	North East	S632KHN	North East	S878SNB	North West & W	T48WUT	Midlands
S355PGA	North West & W	S633KHN	North East	S879SNB	North West & W	T49JJF	Midlands
S356KHN	North East	S634KHN	North East	SCZ9651	Southern Counties	T51JJF	Midlands
S357KHN	North East	S635KHN	North East	SCZ9652	Southern Counties	T52JJF	Midlands
S358KHN	North East	S636KHN	North East	SIB4846	The Shires	T53JJF	Midlands
S426MCC	The Shires	S637KHN	North East	SIB6709	Southern Counties	T54JJF	Midlands
S427MCC	The Shires	S638KHN	North East	SIB6711	Southern Counties	T56AUA	London
S429MCC	The Shires	S639KHN	North East	SIB7480	The Shires	T61JBA	Midlands
S462GUB	Yorkshire	S640KHN	North East	SIB7481	The Shires	T62JBA	North West & W
S463GUB	Yorkshire	S641KHN	North East	SIB8529	The Shires	T63JBA	North West & W
S464GUB	Yorkshire	S642KHN	North East	SJI5569	Midlands	T64JBA	North West & W
S465GUB	Yorkshire	S643KHN	North East	SK52MLE	Midlands	T65JBA	North West & W
S466GUB	Yorkshire	S644KJU	Midlands	SK52MLF	Midlands	T74AUA	North East
S467GUB	Yorkshire	S645KJU	Midlands	SK52MLJ	Midlands	T75AUA	North East
S468GUB	Yorkshire	S646KJU	Midlands	SK52MLL	Midlands	T76AUA	North East
S469GUB	Yorkshire	S647KJU	Midlands	SK52MLN	Midlands	T78AUA	North East
S470GUB	Yorkshire	S648KJU	Midlands	SK52MLO	Midlands	T79AUA	North East
S471GUB	Yorkshire	S649KJU	Midlands	SMK658F	London	T81AUA	North East
S472ANW	Yorkshire	S650KJU	Midlands	SMK660F	London	T82AUA	North East
S473ANW	Yorkshire	S651KJU	Midlands	SMK663F	London	T83AUA	North East
S474ANW	Yorkshire	S652KJU	Midlands	SMK666F	London	T109LKK	Southern Counties
S475ANW	Yorkshire	S653KJU	Midlands	SMK674F	London	T110AUA	London
S476ANW	Yorkshire	S701VKM	Southern Counties	SMK675F	London	T110GGO	London
S477ANW	Yorkshire	S702KFT	North East	SMK678F	London	T110LKK	Southern Counties
S478ANW	Yorkshire	S702VKM	Southern Counties	SMK682F	London	T119AUA	Midlands
S479ANW	Yorkshire	S703KFT	North East	SMK684F	London	T202XBV	London
S480ANW	Yorkshire	S703VKM	Southern Counties	SMK685F	London	T203XBV	London
S481ANW	Yorkshire	S704KFT	North East	SMK686F	London	T204XBV	London
S482ANW	Yorkshire	S704VKM	Southern Counties	SMK688F	London	T205XBV	London
S483ANW	Yorkshire	S705KFT	North East	SMK692F	London	T206XBV	London
S484ANW	Yorkshire	S705VKM	Southern Counties	SMK694F	London	T207XBV	London
S485ANW	Yorkshire	S706KFT	North East	SMK708F	London	T208XBV	London
S486ANW	Yorkshire	S706VKM	Southern Counties	SMK715F	London	T209XBV	London
S487ANW	Yorkshire	S707KFT	North East	SMK716F	London	T209XVO	Midlands
S488ANW	Yorkshire	S708KFT	North East	SMK718F	London	T210XBV	London
S489ANW	Yorkshire	S709KFT	North East	SMK719F	London	T211XBV	London
S490ANW	Yorkshire	S710KFT	North East	SMK726F	London	T212XBV	London
S491ANW	Yorkshire	S711KFT	North East	SMK730F	London	T213XBV	London
S558MCC	North West & W	S712KRG	North East	SMK741F	London	T214XBV	London
S559MCC	North West & W	S713KRG	North East	SMK742F	London	T215XBV	London
S610KHN	North East	S714KRG	North East	SMK746F	London	T216XBV	London
S611KHN	North East	S715KRG	North East	SMK747F	London	T217XBV	London
S612KHN	North East	S822MCC	North West & W	SMK750F	London	T218NMJ	Southern Counties
S613KHN	North East	S823MCC	North West & W	SMK752F	London	T218XBV	London
S614KHN	North East	S824MCC	North West & W	SMK753F	London	T219NMJ	The Shires
S615KHN	North East	S825MCC	North West & W	SMK754F	London	T219XBV	London

Reg	Region	Reg	Region	Reg	Region	Reg	Region
T220XBV	London	T492KGB	The Shires	T829NMJ	The Shires	V214PCX	Yorkshire
T273JKM	Southern Counties	T493KGB	The Shires	T911KKM	Southern Counties	V215KDA	Midlands
T274JKM	Southern Counties	T494KGB	The Shires	T912KKM	Southern Counties	V215PCX	Yorkshire
T275JKM	Southern Counties	T495KGB	The Shires	T913KKM	Southern Counties	V216KDA	Midlands
T276JKM	Southern Counties	T526AOB	North West & W	T914KKM	Southern Counties	V216PCX	Yorkshire
T277JKM	Southern Counties	T527AOB	North West & W	T915KKM	Southern Counties	V217KDA	Midlands
T278JKM	Southern Counties	T528AOB	North West & W	T916KKM	Southern Counties	V217PCX	Yorkshire
T279JKM	Southern Counties	T529AOB	North West & W	T917KKM	North West & W	V218KDA	Midlands
T280JKM	Southern Counties	T557UOX	The Shires	T918KKM	Southern Counties	V218PCX	Yorkshire
T281JKM	Southern Counties	T560JJC	North West & W	T919KKM	Southern Counties	V219KDA	Midlands
T282JKM	Southern Counties	T561JJC	North West & W	T920KKM	North West & W	V219PCX	Yorkshire
T283JKM	Southern Counties	T562JJC	North West & W	T921KKM	Southern Counties	V220KDA	Midlands
T284JKM	Southern Counties	T563JJC	North West & W	T922KKM	North West & W	V220PCX	Yorkshire
T285JKM	Southern Counties	T564JJC	North West & W	TIB5903	Southern Counties	V221KDA	Midlands
T286JKM	Southern Counties	T565JJC	North West & W	TIB5904	Southern Counties	V221PCX	Yorkshire
T287JKM	Southern Counties	T566JJC	North West & W	TNR812X	North West & W	V223KDA	Midlands
T288JKM	Southern Counties	T567JJC	North West & W	TPC103X	Midlands	V223PCX	Yorkshire
T289JKM	Southern Counties	T568JJC	North West & W	TPD106X	North West & W	V224KDA	Midlands
T293FGN	London	T569JJC	North West & W	TPD116X	Scotland	V224PCX	Yorkshire
T294FGN	London	T570JJC	North West & W	TUP572V	Scotland	V225KDA	Midlands
T295FGN	London	T591CGT	Southern Counties	TWY7	Yorkshire	V225PCX	Yorkshire
T296FGN	London	T592CGT	Southern Counties	UJI2338	Southern Counties	V226KDA	Midlands
T297FGN	London	T612PNC	North West & W	UOI772	North East	V226PCX	Yorkshire
T298FGN	London	T613PNC	North West & W	UWW13X	North East	V227KDA	Midlands
T299FGN	London	T614PNC	North West & W	V141EJR	North East	V227PCX	Yorkshire
T301FGN	London	T615PNC	North West & W	V142EJR	North East	V228KDA	Midlands
T302FGN	London	T616PNC	North West & W	V201KDA	Midlands	V228PCX	Yorkshire
T303FGN	London	T617PNC	North West & W	V201PCX	Yorkshire	V229KDA	Midlands
T304FGN	London	T618PNC	North West & W	V202KDA	Midlands	V229XUB	Yorkshire
T305FGN	London	T619PNC	North West & W	V202PCX	Yorkshire	V230HBH	The Shires
T306FGN	London	T620PNC	North West & W	V203KDA	Midlands	V230KDA	Midlands
T307FGN	London	T621PNC	North West & W	V203PCX	Yorkshire	V231HBH	The Shires
T308FGN	London	T622PNC	North West & W	V204KDA	Midlands	V231KDA	Midlands
T309FGN	London	T623PNC	North West & W	V204PCX	Yorkshire	V232HBH	The Shires
T310FGN	London	T624EUB	Yorkshire	V205KDA	Midlands	V232KDA	Midlands
T311FGN	London	T625EUB	Yorkshire	V205PCX	Yorkshire	V233HBH	The Shires
T312FGN	London	T626EUB	Yorkshire	V206DJR	North East	V233KDA	Midlands
T313FGN	London	T627EUB	Yorkshire	V206KDA	Midlands	V234HBH	The Shires
T314FGN	London	T628EUB	Yorkshire	V206PCX	Yorkshire	V234KDA	Midlands
T314PNB	North West & W	T629EUB	Yorkshire	V207DJR	North East	V235HBH	The Shires
T315FGN	London	T630EUB	Yorkshire	V207KDA	Midlands	V235KDA	Midlands
T315PNB	North West & W	T631EUB	Yorkshire	V207PCX	Yorkshire	V236HBH	The Shires
T316FGN	London	T632EUB	Yorkshire	V208DJR	North East	V236KDA	Midlands
T316PNB	North West & W	T633EUB	Yorkshire	V208KDA	Midlands	V237HBH	The Shires
T317FGN	London	T634EUB	Yorkshire	V208PCX	Yorkshire	V237KDA	Midlands
T317PNB	North West & W	T635EUB	Yorkshire	V209DJR	North East	V238HBH	The Shires
T318FGN	London	T636EUB	Yorkshire	V209KDA	Midlands	V238KDA	Midlands
T318PNB	North West & W	T637EUB	Yorkshire	V209PCX	Yorkshire	V239HBH	The Shires
T319FGN	London	T638EUB	Yorkshire	V210DJR	North East	V239KDA	Midlands
T319PNB	North West & W	T639EUB	Yorkshire	V210KDA	Midlands	V250HBH	The Shires
T320FGN	London	T701RCN	North East	V210PCX	Yorkshire	V251HBH	The Shires
T321PNB	North West & W	T702RCN	North East	V211DJR	North East	V252HBH	The Shires
T322FGN	London	T820NMJ	Southern Counties	V211KDA	Midlands	V253HBH	The Shires
T322PNB	North West & W	T820PNB	North West & W	V211PCX	Yorkshire	V254HBH	The Shires
T323FGN	London	T821NMJ	Southern Counties	V212DJR	North East	V255HBH	The Shires
T323PNB	North West & W	T822NMJ	Southern Counties	V212KDA	Midlands	V256HBH	The Shires
T324FGN	London	T823NMJ	Southern Counties	V212PCX	Yorkshire	V257HBH	The Shires
T324PNB	North West & W	T824NMJ	Southern Counties	V213DJR	North East	V258HBH	The Shires
T325FGN	London	T825NMJ	Southern Counties	V213KDA	Midlands	V259HBH	The Shires
T421GGO	London	T826NMJ	Southern Counties	V213PCX	Yorkshire	V260HBH	The Shires
T490KGB	The Shires	T827NMJ	The Shires	V214DJR	North East	V261HBH	The Shires
T491KGB	The Shires	T828NMJ	The Shires	V214KDA	Midlands	V262HBH	The Shires

V263HBH	The Shires	V404ENC	North West & W	V580DJC	North West & W	V641DVU	North West & W
V264HBH	The Shires	V405ENC	North West & W	V580ECC	North West & W	V641KVH	Yorkshire
V265HBH	The Shires	V406ENC	North West & W	V581DJC	North West & W	V642DVU	North West & W
V266HBH	The Shires	V407ENC	North West & W	V582DJC	North West & W	V643DVU	North West & W
V267HBH	The Shires	V408ENC	North West & W	V583DJC	North West & W	V644DVU	North West & W
V268HBH	The Shires	V409ENC	North West & W	V584DJC	North West & W	V645DVU	North West & W
V270HBH	The Shires	V410ENC	North West & W	V585DJC	North West & W	V646DVU	North West & W
V271HBH	The Shires	V411ENC	North West & W	V586DJC	North West & W	V647DVU	North West & W
V272HBH	The Shires	V412ENC	North West & W	V587DJC	North West & W	V648DVU	North West & W
V273HBH	The Shires	V413ENC	North West & W	V588DJC	North West & W	V649DVU	North West & W
V274HBH	The Shires	V414ENC	North West & W	V590DJC	North West & W	V650DVU	North West & W
V275HBH	The Shires	V415ENC	North West & W	V591DJC	North West & W	V650LGC	London
V276HBH	The Shires	V421DGT	London	V601DBC	Midlands	V651DVU	North West & W
V280HBH	The Shires	V422DGT	London	V601LGC	London	V652DVU	North West & W
V281HBH	The Shires	V423DGT	London	V602DBC	Midlands	V653DVU	North West & W
V282HBH	The Shires	V424DGT	London	V603DBC	Midlands	V653LWT	North East
V283HBH	The Shires	V425DGT	London	V604DBC	Midlands	V654DVU	North West & W
V284HBH	The Shires	V426DGT	London	V605DBC	Midlands	V655DVU	North West & W
V285HBH	The Shires	V427DGT	London	V606DBC	Midlands	V656DVU	North West & W
V286HBH	The Shires	V428DGT	London	V607DBC	Midlands	V657DVU	North West & W
V287HBH	The Shires	V429DGT	London	V608DBC	Midlands	V658DVU	North West & W
V288HBH	The Shires	V430DGT	London	V609DBC	Midlands	V659DVU	North West & W
V289HBH	The Shires	V431DGT	London	V609LGC	London	V660DVU	North West & W
V290HBH	The Shires	V432DGT	London	V610DBC	Midlands	V660LGC	London
V291HBH	The Shires	V433DGT	London	V610LGC	London	V661DVU	North West & W
V292HBH	The Shires	V434DGT	London	V611DBC	Midlands	V662DVU	North West & W
V293HBH	The Shires	V435DGT	London	V611LGC	London	V663DVU	North West & W
V294HBH	The Shires	V501DFT	North East	V612DBC	Midlands	V664DVU	North West & W
V326DGT	London	V502DFT	North East	V612DNL	North East	V665DVU	North West & W
V327DGT	London	V503DFT	North East	V612LGC	London	V667DVU	North West & W
V329DGT	London	V504DFT	North East	V613LGC	London	V668DVU	North West & W
V330DGT	London	V505DFT	North East	V614LGC	London	V669DVU	North West & W
V331DGT	London	V506DFT	North East	V615LGC	London	V670DVU	North West & W
V332DGT	London	V507DFT	North East	V616LGC	London	V671DVU	North West & W
V334DGT	London	V508DFT	North East	V617LGC	London	V672DVU	North West & W
V335DGT	London	V509DFT	North East	V618LGC	London	V673DVU	North West & W
V336DGT	London	V510DFT	North East	V619LGC	London	V674DVU	North West & W
V337DGT	London	V511DFT	North East	V620LGC	London	V675DVU	North West & W
V338DGT	London	V512DFT	North East	V621LGC	London	V676DVU	North West & W
V339DGT	London	V513DFT	North East	V622LGC	London	V701LWT	London
V341DGT	London	V514DFT	North East	V623LGC	London	V703DNL	North East
V342DGT	London	V515DFT	North East	V624DBN	North West & W	V705DNL	North East
V343DGT	London	V530GDS	North East	V625DVU	North West & W	V706DNL	North East
V344DGT	London	V531GDS	North East	V626DVU	North West & W	V707DNL	North East
V345DGT	London	V532GDS	North East	V627DVU	North West & W	V708DNL	North East
V346DGT	London	V533GDS	North East	V628DVU	North West & W	V709DNL	North East
V347DGT	London	V534GDS	North East	V628LGC	London	V710DNL	North East
V348DGT	London	V535GDS	North East	V629DVU	North West & W	V711DNL	North East
V349DGT	London	V536GDS	North East	V630DVU	North West & W	V712DNL	North East
V351DGT	London	V553ECC	North West & W	V631DVU	North West & W	V713DNL	North East
V352DGT	London	V554ECC	North West & W	V632DVU	North West & W	V714DNL	North East
V353DGT	London	V556ECC	North West & W	V633DVU	North West & W	V715DNL	North East
V354DGT	London	V557ECC	North West & W	V633LGC	London	V715LWT	North West & W
V355DGT	London	V571DJC	North West & W	V634DVU	North West & W	V716DNL	North East
V356DGT	London	V572DJC	North West & W	V635DVU	North West & W	V717DNL	North East
V358DGT	London	V573DJC	North West & W	V636DVU	North West & W	V718DNL	North East
V359DGT	London	V574DJC	North West & W	V637DVU	North West & W	V719DNL	North East
V361DGT	London	V575DJC	North West & W	V638DVU	North West & W	V720DNL	North East
V362DGT	London	V576DJC	North West & W	V639DVU	North West & W	V721DNL	North East
V363DGT	London	V577DJC	North West & W	V640DVU	North West & W	V722DNL	North East
V364DGT	London	V578DJC	North West & W	V640KVH	Yorkshire	V723DNL	North East
V365DGT	London	V579DJC	North West & W	V640LGC	London	V724DNL	North East

220

V725DNL	North East	W191CDN	North West & W	W368VGJ	London	W433XKX	The Shires
V726DNL	North East	W192CDN	North West & W	W368XKX	The Shires	W434WGJ	London
V727DNL	North East	W193CDN	North West & W	W369VGJ	London	W434XKX	Southern Counties
V728DNL	North East	W194CDN	North West & W	W369XKX	The Shires	W435WGJ	London
V729DNL	North East	W198CDN	Southern Counties	W371VGJ	London	W435XKX	Southern Counties
V730DNL	North East	W218CDN	London	W372VGJ	London	W436WGJ	London
V731DNL	North East	W226SNR	Midlands	W373VGJ	London	W436XKX	Southern Counties
V732DNl	North East	W227SNR	Midlands	W374VGJ	London	W437WGJ	London
V733DNL	North East	W228SNR	Midlands	W376VGJ	London	W437XKX	Southern Counties
V734DNL	North East	W229SNR	Midlands	W377VGJ	London	W438WGJ	London
V735DNL	North East	W231SNR	Midlands	W378VGJ	London	W438XKX	Southern Counties
V736DNL	North East	W232SNR	Midlands	W379VGJ	London	W439XKX	Southern Counties
V737DNL	North East	W233SNR	Midlands	W381VGJ	London	W441XKX	Southern Counties
V738DNL	North East	W234SNR	Midlands	W382VGJ	London	W442XKX	Southern Counties
V739DNL	North East	W235SNR	Midlands	W383VGJ	London	W443XKX	Southern Counties
V740DNL	North East	W236SNR	Midlands	W384VGJ	London	W445XKX	Southern Counties
V741DNL	North East	W237SNR	Midlands	W385VGJ	London	W446XKX	Southern Counties
V742DNL	North East	W238SNR	Midlands	W386VGJ	London	W447XKX	Southern Counties
V743ECU	North East	W239SNR	Midlands	W387VGJ	London	W451XKX	Southern Counties
V744ECU	North East	W241SNR	Midlands	W388VGJ	London	W452XKX	The Shires
V745ECU	North East	W242SNR	Midlands	W389VGJ	London	W453XKX	The Shires
V746ECU	North East	W243SNR	Midlands	W391VGJ	London	W454XKX	The Shires
V747ECU	North East	W244SNR	Midlands	W392VGJ	London	W457XKX	The Shires
V748ECU	North East	W246SNR	Midlands	W393VGJ	London	W458XKX	The Shires
V749ECU	North East	W247SNR	Midlands	W394OJC	North West & W	W459XKX	The Shires
VBG101V	North West & W	W248SNR	Midlands	W394VGJ	London	W461XKX	The Shires
VBG106V	North West & W	W249SNR	Midlands	W395RBB	North East	W462XKX	The Shires
VLT5	London	W251SNR	Midlands	W395VGJ	London	W463XKX	The Shires
VLT6	London	W269NFF	North West & W	W396RBB	North East	W464XKX	The Shires
VLT12	London	W292PPT	North East	W396VGJ	London	W465XKX	The Shires
VLT25	London	W293PPT	North East	W397RBB	North East	W466XKX	The Shires
VLT32	London	W294PPT	North East	W397VGJ	London	W467XKX	The Shires
VLT88	London	W295PPT	North East	W398RBB	North East	W468XKX	The Shires
VLT244	London	W296PPT	North East	W398VGJ	London	W469XKX	The Shires
VLT275	London	W297PPT	North East	W399RBB	North East	W471XKX	The Shires
VLT295	London	W298PPT	North East	W399VGJ	London	W472XKX	The Shires
VU02TTF	North West & W	W299PPT	North East	W401VGJ	London	W473XKX	The Shires
VU02TTV	North West & W	W301PPT	North East	W402VGJ	London	W474XKX	The Shires
VVN202Y	OLST	W302PPT	North East	W403VGJ	London	W475XKX	The Shires
VVN203Y	OLST	W303PPT	North East	W404VGJ	London	W476XKX	The Shires
VYJ806	London	W304PPT	North East	W407VGJ	London	W477XKX	The Shires
VYJ808	London	W307PPT	North East	W408VGJ	London	W478XKX	The Shires
W76PRG	North East	W308PPT	North East	W409VGJ	London	W479XKX	The Shires
W78PRG	North East	W309PPT	North East	W411VGJ	London	W481XKX	The Shires
W79PRG	North East	W311PPT	North East	W412VGJ	London	W482XKX	The Shires
W81PRG	North East	W312PPT	North East	W413VGJ	London	W483XKX	The Shires
W82PRG	North East	W313PPT	North East	W414VGJ	London	W484XKX	The Shires
W83PRG	North East	W314PPT	North East	W421XKX	The Shires	W485XKX	The Shires
W102EWU	Yorkshire	W315PPT	North East	W422XKX	The Shires	W486XKX	The Shires
W103EWU	Yorkshire	W317PPT	North East	W423XKX	The Shires	W487XKX	The Shires
W104EWU	Yorkshire	W319PPT	North East	W424XKX	The Shires	W488XKX	The Shires
W106EWU	Yorkshire	W359XKX	The Shires	W425XKX	The Shires	W489XKX	The Shires
W107EWU	Yorkshire	W361XKX	The Shires	W426XKX	The Shires	W491YGS	The Shires
W108EWU	Yorkshire	W362XKX	The Shires	W427XKX	The Shires	W492YGS	The Shires
W109EWU	Yorkshire	W363XKX	The Shires	W428XKX	The Shires	W493YGS	The Shires
W136VGJ	London	W364XKX	The Shires	W429XKX	The Shires	W494YGS	The Shires
W137VGJ	London	W365XKX	The Shires	W431WGJ	London	W495YGS	The Shires
W138VGJ	London	W366VGJ	London	W431XKX	The Shires	W496YGS	The Shires
W165HBT	Yorkshire	W366XKX	The Shires	W432WGJ	London	W497YGS	The Shires
W166HBT	Yorkshire	W367VGJ	London	W432XKX	The Shires	W498YGS	The Shires
W183CDN	Southern Counties	W367XKX	The Shires	W433WGJ	London	W501RBB	North East

W601YKN	Southern Counties	WLT897	London	X243HJA	North West & W	X428FGP	London
W602VGJ	London	WLT901	London	X243PGT	London	X428HJA	North West & W
W602YKN	Southern Counties	WLT909	London	X244HJA	North West & W	X429FGP	London
W603VGJ	London	WLT916	The Shires	X244PGT	London	X429HJA	North West & W
W603YKN	Southern Counties	WLT954	North East	X246HJA	North West & W	X431FGP	London
W604VGJ	London	WLT970	London	X246PGT	London	X431HJA	North West & W
W604YKN	Southern Counties	WLT997	London	X247HJA	North West & W	X432FGP	London
W605VGJ	London	WSU475	Scotland	X247PGT	London	X432HJA	North West & W
W605YKN	Southern Counties	WSU476	Scotland	X248HJA	North West & W	X433FGP	London
W606VGJ	London	WWM914W	North West & W	X248PGT	London	X433HJA	North West & W
W607VGJ	London	WYW24T	OLST	X249HJA	North West & W	X434FGP	London
W608VGJ	London	WYW51T	OLST	X249PGT	London	X434HJA	North West & W
W651CWX	Yorkshire	X32KON	North West & W	X251HJA	North West & W	X435FGP	London
W652CWX	Yorkshire	X143WNL	North East	X252HBC	Midlands	X435HJA	North West & W
W653CWX	Yorkshire	X144WNL	North East	X252HJA	North West & W	X436FGP	London
W654CWX	Yorkshire	X201ANC	North West & W	X253HJA	North West & W	X436HJA	North West & W
W656CWX	Yorkshire	X202ANC	North West & W	X254HJA	North West & W	X437FGP	London
W657CWX	Yorkshire	X203ANC	North West & W	X256HJA	North West & W	X437HJA	North West & W
W658CWX	Yorkshire	X204ANC	North West & W	X257HJA	North West & W	X438FGP	London
W659CWX	Yorkshire	X207ANC	North West & W	X258HJA	North West & W	X438HJA	North West & W
W661CWX	Yorkshire	X208ANC	North West & W	X259HJA	North West & W	X439FGP	London
W662CWX	Yorkshire	X209ANC	North West & W	X261OBN	North West & W	X439HJA	North West & W
W663CWX	Yorkshire	X209JOF	North West & W	X262OBN	North West & W	X441FGP	London
W664CWX	Yorkshire	X211ANC	North West & W	X263OBN	North West & W	X441HJA	North West & W
W665CWX	Yorkshire	X211JOF	North West & W	X264OBN	North West & W	X442FGP	London
W667CWX	Yorkshire	X212ANC	North West & W	X265OBN	North West & W	X442HJA	North West & W
W668CWX	Yorkshire	X212JOF	North West & W	X266OBN	North West & W	X443FGP	London
W669CWX	Yorkshire	X213ANC	North West & W	X267OBN	North West & W	X443HJA	North West & W
W671CWX	Yorkshire	X213JOF	North West & W	X268OBN	North West & W	X445FGP	London
W672CWX	Yorkshire	X214ANC	North West & W	X269OBN	North West & W	X445HJA	North West & W
W673CWX	Yorkshire	X214JOF	North West & W	X271OBN	North West & W	X446FGP	London
W674CWX	Yorkshire	X215ANC	North West & W	X271RFF	North West & W	X446HJA	North West & W
W69PRG	North East	X215JOF	North West & W	X272OBN	North West & W	X447FGP	London
W72PRG	North East	X216ANC	North West & W	X272RFF	North West & W	X447HJA	North West & W
W751SBR	North East	X216JOF	North West & W	X273RFF	North West & W	X448FGP	London
W752SBR	North East	X217ANC	North West & W	X274RFF	North West & W	X448HJA	North West & W
W753SBR	North East	X217JOF	North West & W	X295MBH	The Shires	X449FGP	London
W754SBR	North East	X218ANC	North West & W	X296MBH	The Shires	X449HJA	North West & W
W756SBR	North East	X218JOF	North West & W	X297MBH	The Shires	X451FGP	London
W757SBR	North East	X219ANC	North West & W	X415FGP	London	X452FGP	London
W758SBR	North East	X221ANC	North West & W	X416AJA	North West & W	X453FGP	London
W759SBR	North East	X223ANC	North West & W	X416FGP	London	X454FGP	London
WFC214Y	North East	X224ANC	North West & W	X417AJA	North West & W	X457FGP	London
WIB1113	The Shires	X226ANC	North West & W	X417FGP	London	X458FGP	London
WLT348	London	X227ANC	North West & W	X418AJA	North West & W	X459FGP	London
WLT385	London	X228ANC	North West & W	X418FGP	London	X471GGO	London
WLT531	London	X229ANC	North West & W	X419AJA	North West & W	X475GGO	London
WLT652	London	X231ANC	North West & W	X419FGP	London	X478GGO	London
WLT664	London	X232ANC	North West & W	X421AJA	North West & W	X481GGO	London
WLT676	London	X233ANC	North West & W	X421FGP	London	X485GGO	London
WLT719	London	X234ANC	North West & W	X422AJA	North West & W	X501GGO	London
WLT807	London	X235ANC	North West & W	X422FGP	London	X502GGO	London
WLT838	London	X236ANC	North West & W	X423AJA	North West & W	X503GGO	London
WLT871	London	X237ANC	North West & W	X423FGP	London	X504GGO	London
WLT875	London	X238ANC	North West & W	X424AJA	North West & W	X506GGO	London
WLT882	London	X239ANC	North West & W	X424FGP	London	X507GGO	London
WLT884	London	X239PGT	London	X425FGP	London	X508GGO	London
WLT888	London	X241ANC	North West & W	X426AJA	North West & W	X519GGO	London
WLT892	London	X241PGT	London	X426FGP	London	X521GGO	London
WLT895	London	X242ANC	North West & W	X427AJA	North West & W	X522GGO	London
WLT896	London	X242PGT	London	X427FGP	London	X523GGO	London

X524GGO	London	X811AJA	North West & W	Y346UON	Midlands	Y482UGC	London
X526GGO	London	X812AJA	North West & W	Y347UON	Midlands	Y483UGC	London
X527GGO	London	X813AJA	North West & W	Y348UON	Midlands	Y484UGC	London
X529GGO	London	X814AJA	North West & W	Y349UON	Midlands	Y485UGC	London
X531GGO	London	X815AJA	North West & W	Y351UON	Midlands	Y486UGC	London
X532GGO	London	X816AJA	North West & W	Y352UON	Midlands	Y487UGC	London
X533GGO	London	X817AJA	North West & W	Y353UON	Midlands	Y488UGC	London
X534GGO	London	X818AJA	North West & W	Y354UON	Midlands	Y489UGC	London
X536GGO	London	X819AJA	North West & W	Y356UON	Midlands	Y491UGC	London
X537GGO	London	X821AJA	North West & W	Y357UON	Midlands	Y492UGC	London
X538GGO	London	X822AJA	North West & W	Y358UON	Midlands	Y493UGC	London
X541GGO	London	X956DBT	North West & W	Y361UON	Midlands	Y494UGC	London
X546GGO	London	XSV691	North East	Y362UON	Midlands	Y495UGC	London
X646WTN	North East	XVS851	London	Y363UON	Midlands	Y496UGC	London
X647WTN	North East	XYJ418	London	Y364UON	Midlands	Y497UGC	London
X648WTN	North East	XYJ427	London	Y365UON	Midlands	Y498UGC	London
X649WTN	North East	Y22CJW	North West & W	Y366UON	Midlands	Y499UGC	London
X651WTN	North East	Y32TDA	North West & W	Y367UON	Midlands	Y501UGC	London
X652WTN	North East	Y36TDA	North West & W	Y451KBU	North West & W	Y502UGC	London
X653WTN	North East	Y37TDA	North West & W	Y451UGC	London	Y503UGC	London
X654WTN	North East	Y38TDA	North West & W	Y452KBU	North West & W	Y504UGC	London
X656WTN	North East	Y39TDA	North West & W	Y452UGC	London	Y506UGC	London
X657WTN	North East	Y42HBT	The Shires	Y453KBU	North West & W	Y507UGC	London
X675YUG	Yorkshire	Y42TDA	North West & W	Y454KBU	North West & W	Y508UGC	London
X676YUG	Yorkshire	Y46HBT	The Shires	Y457KBU	North West & W	Y509UGC	London
X677YUG	Yorkshire	Y46TDA	North West & W	Y457KNF	North West & W	Y511UGC	London
X678YUG	Yorkshire	Y47HBT	The Shires	Y458KBU	North West & W	Y512UGC	London
X679YUG	Yorkshire	Y48HBT	The Shires	Y458KNF	North West & W	Y513UGC	London
X681YUG	Yorkshire	Y49HBT	The Shires	Y459KBU	North West & W	Y514UGC	London
X682YUG	Yorkshire	Y102TGH	London	Y461KNF	North West & W	Y516UGC	London
X683YUG	Yorkshire	Y184TUK	Midlands	Y461UGC	London	Y517UGC	London
X684YUG	Yorkshire	Y189RJU	Midlands	Y462KNF	North West & W	Y518UGC	London
X685YUG	Yorkshire	Y207RJU	Midlands	Y462UGC	London	Y519UGC	London
X686YUG	Yorkshire	Y241KBU	North West & W	Y463KNF	North West & W	Y521UGC	London
X687YUG	Yorkshire	Y242KBU	North West & W	Y463UGC	London	Y522UGC	London
X688YUG	Yorkshire	Y243KBU	North West & W	Y464KNF	North West & W	Y523UGC	London
X689YUG	Yorkshire	Y253YBC	Midlands	Y464UGC	London	Y524UGC	London
X691YUG	Yorkshire	Y254YBC	Midlands	Y465KNF	North West & W	Y526UGC	London
X692YUG	Yorkshire	Y256YBC	Midlands	Y465UGC	London	Y527UGC	London
X693YUG	Yorkshire	Y257YBC	Midlands	Y466KNF	North West & W	Y529UGC	London
X694YUG	Yorkshire	Y258YBC	Midlands	Y466UGC	London	Y531UGC	London
X695YUG	Yorkshire	Y259YBC	Midlands	Y467KNF	North West & W	Y532UGC	London
X696YUG	Yorkshire	Y261YBC	Midlands	Y467UGC	London	Y533UGC	London
X701DBT	North West & W	Y262YBC	Midlands	Y468KNF	North West & W	Y538VFF	North West & W
X702DBT	North West & W	Y263YBC	Midlands	Y468UGC	London	Y539VFF	North West & W
X703DBT	North West & W	Y264YBC	Midlands	Y469KNF	North West & W	Y541UGC	London
X704DBT	North West & W	Y265YBC	Midlands	Y469UGC	London	Y541UJC	North West & W
X705DBT	North West & W	Y266YBC	Midlands	Y471KNF	North West & W	Y542UGC	London
X706DBT	North West & W	Y267YBC	Midlands	Y471UGC	London	Y542UJC	North West & W
X707DBT	North West & W	Y291TKJ	Southern Counties	Y472KNF	North West & W	Y543UGC	London
X708DBT	North West & W	Y292TKJ	Southern Counties	Y472UGC	London	Y543UJC	North West & W
X709DBT	North West & W	Y293TKJ	Southern Counties	Y473KNF	North West & W	Y544UGC	London
X801AJA	North West & W	Y294TKJ	Southern Counties	Y473UGC	London	Y544UJC	North West & W
X802AJA	North West & W	Y295TKJ	Southern Counties	Y474UGC	London	Y546UGC	London
X803AJA	North West & W	Y296TKJ	Southern Counties	Y475KNF	North West & W	Y546UJC	North West & W
X804AJA	North West & W	Y297TKJ	Southern Counties	Y475UGC	London	Y547UGC	London
X805AJA	North West & W	Y298TKJ	Southern Counties	Y476UGC	London	Y547UJC	North West & W
X806AJA	North West & W	Y299TKJ	Southern Counties	Y477UGC	London	Y548UGC	London
X807AJA	North West & W	Y301TKJ	Southern Counties	Y478UGC	London	Y548UJC	North West & W
X808AJA	North West & W	Y302TKJ	Southern Counties	Y479UGC	London	Y549UGC	London
X809AJA	North West & W	Y303TKJ	Southern Counties	Y481UGC	London	Y549UJC	North West & W

Y551UJC	North West & W	Y715KNF	North West & W	YD02PXY	Yorkshire	YJ03PFX	Midlands
Y552UJC	North West & W	Y716KNF	North West & W	YD02PXZ	Yorkshire	YJ04BKF	Midlands
Y581UGC	London	Y717KNF	North West & W	YD02PYU	Yorkshire	YJ04HJC	Yorkshire
Y685EBR	North East	Y718KNF	North West & W	YD02PYV	Yorkshire	YJ04HJD	Yorkshire
Y686EBR	North East	Y719KNF	North West & W	YD02PYW	Yorkshire	YJ04HJE	Yorkshire
Y687EBR	North East	Y721KNF	North West & W	YD02PYX	Yorkshire	YJ04HJF	Yorkshire
Y688EBR	North East	Y722KNF	North West & W	YD02PYY	Yorkshire	YJ04HJG	Yorkshire
Y689EBR	North East	Y723KNF	North West & W	YD02PYZ	Yorkshire	YJ53VFY	Midlands
Y691EBR	North East	Y724KNF	North West & W	YG52CFA	Yorkshire	YN04LXF	The Shires
Y692EBR	North East	Y726KNF	North West & W	YG52CFD	Yorkshire	YN04LXG	The Shires
Y693EBR	North East	Y727KNF	North West & W	YG52CFE	Yorkshire	YN04LXH	The Shires
Y694EBR	North East	Y728KNF	North West & W	YG52CFF	Yorkshire	YO53OUH	North West & W
Y701XJF	Midlands	Y729KNF	North West & W	YG52CFJ	Yorkshire	YO53OUJ	North West & W
Y702XJF	Midlands	Y733KNF	North West & W	YG52CFK	Yorkshire	YP52JWO	North West & W
Y703XJF	Midlands	Y744KNF	North West & W	YG52CFL	Yorkshire	YP52JWU	North West & W
Y704XJF	Midlands	Y801DGT	London	YG52CFM	Yorkshire	YP52JWW	North West & W
Y705XJF	Midlands	Y802DGT	London	YG52CFN	Yorkshire	YPJ207Y	Midlands
Y706XJF	Midlands	Y803DGT	London	YG52CFO	Yorkshire	YS02UBX	The Shires
Y707XJF	Midlands	Y804DGT	London	YG52CFP	Yorkshire	YS02UBY	The Shires
Y709XJF	Midlands	Y805DGT	London	YG52CFU	Yorkshire	YS51HDN	The Shires
Y711KNF	North West & W	Y806DGT	London	YG52CFV	Yorkshire	YS51HDO	The Shires
Y712KNF	North West & W	YAU126Y	Midlands	YG52CFX	Yorkshire	YSU870	North East
Y713KNF	North West & W	YD02PXW	Yorkshire	YIB2396	The Shires	YSU871	North East
Y714KNF	North West & W	YD02PXX	Yorkshire	YIB2397	The Shires		

ISBN 1 897990 93 6

© Published by *British Bus Publishing Ltd*, July 2004
British Bus Publishing Ltd, 16 St Margaret's Drive, Wellington, Telford, TF1 3PH
Telephone: 01952 255669 - Facsimile: 01952 222397

www.britishbuspublishing.co.uk E-mail address: bill@britishbuspublishing.co.uk